Post-Popperian Methodology of Economics

Recent Economic Thought Series

Editor:

Warren G. Samuels
Michigan State University
East Lansing, Michigan U.S.A.

Other books in the series:

Feiwel, G.: *Samuelson and Neoclassical Economics*
Wade, L.: *Political Economy: Modern Views*
Zimbalist, A.: *Comparative Economic Systems: Recent Views*
Darity, W.: *Labor Economics: Modern Views*
Jarsulic, M.: *Money and Macro Policy*
Samuelson, L.: *Microeconomic Theory*
Bromley, D.: *Natural Resource Economics: Policy Problems and Contemporary Analysis*
Mirowski, P.: *The Reconstruction of Economic Theory*
Field, A.: *The Future of Economic History*
Lowry, S.: *Pre-Classical Economic Thought*
Officer, L.: *International Economics*
Asimakopulos, A.: *Theories of Income Distribution*
Earl, P.: *Psychological Economics; Development, Tensions, Prospects*
Thweatt, W.: *Classical Political Economy*
Peterson, W.: *Market Power and the Economy*
DeGregori, T.: *Development Economics*
Nowotny, K.: *Public Utility Regulation*
Horowitz, I.: *Decision Theory*
Mercuro, N.: *Law and Economics*
Hennings, K. and Samuels, W.: *Neoclassical Economic Theory*
Samuels, W.: *Economics as Discourse*
Lutz, M.: *Social Economics*
Weimer, D.: *Policy Analysis and Economics*
Bromley, D. and Segerson, K.: *The Social Response to Environmental Risk*
Roberts, B. and Feiner, S.: *Radical Economics*
Mercuro, N.: *Taking Property and Just Compensation*

Post-Popperian Methodology of Economics:

Recovering Practice

edited by

Neil de Marchi

Duke University

Springer Science+Business Media, LLC

Library of Congress Cataloging-in-Publication Data

Post-Popperian methodology of economics : recovering practice / edited by Neil de Marchi.
p. cm. -- (Recent economic thought series)
Includes bibliographical references and index
ISBN 978-94-010-5307-5 ISBN 978-94-011-2942-8 (eBook)
DOI 10.1007/978-94-011-2942-8
1. Economics--Methodology. I. de Marchi, Neil. II. Series.
HB131.P67 1992
330.1--dc20 92-9323
CIP

Originally published by Kluwer Academic Publishers in 1992
Softcover reprint of the hardcover 1st edition 1992

Printed on acid-free paper.

Contents

Contributors

Cristina Bicchieri, Carnegie-Mellon University, USA
Mark Blaug, University of Buckingham and University of Exeter, UK
Bruce Caldwell, University of North Carolina at Greensboro, USA
A.W. Coats, Duke University, USA
Bert Hamminga, University of Brabant, The Netherlands
D. Wade Hands, University of Puget Sound, USA
Maarten C.W. Janssen, Erasmus University, The Netherlands
Arjo Klamer, George Washington University, USA
Donald N. McCloskey, University of Iowa, USA
Uskali Mäki, University of Helsinki, Finland
Neil de Marchi, Duke University, USA
Philip Mirowski, University of Notre Dame, USA
Alan Nelson, University of California at Irvine, USA
Alex Rosenberg, University of California at Riverside, USA
Jane Rossetti, Franklin and Marshall College, USA
Janet A. Seiz, Grinnell College, USA
E. Roy Weintraub, Duke University, USA

Post-Popperian Methodology of Economics

INTRODUCTION*

Neil de Marchi

METHODOLOGY AS ATTEMPT TO UNDERSTAND PRACTICE

Economic methodology may be understood in a variety of ways. Sixty years ago individuals whom we could easily call methodologists busied themselves with the question: what is the special nature and significance of economics as a separate scientific discipline (Robbins, 1932; cf. John Stuart Mill, 1836 and, in a surprising revival of this tradition, Hausman, 1992)? More recently, with economics itself firmly established, methodology has come to mean "how economists explain" (Blaug 1980) or, in a variant of that, "the careful study of theory structure and theory development in economics." (Hamminga 1983, Introduction)

Many practicing economists, of course, use the word methodology as shorthand for the methods they employ. Most methodologists, however, would prefer to make a distinction between methods and the application of critical standards to whatever methods are used. These standards typically have been derived from philosophy or philosophy of science. Such external borrowing has always been a little suspect. But in the past decade or so the very idea of standards has been subjected to questioning. In part the challenge stems from the consideration that there is no basis for privileging any particular critical point of view. That is, there is no *argument* by which any one set of standards could be elevated to become THE measure of adequacy (Rorty, 1979).

Among recent economic methodologists the first to take issue with standards was Lawrence Boland (1982). Boland identified a presumption underlying much methodological discussion in economics, that we are in search of the 'best' theory. This is problematic if, as Boland maintained, the predominant methodological stance in economics also happens to be conventionalism. Conventionalists hold that, in matters of theory choice, the evidence doesn't force us to accept one theory over another, so that we are thrown back on rules of thumb, or conventions, which themselves merely promote one or another interest—in scope, accuracy, novelty, and so on (see Laudan, 1990, 57, 66). The conventionalist, it follows, is hard put to come up with an unequivocal and universal ranking of theory quality.[1] Boland eschews both inductivism (in its simplest version, the idea that the evidence will 'prove' a theory true) and the conventionalism that he sees as its weakened expression, preferring to follow Popper in viewing science as "a *learning* enterprise whose sole objective is to find errors in our understanding." (1982, 168) Scientists, by this reckoning, are in the business of attempting solutions to problems, rather than seeking to add to a stock of well-founded truths.

Boland receives unexpected (and possibly unwelcome) support from philosopher Richard Rorty. Boland, recall, claims that economists, and the economic methodologists who go along with them, are interested primarily in consensus. That is the idea behind the search for the 'best' theory. To conduct such searches, though, requires a prior agreement as to the 'right' method of inquiry (1982, 26 and ch. 12) Rorty makes much the same point: "we can get epistemological commensuration only where we already have agreed-upon practices of inquiry." (1979, 321) Rorty's argument is straightforward. For epistemology, or inquiry into the grounds of knowledge, "to be rational is to find the proper set of terms into which all the contributions should be translated if agreement is to become possible" (ibid., 318). But getting agreement on which terms are proper, 'basic' or foundational—as, for example, Popper's singular or 'basic statements': "Lo, a black swan," to borrow Newton-Smith's illustration—will not be possible without "prior knowledge of the whole fabric within which these elements occur." (Rorty 1979, 319) This marks a sharp division between Boland and Rorty.

Rorty is here invoking a holistic line of argument: understanding a theory is like understanding a culture or a language; we cannot understand the parts without knowing how the whole thing works. There is also the problem of the 'hermeneutic circle'; for it is equally true that we can't understand the whole until we know something about the parts. If we accept this holistic approach, and the reality of the hermeneutic circle, then a theory is not so much a structure erected upon certain basic elements or foundations, to be legitimated by the objective testing of its piece-by-piece reconstruction; it is more an expression of social or conversational conventions and practices. But then it also follows that methodology is not concerned with the foundations of knowledge; it is concerned with understanding practice. Thus Rorty: "For epistemology, conversation is implicit inquiry. For hermeneutics, inquiry is routine conversation." (ibid., 318)[2]

It is precisely at this point that methodological debate in economics is joined today (Hands, 1992 agonizes through the arguments on both sides). A number of individuals interested in economic methodology have followed Rorty's lead: McCloskey (1986, 1989), Klamer (1988), Weintraub (1991), to mention just three. Speaking generally, they all protest the elevation of selected conventions to the status of universal rules (for determining how, whether and when we know). The tradition they reject is most familiar to economists through the work of Sir Karl Popper (and Imre Lakatos).

POPPER'S METHODOLOGY OF REGULATIVE IDEALS

Karl Popper, whatever other views he may have promulgated, is above all an advocate of the position that science is what it is by virtue of adhering to certain ideals. The methodology of science is therefore not empirical or descriptive; it is not concerned with understanding scientists' practices; it is, rather, a set of rules for producing 'rational', or 'objective knowledge'. What is objective, in turn, is what has had the personal and subjective elements in it reduced to a minimum: objective knowledge is "independent of anybody's claim to know," that is, independent of belief (Popper, 1972, 109; quoted by Pera, 1989, 176).[3] It is not that Popper is primarily interested in criteria of 'good' science; but he does wish to demarcate science from nonscience, as being qualitatively different. He admits that there is no way to guarantee truth, nor even a way for the scientist to 'know' that it has been found. What the rules of method do guarantee is a negative.[4] As a matter of logic, they ensure that false claims—claims in which beliefs masquerade as objective knowledge—will be shown up. To give up the rules is to forego that guarantee and to run the (unnecessary) risk of confusing passions and beliefs with science, with all the political consequences that may follow.

Acceptance of Popper's rule-based approach has led students of economic methodology to focus on a limited range of questions: are economic theories falsifiable (Klant, 1984)? are they being 'severely' tested (Blaug, 1980)? does the history of economic thought show that progress towards 'better' theories has occurred, in the sense that error has been identified and dealt with, appeals to psychology and induction abandoned (Boland, 1986), and that theories of greater corroborated content have replaced theories with less (Blaug, 1990)? Others have begun to urge that these questions are unduly restrictive (Klamer, 1988; Mäki, 1990; Hands, below).

One can support this view *without* taking the Rortian perspective to mean that it is necessarily or always mistaken and pointless to investigate testing, assess problem-solutions, or write an internal history of theory. That at any rate is my position. It is shared by several of the authors in this collection; more importantly, it seems to be implied by taking the hermeneutic circle seriously: one has to start at both ends, with the whole *and* with the parts. The only things ruled out by a holistic perspective are an exclusive emphasis on the parts; and the notion that the parts are somehow basic or foundational.

It is as well to be clear on this point. I will presently offer some reasons why Popper's rule-based approach to methodology appears not to be workable; but his focus on problems, and on learning through a critical examination of competing solutions, is attractive and can be made compatible with all but that variant of the interpretative alternative which rejects any attempt to attach 'better'/'worse' rankings to interpretations. A stress on problems does not oblige one to think that problems have an identity distinct from the concerns and conceptual apparatus of the scientist. Problems are part of their time; and what is problematic is irreducibly context-dependent. It is also true that by paying full attention to the social and personal we can discover great amounts of value for understanding how problems come to be identified; how (and which) solutions come to be tried out; how the inscriptions of scientific efforts represented by research papers, and claims of facticity, and credibility, are 'produced'. Buying into the problem-based approach does, however, involve accepting that some solutions 'work', or that some work better than others.

Again, accepting that some ranking is possible does not require asserting timelessness, or objectivity; nor does it, even implicitly, require the privileging of some standard. All talk about alternatives requires adopting and comparing points of view; and obviously these are chosen, imposed, used for the sake of illumination, and so on. Within the chosen perspective, clearly a ranking of solutions is possible. But there is also a record—or so the problem-based approach insists—of evidence which enables ranking, to some degree, across local and personal perspectives. Houses do or do not fall down;

for the economy, we have similar records of observations (e.g., stock prices). These can be empirically modelled and 'explained'. True, those who believe that stock markets exist to perform arbitraging functions, and little else, will be more readily satisfied with an empirical finding that markets seem to be 'efficient' than will those who are interested in origins, adaptation, 'learning' by market participants, hence in quirks, imperfections, and the evolution of rules and practices. The so-called historical record is, of course, only one of the possible records that might have been made; and much of it might be our own construct. Yet the range of admissible interpretations is constrained by the traces of evidence we have, including the records of prices kept and other pieces of relevant information, such as traces of manipulative behaviors (to stick to the stock prices example). It is not true that very many interpretations are capable of being inserted into the past that has survived or that can be extracted (the 'real' past). Therefore the ranking of solutions within economics, for example, is conditional, and context- and community-bound; yet members of different sub-communities among economists frequently—not always—understand each other's language games, and cross-community rankings of solutions are criticised precisely by making explicit the commitments and criteria being employed by each. Hence, too, the conditional nature of rankings does not mean that they are either solipsistic or all separate *and* equal.

I would like to think that the only objection a holist could make to all this would be to point out that, all too often, insisting on the possibility of impersonal rankings has gone together with the employment of familiar notions such as: facts simply *are*, and there's an end of it. But that is an empirical (or historical) objection; it didn't have to be that way. Popper himself acknowledges that we stop probing not because we have hit rock-hard facts, but because "we are satisfied" that the resistances we encounter will support the structure we have erected, "at least for the time being" (1959, 111). This can be taken as a virtual invitation to explore just who the 'we' are, and why 'we' might be satisfied.

At the same time, Popper's methodology has lent itself to misuse by economists. The idea that there simply *are* facts invites belief in the idea that knowledge can be progressive; after all, there is in 'the facts' a standard for assessment to which every candidate solution can be brought. These ideas Popper will have no part of; but his methodological conviction that false solutions can be identified and either improved or dropped, combined with his view that situational analysis is a sort of model for the social sciences (see Hands, below), can easily be turned into the belief that *surviving* solutions (theories) are the most appropriate in some larger sense: they are *best*. Economists have a long tradition of linking survival with efficient outcomes. But if observed survivors are the best then "optimality covers the tracks of history." (Gould 1989, 300) There is no place in perfectness for distortions and malformations, whether produced by bumbling ineptitude or venality.

Popper cannot be blamed for this misapplication of his methodology by some practicing economists. Nonetheless—getting at last to the reasons I said would presently be given—following him becomes problematic if it is maintained, as Popper does maintain, that the social, cultural, language- and communication-related aspects of the production of knowledge by real live scientists are in a category that is quite distinct from the end product, 'objective knowledge'; that the one is in World 2, the other in World 3, and the object of inquiry in World 3 is in no way dependent upon what goes on in World 2. It is important to understand what is being claimed here. The claim is that the knowledge *status* of the product, by virtue of its being logical, universal, not context-bound, is other than that of the beliefs of the scientists doing the producing. Beliefs may be personal, political, cultural; but whatever they are, they constitute no part of scientific knowledge.

This *does* involve privileging, and it does involve claims for ranking which go far beyond what I suggested earlier would be acceptable to (most) holists. There are practical and logical difficulties in maintaining Popper's distinction, and I rehearse two lines of objection here which combine elements of both. I have selected what I consider to be fairly telling arguments.

1. **There is evidence that the inter-subjectivity requirement for World 3 knowledge cannot be met.** Replication of that which turns on particular, local, non-recurrent elements of the situation is impossible. One such element is the individual scientist, whose judgement and choices frequently are constitutive of the result. Harry Collins has made this case using the example of replicating laser technology (1985, esp. ch. 3. See also pp. 247-52, below). An instance within economics involves well known tests in the 1970s by American economists of the natural rate hypothesis. The econometric tests employed empirical models which were quite particular, and which the authors of the tests

did not claim to be representative of a single class of theory. That being the case, however, there was no way that the test results could be considered knowledge in a sense wholly distinct from the convictions held by the individual economists doing the testing and embodied in the particular models they selected for use (Kim, de Marchi and Morgan, 1992). To go beyond this would require a negotiated agreement on what is to count as representative. The negotiation, it is clear, not a test result, takes priority (cf. pp. 364-5, below).

2. **Efforts to render 'applicable' Popper's notion of verisimilitude or truthlikeness for judging theories have failed.** In principle, verisimilitude has nothing to do with evidence. It is expressed strictly in terms of the relative truth- and falsity-content of theories (Popper, 1965, 233, 234). This, in turn, is meant to be a logical, not a substantive, relation. As with so much else in Popper, verisimilitude was to serve as a way of facilitating criticism, in this case of guesses as to which of two theories is the more truthlike. Popper no more wanted to claim that he could know degrees of truthlikeness than that he could know in general (Miller, 1972, 53). Nonetheless, we have a need for some workable rule for comparing theories, and the fact is that efforts to produce a formal (set-theoretic) "canon of comparison" have been unsuccessful (Miller, 1975b, 207). The problem is that rival theories normally contradict each other, hence *cannot* be compared for verisimilitude (Miller, 1975a, 161).

Matters are no better with attempts to find a language within which to express and compare the substance of rival theories. If we are to compare theories—the search for the 'best', once again—we need to suppose a neutral language, so that we do not fall into the trap of merely translating one theory into the terms of the other, or vice versa. One possibility is to deploy what philosophers call a nominalistic language, or one which functions in terms of enumerated characteristics giving the meaning of words. Such a language, however, enables us to say that assertions are analytically true or contradictory, but it does not suffice to capture scientific (empirical) hypotheses. A scientific hypothesis is deemed better in Popperian terms the more vulnerable (falsifiable) it is; hence it should have as wide a range over observable facts as possible. But we run into the problem that to give hypotheses factual content, and even to express them, we need to use language in a more context-related way than a nominalistic language supposes. In economics the closest approach to nominalistic language use is to be found in axiomatic choice theory (for example, Debreu 1959). Even Debreu, however, though he is not concerned with refutable hypotheses, cannot avoid context-laden—i.e., *not* neutral—terms: commodity, agent, price system, 'action' (35). His mathematical language nominates quite restricted meanings for such terms, the aim being to ensure that "the theory...is logically entirely disconnected from its interpretations" (x). Yet the logic of the theory is said also to be developed so as facilitate possible interpretations (35), and in fact interpretation takes up most of the space in Debreu's *Theory of Value*. Debreu insists that different interpretations are possible without the theory's being altered; but debate inevitably centers on competing interpretations, and this necessarily involves *comparing* interpretations with the original meanings assigned to concepts. In short, the logic of the theory is no longer a distinct entity as soon as we begin interpreting it; what we have, rather, is a whole series of logic/interpretation pairs.

Besides this, enumerated characteristics are prior restrictions that eliminate potential falsifiers and thereby also restrict the possibilities of our learning through error. Not surprisingly, Popper himself objects that a purely nominalistic language cannot be a language adequate for science (1965, 262).

In short, attempts to find language-independent ways to compare theories, while preserving the scientific character of their hypotheses, have failed as completely as the searches for formal canons of comparison. As Miller puts it, appearances that two theories can be expressed so as to give answers to the 'same' question, or values for the 'same' quantity, are just that: the theories turn out to be "not invariant under trivial changes of language." (1975a, 166)[5] That leaves verisimilitude hanging in the air.[6]

What I infer from these considerations is that there is no *workable* separation possible between Worlds 2 and 3. Hence there is no *workable* basis for opposing universal, objective knowledge to local, contingent knowledge (cf. Herrnstein Smith, 1988).

But if regulative ideals and rules, such as "regard only that which deals in objective knowledge as scientific," or "progressive theories must have excess content," cannot be translated into operational procedures, quite obviously they still may be defended for their value as ideals. Popper, and his followers, faced with the objections just discussed, tend to fall back to this position. As Blaug (1991, 503) says: "the normative case for falsificationism might stand up even if the positive one fell to the ground." And when Popper expresses his preference for a society in which there is an agreed standard of freedom, which facilitates the picking out of infringements of liberty (1965, 5; cf. 375), he acknowledges that he is in fact only affirming "*an irrational faith* in the attitude [ideal] of reasonableness" (ibid., 357; emphasis added). Popper and Blaug fear that without their particular regulative ideals the tower of scientific achievement would come crashing down. I would expect that, if they are so concerned about the negative consequences of lapses from the ideal, they might be more seriously interested in understanding practice.[7] At any rate, whether for that reason, or because there is no workable separation possible between Worlds 2 and 3, methodologists simply cannot avoid trying to understand practice.

RECOVERING PRACTICE

Part I This collection of essays starts off with two critical surveys. The first, by Hands, underscores the problems with methodology of the Popperian sort. Hands includes Lakatos in this rule-based methodological tradition. He argues that precisely at one of the points where Lakatos is most Popperian—where he insists, for example, on assessing theories by the criterion of 'novelty'—Lakatos seems most out of touch with the way economists actually behave. By contrast, Popper, notably in his espousal of situational analysis, is virtually summarizing the neo-classical economist's actual method of analysis, yet the rationality principle, central in that method, is by his own admission unfalsifiable.

Tradition, belief and context are not on a par with objective knowledge in Popper's way of thinking. Yet it seems difficult to deny that social conditioning plays a role in the invention, introduction, persistence, acceptance, modification and rejection of statements in economics. Mäki, in the second survey essay, argues that if social conditioning does occur, we will not be able to understand how economics is done without "a descriptive statement of the actual situation [of the economist]." This is an extremely modest admission of the need to pay attention to context, and those sceptical of methodological ideals or rules, because underlying them is the presumption of a privileged position for making judgements about truth, would want to go much further.[8] Mäki is a Realist; more precisely, he believes in relating theoretical convictions to some ontic core of economic reality. He is therefore inclined to accept the idea that truth might emerge, whatever the goals, beliefs, and practices of scientists (and even independently of the existence of Popper-type methodological ideals). Radical social constructivists—those who hold that knowledge is not merely influenced by but *is* itself a social construct—will challenge the underlying notion of a separate truth. But Mäki's concern with truth leads him also to ask: are there social conditions that help successful truth-seeking? If the answer is yes, and if it is also the case that not all social conditions are equal in this regard, then the methodologist who believes in a real world and is interested in truth cannot do without a sociology of science.

Part II Part II comprises a pair of papers dealing with the auxiliary hypotheses needed to link rational choice at the social and the individual level. Nelson is concerned with the necessary distributional restrictions on individual behavior if the economist is to use market data to infer individual behavior, as is done in the molecular theory of gases. Bicchieri wants to know what additional hypotheses about players' knowledge and beliefs must be introduced if one is to be able to use the rationality postulate to reach social outcomes in cases involving strategic interaction between individuals. Both papers are about practice, but practice in the form of the sorts of theories economists produce.

Part III Most of the contributors in Part III stress the tension between holism and any methodology that tends to privilege some one standard or perspective. Rossetti argues that it is not possible to position oneself 'outside' practice. Mirowski pursues this further. The rhetoric project, he suggests, should be construed as a way of raising economists' awareness that the inside/outside distinction is not only suspect, but that this has consequences for a 'mainstream' economist. (McCloskey demurs: there is no necessary connection between one's particular 'politics' and one's acknowledgement of contingency.) Seiz asks: if genderedness in economic writings is ignored or downplayed, should we interpret this phenomenon as a special expression of the view that the social *can* be excluded in scientific inquiry? Her answer is No, because problems are always problems *for* someone or some group. Hamminga is less troubled by the matter of finding standards. He treats methodological ideas as subject to the test of history, the history of economists' theoretical constructs. This looks like an effort to make methodology subject to economic practice, but it is itself subject to the difficulties of establishing that the history is able to function as a standard; difficulties I have hinted at earlier, but which Hamminga doesn't openly address.

This third group of essays raises the question: What are the gains and losses from tempering our long-standing concern with regulative ideals and privileged standards? We surely lose a sense of (economic) science as something more solid, objective, and universal than the knowledge that is based inextricably in particular language communities and is therefore local, culture-bound. But that is, after all, only a loss of *sense*; nothing else is changed. What is gained is an opening up of the study of practice to a broader range of concerns; not a superior epistemology, note, but an admission of categories and topics for which previously there was no place.

New categories and topics help make way for new causal explanations. This is both more exciting and more challenging than might at first appear. That's because more is involved than simply accepting that there is a large array of possibilities: possible worlds, possible interpretations. Possibilities have to be rendered plausible, by which I mean more than that arguments are found persuasive; also involved is seeking out and applying constraints arising from data, the agents actually present, the sorts of questions of interest, the requirement of coherence. We are back at the idea of resistances introduced in passing earlier; only now the thought can be pressed a little further. Two illustrations: (1) If the household is viewed not as an undivided decision-making unit, or as a two-person unit with a dominant 'head', but as a grouping of two or more agents, each with a quit threshhold, how does this modify the issues that can be addressed? For one thing, in development economics (though not only there), fertility issues may be seen to take on a different caste, contingent upon whether the woman is or is not economically independent. What does it take, however, to get this altered concept into standard analysis? If lying behind the change are large social movements, reflected perhaps in increased workforce participation by women, at the very least understanding analytical change seems to require a grasp of political and social demands and responses to them. (2) What is at stake, governing a decision to treat stock prices as describable by a 'martingale' process rather than, more 'loosely', as a random walk? If what is involved is one's belief that economic processes must be law-governed, what kind of outlook does it take to commit to the still more 'radical' idea that distributions of stock prices may display increasing variance? What would have to be different about the history of economists' intellectual and cultural borrowings, and their aspirations for economics itself, to enable a debate to occur over this radical challenge?

It should be clear from these quick illustrations that the methodologist, wanting to understand practice, is directly or indirectly involved in a host of intellectual, cultural, historical, language-related, political and other considerations. These considerations collectively determine what will be found plausible by a group of economic thinkers at any one time and place.

I tentatively characterized the current methodological debate as one involving opposites. But that is actually misleading. Neither pole of the opposition gives us much warrant for conviction, neither the notion of science as ideals with no traceable link to practice, nor the idea that interpretation is all there is, the only game in town. Exploring what makes for plausibility, in the enlarged sense (involving resistances, hence some potential for ranking), occupies the somewhat neglected middle ground, and that's where methodologists interested in understanding practice will find themselves in the next few years.

NOTES

*My thanks to Bob Coats, Wade Hands and Roy Weintraub for direct critical input, and to Arjo Klamer, Marina Bianchi and Barbara Herrnstein Smith for generous instruction through conversation.

1. If two theories are indeed observationally equivalent, then "there is no matter of fact at stake" and the choice between them must be made on some other ground(s). Which? Since a decision must be made, which theory is counted 'in' and which 'out' is not independent of some property or properties over which *we* control the choice. For a useful, brief discussion, which also urges that there is an ineradicable conventionalist element in Popper's position, see Newton-Smith (1981), 61 ff.

2. Below I shall argue that the elements that Popper uses for rationally judging theories—not just 'basic' statements, but criteria such as verisimilitude—cannot be separated from language which, in turn, is context-laden. It is startling to realize how problematic this is for all formal epistemologies, all attempts to 'stand back

from' and *judge* what we 'know'. The attempts (for example by Carnap, and the English language-analytic school of philosophy) to treat philosophical problems as problems of formal syntax are now seen to have been ill-conceived. Even Popper acknowledges this (1976, 30).

3. I am indebted to Pera (1989) for his clarification of both the history and the implications of rule-based methodology, especially in the work of Imre Lakatos.

4. It is worth stressing this in connection with Popper, because the protests of McCloskey and others about Methodology (capital M) rest on its alleged pretensions to tell us what Good Science is. This confuses epistemology with methodology, a confusion that cannot be charged to Popper's account.

5. If one tries to do without the positive ideas content of theories and sticks strictly to comparisons in terms of the (non-quantitative) *answers to questions* yielded by the one and by the other, the problem arises that unless one theory is complete (which is never the case) we can always find a consequence of the other which neither follows from the first nor contradicts it (Miller, 1975a, 165). Finally, if one sticks to *numerical consequences*, something similar blocks our way: "there will always be quantities evaluated by the one but not by the other." (ibid., 166)

6. Odd though it may seem, Popper apparently wants there to be some connection back from World 3 to World 2. He invokes for this purpose a "transference principle," according to which "what is true in logic is true in scientific method *and in the history of science*." (1972, quoted by Pera 1989, 176; emphasis added) But with verisimilitude hanging in the air it is difficult to see what the basis could be for making this connection.

7. Blaug (1980) is replete with case studies of modern economic practice, but it is clear that he is less interested in understanding the practice than in showing how far it has deviated from Popperian ideal science. The record is one of abysmal failure. But instead of concluding that maybe economists' practices should be understaood in a different way, Blaug draws the lesson that they should try

harder to live up to Popper's ideals.

8. Anti-foundationalist views are represented in this volume by McCloskey, Rossetti, Mirowski, Klamer and Weintraub.

REFERENCES

Blaug, M. (1980). *The methodology of economics. Or, how economists explain.* Cambridge: Cambridge University Press.

__________________ (1991a). "Second Thoughts on the Keynesian Revolution." *History of Political Economy*, 23, 171-92.

__________________ (1991b). "Afterword." In *Appraising Economic Theories: Studies in the Methodology of Research Programs*, Neil de Marchi and Mark Blaug (eds). Aldershot: Edward Elgar, 499-512.

Boland, L. A. (1982). *The Foundations of Economic Method.* London: Allen and Unwin.

__________________ (1986). *Methodology for a New Microeconomics. The Critical Foundations.* Boston: Allen and Unwin.

Collins, H. M. (1985). *Changing Order. Replication and Induction in Scientific Practice.* Beverly Hills, Calif.: Sage.

Debreu, G. (1959). *Theory of Value. An Axiomatic Analysis of Economic Equilibrium.* New Haven: Yale University Press.

Gould, S. J. (1989). *Wonderful Life. The Burgess Shale and the Nature of History.* New York: Norton.

Hamminga, B. (1983). *Neoclassical Theory Structure and Theory Development.* New York: Springer.

Hands, D. W. (1992). *Testing Rationality and Progress. Essays on the Popperian Tradition in Economic Methodology.* Totowa, N.J.

Herrnstein Smith, B. (1988). *Contingencies of Value. Alternative Perspectives for Critical Theory.* Cambridge, Mass.: Harvard University Press.

Hausman, D. M. (1992). *The Inexact and Separate Science of Economics.* Cambridge: Cambridge University Press.

Kim, J., de Marchi, N. and Morgan, M. (1992). "Empirical Model Particularities and Beliefe in the Natural Rate Hypothesis." Mimeo.

Klamer, A. (1998a). "Economics as Discourse." In Neil de Marchi (ed.) *The Popperian Legacy in Economics.* Cambridge: Cambridge University Press, 259-78.

______________ (1988b). "Negotiating a new conversation about economics." In Klamer, A., McCloskey, D. N., and Solow, R. M. (ed's) *The consequences of economic rhetoric.* Cambridge: Cambridge University Press.

Klant, J.J. (1984). *The Rules of the Game. The Logical Structure of Economic Theories.* Cambridge: Cambridge University Press.

Laudan, L. (1990). *Science and Relativism. Some Key Controversies in the Philosophy of Science.* Chicago: University of Chicago Press.

McCloskey, D. N. (1986). *The Rhetoric of Economics.* Madison: University of Wisconsin Prtess.

______________ (1989). "Formalism in Economics, Rhetorically Speaking." *Ricerche Economiche*, XLIII, 57-75.

Mäki, U. (1990). "Methodology of economics: complaints and guidelines." *Finnish Economic Papers*, 3, 77-84.

Mill, J.S. (1836). "On the Definition of Political Economy; and on the Method of Investigation Proper to It." Available in *The Collected Works of John Stuart Mill*, J.M. Robson (ed.), vol. IV, *Essays on*

Economics and Society. Toronto: University of Toronto Press, 1967, 309-39.

Miller, D. (1972). "The Truth-likeness of Truthlikeness." *Analysis*, 33, 50-55.

__________ (1975a). "The Accuracy of Predictions." *Synthese*, 3, 159-91.

__________ (1975b). "The Accuracy of Predictions. A Reply." *Synthese*, 30, 207-19.

Pera, M. (1989). "Methodological Sophisticationism: A Degenerating Project." In K. Gavroglu, Y. Goudaroulis and P. Nicolacopoulos (ed's) *Imre Lakatos and Theories of Scientific Change*. Boston: Kluwer Academic Publishers, 169-87.

Popper, K. (1959). *The Logic of Scientific Discovery*. London: Hutchinson.

__________ (1965). *Conjectures and Refutations*. London: Routledge & Kegan Paul.

__________ (1972). *Objective Knowledge*. Oxford: Clarendon.

__________ (1976). *Unended Quest. An Intellectual Biography*. Glasgow: Collins.

Robbins, L. (1932). *An Essay on the Nature & Significance of Economic Science*. London: Macmillan.

Rorty, R. (1979). *Philosophy and the Mirror of Nature*. Princeton: Princeton University Press.

Newton-Smith, W.H. (1981). *The Rationality of Science*. London: Routledge & Kegan Paul.

Weintraub, E. Roy (1991). *Stabilizing Dynamics. Constructing Economic Knowledge*. Cambridge: Cambridge University Press.

I. Rules and Constructions

CHAPTER 1

FALSIFICATION, SITUATIONAL ANALYSIS AND SCIENTIFIC RESEARCH PROGRAMS: THE POPPERIAN TRADITION IN ECONOMIC METHODOLOGY

D. Wade Hands

INTRODUCTION

No other philosopher and his work have influenced economic methodology as much as Karl Popper; yet, in over fifty years of philosophical writing Popper explicitly considered economics in only a few rare cases. From the economic profession's introduction to falsificationist ideas in Hutchison (1938) to the recent spate of Lakatosian case studies in the history of economic thought,[1] no major issue in economic methodology has been discussed without a significant Popperian "voice."[2]

It is the purpose of this essay to critically re-examine the Popperian influence in economic methodology. The presentation will be in three parts, each corresponding to one of the three main points of contact between the Popperian tradition and the literature on economic methodology. The first section examines falsificationism: Popper's well-known approach to the philosophy of natural science. The second section discusses "situational analysis": Popper's less well-known approach to the social sciences. The final topic considered is the work of Imre Lakatos and how it has been applied to the history of economic thought. Lakatos' philosophical position is certainly different than Popper's, but his work is clearly enough within the general Popperian tradition to be included in this re-examination of Popper. In each of the three areas the focus will be on the literature that explicitly concerns economics; there will not be any effort to discuss general philosophical arguments or evaluations based on other scientific disciplines. Throughout the chapter survey material is provided to help familiarize the reader with the relevant literature, but the chapter does not provide an exhaustive survey of any of the three topics.

FALSIFICATIONISM

No doubt economists, philosophers, and members of the academic community in general, know Karl Popper best for his falsificationist approach to the philosophy of science. First presented in *Logik der Forschung* in 1934 (English translation, Popper (1968)), falsificationism represents Popper's approach to the growth of knowledge as well as his solution to (or dissolution of) the traditional problem of induction. It is for his falsificationism that Popper claims responsibility for the death of logical positivism.[3]

Actually, Popperian falsificationism is composed of two separate theses: one demarcational (concerned with demarcating science from nonscience) and one methodological (concerned with how science should be practiced). The demarcation thesis is that for a theory to be "scientific" it must be at least potentially falsifiable, that is, there must exist at least one empirical basic statement that is in conflict with the theory.[4] This potential falsifiability is a logical relationship between the theory and a basic statement; in particular, the demarcation criterion does not require that anyone has actually tried to falsify the theory, only that it would be logically possible to do so. Popper's demarcation criterion has been the subject of extensive debate in the philosophical literature, but it is seldom an issue in economics—possibly because most commentators feel that economic theories are potentially falsifiable.[5] For economists who advocate a falsificationist position, the more important issue is methodology rather than demarcation, and Popperian *methodology* requires the practical (rather than merely the logical) falsifiability of scientific theories.

Briefly, and neglecting a host of philosophical issues, Popper's falsificationist methodology requires the search for scientific knowledge to proceed in the following way. Start with a scientific problem situation: something requiring a scientific explanation.

Second, propose a bold conjecture that might offer a solution to the problem. Third, severely test the conjecture by comparing its least likely consequences with the relevant empirical data. The notion here is that a test is *more severe* the more prima facie *unlikely* the consequence tested; the theory should be forced to "stick its neck out," to "offer the enemy, namely nature, the most exposed and extended surface."[6] Finally, the last move in the game depends on how the theory performed during the third testing stage. If the implications of the theory were not supported by the evidence, the conjecture is falsified and it should be replaced by a new theory that is *not ad hoc* relative to the original.[7] If the theory was not falsified then it is considered corroborated by the test and it is accepted provisionally. It should be noted that given Popper's fallibilism, this acceptance is provisional forever; the method does not guarantee the surviving theory is true, only that is has faced a tough opponent and won.

There are a number of reasons why such a falsificationist methodology might be particularly appealing to economic methodologists. If the task of economic methodology is viewed (as it has been until quite recently) as "choosing" among various philosophies of natural science in order to "apply" one to economics, then Popperian falsificationism has some clear advantages over anything that might be borrowed from the positivist tradition. For one thing, falsificationism is eminently more straightforward and intuitive than the inductive logic of the later logical empiricists. Perhaps more important is the fact that Popper's falsificationism is truly a *methodology*. Unlike philosophers in the positivist tradition, Popper was not trying to provide an epistemic justification for the knowledge claims of science. Popper's goal was the more mundane task of characterizing a set of rules (a method) which would allow us to learn from experience. This distinction between methodology and justification is critical to understanding the Popperian preference of the economics profession. The reason is that by and large the positivist tradition was *not* a tradition of methodological rule making. Most logical empiricist philosophers were entirely convinced that science proceeded by induction; their philosophical task was to *justify* that procedure. Such a justificationist philosophy of science provides little or no guidance to an economics profession in search of scientific rules. The question for economic *methodology* is not to provide a philosophical justification for science, but rather to find a set of rules that can be followed so that economists can do whatever it is that scientists do.[8]

Another reason for the support of Popperian falsificationism among economists is that it seems to solve (or dissolve) the old induction versus deduction debate in economics; it provides a tidy way out of the *methodenstreit* without making either side the overall winner. Consistent with the apriorist/deductivist tradition in economics, the falsificationist method would allow hypotheses based on introspection and/or the supposition of rational action. Consistent with the historical/inductivist tradition in economics, falsificationism requires empirical testing and the discipline of the data. Popperian falsificationism seems to allow the profession to take advantage of what is best in each of these traditional approaches to economic research. It is permissible to leap to conjectures about economic behavior without the extensive accumulation of empirical data which would be required if only inductive generalizations were allowed, while at the same time (unlike the Misesian approach) the facts do matter and acceptable hypotheses must survive severe tests. This "best of both worlds" property makes falsificationism a natural philosophical companion to the Marshallian tradition in economics, a characteristic that provides for its support by many methodologists.

In addition to these philosophical issues there are possibly some forces of attraction that should be classified as "sociological" (and/or personal, and/or ideological). In particular, Popper's direct influence on a number of influential London School of Economics economists,[9] and his longstanding relationship with Hayek, may have contributed to Popper's popularity among economists. Certainly, citations originating from these two sources made Popper's name familiar to many economists who would not have otherwise been aware of his work. Finally, it is possible to find an ideological connection. Popper's own work in social and political philosophy[10] is decidedly antihistoricist and antiMarxist: views that are (at the very least) not inconsistent with those of most mainstream economists. These "sociological" and/or "ideological" factors do not directly support a falsificationist methodology for economics; rather, they explain why economists might consider Popper an "acceptable" philosopher and thereby (since falsificationism is Popper's most well-known view) lend indirect support to falsificationism in economics.[11]

Now despite all of these reasons why falsificationism might be a desirable methodology for economics, the fact is that *falsificationism is seldom if ever practiced in economics*. This seems to be the one point generally agreed upon by recent methodological commentators.

In fact, this (empirical) claim is supported at length by the case studies in Blaug (1980), a work that consistently advocates falsificationism as a normative doctrine. The disagreement between critics and defenders of falsificationism is *not whether it has been practiced*, basically it has not, but rather *whether it should be practiced*. The real questions are whether the profession should "try harder" to practice falsificationism, though it has failed to do so in the past, and would the discipline of economics be substantially improved by such falsificationist practice.[12]

One way to answer such queries about the appropriateness of falsificationism in economics would be to consider the appropriateness of Popper's falsificationist methodology as a *general* approach to the growth of scientific knowledge. Falsificationism may not be appropriate for economics, even if it is a good model for the growth of knowledge in natural science, but if it fails in natural science then its usefulness in economics is surely in doubt. Unfortunately, such an excursion into the vast philosophical literature criticizing Popperian falsificationism is far beyond the scope of the current essay.[13]

Rather than delving into the more general philosophical literature, the next section will simply list some of the criticisms of falsificationism that can and have been raised explicitly within the context of economics. These criticisms may of course overlap with more general concerns, but even so, only economics will be discussed. The list is not exhaustive, but it does capture many of the problems exhibited by a falsificationist methodology in economics. They are not listed in any particular order of importance.[14]

1. The Duhemian problem[15] and related issues pose insuperable problems for falsificationist practice in economics. There are a number of reasons why this is the case. First, the complexity of human behavior requires the use of numerous initial conditions and strong simplifying assumptions. Some of these restrictions may actually be false, such as the differentiability of production functions or the infinite divisibility of commodities. Some of these restrictions may be logically unfalsifiable, such as the assumptions of eventually diminishing returns or eventually decreasing returns to scale. Still others of these assumptions may be logically falsifiable but practically unfalsifiable, such as the completeness assumption in consumer choice theory. And finally, most of these restrictions are extremely difficult to test for because of the absence of a suitably controlled laboratory

environment. The presence of such a variety of restrictions makes it virtually impossible to "aim the arrow of *modus tollens*" at one particular problematic element of the set of auxiliary hypotheses when contrary evidence is found.

Secondly, in addition to these problems with auxiliary assumptions, there is no consensus regarding the empirical basis in economics. It is always possible to argue that what observed was "not really" involuntary unemployment or "not really" economic profit, etc. Now, it is a fundamental part of the Popperian program that the empirical basis need not be incorrigible, but Popper does require a generally accepted convention on the empirical basis.[16] In economics, such a conventionally accepted empirical basis often does not exist.

Finally, it should be noted that social sciences can have feedback effects that do not exist in the physical sciences. The test of an economic theory may itself alter the initial conditions for the test. Conducting a test of the relationship between the money supply and the price level may alter expectations in such a way that the initial conditions (which were true "initially") are not true after the test (or if the "same" test were conducted again).[17]

2. The qualitative comparative statics technique used in economics makes severe testing very difficult and cheap corroborational success "too easy." Even with the auxiliary assumptions discussed in (1.) still, it is very often the case that the strongest available prediction is a qualitative comparative statics result that only specifies that the variable in question increases, decreases, or remains the same. Since being of the correct sign is much easier than being of the correct sign and magnitude, this qualitative technique generates theories that are low in empirical content, have few potential falsifers, and are difficult, if not impossible, to test severely. The result is often economic theories that are corroborated, but trivial.[18]

3. Popper's "admitted failure" (1983, xxxv) to develop an adequate theory of verisimilitude[19] presents problems for a falsificationist methodology in economics. The problem of verisimilitude developed in an attempt to reconcile Popper's falsificationist methodology with his scientific realism. For a realist the aim of

science is "true" theories; according to falsificationism, scientific theories should be chosen if they have been corroborated by passing severe tests. If the falsificationist method is to fulfill the realist aim of science, it should be demonstrated that more corroborated theories are closer to the truth; this is the goal of Popper's theory of verisimilitude.

Actually, a satisfactory theory of verisimilitude would serve Popperian philosophy in two separate ways. The first, mentioned above, would be to provide an epistemic justification for playing the game of science by falsificationist rules. This issue is extremely important for Popperian philosophy since it means that without a theory of verisimilitude there are philosophically "no good reasons" (Popper, 1972, 22) for choosing theories as Popper recommends. The second function of a theory of verisimilitude is more practical; it would provide some rules for choosing the "best" theory in troublesome cases. This is because a theory of verisimilitude would provide rules for discovering which of two theories has more verisimilitude, which is a better approximation to the truth. Thus, if we had two theories and both had been falsified, we could choose the one with more verisimilitude. Notice that falsificationism without a theory of verisimilitude is of no help in such cases; since both are false, both are *out* (similarly for cases involving a choice between a falsified but bold theory and a corroborated but modest theory).[20] Again having a way to determine which is closer to the truth might allow us to choose a theory more consistent with the aims of science than simple falsificationist rules.

This second, more practical, function of the theory of verisimilitude is extremely important for economic methodology. For all the reasons discussed above, and perhaps others as well, economists are almost always faced with choosing between two falsified theories or between a bold falsified theory and a more modest corroborated one. If Popper's theory of verisimilitude had been a success, and it could be added to the norms of simple falsificationism (both to justify the norms and to help in making the practical decisions of theory choice) then falsificationism might have an important role in economics. Without the link between severe testing and truthlikeness, the method is of limited value in pursuing the realist aim of science.

4. Popper's rules for progressive theory development (non *ad hocness*) are often inappropriate in economics. Popper argues that if one theory is to constitute "progress" over a predecessor, the new theory must be "independently testable"; it must have "excess empirical content," predict "novel facts."[21] This issue will be examined in more detail in the Lakatos section below, but for now let it be said that while progress of this Popperian type may sometimes be of interest to economists, often progress in economics is (and should be) much different. Often economists are concerned with finding new explanations for well-known stylized (non novel) facts, or alternatively, economists are concerned with explaining the same phenomena with fewer theoretical restrictions. What consititutes "progress" in economic theory (or what should constitute progress) is a complex and ongoing question, but it is apparent that any suitable answer will require a much more liberal set of standards than those offered by strict Popperian falsificationism.

All of these criticisms do not bode well for a falsificationist economic methodology. Despite all of the reasons why a falsificationist methodology might be attractive, it fails to provide an adequate set of rules for doing economics. Strict adherence to falsificationist norms would virtually *destroy all existing economic theory* and leave economists with a rule book for a game unlike anything the profession has played in the past. This high cost would be paid without any guarantee that obeying the new rules would result in theories any closer to the truth about economic behavior than those currently available.

Now, of course, denying that falsificationism provides the proper methodological rules for conducting economics does *not* mean that "the facts" should not matter in economic theory choice or that empirical testing is not important. This type of argument is a quite common red herring in methodological discussion involving falsificationism in economics. Popperian falsificationism is not generic empiricism; it is a *very* specific set of rules about how scientific inquiry should be conducted. Abandoning Popperian falsificationism as a methodology does not mean abandoning learning from experience.

SITUATIONAL ANALYSIS

While economic methodologists have long been concerned with Popperian falsificationism, Popper's views on situational analysis have only recently become an explicit part of the literature on economic method. The most likely reason for this neglect is the relative (to falsificationism) inaccessibility of Popper's work on the topic. The staunchest supporters of situational analysis have been social science oriented philosophers, such as I. C. Jarvie, who became familiar with the argument through Popper's lectures,[22] and while the central thesis was presented in Popper's work on social and political philosophy (1961, 1966), the clearest presentation of the argument is Popper (1967), a paper only recently translated from the original French (Popper 1985). Other presentations of the topic are scattered about in works such as Popper (1976a); a paper written as part of a debate with the Frankfurt School of sociology.

Situational analysis is Popper's method for the social sciences.[23] In fact, he argues that situational analysis is the *only* method appropriate for the social sciences.[24] Now, since economics is surely a *social* science, there is a paradox in the fact that economic methodologists have focused almost exclusively on falsificationism, Popper's philosophy of natural science, and neglected situational analysis. This paradox, though explicable in terms of the relative inaccessibility of Popper's writings on situational analysis, is even more pronounced since situational analysis *is the method of economic analysis.*[25]

According to Popper's situational analysis, explanations of human behavior should proceed as follows. Suppose the problem is to explain why agent A engaged in some particular type of behavior, say X. The first step in explaining this behavior is to describe the "situation" of the agent at the time the behavior in question took place. This description of the agent's situation will normally include both subjective components (the agent's goals, beliefs, desires, etc.) as well as objective components (physical and social constraints the agent faces). The second step in the explanation is to provide an analysis of the situation; to specify what type of behavior would be appropriate (i.e. rational) given the agent's situation. The third part of the explanation is to add, and this is the key, the *rationality principle* (RP), which asserts that *all* individuals *actually act in a way that is appropriate* to their situation (that is they act rationally). This RP allows us to deduce the act of the agent from the description of his/her "situation" and our analysis of what constitutes appropriate behavior. The RP is a bridge-principle that connects the "situation" with an "action;" it "stands in for the 'law' that 'animates' the otherwise inert collection of situational features" (Latsis 1983, 133).

Schematically then, the situational analysis explaining why agent A did X has the following form.[26]

I. Description of the Situation:	Agent A was in situation S.
II. Analysis of the Situation:	In situation S the appropriate (rational) thing to do is X.
III. The RP:	Agents always act appropriately (rationally) given their situations.
-----------------	-------------------------
IV. Explanandum:	Therefore: A did X.

It is easy to see that situational analysis is the method of microeconomics (and any macroeconomics based on micro foundations). Economists specify the situation of the agent (individual or firm) usually in terms of the preferences and/or technology and the relevant constraints (prices, income, factor constraints, etc.). Included in the description of the situation is some "motivating" consideration (maximizing utility, maximizing profit, etc.). The second step is to deduce the appropriate behavior of the agent given the situation specified (buy more, buy less, increase production, decrease production, etc.). This second step is what constitutes most of economic *theory*, the formal deduction (usually mathematical) of the "appropriate" behavior in a particular "situation." Finally, if the economist's task is to explain an observed action, the RP is activated to connect the analysis of the situation with the action to be explained. If the task is "pure theory," then this latter step is neglected and the "theoretical result" is technically deducing step II from a hypothetical situation in step I. Comparative statics results are simply performing the deduction from I to II twice, with a slight change in an element of the situation I between the deductions. Aggregative phenomena, such as equilibrium prices, are explained by adding two additional steps to the above scheme: V and VI. Step V adds additional analysis about the aggregate impact of a number of agents (A_1, A_2, ... A_n) each doing the appropriate thing, $X = (X_1, X_2, ... X_n)$. The analysis in step V takes the following form: if all A_i's do X_i; then the aggregate result will be Y. Step VI is then an aggregative explanandum: therefore Y.

Notice that such an explanatory scheme really captures all of (at least micro) economics, not just the textbook versions.[27] For example, the great debates over whether firms maximize profits, or satisfice, or mark-up prime costs, are not debates that alter the above scheme as the basic method of explanation. These are only debates about what constitutes an empirically interesting specification of the situation the agent (in this case the firm) faces. What is rigid about traditional textbook microeconomics is not that it requires adherence to the above scheme, but rather that *only certain things* are permitted in the description of the agent's situation. For instance, the conventions of the profession traditionally allow only preferences and technology as the private parts of the agent's situation, and only prices as the acceptable objective (public) constraints.

In summary then, Popper proposes situational analysis (hereafter SA) as the only general approach for providing explanations in social science and microeconomic explanations satisfy this criterion; microeconomic explanations are special cases of SA explanations. This relationship between SA and economics raises a number of issues; some of these issues involve Popper's SA approach itself (and therefore economics), while others involve the particular form that economic explanations take *within* the general SA framework.

The most important question for SA itself is that it produces "scientific" explanations that do not satisfy Popper's own (falsificationist) criteria for such explanations.[28] According to Popper the falsificationist, the universal generalizations used in a scientific explanation should be scientific theories. This means, as discussed above, that such generalizations should (1) be falsifiable, and (2) have actually passed severe tests (be corroborated). Now consider the RP. It serves as the universal generalization in such a SA explanation, it is the "law" in the explanation, and yet its nomic status is unclear.

Some claim that the RP is simply unfalsifiable; there exists no observation that would require us to give up (would logically conflict with) the claim that the agent is acting appropriately to the situation.

It can always be argued that there is something in (the subjective part of) the situation, unknown to us, that renders the action appropriate. Others (most philosophical commentators on the issue) argue that the RP *is* falsifiable, but that it should never be abandoned; that when faced with a potentially falsifying observation we should "*cling to the rationality principle* and revise or hypothesis about his aims and beliefs" (Watkins 1970, 173).[29] In either case though, whether the RP is unfalsifiable or whether we simply choose by methodological fiat to ignore its falsification, it is not the kind of universal generalization that Popper, the falsificationist, would allow in a scientific explanation. Thus, if we insist on Popper's demarcation criterion, social science explanations relying on the RP "are not *bona fide* scientific explanations" (Koertge, 1974, 201).[30] Or, even more strongly, since philosophers of science have traditionally considered the provision of scientific explanations to be an (possibly *the*) important aim of science, social science, including economics, is not *science* after all. This is certainly relevant to economics, but it is also relevant to the entire Popperian program in philosophy of science since Popper explicitly developed his demarcation criteria to demarcate scientific theories from what he considered pseudo-science: Marx and Freud (Popper, 1976b, 41-44). These social theories can hardly be criticized for not doing what the very best social sciences (in Popper's view) do not do.[31]

Before turning to the second type of questions raised by SA explanations, it should be noted that the above questions are fundamental philosophical issues. Some claim that to give up such explanations in social science would amount to abandoning free will to complete determinism.[32] On the other hand, explanations involving RP, unlike explanations in the physical sciences, are not causal; there is no mechanism connecting the situation with the act. It has been argued that it is precisely this causality avoidance, and thus freedom preserving characteristic, that makes SA explanations so attractive to Popper; "Popper wishes to escape the ugly consequences of what he considers to be Hume's dilemma by developing an account of behavior which is neither random nor determined but somewhere in between" (Latsis, 1983, 137).

Returning now to the more practical concerns of economic methodology, what can be said about microeconomic explanations *as* SA explanations? In other words, what if we disregard the above general criticism of SA explanations and focus on the particular form which SA explanations take in economics? What is the lesson here for economic methodology?

The lesson is that not much can be learned from Popper's writings on SA or related work by other philosophers. If we accept SA explanations as a fact of life in social science, then all of the "action" in economics must occur in the description of the agent's situation, and economists are left with all of the traditional questions regarding theory choice in their discipline. Since the RP (stage III) is in *every* explanation, it is the same from one "theory" to the next. The analysis step (step II) is of course different for each different posited explanation, but since this second step is mostly deduction from the specifications of the agent's situation (step I), it is relatively mechanical (though it may be technically quite complex). It seems the really creative part of economics and the place where different "theories" compete for attention is in the description of the agent's situation (step I). Economists must make decisions about how to specify the (subjective and objective) situation of the agent so that economic behavior may be predicted or explained. Recognizing that explanations in economics are really all Popperian SA explanations doesn't "help" with the fundamental issues of theory choice in economics. Economists must still make decisions about how the facts will influence their choices, how to modify the specification of the agent's situation when a prediction fails, what nonempirical considerations should influence theory choice, etc.

Popper and other philosophers writing on SA have focused on basically two issues. The first, discussed above, has been the question of the nomic status of the RP. The second has been to demonstrate (by example) the success of SA in various social sciences. Now the former question is an important philosophical issue that has an impact on the ultimate epistemic standing of economics, but it seems to have little to do directly with day to day matters of theory choice.[33] The latter issue, no matter how psychologically satisfying the results might be, has no effect on the economics profession since economics is already the source of the most successful applications of SA. Thus while economic explanations are SA explanations, and while such explanations raise important philosophical issues, the Popperian literature on SA has little to offer (at least at this time) economic methodologists concerned with the hard questions of why economists should choose one theory over another.

LAKATOS' METHODOLOGY OF SCIENTIFIC RESEARCH PROGRAMS

Lakatos's work in the philosophy of science first appeared in the early 1970s (Lakatos, 1970, 1971) and it was adopted almost immediately by a number of economic methodologists. Numerous papers on Lakatos appeared in the economics literature, many as a result of the Nafplion Colloquium on Research Programmes in Physics and Economics in 1974.[34] The literature on "Lakatos and economics" has taken basically two (non-mutually exclusive) forms. The first is principally historical, attempting to "reconstruct" some particular episode in the history of economic thought along Lakatosian lines; the second is more in the spirit of traditional work in economic methodology, attempting to appraise Lakatos's methodology of scientific research programs as an economic methodology and/or compare it to other philosophies such as Popper or Kuhn.[35]

In many respects Lakatos's methodology of scientific research programs (MSRP) is an extension of the evolution of the Popperian tradition in the philosophy of science, but in other respects it is very different, addressing issues raised by other philosophers such as Kuhn (1970) and those in the historical tradition. For Lakatos, the primary unit of appraisal in science is the "research program" rather than the scientific theory. A research program is a rather loose amalgam consisting of a hard core, positive and negative heuristics, and a protective belt.[36] The hard core contains the fundamental metaphysical presuppositions of the program; it defines the program, and its elements are treated as irrefutable by the program's practitioners. To participate in the program is to accept and be guided by the program's hard core. For example, in Weintraub's Lakatosian reconstruction of the NeoWalrasian research program in economics, the hard core consists of propositions such as: agents have preferences over outcomes, agents act independently and optimize subject to constraints, etc.[37] The positive and negative heuristics, respectively, are instructions about what should and should not be pursued in the development of the program. The positive heuristic guides researchers toward the right questions to ask and the best tools to use in answering them; the negative heuristic advises on what questions should not be pursued and what tools are inappropriate. Again, using Weintraub's analysis of the NeoWalrasian program as an example, the positive heuristic contains injunctions such as: construct theories where the agents optimize, while the negative heuristic implores researchers to avoid things like theories involving irrational behavior. Finally, the protective belt consists of the program's theories, auxiliary hypotheses, empirical conventions, and the (evolving) "body" of the research program. All of the activity of the program occurs in the protective belt as a result of the interaction of the hard core, the heuristics, and the program's empirical record. For the NeoWalrasian program it is argued that the protective belt includes almost all of applied microeconomics.

A research program is appraised on the basis of the theoretical activity in the protective belt. There is *theoretical progress* if each change in the protective belt is empirical content increasing, if it predicts novel facts.[38] The research program exhibits *empirical progress* if this excess empirical content is confirmed (Lakatos, 1970, 118). Lakatos considers a third type of progress, heuristic progress, that requires the changes to be consistent with the hard core of the program. His definitions of theoretical and empirical progress presuppose that conditions for this latter type of progress have been satisfied.

Lakatos's Popperian lineage is evident in a number of ways. One of these ways is in his characterization of empirical content and novel facts. For Lakatos, like Popper, "The empirical basis of a theory is the set of its potential falsifiers: the set of those observational propositions which may disprove it" (Lakatos, 1970, 98, n. 2). Thus, while Lakatos clearly considers progress to be achieved through empirical confirmation, rather than falsification, his characterization of the tension between theory and fact is fundamentally falsificationist. Also with respect to empirical content, Lakatos is clearly Popperian in his "conventionalism" about the empirical basis.[39] Finally, the Popperian spirit is evident in the way Lakatos defines "metaphysical" and his recognition of the importance of metaphysics in science.[40]

On the other hand, there are some very unPopperian things about the MSRP. Most important is the complete immunity of the hard core to empirical criticism; the idea that it is appropriate to completely immunize any part of scientific theory is in direct conflict with Popper's "nothing is sacred" falsificationist philosophy of science. Certainly, Popper recognizes that science has experienced periods of Kuhnian "normal science" where the critical spirit was temporarily arrested, but for Popper this is something to lament not praise (Popper, 1970). Another point of disagreement is obviously confirmation versus falsification. Other than the way Lakatos defines empirical content, he has little regard for falsification. For Lakatos all theories are "born refuted" (1970, 120-21), and the real task of philosophy of science is to develop a method of theory appraisal that *starts* from this fact. Finally, Lakatos embraces an historical metamethodology whereby the actual history of science can be used to appraise various methodologies of science.[41] For Popper, methodology is purely a normative affair and there is no sense in which the actual history of science can be used to "test" methodologies.

These places where Lakatos splits with Popper are the places where Lakatos is most likely to win the favor of economists since they happen to be areas of substantial tension between falsificationism and economics. Certainly, economics is replete with "hard cores." Not only is the rationality principle protected from refutation, but individual economic theories harbor hard core propositions as well: Weintraub's hard core elements of the NeoWalrasian program being an excellent case in point. While not all economists would agree on exactly what these hard core propositions should be in any particular domain of inquiry, there seems to be a consensus that such hard core presuppositions exist and that they necessarily define alternative research programs in economics. A philosophical program such as Popperian falsificationism, which requires practitioners to be willing to give up any part of their research program at any instant, can hardly provide a guide for doing economics as appropriate as one (such as Lakatos's) that allows for these pervasive hard cores. So too for the issue of confirmation versus falsification. It is clear that falsificationism has not been practiced in economics and to arbitrarily enforce it would essentially eliminate the discipline. On the other hand, there *is* a great amount of empirical activity in economics. The facts do matter, but they matter in a much more subtle and complex way than falsificationism allows. As Weintraub states, "the idea that facts can falsify theories, and that the role of applied work is to produce facts that falsify the theories that the theorists create, is simultaneously to misunderstand facts, theories, tests, and falsification" (1988, 222). Surely, Lakatos' notion of empirical progress is more like what the best empirical work in economics does and should do than Popperian falsificationism.

Finally, Lakatos (unlike Popper) has emphasized the role of the history of science in supporting particular methodological proposals. Of course, this question of the proper relationships between the history of science and the philosophy of science is a very complex issue that continues to be debated in philosophy, but it is clearly the case that economists have recently been sympathetic to methodological proposals that are sensitive to the actual history of their discipline. Economists have produced quite a vast literature that uses the Lakatosian categories to reconstruct various parts of the history of economic thought. Standard practice in such literature is to choose a particular part of economic theory (past or present) and then try to isolate and identify the hard core, the positive and negative heuristics, and the type of theoretical activity occurring in the protective belt. The bottom line in such work is usually a positive or negative appraisal of the "progressivity" of this particular part of economics.[42] Examples of such reconstructions range in topic from Jevons, Menger and Walras (in Fisher, 1986), to rational expectations macro (in Maddock, 1984), to Henry George (in Petrella, 1988).

An overall assessment of this Lakatosian reconstruction literature is very difficult because of its vastness and diversity and also for a more fundamental reason. This second reason is that many economists writing in the field have taken very little care in the way the Lakatosian terminology is used. This lack of fidelity to Lakatos's concepts results in "hard cores," "heuristics," and (particularly) "novel facts" that bear little resemblance to their Lakatosian analogs or how these terms have been used in reconstructions in the physical sciences.[43] It is very difficult to evaluate such literature. Some of it is interesting (possibly creative) history of economic thought, but it is unclear what it says about the MSRP in the particular theories examined. What can be said is that *in the case studies where the relevant language is consistent with Lakatos*, "progress" and the prediction of novel facts it necessarily implies has been a *rare occurrence*. Now there have been some well-researched cases where the prediction of novel facts has actually been uncovered,[44] but such cases correspond to a miniscule portion of the theoretical "advances" of the profession. Lakatos's criterion for "theoretical progress," the prediction of novel facts, may be sufficient for what the profession considers to be theoretical progress but it is surely not necessary. Just as "the development of economic analysis would look a dismal affair through falsificationist spectacles" (Latsis, 1976b, 8), it seems that economics would look almost as bad on a strict Lakatosian view. This argument of course assumes that we actually define such things as "progress" and "novel fact" in the Lakatosian way. If these terms are defined with sufficient vagueness (as some economists have done), then one can produce any Panglossian historical record desired.

Now this claim, that the MSRP has much that is relevant for economics, but that empirical and theoretical advance in economics occur (and should occur) in many other ways than Lakatos specified in the MSRP, reflects very poorly (again) on Popper. The reason is that by and large *where economics is most likely to part ways with Lakatos is precisely where Lakatos borrowed most heavily from Popper.* Lakatos seems to have much to say about economics, and looking for the types of things that Lakatos suggests one should look for in the history of science has produced some excellent historical studies. This work has drawn attention to the discipline's metaphysical hard core and it has reopened the important methodological question of the exact relationship between applied economics/econometrics and pure economic theory. What Lakatos has not produced (and we have good reason to believe will never be produced—but that's another story) is a mechanical model for the growth of scientific knowledge that perfectly fits the development of economics. In Lakatos's case the fit seems to be poorest where older Popperian parts were used without much modification.

CONCLUSION

It appears that in the final evaluation "Popperian" economic methodology must be given low marks. Falsificationism, Popper's fundamental program for the growth of scientific knowledge, seems extremely ill-suited to economics. Popper's situational analysis view of social science is precisely what economists do, but the discussion of the topic in the Popperian literature does not help economics with any real methodological questions. The interest in Lakatos has produced some valuable historical studies but the overall fit of economics into the MSRP is not good; and not good precisely where Lakatos is the most Popperian.

Now despite, and even granting all of the above arguments, there is still a way to save the Popperian tradition from this negative evaluation. The defense is based on the claim that while all of the above may be true, it really doesn't say anything about Popperian philosophy. The argument is that Popper's *really* important work is something quite different from what has been discussed above, that his *real* contribution to philosophy is *critical rationalism*, not falsificationism, and once this is recognized Popper does have something valuable to contribute to economic methodology.

Critical rationalism is Popper's general view of the philosophical method. It is the general method of rational discussion and the critical examination of proposed solutions.[45] Its overarching mandate is *criticize*, not falsify, though falsificationism is a special case of this more general method. Falsificationism is simply critical rationalism applied to the limited case of *empirical* criticism. Outside of this narrow empirical domain, critical rationalism is a quite general approach; metaphysical theories, philosophical theories, natural sciences that do not seem to fit falsificationism (evolutionary biology), and social sciences employing the rationality principle can all be examined, discussed and ultimately appraised through critical rationalism. Applying critical rationalism to economics simply means that we should criticize economic theories and we should be willing to learn from this critical discussion. Strategies that block or evade criticism should be shunned while those that open themselves to criticism should be welcomed. If this is Popper's real position, if this is the heart of Popperian philosophy, then the above criticisms seem to be of little importance, and it does appear that the economics profession has something to learn from Popperian philosophy.[46]

It is certainly difficult to argue against critical rationalism; for one thing it seems eminently reasonable and for another thing any rational argument against critical rationalism seems to presuppose it. One could argue against the exegetical claim that critical rationalism was *really* Popper's main contribution to philosophy but little would be gained by doing so; critical rationalism is actually in Popper (however minimally), and it may be appropriate even if the claim that it was Popper's main thesis is incorrect. The real problem for critical rationalism is not that one can say very much against it, but rather that one cannot say very much with it. Critical rationalism is a view that seems to be palatable by virtue of its blandness, the epistemological analog of the ethical mandate to "live the good life." Recent discussions of critical rationalism in the philosophical literature conclude that the notion is doomed to be a "contentless directive",[47] too amorphous to be of value in any interesting cases. This does not make it wrong or pernicious of course, just not very informative and devoid of the "bite" that is so attractive in Popperian philosophy. Thus, while the role of Popperian philosophy can be saved by turning to critical rationalism and away from falsification and demarcation, the victory is relatively hollow. If one listens carefully behind the roar of such a Popperian victory speech, one can hear Popper's old enemies, Hegel and Marx, chuckling in the dark.

NOTES

1. Blaug (1967, 1990), Brown (1981), Coats (1976), Cohen (1983), Cross (1982), de Marchi (1976), Diamond (1988), Fisher (1986), Fulton (1984), Hands (1985b, 1990), Latsis (1972, 1976b), Leijonhufvud (1976), Maddock (1984), Rizzo (1982), Schmidt (1982), and Weintraub (1985a, 1985b, 1988), is a partial listing of these Lakatosian reconstructions. See also de Marchi and Blaug (1991).

2. Influential books on economic method that fall broadly into the Popperian tradition include Blaug (1980), Boland (1982), Hutchison (1938), Klant (1984), Lipsey (1966), Weintraub (1985b), and (based on Caldwell (1991) Caldwell (1982).

3. Popper (1976b, 88).

4. The expression "basic statement" has a rather narrow meaning in Popperian philosophy. The concept was introduced in chapter V of Popper (1968); it is nicely summarized in Watkins (1984, 247-54).

5. Actually, as will be discussed below, scientific theories are not *by themselves* logically falsifiable. Rather, scientific theories along with (usually numerous) auxiliary hypotheses may form logically falsifiable *test systems* (see Hausman, 1988, 68-9).

6. Gellner (1974, 171).

7. See Hands (1988) for a general discussion of the Popperian notion of *ad hocness.*

8. An exception here is L. von Mises (1949, 1978); the Austrian "methodology" of von Mises seems to be justificationist in origin.

9. See de Marchi (1988b) for a discussion of the LSE connection.

10. Popper (1961) and (1966), for example.

11. An exception here seems to be Hutchison, who considers the link more direct. For him falsificationism is "the epistemological basis for a free, pluralist society" (1976, 203). A similar theme runs throughout Hutchison (1988).

12. This point is argued forcefully in Caldwell (1991).

13. Feyerabend (1975), Grunbaum (1976), Lakatos (1970), Maxwell (1972), and Putnam (1974) provide a small sample of such general criticism.

14. The main sources for this list of criticisms are Caldwell (1984, 1991), Hausman (1981, 1985, 1988), and Latsis (1976b).

15. The Duhemian problem (Duhem, 1954) arises because theories are never tested alone, rather they are tested in conjunction with certain auxiliary hypotheses (including those about the data). Thus if T is the theory, the prediction of evidence e is given by T·A => e, where A is the set of auxiliary hypotheses. The conjunction T·A forms a test system and the observation "not e" implies "not (T·A)" rather than simply "not T"; the test system is falsified, not necessarily the theory. In a scientific context there are a number of possible responses to "not e" (see Koertge, 1978, 255). One could challenge the reliability of the observation "not e." One could reject A or one of the elements of A. One could challenge the validity of the implication from T·A to e. And finally, we could follow Popper's advice and reject the theory T; discarding the theory is but one possibility. This problem is also called the Duhem-Quine problem, though the Duhemian appellation may be exegetically incorrect (see Ariew (1984)). It is a standard concern in the philosophy of science that has more recently been recognized as an issue for economic methodology (see Cross (1982) for instance). Popper clearly recognized the Duhemian problem (1965, 112, 239); and (1972, 353), for instance), but his methodological solution is itself subject to criticism (particularly 3.) below.

16. Popper (1965, 42, 267, 387-88); (1968, 43-44, 93-95, 97-111); (1983, 185-86).

17. This problem, but in reverse, is demonstrated by the examples in

Faulhaber and Baumol (1988). The authors discuss a number of cases where results from microeconomic theory have been "applied" by government and the business community. Of course, the fact that the implications of the theory were "applied" after, because of the economic theory, means that the implications did not hold when the theory was proposed. The microeconomic theories in question can be corroborated today because falsificationism wasn't practiced earlier. It is difficult to imagine such cases in physics.

18. This is one source of the "innocuous falsification" mentioned by Blaug (1980, 128, 259) and Coddington (1975, 542-45). It should be noted that if the parameters in the auxiliary hypotheses are not sufficiently restricted, but allowed to vary freely, then an even more severe problem develops: the so-called "parameter paradox" (Klant, 1984, 153-57); (1988, 108, 110-11). This is because if parameters are truly "variables" then *even* qualitative comparative statics can not be obtained. This results in a theory (or theoretical test system) that is completely unfalsifiable: there exists no observation in conflict with it.

19. Popper's most important writings on verisimilitude are contained in Popper (1965) and (1972). Useful surveys of the topic are Koertge (1979a, 234-38) and Watkins (1984, chapter 8). The question of verisimilitude in Popper's philosophy is examined in more detail in Hands (1991a).

20. This problem is demonstrated nicely by the following anecdote from Koertge (1979b, 237).

> "If two children are told to pick all and only the good cherries off a tree, who has done better: Clara Caution, who picks a tiny thimbleful, nearly all of which are firm and ripe, or Bella Bold, who brings home an enormous tubful, many of which are green or rotten? Which are worse, sins of omission or sins of comission?"

21. These concepts are discussed in detail with appropriate references to Popper's writings in Hands (1988). Other general discussions of these Popperian concepts include Koertge (1978), Watkins (1978,

1984), and Worrall (1978).

22. The argument is "nowhere fully explained outside of lectures" (Jarvie (1972, 5)).

23. General discussions of situational analysis by philosophers other than Popper include Farr (1983), Jarvie (1972, 1982), Koertge (1974, 1975, 1979a, 1985), and Watkins (1970). The methodological discussion regarding economics is contained in Blaug (1985), Caldwell (1991), Hands (1985a), and Latsis (1983) with brief mention in Blaug (1980), Hutchison (1981), Klant (1984, 1988), and Latsis (1976b). Wong (1978) uses situational analysis to criticize the theoretical contribution of an individual economist rather than examining the general implications for economic methodology.

24. Popper (1985, 358); Koertge (1974, 199); Latsis (1983, 136); Watkins (1970, 167).

25. Popper (1966, 97); (1976a, 102-03); (1976b, 117-18).

26. Koertge (1975, 87); (1979a, 440).

27. This scheme is not even restricted to "orthodox" economics. Consider the traditional Marxist answer to the question of why nineteenth century capitalists hired women and children and worked them long hours: Well, the situation of the individual capitalist was that they needed to make their rate of profit as high as possible or they would be pushed out of business and thus become proletariat themselves. The rate of profit is given by $\pi = S/(C+V)$ where S is surplus value, the amount of labor time obtained by the capitalist in excess of V, the amount of labor time necessary to reproduce the workers. Now given C, π can be increased by increasing S or by decreasing V. Working laborers longer hours will increase S, and hiring women and children (since V is based on reproducing the household which sustains the worker) will reduce V. Therefore, since agents always act "appropriately" to their situation, capitalists hired women and children and worked them long hours.

28. This difference prompted the distinction between $Popper_S$ (social science/SA) and $Popper_n$ (natural science) in Hands (1985a) and Caldwell (1991).

29. Popper himself certainly argues that the RP should never be abandoned (Popper (1985), 360). It is unclear though whether this is because the RP is unfalsifiable or simply because of a methodological decision.

30. Actually, SA explanations are *not bona fide* scientific explanations on *any* covering law model of scientific explanations (not just Popper's).

31. This point is made by Koertge (1979a, 84, 93).

32. Latsis (1983), Koertge (1975).

33. This of course assumes that economics is "stuck with" SA. If, on the other hand, one takes seriously the failure of the RP as a causal law, one possibility would be to abandon SA explanations altogether. This would force economists to "start from scratch" and if they are to explain economic behavior at all, to do so on the basis of the type of causal universal laws required in scientific explanations. This is essentially the proposal of Rosenberg (1980).

34. This conference produced the seminal volume Latsis (1976a).

35. See note 1 for references to the former literature. The latter literature also includes some of these same references as well as others such as, Archibald (1979), Goodwin (1980), Hands (1979, 1984, 1988), Hutchison (1976, 1981), Remenyi (1979), Robbins (1979), and Rosenberg (1986). Lakatos is also discussed in surveys such as Blaug (1980), Caldwell (1982) and Pheby (1988).

36. Many summaries of the MSRP are available in the economics literature (Blaug (1980), Hands (1985a), and Weintraub (1985a, 1985b, 1988) for instance) but the single best presentation of the argument remains Lakatos (1970) himself. As with Popper's falsificationism, only a sketch of the main thesis is provided here.

37. As notes 1 and 35 clearly indicate, there has been a lot of work in "Lakatosian economics." In all of this work, none has been as serious or as careful as Weintraub's work on the NeoWalrasian program (1985b, 1988).

38. The term "novel fact" has a very specific meaning in the Lakatosian (and Popperian) program. See Gardner (1982), Hands (1985b, 1991b) and Worrall (1978) on this issue.

39. This point is emphasized in Hands (1979).

40. Popper, unlike philosophers in the positivist tradition, has always recognized that metaphysics has a role to play in the growth of scientific knowledge. In fact, Popper's lifework is often characterized as a long process of systematically expanding the role of metaphysics in science (a view corroborated by the discussion of metaphysics in Popper (1983)). Philosophers in the Popperian tradition have intermittently considered the question of appraising metaphysics (Koertge (1978), Watkins (1958), Wisdom (1963, 1987) for example) but the topic remains underdeveloped. The issue will be raised again in the conclusing section.

41. "A general definition of science, thus, must reconstruct the acknowledgedly best gambits as 'scientific': if it fails to do so, it has to be rejected" (Lakatos (1971), p. 111).

42. These case studies use Lakatos to appraise economics; the exception is Hands (1985b) where economics is used to appraise Lakatos.

43. Rather than singling out the worst perpetrators of this terminological infidelity, I will take the opposite approach. In the reconstruction literature, certain economists have been careful in the way the Lakatosian terminology is used and in the way the economic and empirical concepts are mapped into these Lakatosian notions; a list of such work would need to include Blaug (1987), de Marchi (1976), Latsis (1976b), Maddock (1984) and Weintraub (1985a, 1985b, 1988).

44. See the references in note 43.

45. Critical rationalism has been an underlying theme throughout Popper's life's work. It is more pronounced in later work than earlier (esp. (1972, 1983)) but not even *The Logic of Scientific Discovery* is without it.

> "And yet I am quite ready to admit that there is a method which might be described as 'the one method of philosophy.' But it is not characteristic of philosophy alone; it is, rather, the one method of all *rational discussion*, and therefore of the natural sciences as well as philosophy. The method I have in mind is that of stating one's problem clearly and of examining its various proposed solutions *critically*" ((1968), 16).

46. According to Caldwell (1991), critical rationalism is how his "pluralism" in (1982, 1988) should be interpreted and it is also how Klant interprets his "plausibilism" in (1984) (see Klant, 1988, 108).

47. Nola (1987, 497).

REFERENCES

Archibald, G. C. (1979), "Method and Appraisal in Economics," *Philosophy of the Social Sciences*, 9, 304-15.

Ariew, R. (1984), "The Duhem Thesis," *British Journal for the Philosophy of Science*, 35, 313-325.

Blaug, M. (1976), "Kuhn versus Lakatos, or Paradigms versus Research Programmes in the History of Economics," in S. J. Latsis (1976a), 149-80.

__________________. (1980), *The Methodology of Economics*. Cambridge: Cambridge University Press.

__________________. (1985), "Comments on D. Wade Hands, 'Karl Popper and Economic Methodology: A New Look'," *Economics and Philosophy*, 1, 286-88.

__________________. (1990), "Second Thoughts on the Keynesian Revolution," in Blaug.

Boland, L. (1982), *The Foundations of Economic Method*. London: Allen & Unwin.

Brown, E. K. (1981), "The Neoclassical and Post-Keynesian Research Programs: The Methodological Issues," *Review of Social Economy*, 34, 111-32.

Caldwell, B. J. (1982), *Beyond Positivism: Economic Methodology in the Twentieth Century*. London: Allen & Unwin.

__________________. (1984), "Some Problems with Falsificationism in Economics," *Philosophy of the Social Sciences*, 14, 489-95.

__________________. (1988), "The Case for Pluralism," in de Marchi (1988a), 231-44.

__________________. (1991), "Clarifying Popper," *Journal of Economic Literature*, 29, 1-33.

Coats, A. W. (1976), "Economics and Psychology: The Death and Resurrection of a Research Programme," in S. J. Latsis (1976a), 43-64.

Coddington, A. (1975), "The Rationale of General Equilibrium Theory," *Economic Inquiry*, 13, 339-58.

Cohen, A. (1983), "The Laws of Return Under Competitive Conditions: Progress in Microeconomics Since Sraffa," *Eastern Economic Journal*, 9, 213-20.

Cross, R. (1982), "The Duhem-Quine Thesis, Lakatos, and the Appraisal of Theories in Macroeconomics," *Economic Journal*, 92, 320-40.

de Marchi, N. (1976), "Anomaly and the Development of Economics: The Case of the Leontief Paradox," in S. J. Latsis (1976a), 109-27.

__________________. (ed.) (1988a), *The Popperian Legacy in Economics*. Cambridge: Cambridge University Press.

___________________. (1988b), "Popper and the LSE Economists," in de Marchi (1988a), 139-66.

___________________ and Blaug, M. (eds.). (1991), *Appraising Economic Theories: Studies in the Methodology of Research Programs*. Aldershot: Edward Elgar.

Diamond, A. M. Jr. (1988), "The Empirical Progressiveness of the General Equilibrium Research Program," *History of Political Economy*, 20, 119-35.

Duhem, P. (1954), *The Aim and Structure of Physical Theory*. Translated by P. P. Wiener, Princeton, NJ: Princeton University Press.

Farr, J. (1983), "Popper's Hermeneutics," *Philosophy of the Social Sciences*, 13, 157-76.

Faulhaber, G. R. and Baumol, W. J. (1988), "Economists as Innovators: Practical Products of Theoretical Research," *Journal of Economic Literature*, 26, 577-600.

Feyerabend, P. K. (1970), "Consolations for the Specialist," in *Criticism and the Growth of Knowledge*. I. Lakatos and A. Musgrave (eds.). Cambridge University Press, 197-230.

___________________. (1975), *Against Method*. London: New Left Books.

Fisher, F. M. (1986), *The Logic of Economic Discovery*. Washington Square, NY: New York University Press.

Fulton, G. (1984), "Research Programmes in Economics," *History of Political Economy*, 16, 187-205.

Gardner, M. R. (1982), "Predicting Novel Facts," *British Journal for the Philosophy of Science*, 33, 1-15.

Gellner, E. (1974), *Legitimation of Belief*. Cambridge: Cambridge University Press.

Goodwin, C. (1980), "Towards a Theory of the History of Economics," *History of Political Economy*, 12, 610-19.

Grunbaum, A. (1976), "Is Falsifiability the Touchstone of Scientific Rationality? Karl Popper Versus Inductivism," in *Essays in Memory of Imre Lakatos*. R. Cohen et. al. (eds.), Dordrecht, Holland: D. Reidel.

Hands, D. W. (1979), "The Methodology of Economic Research Programmes," *Philosophy of the Social Sciences*, 9, 293-303.

__________________. (1984), "Blaug's Economic Methodology," *Philosophy of the Social Sciences*, 14, 115-25.

__________________. (1985a), "Karl Popper and Economic Methodology," *Economics and Philosophy*, 1, 83-99.

__________________. (1985b), "Second Thoughts on Lakatos," *History of Political Economy*, 17, 1-16.

__________________. (1988), "Ad Hocness in Economics and the Popperian Tradition," in de Marchi (1988a), 121-37.

__________________. (1990), "Second Thoughts on 'Second Thoughts': Reconsidering the Lakatosian Progress of *The General Theory*," *Review of Political Economy*, 2, 67-81.

__________________. (1991a), "The Problem of Excess Content: Economics, Novelty and A Long Popperian Tale," in de Marchi and Blaug (1991), 58-75.

__________________. (1991b), "Reply to Hamminga and Mäki," in de Marchi and Blaug (1991), 91-102.

Hausman, D. M. (1981), *Capital, Profits and Prices: An Essay in the Philosophy of Economics*. New York: Columbia University Press.

__________________. (1985), "Is Falsificationism Unpracticed or Unpracticable?" *Philosophy of the Social Sciences*, 15

313-19.

__________. (1988), "An Appraisal of Popperian Economic Methodology," in de Marchi (1988a), 65-85.

Hutchison, T. W. (1938), *The Significance and Basic Postulates of Economic Theory*. London: Macmillan (reprint, New York: Augustus M. Kelly, 1960).

__________. (1976), "On the History and Philosophy of Science and Economics," in S. J. Latsis (1976a), 181-205.

__________. (1981), "On the Aims and Methods of Economic Theorizing," in *The Politics and Philosophy of Economics*. T. W. Hutchison (ed.) New York: New York University Press, 266-307.

__________. (1988), "The Case for Falsificationism," in de Marchi (1988a), 169-81.

Jarvie, I. C. (1972), *Concepts and Society*. London: Routeledge and Kegan Paul.

__________. (1982), "Popper on the Difference Between the Natural and Social Sciences," in *In Pursuit of Truth: Essays on the Philosophy of Karl Popper on the Occasion of His 80th Birthday*. B. Levinson (ed.), Atlantic Highlands, NJ: Humanities Press, 83-107.

__________. (1984), *The Rules of the Game*. Cambridge: Cambridge University Press.

Klant, J. J. (1988), "The Natural Order," in de Marchi (1988a), 87-117.

Koertge, N. (1974), "On Popper's Philosophy of Social Science," in *PSA 1972*. K. F. Schaffner and R. S. Cohen (eds.)., Dordrecht, Holland: D. Reidel, 195-207.

__________. (1975), "Popper's Metaphysical Research Program for the Human Sciences," *Inquiry*, 19, 437-62.

__________. (1978), "Toward a New Theory of Scientific Inquiry," in *Progress and Rationality in Science*. G. Radnitzky and G. Anderson (eds.), Dordrecht, Holland: D. Reidel, 253-78.

__________. (1979a), "The Methodological Status of Popper's Rationality Principle," *Theory and Decision*, 10, 83-95.

__________. (1979b), "The Problems of Appraising Scientific Theories," in *Current Research in Philosophy of Science*. P. D. Asquith and H. E. Kyburg, Jr. (eds.), East Lansing, MI: Philosophy of Science Association, 228-251.

__________. (1985), "On Explaining Beliefs," *Erkenntnis*, 22, 175-86.

Kuhn, T. S. (1970), *The Structure of Scientific Revolutions*. 2nd ed., Chicago: University of Chicago Press.

Lakatos, I. (1970), "Falsification and the Methodology of Scientific Research Programmes," in *Criticism and the Growth of Knowledge*. I. Lakatos and A. Musgrave (eds.), Cambridge: Cambridge University Press, 91-196.

__________. (1971), "History of Science and Its Rational Reconstructions," in *Boston Studies in the Philosophy of Science*, Vol. 8. R. C. Buck and R. S. Cohen (eds.), Dordrecht, Holland: D. Reidel, 91-136.

Latsis, S. J. (1972), "Situational Determination in Economics," *The British Journal for the Philosophy of Science*, 23, 207-45.

__________. (1976a), *Method and Appraisal in Economics*. Cambridge: Cambridge University Press.

__________. (1976b), "A Research Programme in Economics," in S. J. Latsis (1976a), 1-41.

__________. (1983), "The Role and Status of the Rationality Principle in the Social Sciences," in *Epistemology, Methodology and the Social Sciences*. R. S. Cohen and M. W. Wartefsky (eds.), Dordrecht, Holland: D. Reidel, 123-51.

Leijonhufvud, A. (1976), "Schools, 'Revolutions,' and Research Programmes in Economic Theory," in S. J. Latsis (1976a), 65-108.

Lipsey, R. G. (1966), *An Introduction to Positive Economics*, 2nd ed., London: Weidenfeld and Nicolson.

Maddock, R, (1984), "Rational Expectations Macrotheory: A Lakatosian Case Study in Program Adjustment," *History of Political Economy*, 16, 291-309.

Maxwell, N. (1972), "A Critique of Popper's Views on Scientific Method," *Philosophy of Science*, 39, 131-52.

Mises, L. von (1949), *Human Action: A Treatise on Economics*. New Haven: Yale University Press.

________________. (1978), *The Ultimate Foundation of Economic Science*. 2nd ed., Kansas City: Sheed Andrews and McMeel.

Nola, R. (1987), "The Status of Popper's Theory of Scientific Method," *British Journal for the Philosophy of Science*, 38, 441-480.

Petrella, F. (1988), "Henry George and the Classical Scientific Research Program: The Economics of Republican Millennialism" *American Journal of Economics and Sociology*, 47, 239-56.

Pheby, J. (1988), *Methodology and Economics: A Critical Introduction*. London: Macmillan.

Popper, K. R. (1961), *The Poverty of Historicism*. 3rd ed., New York: Harper and Row.

________________. (1965), *Conjectures and Refutations*. 2nd ed., New York: Harper and Row.

________________. (1966), *The Open Society and Its Enemies*. Vol. I and II, 2nd ed., New York: Harper and Row.

__________. (1967), "La Rationalité et le Statut du Principle de Rationalité," in *Les Fondements Philosophiques des Systemes Economiques*. E. M. Classen (ed.), Paris: Payot, 142-50.

__________. (1968), *The Logic of Scientific Discovery*. 2nd ed., New York: Harper and Row.

__________. (1970), "Normal Science and Its Dangers," in *Criticism and the Growth of Knowledge*. I. Lakatos and A. Musgrave (eds.), Cambridge: Cambridge University Press, 51-8.

__________. (1972), *Objective Knowledge*. Oxford: Oxford University Press.

__________. (1976a), "The Logic of the Social Sciences," in *The Positivist Dispute in German Sociology*. T. W. Adorno et al. (eds.), translated by G. Adey and D. Frisby, New York: Harper and Row, 87-104.

__________. (1976b), *Unended Quest*. LaSalle, IL: Open Court.

__________. (1983), *Realism and the Aim of Science*. W. W. Bartley III (ed.), Totowa, NJ: Rowman and Littlefield.

__________. (1985), "The Rationality Principle," English translation of Popper (1967) in *Popper Selections*. D. Miller (ed.), Princeton: Princeton University Press.

Putnam, H. (1974), "The 'Corroboration' of Theories," in *The Philosophy of Karl Popper*. P. A. Schilpp (ed.), LaSalle, IL: Open Court.

Remenyi, J. V. (1979), "Core Demi-core Interaction: Towards a General Theory of Disciplinary and Subdisciplinary Growth," *History of Political Economy*, 11, 30-63.

Rizzo, M. J. (1982), "Mises and Lakatos: A Reformulation of Austrian Methodology," in *Method, Process and Austrian Economics*. I. M.

Kirzner (ed.), Lexington, MA: Lexington Books.

Robbins, L. (1979), "On Latsis's Method and Appraisal in Economics: A Review Essay," *Journal of Economic Literature*, 17, 996-1004.

Rosenberg, A. (1980), *Sociobiology and the Pre-emption of Social Science*. Baltimore: Johns Hopkins University Press.

__________________. (1986), "Lakatosian Consolations for Economists," *Economics and Philosophy*, 2, 127-39.

Schmidt, R. H. (1982), "Methodology and Finance," *Theory and Decision*, 14, 391-413.

Watkins, J. (1958), "Confirmable and Influential Metaphysics," *Mind*, 67, 344-65.

__________________. (1970), "Imperfect Rationality," in *Explanation in the Behavioral Sciences*. R. Borger and F. Cioffi (eds.), Cambridge: Cambridge University Press, 91-121.

__________________. (1978), "The Popperian Approach to Scientific Knowledge," in *Progress and Rationality in Science*. G. Radnitzky and G. Anderson (eds.), Dordrecht, Holland: D. Reidel, 23-43.

__________________. (1984), *Science and Skepticism*. Princeton, NJ: Princeton University Press.

Weintraub, E. R. (1985a), "Appraising General Equilibrium Analysis," *Economics and Philosophy*, 1, 23-37.

__________________. (1985b), *General Equilibrium Analysis: Studies in Appraisal*. Cambridge: Cambridge University Press.

__________________. (1988), "The NeoWalrasian Program is Empirically Progressive," in de Marchi (1988a).

Wisdom, J. O. (1963), "The Refutability of 'Irrefutable' Laws," *British Journal for the Philosophy of Science*, 13, 303-306.

_____________________, J. O. (1987), *Challengeability in Modern Science*. Aldershot, England: Gower Publishing.

Wong, S. (1978), *The Foundation of Paul Samuelson's Revealed Preference Theory*. London: Routledge and Kegan Paul.

Worrall, J. (1978), "The Ways in Which the Methodology of Scientific Research Programmes Improves on Popper's Methodology," in *Progress and Rationality in Science*. G. Radnitzky and G. Anderson (eds.), Dordrecht, Holland: D. Reidel, 45-70.

COMMENTARY BY MARK BLAUG

Wade Hands has been chipping away at Popper and Lakatos in a number of provocative papers for the last few years. In the present essay, he continues to hammer the Popperian tradition in economic methodology: he denies that Popperian falsificationism is practiced in economics, doubts that it should be practiced, and contends that if it were practiced it would simply destroy the subject. These are strong claims, but they rest on a punctilious interpretation of the methodology of falsificationism.[1] In a key passage, Hands distinguishes between falsificationism and a commitment to empirical testing:

> Now, of course, denying that falsificationism provides the proper methodological rules for conducting economics does *not* mean that "the facts" should not matter in economic theory choice or that empirical testing is not important. This type of argument is a quite common red herring in methodological discussion involving falsificationism in economics. Popperian falsificationism is not generic empiricism; it is a *very* specific set of rules about how scientific inquiry should be conducted. Abandoning Popperian falsificationism as a methodology does not mean abandoning learning from experience (26).

Without precisely defining falsificationism, Hands, nevertheless, offers a general description of it (20-2), emphasizing such elements as potential refutability of the predictions deduced from scientific theories, the preference for unlikely predictions, the ban on *ad hoc* "immunizing stratagems" in the event of refutations, and so forth. In other words, falsificationism is a severe methodology that seeks to maximise the vulnerability of scientific theories; in that lies all the resistance to it.

Being a normative doctrine, a set of rules about how scientific inquiry should ideally be conducted; falsificationism cannot be reduced to a mechanical filter for separating acceptable from unacceptable theories. Whether a theory has been severely tested, whether it is well corroborated, whether *ad hoc* stratagems have been avoided, and sometimes even the basic question of whether it is indeed potentially falsifiable, are all matters of judgment that cannot be assigned to a computer programme. Hands insists that falsificationism is "a *very* specific set of rules" about the conduct of scientific inquiry but it would be better to say that it is a particular attitude to the results of scientific inquiry. How then does falsificationism differ from "generic empiricism"? It differs from it solely in degree, not in kind.

Why should "facts" matter in theory choice? Why bother with empirical testing? We are sometimes told that social scientists cannot "explain," they can only "understand." Social science can at best weave together the known "facts" in a plausible pattern, thus relating the unknown to what is already familiarly known; as for peering into the future, or "testing" the predictions deduced from theories, that is to be condemned as old-fashioned "positivism."[2] The empiricism of old-fashioned "positivism" was grounded in the philosophy of realism: there *is* "objective knowledge" and the aim of science is to come ever closer to a "true" grasp of both the natural and the social world. It is for this reason that realists are necessarily committed to empirical testing as the decisive check on the verisimilitude of scientific theories. Of course, realists demand that theories be logically consistent—if only to guarantee that one knows what one is talking about. Of course, they prefer simple and elegant theories, everything else being the same, to complex and clumsy theories. Of course, they prefer theories that are plausible, in the sense of being consonant with background knowledge, to those that are implausible. And needless to say, they usually require theories to be confirmed by such data as are already at our command. But neither simplicity, nor elegance, nor plausibility, nor confirmability in any way guarantees the attainment of truth. Only by using the theory to predict a "novel fact" can we hope to discover whether it has obtained a glimpse of objective reality.

But empirical testing is never conclusive, if only because of the Duhem-Quine thesis: the fact that we always test the conjunction of the theory and at least one auxiliary hypothesis. The inconclusiveness of empirical testing is even greater in the social than in the natural sciences, if only because the social sciences lack universal empirical laws or what Hands calls "a conventionally accepted empirical basis" (24). In addition, we in economics are frequently satisfied with qualitative predictions, and qualitative predictions will frequently pass almost any test we can devise: every demand curve turns out to be negatively inclined, and yet, we can rarely tell whether the price-elasticity of a particular demand curve is less than or greater than unity at some particular price.

But all this implies that getting away with murder is so much easier in economics than in physics, and hence, that methodological vigilance is more important to us than it is to physicists. In short, we need to do a little more than to insist on empirical testing, although even that insistence is never idle in the social sciences where so many would like to be issued with a philosophical license to say whatever they wish to say. Falsificationism is precisely that: it insists on empirical testing as the litmus paper of verisimilitude, but it goes beyond it in specifying what to do when our tests fail to support a theory.

To be sure, Popper did *not* succeed in solving "the problem of verisimilitude," meaning the provision of a scalar measure of the "degree of corroboration" of a theory. This implies that we will frequently be unable to choose between rival theories in a compelling, demonstrable manner, having to fall back once again on judgment, in this case a judgment about which a number of only partly commensurate theories are better corroborated. Nevertheless, the difficulty of making such a judgment is not a sufficient reason for giving up falsificationism and relying instead on a vague appeal to the importance of empirical testing, particularly as we are not told why it should be thought of as important.

Those of us, like myself, who have advocated falsificationism as a normative methodology for economics have done so in order to improve economics, to weed out ideological doctrines dressed up as scientific truths, and to provide the discipline of striving for law-like explanations of economic behavior. That economists rarely practice falsificationism only demonstrates the need to preach falsificationism day in and day out, always assuming that falsificationism is in fact practicable in economics that the history of our subject displays some instances of it. Nothing in Hands' succinct summary of the criticisms that have been levelled at falsificationism in economics (23-26) convinces me that what economics needs is less and not more of Popper's bitter pill—on the contrary.

In the fourth section of his chapter, Hands turns from Popper to Lakatos, arguing that there are some elements in Lakatos that are decidedly unPopperian (32-4). His account of these differences is overdrawn, but nevertheless, the drift of his argument is perfectly correct: Lakatos is more persuasive than Popper, and in addition, there is Lakatos' "methodology of historiographical research programmes" (the notion of using the history of science to appraise methodologies of science), which is only implicit in Popper.[3] If the history of economics failed to correspond in any way to Lakatos' methodology, and in particular to his criterion of progress in scientific knowledge, I for one would be prepared to abandon Lakatos and, by implication, Popper. But isn't the number of carefully conducted case studies to date, surely, too small to conclude as Hands does that economics does not fit the Lakatosian mold (36)? We have been at this game for, say, 16 years (counting from the Latsis volume of 1976), and this suggests that to reject Lakatos now is to indulge in the very "naive falsificationism" that Popper is sometimes accused of. Hands is too eager to kill the baby before it is out of the cradle. I recommend that we suspend judgment about Lakatos' MSRP until we have seen more evidence in the form of additional case studies.

I shall leave for another time the third section of Hands' chapter on "situational analysis," in part, because I have reacted to Hands' thought on this topic before (Blaug, 1985), and in part, because it would take me too far afield. Let me close by praising Hands' final pages dismissing "critical rationalism" as a post-Popperian reading of the essence of Popper (36-38). The demand that all ideas should be criticized and that we should be willing to learn from criticism is so bland as to be meaningless. But the same charge of methodological blandness applies to Hands' insistence on the importance of empirical testing, even while rejecting those philosophers of science who have built their methodologies on the bedrock of empirical testing. If Hands wants to discard Popper and Lakatos, will he kindly tell us why we should even bother testing theories, and in particular, what we should do when those tests go against a theory?

NOTES

1. He is not alone in making these claims. For example, Caldwell (1982) contains a number of similar but less boldly expressed sentiments.

2, See numerous articles on methodology in the *Journal of Economic Issues*.

3. Although Popper insists that methodology is normative, deriving from epistemological considerations and not inferred from the history of science, his writings are, nevertheless, replete with flattering references to Newton and Einstein and damning references to Marx and Freud, references which are clearly designed to support his methodological pronouncements; in other words, there is an unresolved tension in Popper on the famous question of the relationship between the history and the methodology of science, which Lakatos exploited.

REFERENCES

Blaug, M. (1985), "Comments on D. Wade Hands," Karl Popper and Economic Methodology: A New Look." *Economics and Philosophy*, 1, 286-88.

Caldwell, B. J. (1982), *Beyond Positivism: Economic Methodology in the Twentieth Century*. London: Allen and Unwin.

REPLY BY D. WADE HANDS

One problem associated with the standard paper-comment-reply format for scholarly exchange is that it seems to exaggerate the amount of disagreement between authors. In this particular case, as with many of our other exchanges during the last few years,[1] Mark Blaug and I appear to be grossly at odds over fundamental philosophical issues. I think these philosophical differences appear to be greater than they really are. We do in fact disagree about economic *methodology*, but I also think that we are much closer in our *general philosophical views* than these exchanges would indicate.

If I were forced to identify my beliefs with a single school of modern philosophy—to give myself a single label—I too would be "Popperian." I am a fallibilist and a nonfoundation-alist empiricist. I believe that we learn about the world by trial and error, and that the differences between the natural and social sciences are matters of degree rather than kind. I find little of value and much that is pernicious in recent rhetorical and neopragmatist trends, and while modern instrumentalism is often impressive in its sophistication, I find it unconvincing. Basically, I am Popperian in the same sense that most members of the "Popperian school" are Popperian.

What I do *not* advocate is a falsificationist *methodology* for economics or any other science. Even the paradigm cases of natural sciences could not live up to falsificationist standards; if they had, Lakatos would never have written the MSRP. The MSRP was an attempt to overcome some of the well-known difficulties of falsificationism, and in many respects, it was successful.[2] In other respects though, it inherited the problems of its predecessor and even generated some new ones of its own. To me, these difficulties with falsificationism and the MSRP are simply a call to continue working, a call to develop a methodology that is consistent with basic philosophical goals of Popper and Lakatos but devoid of their problems. I do not think this much different from the attitude of most members of the "Popperian school."

Mark Blaug, I would argue, shares my general philosophical perspective, but he sees our methodological task much differently. For him economics is constantly on the brink of being overrun by ideologues and pamphleteers, and a strict methodology like falsificationism is needed to "weed out ideological doctrines dressed up as scientific truths." A constant roar of methodological admonition is required to keep the economic profession's nose to the empirical grindstone and prevent it from being seduced by the ideological dark side. To borrow Feyerabend's phrase (1970, 229), falsificationism is a "stern and demanding mistress," and for Blaug, therein lies its strength.

Now I share Blaug's concerns. I too want a methodology that can reject some theories, but I also want one that will leave much (most) of current economic theory intact and allow for new theories to develop. I am as much concerned with "letting the field grow" as "weeding it out." Falsificationism (or the MSRP if strictly applied) is not a good methodology for letting theories grow, weeding out yes—but letting grow—no. As I have argued elsewhere,[3] falsificationism is a great methodology for avoiding type II errors--it makes it impossible to ever accept a bad theory. On the other hand, since nothing seems to be able to pass the falsificationist test, it makes the chances of a type I error (rejecting a good theory) quite high. Blaug's main concern is avoiding type II errors, making certain the ideologues stay out; I am equally concerned with type I errors. I do not want a methodology that would force us to abandon most of modern economic theory, or one that would become a prohibitive barrier to the development of any new ideas. As I stated in my review of Blaug (1980): "Strict falsificationist rules certainly keep the riff-raff out of science, they also keep science out of science. In the case of economics, Blaug's methodology leaves the greatest theorists of history with no more sanctity than the most trivial of pamphleteers, since both fail to meet his standards," (1984, 123). I think that Mark Blaug and I share many of the same basic (Popperian) philosophical preferences, but as long as we differ fundamentally regarding which type of error is more important to avoid, I am afraid we are forever doomed to disagree about economic *methodology*.

NOTES

1. For instance the exchanges, Blaug (1980)/Hands (1984); Blaug (1976)/Hands (1985b)/Blaug (1990)/Hands (1990); and Hands (1985a)/Blaug (1985).

2. This is documented nicely in Worrall (1978).

3. Hands (1984, 123).

REFERENCES

Blaug, M. (1980), *The Methodology of Economics.* Cambridge: Cambridge University Press.

Hands, D. W. (1984), "Blaug's Economic Methodology," *Philosophy of the Social Sciences*, 9, 293-303.

Feyerabend, P. K. (1970), "Consolations for the Spcialist," in *Criticism and the Growth of Knowledge.* I. Lakatos and A. Musgrave (eds.). Cambridge University Press, 197-230.

CHAPTER 2

SOCIAL CONDITIONING OF ECONOMICS

Uskali Mäki

SOCIAL CONDITIONING OF SCIENCE

Contemporary sociology of science usually takes it for granted that science is, all down the line, social in character, and that fatal consequences follow from this in regard to traditional philosophical views of the nature of scientific knowledge and practice. There are a number of different accounts of science being social. All such accounts appear to be more or less unclear as to what the social character of science precisely amounts to. In what follows, some features of a few recent accounts will be surveyed, and some of their critical implications will be pointed out in regard to other conceptions of science, Popperian methodology in particular. Preliminary attempts will also be made to point out some of the ways that science is being viewed as social or socially conditioned (or socially constructed, socially shaped, socially constituted), as implied in those accounts. Towards the end of the chapter, the intriguing issue of relativism will be briefly addressed. The major part of the current sociology of science focuses on the natural sciences; the social sciences have received much less attention. In the course of the following survey, economics and economic methodology will be kept in mind.

I propose to use the formulation "science is socially conditioned" as an umbrella expression that should be taken as intentionally neutral in regard to the precise character of the relation between science and "the social." As such, the formulation is multiply ambiguous. Three clarifying questions have to be answered. First, what is there in science that is so conditioned? Second, what is it that does the conditioning? In other words, what is the character and range of the social? Third, what is the relation or process of conditioning like? Each of these three elements in the key statement can be specified in a number of different ways.

Without attempting to be exhaustive, I will show that, among others, the following three alleged kinds of social conditioning are implied in some recent sociologies of science. Each of them involves implicit specifications of the above three elements.

1. The content of accepted theory or belief (or its metaphysical and epistemological presuppositions) is caused (in an unspecified way) by social factors (such as cultures or interests internal or external to science). Here, a social fact causally generates an aspect of science (namely, scientific knowledge).

2. The goals of scientists' actions are social states or processes (such as credibility or power and their growth). Here a social fact constitutes an aspect of science (namely, scientists' goals).

3. The process of the justification of scientific claims is a social process of negotiation and rhetorical persuasion. Again, a social fact constitutes an aspect of science (namely, the process of justification).

Of these, (1.) has been endorsed by the so-called strong program of the Edinburgh School, while (2.) and (3.) have been more emphatically studied by the so-called ethnographic and constructivist approaches, and elsewhere. While there are incompatibilities between various approaches and research techniques relating to theses (1.)-(3.), the theses as such seem to be mutually compatible, suitably interpreted. On the other hand, it would be much more implausible to argue that theses (1.)-(3.) are compatible with the Popperian norms of science, for example.

THE STRONG PROGRAM

Much of the earlier sociology of science was preoccupied largely with the institutional organization of sciences, its changes and its relationship to the growth and direction of research. Unlike these streams within the field, the primary aim of the "strong program" is to attempt to provide sociological explanations of the propositional contents of beliefs or theories held by scientists. This pursuit is something that the strong program shares with such classics in the original field as Marx, Durkhem, Mannheim, and Sohn-Rethel. Besides the Edinburgh core, consisting of Barry Barnes, David Bloor, and Steven Shapin, there are other adherents such as Harry Collins, Donald MacKenzie, Andrew Pickering, and Trevor Pinch. They do not constitute a homogeneous group. For example, Barnes, inspired by Habermas, tends to cite social interests as explanantia, while Bloor, more in a Durkheimian fashion, puts stress on the culture of science. While most, if not all, would characterize themselves as relativists, Collins, for instance, seems to be a more radical relativist than Barnes or Bloor. (See, Barnes 1974, 1977, 1982; Bloor, 1976, 1983; Collins, 1983; for a survey of empirical studies, see Shapin, 1982.)

If, within the socially conditioned entity, an analytic distinction is drawn between scientific knowledge and scientists' actions, it can be seen that the strong program is primarily—although not exclusively—interested in explaining the former. Thus, the sociology of science endorsed by the Edinburgh School is a sociology of scientific knowledge, or belief in a strict sense.

From the point of view of the standard methodology of economics, it is noteworthy that the strong program, at least in its most representative formulations (such as in Bloor, 1976), is directed against a philosophical understanding of science. In this opinion, philosophers, both in general epistemology and in the philosophy of science, have monopolized the study of rational production of knowledge, while leaving the irrational residuum in scientists' behavior to sociologists and psychologists. It is claimed to be characteristic of these philosophical approaches that they are hopelessly unempirical, that is, unscientific. Unlike the sociological approach, they do not aim at empirical accounts for scientific beliefs. The sociological approach proceeds from the premise that knowledge, scientific knowledge included, is a social phenomenon and should be studied (described, explained) just as other social phenomena are studied by sociologists.

Bloor's (1976, 4-5) four tenets for the sociology of scientific knowledge define a version of the Edinburgh approach or the strong program:

1. The principle of causality: "It would be causal, that is, concerned with the conditions which bring about beliefs or states of knowledge."

2. The principle of impartiality: "It would be impartial with respect to truth and falsity, rationality or irrationality, success or failure. Both sides of these dichotomies will require explanation."

3. The principle of symmetry: "It would be symmetrical in its style of explanation. The same types of cause would explain, say, true and false beliefs."

4. The principle of reflexivity: "It would be reflexive. In principle its patterns of explanation would have to be applicable to sociology itself."

It is believed by Bloor that all this amounts to applying the principles of science to science itself. The program is radically pro-science. More particularly, it is based on a naturalistic methodological monism. Unlike some other currents in the sociology of science, Bloor's program is strongly anti-hermeneutic.

Bloor (ibid., 5-10) is critical of the idea that there can only be a sociology of error (falsity, irrationality) and that rational pursuit of truth is self-explanatory, in need of no further explanation—that only errors would be caused, while true beliefs would have no causes. This exemplifies his distinction between the causal and "teleological" approaches to knowledge. What Bloor regards as the dubious teleological approach takes true knowledge as an end product of a natural course of the rational process of human reasoning, as an embodiment of goal-directed activity with no causal history, while irrational and false beliefs are deviations that can be causally explained. This is the sort of asymmetry that is rejected by the strong program.[1] As Bloor puts it, the strong program, following the example of all scientific approach, is claimed to be "morally" neutral in regard to the epistemic qualities of human beliefs, whereas the teleological view is unscientific in giving rational and true beliefs a morally privileged position. These ideas are expressed in tenets (2.) and (3.), which are most widely accepted among sociologists of science. (For critical discussions of Bloor's tenets, see Laudan, 1981, Bloor, 1981, Collins, 1981a, Hesse, 1980, Newton-Smith, 1981.)

As pointed out above, the Edinburgh School is concerned with the sociology of scientific knowledge rather than the sociology of scientists' actions. The concept of knowledge needs to be roughly specified in this context. According to the standard philosophical definition, knowledge is rationally justified *true belief*. Bloor's specification of what he means by "knowledge" differs from the standard notion. Hence, it is worthwhile to cite him at length: "Instead of defining it as true belief, knowledge for the sociologist is whatever men take to be knowledge. It consists of those beliefs which men confidently hold and live by. In particular the sociologist will be concerned with beliefs which are taken for granted or institutionalized, or invested with authority by groups of men. Of course knowledge must be distinguished from mere belief. This can be done by reserving the word "knowledge" for what is collectively endorsed, leaving the individual and idiosyncratic to count as mere belief." (Bloor, 1976, 2-3; cf. Barnes, 1977, 1) Thus, beliefs become knowledge as individually held ideas receive collective support. Note that no reference to truth is presupposed by this notion and that the idea of rational justification is replaced by unspecified collective endorsement. Such a consensus theory of knowledge makes the very phenomenon of knowledge socially conditioned in the sense of being constituted by attitudes held by a collectivity of individuals.

There is a further sense in which scientific knowledge is claimed to be socially conditioned. Bloor (ibid., 44-47) puts forth the Durkheimian idea that the way we typically conceive of the nature of scientific knowledge is a reflection of the way we see the structure of society. The latter perception gets an expression in various social ideologies, religion included. Theories of knowledge typically "depend on social images and metaphors" (47). In particular, our experience of the structures of social authority and power provide the familiar framework on which conceptions of knowledge can be modelled. This, Bloor thinks, helps to account for the sacred character that is attributed to branches of scientific knowledge. Here, it is not the content of scientific knowledge-claims or beliefs "directly" that are allegedly socially conditioned, but rather the very general forms of belief and principles of justification that somehow "reflect" social structures external to science.

Typically, the factors cited in the applications of the Edinburgh approach as causes of scientific knowledge are "macrosocial" factors external to science. The program is largely macrosociological or even holistic: explanations are framed in terms of the impact on scientists' theories of systems of social relations, of cultural values, of social power and communal interest, of political ideologies.[2] It is implied in the agenda of a typical application of the Edinburgh program that, for example, when scientists cite compelling evidence as the reason for their theoretical beliefs, this is, to say the least, superficial or perhaps indicative of ideological concealment because, in fact, their beliefs have been shaped by cognitive interests that are causally dependent on social interests that, in turn, are determined by social structures.

Interests ascribed to communities or institutions are viewed as theoretical entities in the same way as are forces, fields, and molecular structures, and they are cited as causal conditions of beliefs. No modally deterministic connection is claimed to prevail here by a major representative of this line of thought, just a "temporal co-variation of beliefs, interests and social structure" with the specification that "it is claimed that interests inspire the construction of knowledge out of available cultural resources in ways which are specific to particular times and situations and their overall social and cultural contexts. As for the relationship of interests and social structure, it is accepted that some interests are indeed structurally generated." (Barnes, 1977, 58; see also Barnes and MacKenzie, 1979)

According to Barnes, interests fall into two categories, "an overt interest in prediction, manipulation and control, and a covert interest in rationalization and persuasion." (ibid., 38) When the latter is in operation, the resulting idea or belief is "ideologically determined." In Barnes's definition, "[k]nowledge or culture is ideologically determined in so far as it is created, accepted or sustained by concealed, unacknowledged, illegitimate interests." (ibid., 33)

There are a number of conceptual and methodological issues involved in the interest approach. They relate, among other things, to the precise meaning(s) of the very notion of interest; to whether some interests (such as the instrumental interest in prediction and control) have a transcendental status or whether all interests are socially contingent and open to rival interpretations; to whether interests are nothing but artifacts of the sociologist of science; to the role of interests in the discourse of the scientists studied by sociologists; to the kind of link allegedly connecting interests and beliefs; etc. (For discussions of some of the ambiguities and other problems inherent in the interest approach to scientific knowledge, see Yearley, 1982, Woolgar, 1981, Barnes, 1981, MacKenzie, 1981.)

Marx's attempt to give an account of what he called the "vulgarization" of economics after the classical period might be viewed as an early and crude application of something like the strong program. Its main ideas can be reconstructed briefly as follows. Commodity fetishism as a reflection of a powerful structural feature of the capitalist economy generates a tendency to the origination and establishment of "vulgar" economic theories (which depict market exchange as fundamental to the economy), while this tendency or potency is actualized by changed relations in class struggle external to science (because "vulgar" theories serve the apologetic and threatened interests of the bourgeois class). It is part of that story that the vulgar and apologetic character of those theories was concealed, thus making them ideologically conditioned. Despite some affinities, the Edinburgh School is not straightforwardly Marxist, however. While a Marxist would pursue explanations of at least some important scientific ideas in terms of reference to the fundamental or "base" structure of society, the social facts that applications of the Edinburgh program cite as potential causes of scientific beliefs are typically such matters as rank and status in an educational system or religious affiliation of those involved in the scientific enterprise.

A famous (and controversial) example that shares the general approach of the strong program is Paul Forman's attempt to show that the reason why the German physicists of the Weimar Republic embraced a noncausal, indeterministic view of physical processes had little to do with the experimental and theoretical demands of their scientific inquiries, but that it was rather an expression of the *Zeitgeist.* The social environment was impregnated with romanticism, the general atmosphere was mystical and antirational. The public sentiments were hostile to science and technology, the essential ingredient of which was believed to be the principle of causality. To regain the public approbation and prestige they used to have, the physicists as members of the German academic community dispensed with the principle of causality. All this happened, Forman argues, before the advent of a fundamentally acausal quantum mechanics (Forman, 1971).

I do not know of any such explicit applications of the strong program to economics, but it is clear that an Edinburghian explanation of the reign of the neoclassical orthodoxy would not refer to its having survived severe attempts at falsification, nor to its coming closest of all alternative schools of economic thought to formulating theories in a falsifiable form, nor to its constituting a progressive research program in the Lakatosian sense. Instead, such an explanation might argue that "in some way, and for some as yet unexplained reason, the neoclassical ideology is a part of—or, indeed, the best representative of—Anglo-American ideology." (Burkhardt & Canterbery 1986, 245)

For instance, the individualist commitment in neoclassical theory would be accounted for as a reflection of general ideological individualism in Anglo-American society. One possible way of specifying this is to use the notion of legitimation and to try to show that in order to legitimate themselves as a profession, orthodox economists have to legitimate the prevailing social ideology by giving it a theoretical formulation that is put beyond doubt (ibid., 231-237).

Typically, the precise nature of the allegedly causal connection between social facts and scientific knowledge remains unspecified in the formulations and applications of the strong program. For instance, Bloor claims that "the impact of practical developments in water and steam technology on the content of theories in thermodynamics has been studied in great detail. The causal link is beyond dispute." (Bloor, 1976, 3) However, the question of the exact nature of the causal link remains unsettled here and elsewhere. The problem is also present in those suggestions that connect the popularity or wide acceptance of the standard economic assumptions about the features of individual actors with the established Western ideas of the nature of individuals. As Barnes (1982, 103) admits, "we lack a precise and detailed account of the relationship between goals and interests on the one hand, and concepts and beliefs on the other." At a general level, one radical position is ruled out, though: "no laws or necessary connections are proposed to link knowledge and the social order" (Barnes, 1977, 85).

It may well be that there is some sort of loose *correlation* or *analogy* between some social facts and some scientific theories that the protagonists of the Edinburgh program see as being related to one another. It is, however, much more ambitious and demanding to argue that social interests and structures can causally generate the contents of theories and the involved metaphysical presuppositions held by scientists. Correlation and analogy do not imply causation, nor are they obvious instances of what I have called conditioning. A successful argument for the existence of a genuinely causal relation would have to indicate the existence and functioning of a mediating mechanism that would make it possible for the cause to produce the effect. Bloor, Barnes, and others have been unable to theorize such a causal mechanism. To say the least, their suggestion remains incomplete until a satisfactory account of the causal intermediaries is provided.

The so-called ethnographic approach, and some other recently practiced microsociological approaches, might be taken as complementing the Edinburgh program precisely where the latter encounters some of its worst problems.

ETHNOGRAPHIC AND RELATED APPROACHES

What are often called the ethnographic (or, from a different perspective, constructivist) approaches to studying science provide specific meanings to the statement "science is socially conditioned." Among some of the major representatives are Karin Knorr-Cetina, Bruno Latour, Steve Woolgar, Michael Mulkay, Nigel Gilbert, and Michael Lynch. Four differences between the Edinburgh program and the ethnographic approaches may be sorted out as an introduction to the latter. Note that neither approach is internally homogenous and that the dividing lines between them are not always very sharp.

First, if we draw a (nonabsolute) distinction between internal and external in regard to science, we may say that the scope of the Edinburgh approach encompasses social factors external to science, while the ethnographic analyses put stress on internal social factors. This is accompanied by a difference between more macrosociologically oriented and more microsociologically oriented perspectives.

Second, the Edinburgh program pursues causally explanatory accounts of science, whereas the ethnographic analyses and related (such as ethnomethodological) approaches are more intent on descriptive interpretations of the life processes of scientists and their communities.

Third, applications of the Edinburgh program have typically consisted of sociological reconstructions of historical materials related to past episodes in the development of science, while the ethnographic approaches support concentrated attempts at detailed observation of the situated day-to-day practices of contemporary scientific communities. Not the literary residues, but rather the material and social process of their production as actually observed, is the source of data and primary locus of analysis.

Fourth, we say that the strong program of the Edinburgh school views scientists primarily as holders of beliefs or knowledge-claims. We shall next see that the ethnographic approaches switch the focus of emphasis more to scientists' actions, their everyday practices in their ordinary settings. The title of Latour and Woolgar's *Laboratory Life* is revealing in this respect. This is not to say that concern with belief and knowledge has been excluded, but that it is now given a secondary, derived role; hence, I suppose it would be right to put the stress on "manufacture" in the title of Knorr-Cetina's book, *The Manufacture of Knowledge.*

The ethnographic and constructivist approaches do not postulate anything akin to a set of autonomous social structures or interests external to the scientific community to explain scientists' beliefs and actions. The acting subject with his or her intentions, beliefs, and actions in social settings is the starting point of analysis. It is the scientists with routinized recurrent actions and interactions based on tacit principles who produce, reproduce, and alter the social order of the life-worlds of science. The basic activity is that of the construction of scientific facts and theories in such local and artificial contexts as the laboratory. (For examples of the so-called laboratory studies, see Latour & Woolgar, 1986 (1979), Knorr-Cetina, 1981, Lynch, 1985.) Facts and theories in science are viewed as conventional "fabrications" based on selections, interpretations, and negotiations within research groups. The process of negotiation involves factors like rhetorical persuasion and use of power. Science may be depicted as a game with players using different strategies and tactics for the purpose of maximizing a specific social attribute of individual scientists (or groups thereof), for instance what Latour and Woolgar (ibid.) call "credibility." Both the laboratory and the scientific community at large are viewed in quasi-economic terms as markets in which actors attempt to sell their products, "papers," in order to maximize their own credibility. (For a useful brief account of an ethnographic-constructivist approach, see Knorr-Cetina, 1983.)

It should come as no surprise that the picture provided by the ethnographic studies of laboratory life is radically nonfalsificationist. The laboratory is not an arena of bold conjectures and attempted falsifications organized on the basis of compelling arguments designed in terms of formal logic with the aim of seeking and substantiating the truth or eliminating falsehoods. Rather, the aim of laboratory operations is to "make things work," that is, to achieve a pragmatically satisfactory balance between chemicals, instruments, statistical and other procedures, human participants, and other elements in the complex institution of the laboratory. The thrust of research work is not in the least to test theories. The suggestion that economics is not much different in this regard should not be found startling.

Participant observation is the approach that the ethnographic studies have adopted. Woolgar (1981, 482) complains that most of the social studies of science, even those that are concerned with the contents of scientific claims, rely on such secondary sources as interviews with scientists and published scientific papers. For the most part, this also applies to some recent attempts to find out what actually goes on in economics; they are based on interviews or questionnaires (Klamer, 1983; Colander and Klamer, 1987) or on the published or unpublished work of economists (McCloskey, 1985). Woolgar recommends instead the *in situ* observation of scientific activity, in which the sociological analyst adopts the role of a participant observer. This is what has been practiced in the ethnographic laboratory studies. They are fashioned after the image of anthropological studies of alien tribes. It is claimed that such *in situ* observation provides analysts with more direct access to the actual processes of scientific practice than do interview responses or written documents. As Woolgar (ibid., 483-484) puts it, "more is to be gained from being on the spot than from attempting interpretation from a secondary perspective," such as from actors removed from the scene.

There is no doubt that Axel Leijonhufvud's entertaining piece, "Life among the Econ" (1981 (1973)) is based on observations stemming from being on the spot. This amusing narrative also emulates a kind of ethnographic or anthropological approach with references to the Econ "tribe's" network of "caste and status," "totems and myths," "taboos against association with the Polscis, Sociogs, and other tribes." The status pursued by the members of castes ("fields") is dependent on the manufacture of certain kinds of sacred implements, namely "modls" (ibid., 349). "Each caste has a basic modl of simple pattern and the modls made by individual members will be variations on the theme set by the basic modl of the caste." The basic modl is the "totem" of the caste; for instance, the totem of the "Micro-Econ" consists of intersecting S- and D-lines, while the totem of the "Macro-Econ" consists of intersecting LM- and IS-lines, where both resemble "two carved sticks joined together in the middle somewhat in the form of a pair of scissors" (ibid., 351-353). What is important for our purposes is the claim that modls are in present times produced "more for ceremonial than for practical purposes." This trend among the Econ towards "more ornate, ceremonial modls" is related to the rise of the "Math-Econ" to the "priestly caste" that make "exquisite modls finely carved from bones of walras" (ibid., 349-350, 355). When the ceremony fails to produce concrete results in "prospecting," the Econ adopt strategies through the use of which "the role of the totem in the belief-system of the caste remains unassailed" (ibid., 354), a very non-Popperian feature of the tribe, to be sure.

Most of those who have written on the "culture" of economics (Leijonhufvud, 1981 (1973); Ward, 1972; Earl, 1983) are themselves economists and, hence, in a genuine sense participant observers. There are, however, at least three differences between these attempts and those of the ethnographic sociologies of science. First, these economists do not enter the culture they study as aliens, as do those sociologists who have studied, for instance, the day-to-day practices of biochemists. Second, these economists have not themselves engaged in highly systematic studies based on data collection and empirically controlled theory formation. They have come up with something akin to theories, but these accounts are often more intuitive than in the case of the ethnographic studies. Third, unlike the studies written by economists about their own discipline, the ethnographic approach has produced accounts that reveal the technical or craft character of science by portraying the scientist located at the laboratory bench. Similar studies of economics should provide analyses of what takes place, for example, at economists' desks. Concentration on classrooms, conference sessions, and journal publications is insufficient from this perspective.

SCIENCE AS A RHETORICAL GAME

Much of the recent sociology of science puts considerable emphasis on the linguistic behavior of scientists and its social character. This is well exemplified by Latour and Woolgar's study (1986 (1979)). To them, scientific work is a form of writing, it is production of what they call "literary inscriptions," such as computer printout data sheets, tables of figures, curves and diagrams, and, as the final product, written reports. Science is based on the rhetorical use of language in social contexts, it is "the organization of persuasion through literary inscription" (ibid., 88).

One type of epistemological foundationalism amounts to the doctrine that takes the structure of justification of beliefs as being built upon a set of basic beliefs that are somehow given or warranted but not socially produced—for instance, pure observation reports. The social theories of knowledge production, such as Latour and

Woolgar's and Knorr-Cetina's, reject such foundationalism. They argue that the basic factual representations, or "data," in laboratory research are socially constructed through a process of selection, interpretation, and negotiation. Instead of being given, the data belong to the set of negotiable literary inscriptions.

The winning of the status of a generally accepted representation is a peculiar social process of persuasion whereby the traces of the process itself are hidden. "The function of literary inscription is the successful persuasion of readers, but the readers are only fully convinced when all sources of persuasion seem to have disappeared. In other words, the various operations of writing and reading which sustain an argument are seen by participants to be largely irrelevant to 'facts,' which emerge solely by virtue of these same operations." (ibid., 76)

Latour and Woolgar (ibid., 76-86) claim to have observed a process of gradual transformation of statements from hotly contested conjectures to self-evident facts. They give a fivefold classification of statement types. Type 5 statements correspond to taken-for-granted facts that do not figure in discussions among established members of the laboratory. Type 4 statements are also uncontroversial, but the relation stated is made explicit here. They are typical of teaching texts. Type 3 statements are like type 4 statements with modalities, that is, statements of other statements, such as including a reference to the scientists who discovered the relation stated and the date when the relation was reported to have been found. Type 2 statements are claims rather than uncontroversially established assertions. They contain modalities which "draw attention to the generality of available evidence (or lack of it)." Finally, type 1 statements are conjectures or pure speculations "which appear most commonly at the end of papers, or in private discussion."

From this perspective, science appears as a rhetorical game or struggle with the aim of the participants being to persuade their colleagues to drop all modalities involved in their favorite statements. The aim is to transform as many statements as possible to the status of type 4 statements. In the process of increasing "facticity," or of the establishment of statements as self-evident, all traces of authorship and the rhetorical background disappear. This is why the outcome is dependent on "hiding" the process of its origination.

This insight easily leads to what may be called social coherence theories of justification. Scientific claims become justified when related to other statements that enjoy strong support in a scientific community as a result of socially conditioned processes of selection, persuasion, and negotiation. That is, if there are any "foundational" or "basic" beliefs in science, they are not given, incorrigible, or in any absolute sense privileged; what makes them more basic than other beliefs is the social fact of having won plenty of communal support.

It is then a most natural thing to suggest that these social selection mechanisms should be sociologically investigated. What has been found in such studies is a plethora of various factors, mechanisms, and processes that work towards support-formation, such as persuasive skills, authority and power, tenacity of tradition, use of culturally rooted metaphors, and other such socially loaded facts. They contribute to "closing down" controversies that otherwise would continue without limits due to the unlimited interpretive flexibility of data (Collins, 1981b). What emerges is a picture of scientific justification as a social process that is irreducible to the falsificationist process of deductive reasoning. On this view, the mechanisms of closure are social, not logical.[3]

Still, scientists themselves often appeal to metatheoretical notions such as Popperian falsificationism in giving accounts of their research practices. Having studied the way a group of biochemists construe accounts of actual procedures of theory choice, Michael Mulkay and Nigel Gilbert report that there is a systematic symmetry between how these scientists account for what they regard as correct beliefs and incorrect beliefs. Correct beliefs (usually those of the interpreter and of those with whom the interpreter agrees) are interpreted as being objective and guided by scientifically reliable experimental evidence, while incorrect ones (usually held by those with whom the interpreter disagrees) are viewed as having been influenced by the intrusion of distorting social factors into the scientific domain. (Mulkay and Gilbert, 1982a, 1982b; Gilbert and Mulkay, 1984.)

Mulkay and Gilbert (1981) show that Popperian rules of science are often appealed to in such accounts since conclusions with which the accountant agrees are portrayed as results of actions that obey those rules, while those with which the accountant disagrees are claimed to contravene them. Because the Popperian norms are extremely abstract, they can be, and in fact are, flexibly interpreted to support scientists' varying objectives in different social situations. Mulkay and Gilbert argue that almost any action, belief, or judgment can be made compatible with loose Popperian ideas and that this opportunity is in fact used by scientists. Of course, such discourse by scientists does not yet suffice to establish the idea that good scientific research follows Popperian canons. Not surprisingly, Mulkay and Gilbert argue that scientists' accounts of their own practice should not be accepted at face value. Instead, they appear to be extremely unreliable in that they are incoherent, diverse, variable, and contingent upon contexts. They should be viewed as part of the metatheoretical rhetoric or discourse that scientists practice in persuading others to accept their views and to reject those of their opponents. It is regarded as a task of a sociologist of science to analyze such discourse for what it is.

SCIENTISTS' ACTION AS A PURSUIT OF SOCIAL ENDS IN A MARKET

It is interesting from our point of view that much of recent sociology of science is built upon analogies drawn from economics. In these suggestions science is viewed as analogous to a capitalist market economy in which agents are maximizing producers who competitively and greedily pursue their self-interest. The point of emphasis in these suggestions is on scientists' action and on the ends involved in that action.

The ethnographic studies view the laboratory as a local site of a production process that yields published research reports as final outputs. Formal publications are products of complicated social processes with informal interactions and flows of information involved within a community of research workers. Both the laboratory and the scientific community at large are considered in quasi-economic terms as markets in which participants do their best to market their products, that is, "papers," and in that way to maximize an asset, namely what Pierre Bourdieu (1975) calls "credit" and "symbolic capital," and what Latour and Woolgar (1986 (1979)) call "credibility."

Scientific credit in Bourdieu's sense is symbolic capital that consists of both scientific competence and social authority and that can be converted into various kinds of resources needed for carrying on scientific production. Credit is pursued by scientists in an exclusively rivalrous manner in the market of science by using an investment strategy that would bring them a monopoly of authority in a given field of research, "defined inseparably as technical capacity and social power" (Bourdieu 1975, 19).

The notion of credibility as developed by Latour and Woolgar is indebted to Bourdieu's suggestions, although they are critical of the latter's idea of credit for failing to provide an account of "the way in which technical capacity is linked to social power" (Latour and Woolgar 1986 (1979), 206). Credibility is more than just reward for past achievements. It also refers to future capabilities of scientists to practice science with success. Credibility is a resource that can be cashed in. Scientists are maximizers who invest their energies in the research fields and topics that are anticipated to yield the best return, that is, in those for which there is demand in the "market." The credibility they acquire by doing so leads to new rewards such as research grants, appointments, accepted publications, and so on. These, in turn, generate more credibility. As Latour and Woolgar (ibid., 197) put it, "scientists' behavior is remarkably similar to that of an investor of capital. An accumulation of credibility is prerequisite to investment. The greater this stockpile, the more able the investor is to reap substantial returns and thus to add further to his growing capital." The ensuing process of what they call the "cycle of credibility" constitutes the ultimate dynamics of science.[4]

The point of emphasis in the credibility model is on scientists' action (although, to be sure, there are hints of some kind of systemic teleology in the way the "cycle of credibility" is being characterized). There are two important senses in which scientists' action is understood here as being social in character or socially conditioned. First, the goal scientists pursue by their action—namely, credibility—is a social property. One's credibility is dependent for its existence and utility-yielding properties on other persons in a social context. Second, action oriented towards achieving this goal is in fact a process of social interaction. Scientists choose their strategies and tactics constrained by the actual and anticipated reactions of other scientists.

What kind of a thing, ultimately, is credibility as the property to be maximized, and why is it that scientists would be interested in maximizing it? Latour and Woolgar do not have much to say about this. They say that "there is no ultimate objective to scientific investment other than the continual redeployment of accumulated resources" (ibid., 198) and that "[t]he objective of market activity is to extend and *speed up the credibility cycle as a whole*" (ibid., 207). Presumably, they do not think that credibility is maximized for its own sake. Even though they say that there is no objective beyond "the continual redeployment of accumulated resources," they might be prepared to think that credibility is an instrumental entity that is maximized because it can be used to acquire other things that yield utility. That they do not discuss these questions may be unfortunate, as the picture they give about scientists' action has now been painted in very monotonous colors. Indeed, it would seem that if scientists were viewed as utility maximizers, Latour and Woolgar's scientists would have only one argument in their utility function, namely, credibility. It is, of course, true that this is compatible with a variety of factors that may motivate scientists, but it is also clear that it does not encompass everything that might motivate scientists to act.

It has been suggested by Williams and Law (1980, 313) that "[t]o view science as the disinterested search for credibility is, in its own way, as misleading as to view it as the disinterested search for truth." They argue that science is more broadly social in character than suggested by the credibility model; calculations about credibility usually are moderated by the social context, loaded with non-credibility issues, in which they occur. There is a broader interactional order with contingent entanglements and commitments that shapes considerations of credibility. "Actors come to value their colleagues as friends, confidants or opponents. Time and effort are invested in these other involvements, public positions are adopted, and the network of side-bets grows and becomes constraining." (ibid., 313) While the market analogy of the credibility model depicts science as social action, these remarks propose to give it more concrete sociopsychological content.

Williams and Law do not develop their suggestion into a well-formulated notion. In this respect, Peter Earl's (1983) "behavioral model of economists' behavior" goes further. It specifies the goal component of scientists' actions more richly than do Latour and Woolgar, in terms of subcomponents of psychic and monetary cost and return. Furthermore, unlike the latter, Earl is interested in the motivations underlying scientists' actions. Earl considers the academic economist's position as analogous to that of managers in business firms as conceptualized in a behavioral framework.

Earl's model depicts scientists as having lexicographic preferences so that their choices are based on certain priorities rather than trade-offs among their goals. The set of goals that "an academic economist will rank highly" includes predictive power, fame and prestige, high income and certain lifestyle, nice (social, natural, academic) environment, minimum effort and avoidance of anxiety (Earl, 1983, 94). Most of these goals have social content or are dependent on social matters. This is the case, for instance, with Earl's notion of fame, which is close to that of credibility in Latour and Woolgar. Thus, we have here another example of a social theory of science built upon the idea that (at least some of) the ends of scientists' action have a social character.

Earl's point is that "ideas find academic acceptance not necessarily because of their intrinsic scientific worth . . . but rather because they are salable as tools which enable their users more easily to reach their goals" (Earl, 1983, 90).[5] Earl argues that his model can be utilized to explain facts such as the reign of neoclassical equilibrium theorizing by referring to the alleged fact that economists "will tend to be attracted by the leisure or promotion advantages that come from practicing as a technically competent equilibrium theorist rather than attempting to swim against the tide as, say, a behavioral economist" (ibid., 101).

That economists are not critical Popperians is characterized by Earl in the following way: "If an anomaly is discovered, information overloads are avoided by not asking difficult questions. A limited rule-guided search will usually provide a way of coping with a difficulty without challenging fundamental questions . . . . As long as (the rules) seem to be working and the scientist is able to meet her aspirations she will have no obvious reason to question them" (ibid., 101). The way Earl depicts economists' behavior is closer to Lakatosian ideas, but there are important differences here, such as the latter's neglect of "the role played by scientists' personal motivations" (ibid., 102). Economists are too conservative and too much guided by their personal aspirations to be real Lakatosians. "If a switch to a new (scientific research program) would have no positive career payoff, yet would involve an admission that she believes she has hitherto been foolishly wasting her time (thus hurting her self-image), the economist may carry on as before" (ibid., 103). In general, Earl's thesis is that "choice between theories ultimately rests on personal preferences and perceptions, shaped as they are by predispositions, by upbringing in a social/academic/economic context, and by the selectivity of cognitive processes" (ibid., 118). Note that this statement contains not only the idea that some of the ends of economists' action are social states and processes, but also the idea that the ends and means of economists' action are shaped by social factors. This makes such action doubly socially conditioned.

From our point of view, one important idea involved in these models of scientists' behavior is the implied dependence of acceptance and rejection on socially loaded factors. Scientists tend to be committed to particular theories and approaches to the extent that they have made prior investments of time, effort, and money in the acquisition of the mastering of those theories and techniques. In the early stages of those prior investments it is relatively easier to change one's beliefs and orientation, but once they become established in the form of institutions and traditions, a change will be more difficult; however, it should not be impossible. The credibility of scientists and the research groups they form is dependent on their continued ability to produce new marketable results. This ability depends on both the investments made and the demand in the market. This demand is not, of course, pregiven, that is, independent of the marketing efforts of the producers of those results, but it is not completely determined by them either. In any case, if the demand or marketability of a particular kind of result decreases considerably, the only option available to a scientist willing to stay in the business may be to change his beliefs. In general, beliefs or methods are not rejected if the cost of such rejection is too high to the standing of the scientist or his research grou Obviously, in this picture, if there are rejections, they are not based on falsifications.

It is noteworthy that, to a large extent, Earl's model is intended as an account of the behavior of economists making "conservative" choices, i.e., sticking to already established ("mainstream") frameworks and techniques and thereby contributing to their further entrenchment. This means that the contents of those frameworks and their origination and winning of a ruling position remain unaccounted for. The model attempts to chart the social and psychological mechanisms of maintenance while leaving the mechanisms of genesis uncharted.

While Earl's sketch model fills in some gaps in Latour and Woolgar's view of scientific action, there are some shared assumptions. Both models are agent-centered and internalist; their focus is on scientists acting in the intellectual market within the boundaries of their discipline. Furthermore, both assume an integrated agent with a well-formulated decision problem in the single scientific game in which he participates. These assumptions have been challenged by Knorr-Cetina, among others (see also, Latour, 1987).

TRANSSCIENTIFIC ARENAS

Knorr-Cetina (1981, 1982) argues that it is not only the laboratory that constitutes the field or market in that scientists play their games. There are other fields or arenas of scientists' action which she calls "transscientific fields" (1981) and "transepistemic arenas" (1982).[6] "It is crucial to realize that the moves which are made in the various arenas of action need not add up to one particular game played according to a coherent set of rules in pursuit of a definite goal. The picture we get is more that of a field on which different games are played at the same time by a variety of people." (Knorr-Cetina, 1982, 118.) Scientists do not play merely with their disciplinary colleagues, but also with other people such as those who have power over the resources of research, such as funding, careers, etc.

This implies that the notion of a scientific community as a specialty network, as something that is restricted to the relationships between specialists in a field, becomes obsolete (see ibid., 114-116).

Knorr-Cetina's suggestion implies, of course, an extension of sociological considerations to encompass social realms external to science. It is, however, different from some of the applications of the Edinburgh program in that it does not imply an agenda for searching for the causal imprints of wider social relations on the contents of scientific theories. Knorr-Cetina's point is, so to speak, to enlarge the market of scientists' action beyond the boundaries of specific scientific fields. To argue that scientists act in several arenas, including extrascientific ones, is to suggest that, if viewed as rhetoric, scientists' action has what may be called a *multiple-auditorial* character in that acts of persuasion may and have to be directed to different audiences using different strategies adapted to the qualities of the respective audiences.

There is no doubt that economics is multiple-auditorial in such a sense. Some of the typical audiences confronted by economists are: the like-minded within academic economics; their critics within the discipline; their students, both undergraduate and graduate; scholars other than economists within academia; their sponsors, both in asking for support and in reporting their successes; the sophisticated members of the public such as journalists, politicians, business managers, and bureaucrats; and the larger public unfamiliar with their message and language (see Coats, 1988, 70; Goodwin, 1988, 209-210). This list could, of course, be extended and its items divided further into smaller and more specific audiences.

While it may be that sciences typically are multiple-auditorial, it is probable that not all sciences are so to the same extent and in the same way. For instance, it would seem obvious that there are differences between physics, economics, and management research in this respect. Richard Whitley's framework, to be discussed next, draws attention to these and other important differences.

ECONOMICS AS A PARTITIONED BUREAUCRACY

Whitley has developed a framework, based on the so-called contingency approach to studying organizations, which gathers together, renames, and modifies many of the ingredients that we have found in the sociologies of science considered so far. While many of the theories considered above build upon generalizations based on findings from one or more disciplines, what makes Whitley's work particularly interesting from our point of view is his attempt at a classification or taxonomy of different kinds of disciplines, in which economics also finds a place (Whitley, 1984a, 1986; see also Coats, 1984, Loasby, 1986).

Whitley considers scientific disciplines as "reputational work organizations" oriented towards knowledge production. They are organized on the basis of structures of coordination and uncertainty inherent to scientific communities and conditioned by their external social contexts. Disciplines vary as to the ways in which and degrees to which they are so organized and conditioned. This major insight allows Whitley to make attempts to find out what is peculiar about each individual discipline, such as post-war physics, management studies, and post-1870 economics.

The first notion in Whitley's framework that makes any science essentially a social enterprise is the idea that scientists pursue positive reputations from particular groups within (or, in some cases, without) their disciplines. This is a matter of the goals of scientists' actions seen as social action: positive reputation as one of the goals has a social character.

The acquisition of reputations is controlled by other features related to each discipline. These features are conceptualized by Whitley to form a framework for concrete analysis. Mutual dependence and task uncertainty are the two key concepts in the framework. These help organize the idea of the social character of the structure of disciplinary action.

The concept of *mutual dependence* refers to "the extent to which scientists have to coordinate and specifically interrelate their research with that of a well-defined and bounded group of fellow specialists"

(Whitley, 1984a, 86). Mutual dependence is divided into two subcategories. The degree of *functional dependence* is concerned with "the extent to which researchers have to use the specific results, ideas, and procedures of fellow specialists in order to construct knowledge claims which are regarded as competent and useful contributions" (ibid., 88). This is a matter of coordinating the outcomes and competence standards of research. The degree of *strategic dependence* is "the extent to which researchers have to persuade colleagues of the significance and importance of their problem and approach to obtain a high reputation from them" (ibid., 88). This is a matter of coordinating goals and strategies of research.

The degree of these two aspects of dependence vary from field to field (from "low" to "high"). To connect these notions to our concerns, in a sense, we may say that the higher the degree of mutual dependence, the stronger the social conditioning of research.

The second of the two key categories in Whitley's framework is that of *task uncertainty.* It is also divided into two subcategories. The degree of *technical task uncertainty* varies in accordance with the extent to which the use of research techniques is either well established and standardized or open to personal, fluid choices and the extent to which the interpretation of results is either straightforward and uniform or ambiguous and open to conflict (ibid., 121). The degree of *strategic uncertainty* "encompasses uncertainty about intellectual priorities, the significance of research topics and preferred ways of tackling them, the likely reputational pay-off of different research strategies, and the relevance of task outcomes for collective intellectual goals" (ibid., 123).

Again, the degree of these two aspects of uncertainty varies across disciplines (from "low" to "high"). It is easy to see that both of them have been defined by Whitley in a way that makes them irreducibly socially loaded notions.

On the basis of these two dimensions of dependence and uncertainty and the respective variables, each with two values, Whitley is able to construe a typology of scientific fields in which economics represents a specific type. To give examples, post-1945 physics belongs to the type of "conceptually integrated bureaucracy" with high functional and strategic dependence and low technical and strategic uncertainty, while management studies and British sociology are "fragmented adhocracies," characterized by low functional and strategic dependence and high technical and strategic uncertainty (see

Whitley, 1984b). Economics occupies a category of its own, called a "*partitioned bureaucracy*" by Whitley, and characterized by low functional and high strategic dependence combined with high technical and low strategic task uncertainty.

Economics is claimed to be a partitioned bureaucracy in the sense that it "seems to combine considerable mutual dependence and task predictability in the analytical core of the subject with rather less coordination and integration of research results in peripheral 'applied' subfields where the meaning and implications of research are often ambiguous and open to conflicting interpretations" (Whitley, 1986, 191). Whitley relies on the testimonies by many witnesses in making the point that "this combination of relatively strong collective control over 'hard-core' . . . assumptions and principles with uncertainty and 'anomalous' peripheral areas would be unstable if reputations in the analytical core were dependent upon success in controlling and coordinating empirical phenomena. However, research involving statistical data and empirical indicators seems to be separated from theoretical model-building activities in economics and to have lower intellectual prestige . . . . Thus, theoreticians can obtain high reputations by producing highly abstract and general models of 'ideal' worlds without considering how they are related to economic phenomena in actual worlds; their work is partitioned from empirical economic studies, and they do not need to demonstrate any systematic connection to them" (ibid., 191-192).

A possibility of misunderstanding may lurk behind Whitley's more categorical pronouncements and I suppose he would agree on the need to eliminate it. This is the reading of Whitley's framework implying that there are strictly and qualitatively separate types of sciences, each with an unshakable identity of their own. However, as should be clear from the way the typology is constructed, the differences between kinds of disciplines are not very strict and clear. The crucial point is that the degree of mutual dependence and task uncertainty are said to vary from "low" to "high," and this, of course, leaves plenty of room for differences of degree, intermediate cases, overlap, etc. Consequently, physics as a "conceptually integrated bureaucracy" is obviously not completely devoid of the sort of partition that is claimed to characterize modern Anglo-Saxon economics as a "highly rule-governed field which separates the stable and controlled analytical core from the uncertain and ambiguous periphery" (Whitley, 1986, 192). The point has to be that there is a difference of degree between economics and physics as to the separation of theory from empirical work.

Another point to be made is that the features we take to characterize a given discipline or field of research are dependent on how we mark off that field. Whitley's "post-1870 economics" is a case in point. An obvious criticism of his account of this field is that he has an unnecessarily restricted view of the extent to which the theoretical core of post-1870 economics is uniform and coherent and has control over all research, thus underestimating the role of dissenting traditions (Coats, 1984, 225). However, it seems to me that Whitley has defined "post-1870 economics" as denoting only the mainstream orthodoxy so as to save the notion from such charges. Still, one may ask whether, after all, a sensible definition can be given to the notion of mainstream economics such that the alleged degree of unity could be preserved.[7]

The notions of mutual dependence and task uncertainty imply that sciences are socially conditioned on the level of scientists' actions and interactions within their disciplines. There is more to the social conditioning of sciences, namely, the role of the determinants that Whitley calls *contextual factors*, which include wider social facts external to science plus other factors: *reputational autonomy* (which concerns performance standards, significance standards, and problem formulation and descriptive terms); *concentration of control over the means of intellectual production and distribution;* and *audience structure* (consisting of audience variety and audience equivalence) (Whitley, 1984a, 220-238). These contextual factors have an impact on the degrees of mutual dependence and task uncertainty (ibid., 104-112, 139-147). These notions make it possible to view much of scientists' actions being performed in transscientific arenas in Knorr-Cetina's sense, albeit to a varying extent—more so in management studies than in economics, for example. Research in the field of management studies is more strongly multiple-auditorial than that in economics since the degree of audience variety and audience equivalence in acquiring reputations is higher in the former. Reputational autonomy is low in fragmented adhocracies and also in the applied periphery of economics as a partitioned bureaucracy, while it is high in the theoretical core of economics.

In conclusion, if post-1870 mainstream economics were a partitioned bureaucracy in Whitley's sense, then we would have here an account that characterizes theory appraisal in economics as a socially conditioned process that has nothing to do with Popperian or Lakatosian standards of rational science, or, even more radically, that is not systematically constrained by empirical evidence.

SOME LESSONS

As pointed out by many commentators, economists do not behave according to the norms prescribed by falsificationist methodology even though they often preach that same methodology. Mark Blaug (1980), for instance, makes this observation and also insists that economists should try to do their best to obey the falsificationist prescriptions, to which, after all, they themselves subscribe in their own methodological declarations.

What should be said about these ideas in light of the findings and suggestions of the recent sociology of science? We have learned that sociologists depict science as socially conditioned in that, for instance, scientists are viewed as pursuing social ends in an interactive process of negotiation and persuasion, shaped by the social context. What conclusions do these insights suggest?

First, the negative observation that the grounds on which economists "choose" theories are not falsificationist grounds conforms to what seems to be the case in other disciplines, too. Thus, it might give some consolation to economists to find that at least they are not much less "scientific" in this sense than researchers in other fields. Furthermore, falsificationist rhetoric by participants, not adequately reflecting their actual research practices, seems to be a typical characteristic of other disciplines as well; again, there seems to be nothing peculiar about economics in this regard.

Second, while neither Blaug nor many others unhappy with the situation have shown what in fact takes place in economics and why, work designed after the example of the sociological accounts of science might be able to contribute to describing and explaining some of the facts about economics. This concerns not only the negative fact of economists not obeying falsificationist norms but also positive facts related to how economists do behave and believe and why.

As to the negative fact, what we have learned is that there seems to be something in the way sciences are socially organized that gives support to the fact that scientists behave in ways that systematically diverge from falsificationist canons. Action animated by credibility and interaction, amounting to negotiation and persuasion, do not appear to fit the categories of bold conjecture, falsification, corroboration, and progressive problem-shift. In particular, if economics were a "partitioned bureaucracy," conditioned by contextual factors in the way Whitley suggests, this would give us further reasons for describing and explaining phenomena within this discipline in nonfalsificationist terms.[8]

One particular doctrine of Popperian epistemology that threatens to be undermined can be separately mentioned: namely, the distinction between the context of discovery and the context of justification. For Popper, only the latter is characterized by systematic rationality, while the discovery process is open to various nonrational influences the workings of which cannot be systematized philosophically but should be studied by sociology, psychology, even political science. This distinction, with all the epistemological burden it is supposed to carry, gets blurred by the findings of sociologists. "Whether a proposed knowledge claim is judged plausible or implausible, interesting, unbelievable or nonsensical, may depend upon *who* proposed the result, *where* the work where done, and how it was accomplished .... Thus, the scientific community itself lends crucial weight to the context of discovery in response to a knowledge claim" (Knorr-Cetina, 1981, 7).

It may be maintained that the rationality of Popperian norms remains intact even though actual practice does not, as a contingent fact, conform to them. The third point to make is that recent sociology of science alerts us to the possibility, or even high likelihood, that (at least some of the) Popperian norms will inevitably prove ineffectual. Again, if economics is a drastically partitioned discipline, due to its social structure, there would seem to be little hope of getting falsificationist criteria applied, even approximately, in the field. This state of affairs would be rooted in the social organization or economics and would be independent of any single economist's possible endeavors to act in a contrary fashion. Therefore, the mere prescribing that falsificationism be adopted by economists in actual practice would fall on deaf ears. Blaug's prescriptive statement to the effect that economists should try harder to satisfy the falsificationist norms of ideal science may prove utterly utopian in the absence of a radical (probably itself utopian) revolution in the social organization of economics. One would then have to ask about the grounds for insisting on the imposition of such norms.

The minimum point made by the sociological theories is that *the fate of a scientific statement is at least partly dependent on the social context* (where by "fate" I mean such things as invention, introduction, persistence, acceptance, rejection, modification, etc.). The minimum point is a descriptive statement of the actual situation in the actual past, present, and future of science. The extent to which various statements in various branches of a discipline, like economics, in various stages of their development are socially conditioned in one or more ways is not, of course, decidable a priori. Still, the minimum point seems to me plausible enough to be taken seriously. It just requires a lot of empirical work to find out where, when, and how in economics the point might hold. Here we encounter the fact that the sociology of economics as a field of inquiry is still in its infancy.

There are two questions of a philosophical sort that can be discussed, if not settled, prior to extensive empirical evidence. First, are there standards of rationality that surpass or are independent of the actualities summarized by the minimum point? Popperian and many other methodologists think there are such standards. I will not tackle this important issue directly here. Second, does admitting that (at least much of) science is socially conditioned necessarily lead one to the idea that the truth value of scientific statements is similarly indexical or context-dependent, or that the pursuit and attainment of objective truth is a meaningless or useless notion? It is this antirealist conclusion suggested by some relativist sociologists that I do not buy. Here I side with the Popperians. The final section is devoted to this issue.

RELATIVISM AND REALISM

Much of the recent sociology of science explicitly declares itself as adhering to "relativism." Since this has caused both confusion and contempt, I will conclude this chapter with a brief discussion of some aspects of this philosophically interesting notion. Relativism appears in a great variety of versions. Building upon the statement "X is relative to Y," relativism takes on different forms depending on how "X" is specified (as the contents of beliefs, aims of research, criteria of acceptance and rejection, truth, reality, etc.) and on how "Y" is specified (as language, professional interests, audience, culture or form of life, etc.). My focus will be on those versions that are related to the realist notion of truth as something that hinges upon the objective structure of the world.

The question we have to face is this: If we accept the idea that a scientific discipline, such as economics, is bound to be socially conditioned in a number of ways, can we still take it as actually, or at least potentially, constituting or providing true knowledge about the way the preexisting economy is? I am inclined to answer this question positively, while some contemporary sociologists of science have either an indifferent or a negative position. In what follows, no penetrating arguments can be formulated to back up any of these answers. Only some of the issues and outlines of some of the arguments will be laid down in somewhat simplified terms.

One way of giving truth a role in a socially conditioned science is to postulate it as one of the ends that scientists pursue. This might be what Whitley suggests. In the second sentence of his book, he says that modern sciences "attempt to monopolize the production of true knowledge of the world" (Whitley, 1984a, 1). This might be taken to amount to the assumption that individual scientists or the groups they constitute have truth about the world as one of their ends. On this assumption, scientists would pursue strong epistemic goals in addition to being activated by the social goal of high positive reputation. This combination appears as completely possible. It seems to me, however, that if this were Whitley's idea, the notion of knowledge defined in terms of truth would be an external element in his framework. It would not have an intimate connection to the other elements.

Alternatively, it may also be that Whitley is among those sociologists of science who relegate the notions of truth and reality merely to scientists' own ideological discourse by means of which the participants try to justify their beliefs and actions. Rhetorical usage of "true," "false," and "real" does not, on this view, have any other function beyond that involved in the persuasion and negotiation by practicing scientists. As Collins (1981a, 218) puts it, these terms (and others, such as "rational" and "progressive") are used in sociological explanations exclusively as "actor's categories." They would have no role among the explanantia of actors' beliefs.

In general, however, regarding science as a social process of rhetorical persuasion does not in itself threaten in any way the idea of science having a veristic dimension. Beliefs marketed by using whatever rhetorical means are found efficient (or inefficient) for that purpose may be true or may be false, and scientists may or may not have the truth as an end of their rhetorical actions. Thus, the recent suggestion that economics has a rhetorical character does not, without additional premises, undermine the realist intuitions about truth and reality (see Mäki, 1988).

Truth does not have to be postulated as a goal of scientists' action in order for it to emerge as an outcome of the interactions between scientists (as an invisible-hand consequence, as it were). Neither of these roles is reserved for truth in Latour and Woolgar. While Bourdieu (1975) postulated that the pursuit of symbolic capital or credit by scientists in a competitive universe would ultimately promote the attainment of the truth, in Latour and Woolgar's (1986 (1979)) framework there is no connection between investments in credibility on the one hand and truth seeking, or truth finding, or truth approaching, on the other. Investments are made only for the purpose of accumulating one's credibility, which is to be reinvested again with the same purpose. And the "cycle of credibility" does not include an invisible-hand teleology towards the truth.

The legitimacy of talk about truth is sometimes questioned by appealing to the socially conditioned nature of the standards of justification. Some representatives of the current sociology of science seem to think that a meaningful notion of truth presupposes the existence of final, and presumably infallible, criteria or procedures of deciding whether a given knowledge claim is in fact true or false. Because no one has been (nor, most probably, will be) able to provide such unambiguous, compelling, and universally valid criteria, some sociologists of knowledge conclude that truth itself is dependent on those same social factors that have a role in conditioning which claims are accepted and which are rejected in a scientific community. This amounts to confusing the truth and justification components of knowledge with each other. Even if it were the case that the rules of argument and the criteria of justification are to be defined in terms that are internal to a social order, it would not yet follow from this that the very notion of truth should be so defined. It may be argued that whether or not our reasons for accepting a given statement as true are good or bad, socially conditioned or unconditioned, the truth value of that statement remains stable by virtue of its relation to its object.

Truth in the realist sense as something that characterizes the relation between a representation and its object in the preexisting world has been questioned by some constructivist sociologists by forwarding the argument that the objects of scientific representations are socially constructed. Science as a process of manufacture or construction of *knowledge* also often appears to the constructivists as a process of construction of the *world*, or worlds. Science is not an attempt to truly represent the preexisting reality, as science never in fact "touches" reality: "Where in the laboratory . . . do we find . . . nature? Most (!) of the reality with which scientists deal is highly preconstructed, if not wholly artificial" (Knorr-Cetina, 1984, 225). Here, it sounds as if reality itself were relative to the social processes of investigating it.

It seems to me that the notion of the constructedness or artificiality of the domain of phenomena studied in laboratories has been left in a considerably obscure state by the constructivists. There seem to be at least two possible ways to specify the meaning of the notion. First, the idea might be given the radical form in which it is stated that whatever it is that scientists encounter in their laboratories, such as the elements, forces, and fields, is ultimately just human construction in a social setting. These items do not have an independent existence. Radical constructivism of this sort is incompatible with realism. Secondly, it might be suggested that it is not the basic constituents of nature, but instead, their specific constellations and modes of interaction that are artificially constructed in the laboratory. It is the substances-and-forces-as-purified-and-isolated-from-"disturbing"-ingredients-and-forces that constitute the artificial objects of study. It is these purifications and isolations, in this interpretation, that are manufactured and in that sense artificial. This position may be called moderate constructivism and it is compatible with realism. On the basis of a suitable interpretation of the word "most" in the above quotation from Knorr-Cetina, she might, after all, count as a moderate constructivist.

Now, this suggestion also has some relevance with respect to the situation in economics. Economic models are typically constructed analogously to the models of laboratory sciences, the analogy being that both are based on purifications and isolations of a few allegedly crucial relations from everything else. The disanalogy is that while in the laboratory circumstances these purifications and isolations can be carried out materially, in economics they are usually possible only conceptually. This is accomplished by means of the use of assumptions such as *ceteris paribus*, which economists know never quite hold true. Thus, one may say, the "worlds" constructed by economists are also artificial. The question that remains is this: in which of the two senses suggested above are the worlds artificial? I suggest that sometimes, at least, it should be possible to take the idea seriously that it is the isolations, closures, and simplifications involved in economic models that are artificial rather than at least all the economic entities, relations, and forces that are postulated. These two interpretive options may be called the realist and the fictionalist reading of economic models. (See Mäki, 1990 and 1991.)

Ian Hacking's comments on Latour and Woolgar's radical constructivism supplement my point. Latour and Woolgar (1986 (1979), 64) state the following: "The central importance of this material arrangement (in the laboratory) is that none of the phenomena 'about which' participants talk could exist without it . . . . It is not simply that phenomena *depend on* certain material instrumentation; rather, the phenomena *are thoroughly constituted by* the material setting of the laboratory. The artificial reality, which participants describe in terms of an objective entity, has in fact been constructed by the use of inscription devices." Hacking (1988, 285) rightly points out that the contrast drawn here between "artificial" and "objective" may be misleading because of the ambiguity of the terms involved. "Artificial" may mean at least two things: first, "produced by man, not occurring naturally"; and second, "made in imitation of a natural product, especially as a substitute—not genuine." Only in the latter sense of the term could we consider the possibility that what is artificial lacks objectivity in some relevant sense. On the other hand, artificial objects in the first sense may exist objectively. As Hacking argues, this concerns shoes as well as the manmade objects (materials, phenomena) of the laboratory. In accordance with what was stated in the preceding paragraph, I would like to suggest that the situation in economics is not much different in this respect, though it may be more complicated.

Some of the popular forms of "relativism" prevalent in the sociological discussions on science are philosophically much less radical than the ontological versions. Barnes and Bloor, for instance, take their own version as being composed of "(i) the observation that beliefs on a certain topic vary, and (ii) the conviction that which of these beliefs is found in a given context depends on, or is relative to, the circumstances of the users," and (iii) the symmetry or equivalent postulate that "all beliefs are on a par with one another with respect to the causes of their credibility" (Barnes and Bloor, 1982, 22-23).

Barnes and Bloor emphasize that the equivalence postulate "is not that all beliefs are equally true or equally false, but that regardless of truth and falsity the fact of their credibility is to be seen as equally problematic" (ibid., 23). Abstracting from other textual evidence, this could be taken to imply that theirs is not relativism about truth. What counts as true is claimed to be relative to social context, that is, reasons for belief are regarded as socially conditioned irrespective of whether the belief is true or false. For the purposes of sociological explanation, the question of truth and falsehood is bracketed; hence, there is no relevant distinction between truth and what counts as true or between what is the case and what is taken to be the case.

The proponents of the Edinburgh approach sometimes sound like straightforward realists about the world and its role in cognition. For instance, Barnes (1977, 25) subscribes to ontological realism and gives it epistemological import: "there is indeed one world, one reality, 'out there,' the source of our perceptions if not their total determinant, the cause of our expectations being fulfilled or disappointed, our endeavours succeeding or being frustrated." He also says that he does not agree with those sociologists (such as Collins and Latour and Woolgar) who "claim that the world has nothing whatsoever to do with what is believed about it" (Barnes, 1984, 122; see also ibid., 124, n12, and his 1974, viii). It is true that, as opposed to Barnes, Collins (1981c, 54) argues that, when designing sociological explanations, it has to be assumed that "the natural world in no way constrains what is believed to be" (see also Collins and Cox 1976, 436-348). Still, Collins (1981a, 218) seems to imply realism about truth when he states that "what is true may be perceived by scientists as being false, and vice versa."

Bloor gives a characterization of the minimum element of his "relativist" program in terms which make it easy for a realist to agree: "Men's ideas about the workings of the world have varied greatly. This has been true within science just as much as in other areas of culture. Such variation forms the starting point for the sociology of knowledge and constitutes its main problem. What are the causes of this variation, and how and why does it change?" (Bloor, 1976, 3) Barnes and Bloor (1982, 34) put it more clearly in realist terms when they say that "reality is, after all, a common factor in all the vastly different cognitive responses that men produce to it. Being a common factor it is not a promising candidate to field as an explanation of that variation." In other words, they subscribe to the realist principle that there is such a thing as the workings of the world about which men have beliefs. No departure from the principle follows from admitting that these beliefs vary and change and often do so because of various sorts of social facts.

It may be granted that at least some variation of beliefs and standards is socially conditioned. This poses no threat to the notion that beliefs may be true or may be false. On the contrary, the idea of social conditioning opens up an important dimension in regard to the role of truth in our conception of science. If beliefs are socially conditioned and if beliefs have the possibility of being true of the world, we may ask about the social conditions of the actualization of that possibility. Indeed, it becomes legitimate to pose this question: What are the favorable social conditions, both internal and external to a particular science such as economics, that help direct a discipline to approach the truth (for instance, by inspiring researchers to seek the truth and helping them be successful in that endeavor)? In other words, what are the social conditions for the implementation of realist rationality? Not all social conditions are supposedly equal in this respect, which implies that successful truth hunting is relative to social matters. Whether or not this insight be regarded as still another form of relativism, methodologists interested in the role of truth in science should incorporate it into their investigations. A realist ("absolutist") methodology, in short, cannot do without a ("relativist") sociology of science.

NOTES

1. For a formulation of the asymmetry thesis by one of its advocates, we may cite Laudan (1977, 188-189): "When a thinker does what it is rational to do, we need inquire no further into the causes of his action; whereas, when he does what is in fact irrational—even if he believes it to be rational—we require some further sociological explanation." On this, Popper and Lakatos agree.

2. For a qualification, see Bloor (1981, 203): "The question of the kind or scope of social factors at work in a system of knowledge is entirely contingent and can only be established by empirical study. The important point, however, is that where broad social factors are not involved, narrow ones take over. The sociology of knowledge is still relevant. As well as *external* sociology of knowledge there is also an *internal* sociology of knowledge."

3. In the context of economics, the rhetorical processes of inquiry

have been insightfully studied by Donald McCloskey (1985) and Arjo Klamer (1983). See also Klamer, McCloskey, and Solow (1988).

4. One might add that the earlier generations of sociologists of science had observed similar features in the social process of science. For instance, Merton (1968) discusses the so-called "Matthew effect" that refers to the phenomenon that scientists with a long list of publications are more likely to get their work published than those with no established reputation, although the submissions of the beginners may be superior. To Merton, this is a deficiency in the scientific process. The difference between the two generations is that, for Latour and Woolgar, it is not at all clear in what sense the Matthew effect could be evaluated as a deficiency or a submission could be assessed as superior to another independently of the actual social process of credibility formation.

5. Note that, unlike many contemporary sociologists of science, Earl holds a notion of the "intrinsic scientific worth" of ideas, unimpregnated by the actual social process whereby they are accepted or rejected.

6. I would prefer the terms "transscientific field" or "transscientific arena" to "transepistemic arena," introduced by Knorr-Cetina (1982) to replace the earlier suggestion. The reason is that the latter suggestion appears to imply, first, that scientific arenas are necessarily epistemic, and second, that nonscientific arenas are necessarily non-epistemic. I find both of these implicit presumptions dubious.

7. Provided there would be enough unity in orthodox mainstream economics to warrant most of Whitley's suggestions, one may question whether the discipline as a whole is characterized by high technical task uncertainty, as he maintains. This may be the case in empirical work, but obviously not so in the theoretical core of orthodox economics (Loasby 1986, 224). This, of course, does not undermine the suggested separation between theoretical and empirical work.

8. We have suggested that economics is not much different from "other fields" or "natural sciences" in some regards while in some other respects it is peculiar. One lesson that suggests itself is that from a perspective such as Whitley's it seems clear that methodologists of economics should pay much more attention to fields like biochemistry

and ecology than to physics when preparing assessments about the scientific status of economics. The traditional reference to "natural sciences" when one in fact has physics in mind is often seriously misleading. It may be much more instructive to take into account differences among the natural (and social) sciences when viewing economics from a comparative perspective. And such a perspective certainly is in itself extremely instructive.

REFERENCES

Barnes, Barry (1974), *Scientific Knowledge and Sociological Theory*. London: Routledge and Kegan Paul.

__________________ (1977), *Interests and the Growth of Knowledge*. London: Routledge and Kegan Paul.

__________________ (1981), "On the 'Hows' and 'Whys' of Cultural Change," *Social Studies of Science*, 11, 481-489.

__________________ (1982), *T.S. Kuhn and Social Science*. New York: Columbia University Press.

__________________, and David Bloor (1982), "Relativism, Rationalism and Sociology of Knowledge," in M. Hollis and S. Lukes, eds., *Rationality and Relativism*. Oxford: Basil Blackwell.

__________________, and Donald Mackenzie (1979), "On the Role of Interests in Scientific Change," in Roy Wallis, ed., *On the Margins of Science: The Social Construction of Scientific Knowledge*, Sociological Review Monograph, 49-66.

Blaug, Mark (1980), *The Methodology of Economics*. Cambridge: Cambridge University Press.

Bloor, David (1976), *Science and Social Imagery*. London: Routledge and Kegan Paul.

__________________ (1981), "The Strengths of the Strong Program," *Philosophy of the Social Sciences*, 11, 199-213.

__________________ (1983), *Wittgenstein: A Social Theory of Knowledge*. London: Macmillan.

Bourdieu, Pierre (1975), "The Specificity of the Scientific Field and the Social Conditions of the Progress of Reason," *Social Science Information*, 14:6, 19-47.

Burkhardt, Jeffrey, and E. Ray Canterbery (1986), "The Orthodoxy and Professional Legitimacy: Toward a Critical Sociology of Economics," *Research in the History of Economic Thought and Methodology*, 4, 229-250.

Coats, A. W. (1984), "The Sociology of Knowledge and the History of Economics," *Research in the History of Economic Thought and Methodology*, 2, 211-234.

__________________ (1988), "Economic Rhetoric: The Social and Historical Context," in Klamer, McCloskey, and Solow, eds., *The Consequences of Economic Rhetoric*, 64-84.

Colander, David, and Arjo Klamer (1987), "The Making of an Economist," *Journal of Economic Perspectives*, 1, 95-111.

Collins, H. M. (1981a), "What Is TRASP? The Radical Program as a Methodological Imperative," *Philosophy of the Social Sciences*, 11, 214-224.

__________________ (1981b), "Stages in the Empirical Program of Relativism," *Social Studies of Science*, 11, 3-10.

__________________ (1981c), "Son of Seven Sexes: The Social Destruction of a Physical Phenomenon," *Social Studies of Science*, 11, 33-62.

__________________ (1983), "An Empirical Relativism Program in the Sociology of Scientific Knowledge," in Knorr-Cetina and Mulkay, eds., *Science Observed*, 85-113.

__________________, and Graham Cox (1976), "Recovering Relativity: Did Prophecy Fail?" *Social Studies of Science*, 6, 423-444.

Earl, Peter E. (1983), "A Behavioral Theory of Economists' Behavior," in Alfred S. Eichner, ed., *Why Economics Is Not Yet a Science*. London: Macmillan.

Forman, Paul (1971), "Weimar Culture, Causality, and Quantum Theory, 1918-1927: Adaptation by German Physicists and Mathematicians to a Hostile Intellectual Environment," *Historical Studies in the Physical Sciences*, 3, 1-115.

Gilbert G. Nigel, and Michael Mulkay (1984), *Opening Pandora's Box*. Cambridge: Cambridge University Press.

Goodwin, Craufurd (1988), "The Heterogeneity of Economists' Discourse: Philosopher, Priest, and Hired Gun," in Klamer, McCloskey, and Solow (eds.), *The Consequences of Economic Rhetoric*, 207-220.

Hacking, Ian (1988), "The Participant Irrealist at Large in the Laboratory," *British Journal of the Philosophy of Science*, 39, 277-294.

Hesse, Mary (1980), *Revolutions and Reconstructions in the Philosophy of Science*. Bloomington: Indiana University Press.

Klamer, Arjo (1983), *Conversations with Economists*. Totowa: Rowman and Allenfield.

Klamer, Arjo, Donald McCloskey, and Robert Solow, eds. (1988), *The Consequences of Economic Rhetoric*. Cambridge: Cambridge University Press.

Knorr-Cetina, Karin (1981), *The Manufacture of Knowledge*. New York.

__________________ (1982), "Scientific Communities or Transepistemic Arenas of Research? A Critique of Quasi-Economic Models of Science," *Social Studies of Science* 12, 101-130.

__________________ (1983), "The Ethnographic Study of Scientific Work: Towards a Constructivist Interpretation of Science," in Knorr-Cetina and Mulkay, eds., *Science Observed*, 115-140.

__________ (1984), "The Fabrication of Facts: Toward a Microsociology of Scientific Knowledge," in N. Stehr and V. Meja, eds., *Society and Knowledge.* New Brunswich, N.J.: Transaction Books.

__________, and Michael Mulkay, eds. (1983), *Science Observed. Perspectives on the Social Study of Science.* Sage.

Latour, Bruno (1987), *Science in Action.* Harvard University Press.

__________, and Steve Woolgar (1986), *Laboratory Life. The Construction of Scientific Facts.* 2nd edition. Princeton: Princeton University Press. (1979)

Laudan, Larry (1977), *Progress and Its Problems.* London: Routledge and Kegan Paul.

__________ (1981), "The Pseudo-Science of Science?" *Philosophy of the Social Sciences*, 11, 173-198.

Leijonhufvud, Axel (1981 (1973)), "Life among the Econ," in Leijonhufvud, Axel, *Information and Coordination.* Oxford: Oxford University Press.

Loasby, Brian J. (1986), "Public Science and Public Knowledge," *Research in the History of Economic Thought and Methodology*, 4, 211-228.

Lynch, Michael (1985), *Art and Artifact in Laboratory Science.* London: Routledge and Kegan Paul.

McCloskey, Donald (1985), *The Rhetoric of Economics.* Madison: University of Wisconsin press.

MacKenzie, Donald (1981), "Interests, Positivism and History," *Social Studies of Science*, 11, 498-504.

Mäki, Uskali (1988), "How to Combine Rhetoric and Realism in the Methodology of Economics," *Economics and Philosophy*, 4, 89-109.

__________ (1990), "Friedman and Realism," *Research in the History of Economic Thought and Methodology*, 10.

__________ (1991), "On the Method of Isolation in Economics," *Poznan Studies in the Philosophy of the Sciences and the Humanities*, special issue on *Intelligibility in Science*, ed. Craig Dilworth.

Merton, Robert (1968), "The Matthew Effect in Science," *Science*, 159, 56-63.

Mulkay, Michael, and G. Nigel Gilbert (1981), "Putting Philosophy to Work: Karl Popper's Influence on Scientific Practice," *Philosophy of the Social Sciences*, 11, 389-407.

__________ and __________ (1982a), "Accounting for Error: How Scientists Construct their Social World when they Account for Correct and Incorrect Belief," *Sociology*, 16, 165-183.

__________ and __________ (1982b), "Warranting Scientific Belief," *Social Studies of Science*, 12, 383-408.

Shapin, Steven (1982), "History of Science and Its Sociological Reconstructions," *History of Science*, 20, 157-211.

Newton-Smith, W. H. (1981), *The Rationality of Science*. Boston: Routledge and Kegan Paul.

Ward, Benjamin (1972), *What's Wrong with Economics?* London: Macmillan.

Whitley, Richard (1984a), *The Intellectual and Social Organization of the Sciences*. Oxford: Oxford University Press.

__________ (1984b), "The Development of Management Studies as a Fragmented adhocracy," *Social Science Information*, 23, 775-818.

__________ (1986), "The Structure and Context of Economics as a Scientific Field," *Research in the History of Economic Thought and Methodology*, 4, 179-209.

Williams, R., and J. Law (1980), "Beyond the Bounds of Credibility," *Fundamenta Scientiae*, 1, 295-315.

Woolgar, Steven (1981), "Interests and Explanation in the Social Study of Science," *Social Studies of Science*, 11, 365-394.

__________________ (1982), "Laboratory Studies: A Comment on the State of the Art," *Social Studies of Science*, 12, 481-498.

Yearley, Steven (1982), "The Relationship between Epistemological and Social Cognitive Interests: Some Ambiguities Underlying the Use of Interest Theory in the Study of Scientific Knowledge," *Studies in the History and Philosophy of Science*, 13, 353-388.

COMMENTARY BY A. W. COATS

The complexity, volume, and rate of growth of scholarly and scientific literature is nowadays so great that only the most myopic specialists can remain unperturbed by the problem of deciding what to read carefully, to skim, or to ignore altogether. Reading, research, and writing compete unremittingly for shares of that precious primary commodity: time. And in practice, choices are generally dictated by chance or random professional contacts rather than by the use of systematic information retrieval processes. Under these circumstances, thoughtful and reliable surveys of the state of play in any given discipline or field have added value especially when the subject-matter is controversial, rapidly expanding, and multidisciplinary in its content and relevance. For these reasons Uskali Mäki's analytical review of recent work in the sociology of science is especially welcome for, as he rightly observes, the sociology of economics is still in its infancy. As George Stigler remarked many years ago, "it is a field of high promise and vast challenge";[1] yet few economists—even specialist historians of the discipline, who should know better—are both familiar with and willing to utilize the available menu of sociology concepts and theories applicable to their subject. Partly, no doubt, this is because sociology of any kind still occupies a low position on the economists' totem pole. Yet, a number of these concepts and theories, albeit in half-baked form, underlie much of the profession's conventional wisdom, the day-to-day gossip among busy practitioners, and the mass of often ill-informed, partisan, or quasi-journalistic off-the-cuff commentary on the current "state of economics." In my judgment, as in Professor Mäki's, the sociology of economics deserves to be taken more seriously and studied more systematically and not only by specialist historians and methodologists.

The following comments focus on the main themes and implications of Mäki's report, rather than on the details. This is not the time for nit-picking: there is much constructive work to be done. It should, however, be noted that Mäki approached his task primarily as a philosopher asking philosopher's questions, whereas the reviewer's perspective is basically that of an economic and social historian. Both viewpoints have validity (as do some others, too). They are complementary rather than competitive, and both are fully compatible with the welcome trend towards the convergence of philosophical, historical and sociological studies of science. The new collaborative spirit among these erstwhile warring specialties exemplifies the "blurring of genres" expression coined by the distinguished anthropologist Clifford Geertz.[2]

There are various reasons for believing that economists, more than most social scientists, have much to learn from a more sociological approach than is to be found in most textbook accounts of their subject. By comparison with the other social sciences, economics has an enviably powerful and durable corpus of theory that, despite its widely acknowledged limitations, has successfully withstood innumerable attacks, many of them cogent and penetrating, from a long line of critics, dissidents, outsiders, and—especially in recent years—eminent insiders too. How then are we to account for the orthodox tradition's remarkable survival capacity? Is it simply the absence of an effective alternative approach, as its defenders stoutly maintain? This is, however, too easy an answer. Economists have often, and justly, been accused of intellectual complacency and insularity—a wilful refusal to draw upon and incorporate into their discipline the relative concepts and findings of other social sciences. And this attitude is nowadays epitomized in the more arrogant manifestations of social science imperialism[3]—that is, the view that economics is the only genuinely scientific social science subject, and that its basic apparatus can be infinitely extended to solve a wide range of problems traditionally regarded as falling within other disciplinary domains. From a sociological standpoint, the issue of the validity of these claims is less interesting than the problem of explaining how this viewpoint has evolved, and by what learning and socialization processes it has been sustained. These matters are especially pertinent at the present time when the economics "establishment," both in Britain and in the United States has felt the need to sponsor formal enquiries into the training and professionalization of economists.[4]

For the historian of economics, or indeed anyone who seeks to understand the nature and development of modern economics, the conventional textbook approach in terms of "great men," "great ideas," or even "great systems" is manifestly incapable of coping with the vastly increased number of practitioners, research styles and methods, specialties and subdivisions, schools of thought, and uses of economic theories and data in a bewildering variety of academic and non-academic settings. While the role of the creative individual has undeniably declined considerably, both absolutely and relatively, this is not to deny that, of course, there will always be leaders and followers. We have our heroes (as yet, significantly, no heroines) in the Nobel Hall of Fame, not to mention other less conspicuous assemblies of the profession's great and good. And, curiously enough, there is currently a veritable proliferation of biographical and analytical studies of the works and influence of great outstanding economics, sometimes in multivolume form.[5] Nevertheless, there has also been a growing recognition of the influence of what Mäki terms "social conditioning"—that is the combination of constraints imposed by the economics community, or to be more specific, professional groups and institutional structures that affect such matters as: the form and content of academic instruction; training, recruitment and entry procedures; career patterns, publication outlets and networks for the dissemination of research; the allocation of research resources; and access to the lay public and to significant policymakers. The nature, operation, and intellectual and social significance of these and other components of the economic knowledge industry deserve the serious and sustained study they are at last beginning to receive.

In the present "infancy" of the sociology of economics the greatest need, in my view, is for more thorough, detailed, and in particular, international comparative studies of the recent past development and current state of economics. The field is wide open; the list of potentially fruitful topics is virtually endless—and certainly much too large to be itemized here. For example, to take a very large theme, the worldwide Americanization of economics teaching, training, and the international dissemination of ideas at all levels is virtually *terra incognita*. Yet, this subject is of the greatest interest and importance if we wish to understand the impact of economics as a discipline and profession in business, government, and international agencies around the globe. On a more mundane level, there is the fascinating question of the role of economics journals within the profession—a topic that has been studied intensively with almost infinite ingenuity and variety by a large number of authors.[6] As yet research of this kind has been almost exclusively focused on the

United States, and on the very recent past. Yet, parallel studies undertaken in other countries would shed significant new light on national differences in the nature and functioning of the economics profession and on the spread of economic ideas.[7]

Against this background of rich research possibilities, I am personally much less concerned than Professor Mäki that the sociologists of science, whose works he surveys, have as yet failed to pinpoint and produce satisfactory explanations of the precise nature and impact of social factors on the development of science. As a philosopher, his questions are both apt and legitimate, but as an historian I do not expect—especially at this stage of our knowledge—to find entirely satisfactory explanations. In the interim, as suggested above, there is much constructive investigation to be undertaken and also reinterpretation of our existing knowledge of the discipline.

Before closing, it is appropriate to register some reservations about the term "social conditioning" in Mäki's title. This expression has an undesirably deterministic flavor, as though social and organizational influences on economics, whether operating from within or outside the disciplinary matrix, have such force as to leave no room for individual initiative or creativity. Dr. Mäki surely does not believe this, or wish to convey such an impression, but there is in his paper a strong suggestion of what has been called "an oversocialized concept of man."[8]

A related point that requires more careful exposition is the question of the relationship between the "internal" and the "external" sociology of knowledge. According to Mäki, the Edinburgh "strong" program is "largely macrosociological, or even holistic," and yet, shortly thereafter, he cites David Bloor's strong assertion of the importance of the "internal" social pressures on scientists.[9] Mäki is, of course, well aware of the variety of current research programs in the sociology of science. But the paired terms, "internal"/"external," "macrosociological"/"microsociological," and "holistic"/"individualistic", though perhaps unavoidable, constitute a rich source of confusion. Their interrelationships should be spelled out more fully.

There is one further aspect of the expression "social conditioning" of economics that deserves attention. Properly speaking, the sociology of science (or knowledge) refers to the two-way interaction of science and society, whereas the literature Mäki analyzes generally ignores the impact of science on society. This may indeed be a current fashion, but if so, it is regrettable, for economics is above all a policy science—however great the prestige attaching to theoretical work. And there is a vast scope for detailed (and also indeed more general) research on the impact of economics on modern society, and as elsewhere, there is much scope for fresh work in the sociology of economics.

NOTES

1. In his review of Robert V. Eagley, ed., *Events, Ideology and Economic Theory* (1968) in the *Journal of Economic History*, 29 (June 1969), 337.

2. Cf. "Blurred Genres: The Refiguration of Social Thought," in Clifford Geertz, *Local Knowledge. Further Essays in Interpretative Anthropology* (New York: Basic Books, 1983), 19-35.

3. The term "imperialism" as applied to the relationship between economics and other social science disciplines has been used by, among others, Kenneth Boulding, Geoff Harcourt, George J. Stigler, and Gordon Tullock. It now has widespread currency.

4. See, for example, R. Towse and M. Blaug, *The Current State of the British Economics Profession* (London: The Royal Economic Society, 1988); and the preliminary report by Lee Hansen, "Educating and Training New Economics Ph.D.'s: How Good a Job Are We Doing?" Commission on Graduate Education in Economics, in *American Economic Review*, 80, (May 1990), 437-450.

5. For example, the recent studies of the work of, among others, James Meade, Nicholas Kaldor, Joan Robinson and Paul Samuelson. The practice of interviewing distinguished economists has become fashionable, especially since Arjo Klamer's *New Classical Macroeconomics: Conversations with the New Classical Economists and their Opponents* (Brighton: Wheatsheaf, 1984). The *Banca Nazionale del Lavoro* has published a long series of economists' autobiographical reminiscences, recently collected in two volumes edited by Jan Kregel; and of course the Nobel Laureates have been featured in similar exercises.

6. The author has in process a bibliography of over 110 articles either

analyzing economic journals or using them as a source of data and insight into the economics profession.

7. A pioneering example is David C. Colander and A. W. Coats, *The Spread of Economic Ideas* (Cambridge: Cambridge University Press, 1989).

8. This widely used expression was, I believe, coined by Irving Goffman.

9. Mäki, "Social Conditioning," chapter 2, 69, but cf. footnote 2.

II. Molecules and Games

CHAPTER 3

HUMAN MOLECULES

Alan Nelson

> While it was long possible and sometimes tempting for physicists to deny the usefulness of the molecular hypothesis, we economists have the good luck of being some of the "molecules" of economic life ourselves, and of having the possibility through human contacts to study the behavior of other "molecules".
>
> —Tjalling Koopmans

According to a popular view, the most essential feature of modern economics is that it analyzes phenomena as the outcome of rational choices by individual economic agents. This is obviously correct for microeconomics. Microeconomics deals explicitly with largely isolated individuals in the theory of the consumer and the theory of the firm, and in General Equilibrium Theory (GET) it deals with the interaction of all the rational agents in an economy. Macroeconomics has often been criticized, since its development, as a more or less distinct field of economics because its theories have not been justified as flowing from rational individual choice. Recently, however, economists have even made progress on this front with "microfoundational" models meant to apply to problems of macroeconomic interest—those employing rational expectations, for instance.

There are good reasons for this requirement of understanding all economic phenomena as arising from individual rational choice. Some of the reasons are scientific, while others are more philosophic in nature. Prominent among the scientific reasons are: the benefits of having a unified account of relatively diverse phenomena, the applicability of a well developed mathematical formalism, and the simplicity of maximization as a mechanism of choice. From some philosophical points of view, on the other hand, modern economics presents an attractive picture of human nature. It might be used to support a conception of humans as essentially rational or an ethical position that stresses the prerogatives of individuals against those of society. There is also the fact that economics explains large scale, readily apparent phenomena (equilibrium prices and quantities, for example) in terms of what is smaller, simpler, and more fundamental. These features, which can be broadly characterized as *reductive*, have always been highly prized by most philosophers. Many great philosophical systems are above all means of trying to reduce the way things *appear* to the underlying reality causing the appearance. This is also true of many important scientific theories, especially microphysical theories. It is appealing, therefore, to have what *appears* to result from the action of a mysterious invisible hand reduced to what it *really* is—the net result of the simple maximizing behavior of ordinary individuals.

The explanatory drive towards scientific reduction is certainly not confined to economics. Histories of physics, chemistry, and biology show that reduction is one of the most important theoretical activities in science. Thermodynamics, for instance, has been reductively explained by statistical mechanics, the successes of Newtonian physics by relativity theory and quantum physics, valence theory by quantum chemistry, and Mendelian genetics by molecular genetics.[1] Elsewhere, I have argued that important aspects of the program of providing microfoundations for macroeconomics are illuminated by a general philosophical analysis of scientific reduction[2] (see Nelson, 1984). In particular, I argued that there are strong analogies between many microfoundational explanations on one hand and statistical mechanical explanations of thermodynamics on the other. Since the formal structure of the reduction in physics is fairly well understood, the analogies can be used to clarify what is involved in the economic case.

In this essay, I shall use similar analogies to try to get another result. Instead of examining how macroeconomics might be reduced to GET, or other less systematic microeconomic theories, I shall focus on the reduction of GET to its own foundations in the theory of individual choice.[3] The basic idea is the same. GET and its applications deal with observable features of an entire economy in action: prices and the quantities of commodities that get exchanged and produced.[4] Moreover, all the important theorems are mathematically derived from assumptions about the behavior of the individual consumers and firms that make up the economy. My project is made easier by the fact that we know exactly how to do these derivations in a wide range of cases. Turning to physics, we know that there are two kinds of explanations of the behavior of a confined gas. Thermodynamics deals with the properties of gases that can be measured and determined in the laboratory: temperature, pressure, volume, type of gas, and so on. Statistical mechanics has the same ultimate goal as thermodynamics, but the method is very different. In statistical mechanics, the easily observable properties of a gas are not directly related to each other, instead, they are understood as arising from the properties of the microscopic gas molecules (or atoms) that constitute the sample of gas. The technique employed begins with a theory of the molecular level and proceeds mathematically to derive the equations that apply at the observable level.

The plan of this essay is to develop a new framework for analyzing some traditional problems with the interpretation of microeconomics. I shall be particularly concerned with the status of "assumptions" (or "hypotheses") about individuals used in the derivation of the theories of supply and demand and, ultimately, GET. Are they true, approximately true, or false, and does the answer even matter? At the end, it will be possible to suggest how to move toward a paradigmatically scientific (not philosophical or methodological) resolution of this old issue. To get there, however, we need to see how an analogous issue about assumptions is resolved in physics. This, in turn, is facilitated by a philosophical analysis of theoretical reduction in science.

There is still no entirely satisfactory philosophical model of what constitutes successful reduction, but there is one that seemed so promising for so long that it is often (mistakenly) taken to be definitive of it. I shall call it *The Standard Model of Reduction* (SMR) and loosely follow the treatment given by E. Nagel (1961). It is useful to review it here for two reasons. It is reasonably precise and its strengths and weaknesses are, therefore, readily apparent. Also, it seems *nearly* to work for some important cases in physics, and much of economics fits the model exceedingly well.

The leading idea of SMR is the intuitive and obvious one of *deriving* the reduced theory from the reducing theory by means of mathematics and logic. The extent to which this constrains the two theories is quite surprising. They must both consist of a set of statements, all of which can be expressed in mathematics and a formal logical language. Even this requirement is probably not met for large parts of social science, except for economics, where it seems to be relatively easily met. This condition, which Nagel calls a *formal condition*, ensures that the reduced theory is derivable from the reducing theory in some rigorous sense. It is also necessary to be able to translate the (linguistic) terms of the reduced science to those of the reducing science—another formal condition. For example, to derive the Boyle-Charles law relating the pressure, volume, and temperature of a gas from the kinetic energy of the gas molecules, we must be able to translate temperature and pressure into mechanical terms. The hypothesis identifying temperature with mean kinetic energy serves this purpose. To derive from biochemistry some cognitive psychology containing a law such as "All persons feeling thirst tend to desire drink", we need a biochemical description of "feeling thirst" (and the other terms in the psychological law).

It is this requirement of translatability that has led philosophers of science to be skeptical about whether there are many real instances of SMR. There is even skepticism about the possibility of advancing our scientific knowledge to the point where SMR is instantiated. The now familiar problem arises as follows.[5] Suppose that we do want to reduce to biochemistry a hypothetical psychology containing the law, "All persons feeling thirst tend to desire drink". Let us further suppose that every instance of a person's feeling thirst really is some biochemical event. We can even pretend that the technology exists to determine the biochemical descriptions of these events. Despite these suppositions, a problem still remains with providing the kind of generally applicable translation required by SMR's formal conditions. The crux of the problem is that there are many different *ways* to be thirsty. There is thirst induced by dehydration, by prior consumption of salt, by certain diseases, by habit, by neurosis, etc. So there is no univocal translation of "thirst"; it must be translated as b1, *or* b2, *or* b3, *or* ..., where each of the b_i is a biochemical description of one of the kinds of states constituting thirst. This kind of translation could convince us that "there is nothing more" to being thirsty than being in some biochemical state or other, but it is not enough to satisfy the

SMR. SMR provides for something much stronger, namely, that everything falling under one law or kind of process in the reduced science find a corresponding law or process in the reducing science. But in our imaginary example, the unitary psychological state of feeling thirst can be matched only with states that are widely divergent from the point of view of biochemistry. The same thing occurs in real cases in psychology (Fodor 1974), biology (Hull 1972), and perhaps even in physics (Wilson 1985). The problem, as philosophers like to put it, is that we can envisage identifying every particular "token" of the "type" *feeling thirst* with some particular ("token") biochemical state. We can have "token-token identities", but SMR demands translations that are "type-type identities". The type *feeling thirst* must be identified with some single biochemical *type.*[6]

One reason that the SMR turns out to be relevant to economics is that the proposed reduction of GET to the theory of individual choice is not plagued by the lack of type-type identities that is endemic in other sciences. Consider the translation of the following part of market economics into a simplified theory of individual choice:

$$Q^j = F(p^j, Y) \qquad (1)$$

where Q^j is the market quantity demanded of commodity j, p^j is the price of j, and Y is total income (expenditure) for the economy. The translation of this is simply the sum of all the individual demands in the economy, as every introductory textbook tells us:

$$Q^j = \sum_{i=1}^{n} q_i^j \qquad (2)$$

where there are n individuals in the economy, q_i^j is the ith individual's demand for commodity j, y^i is his expenditure, and

$$q_i^j = f(p^j, y^i) \qquad (3)$$

Equation (2) expresses a type-type identity. Different tokens at the microlevel result in different numerical values of Q^j at the market level, but all of these different values are still tokens of the type Q^j. Since the same is true of demand in each market (that is, for each commodity j) and there are completely analogous type-type identities for the supply side, the whole of market economics (and GET) appears an especially promising candidate for reduction to the theory of individual choice in accord with SMR's formal conditions.

SMR, however, imposes another important condition:

> If the sole requirement for reduction were that the [reduced] science be logically deducible from arbitrarily chosen premises, the requirement could be satisfied with relatively little difficulty. In the history of significant reductions, however, the premises of the [reducing] science are not ad hoc assumptions. Accordingly, although it would be a far too strong condition that the premises must be known to be true, it does seem reasonable to impose as a nonformal requirement that the theoretical assumptions of the [reducing] science be supported by empirical evidence possessing some degree of probative force.
> (Nagel 1961, 358).

It is this Empirical Condition (as I shall call it), that the reducing theory be supported by empirical evidence, that threatens reduction in economics. What evidence is there that (3) is true for every consumer in the economy? The Empirical Condition sensibly prohibits us from relying on the fact that assuming (3) permits the derivation of the well supported (1). Independent evidence is required. The problem posed by meeting this Condition has a long history in economic theory, albeit in somewhat different contexts. It is involved in the old issue of deriving downward sloping demand curves from the theory of individual choice. Here, the question is why market curves almost invariably slope downward when there does not seem to be a principled way of restricting individual preferences to guarantee this result. Nagel's Empirical Condition is also addressed by the long controversy over "realism of assumptions". In this controversy, the "assumptions" being questioned concern individual maximizing behavior, these assumptions are used to derive propositions about larger scale market phenomena, and "realism" is a problem because the assumptions seem to be false about particular individuals.

Thus there has already been considerable discussion of the economic issues raised by Nagel's Empirical Condition. On the face of it, the Condition is not actually met. It is so obvious that most individual people are not perfectly rational or even approximately rational maximizers, that almost no effort has gone into rigorously testing directly the hypothesis that they are. Such an effort would involve compiling data in the laboratory or in carefully controlled markets for the behavior of fully identified individuals over time.[7] Despite this conflict with Nagel's model of reduction, economists have maintained that the theory of individual choice provides a foundation for GET of the kind that is expected from reductions. Market phenomena are seen as *arising* from the combined rational choices of individuals. Let us call the problem of supporting the theory of individual choice by evidence the "Empirical Problem". There are, I think, three basic ways of trying to reconcile the scientific drive for reduction with the empirical gap in the economic theory of the individual. Let us consider them in turn.

The first way is to use reliable data about markets or the whole economy to get indirect evidence for the theory of individuals. The rough, informal idea is that even though individual behavior might be somewhat erratic or, in some cases, systematically different from ideal behavior, real economic agents are rational *on average*. Therefore, we might conclude, if carefully observed market phenomena are shown to be such that they *could* have arisen from behavior that is rational on average, then we might have good evidence that they *did* arise that way. Finally, we might take another step and conclude that a theory that works well for individual behavior on average or, perhaps, works well for some kind of average individual, is a good theory of the individual behavior.

This proposal needs to be made more precise; the use that "averages" are to be put to has been left vague. Moreover, the proposal seems at first to be flawed in principle. We want the reduced theory to be derivable from a theory with foundations that are relatively more secure either theoretically or empirically. But it is being suggested that the reducing theory be confirmed by evidence taken from the domain of the theory that is to be reduced. This might not be ad hoc, but there is a strong suggestion of vicious circularity.

It is very interesting that there does not seem to be any objectionable circularity in the application of a similar strategy in physics. We explain such observational properties of gases, as temperature, in terms of average properties of their microscopic constituents, and this is one favorite example of successful reduction in accord with SMR. What evidence is there for the claims physicists make, for example, about the average velocity of the molecules in a sample of gas? Our epistemic situation, with respect to individual molecules is, on the face of it, even worse than our situation with respect to individual economic behavior. They cannot so much as be seen. Apparently, physicists partially base claims about individual unobservable molecules and about average properties of large groups of molecules on aggregate facts about groups of molecules. The resulting hypotheses about individuals are then used to derive descriptions, explanations, and predictions about the large scale properties of the whole sample of gas. Why shouldn't an analogous procedure work for economics? I think that it might, but before proceeding, let us set aside two other ways of trying to bridge the gap between the evidence and the individualistic foundation of microeconomics that have received a good deal of attention in print. It is worth noting that these other ways can only be justified by the adoption of strong philosophical theses. In the physics example, it can be argued that the solution of the Empirical Problem does not precommit one to a philosophical doctrine. It would be desirable to carry this over to the economic case because the purpose of philosophy of science is to interpret what science produces, not to dictate to scientists what their theories should look like.

One of the other options is to adopt a methodological position akin to what philosophers have called *instrumentalism*. There are many varieties of instrumentalism, but the main idea is usually that theories are to be considered no more than instruments for getting descriptive and predictive results. Most instrumentalists do not take seriously any claims that the theoretical formalism is about actual existing things. Someone who is an instrumentalist with respect to subatomic particles, for example, acknowledges that talk about "electrons" helps scientists in many ways: it provides heuristics for applying and extending the theory, facilitates verbal communication, etc. But he denies that we have any good evidence that electrons *exist*. It then follows that any putative facts *about* existing electrons are of no scientific significance; what is significant are the phenomena that electrons are invoked to account for. In economics, one might be a kind of instrumentalist about individual economic agents. It would be bizarre to maintain that individual humans do not exist,[8] but some will want to say that facts about individuals are irrelevant from the economic point of view. From the economic point of view, they say, individual choice theory is a useful way of deriving descriptions and predictions of observable market phenomena from assumptions that are somehow more basic, but whose truth or realism are not at issue.

Instrumentalist interpretations of economics have been roundly criticized over the years. Many of the critiques have been forceful. I shall make only one remark here. Sophisticated instrumentalism as it is applied to physics, for example, is an *interpretation* of theories, it is not a *methodological* prescription about how to theorize. An instrumentalist and a realist will think of electrons in very different ways, but they will both do the same experiments and obtain the same results. It would be patent nonsense for an instrumentalist to say, "I am interested in the pretense that electrons have charge, not that they have mass, but I'm an instrumentalist, so electrons don't exist and mass can be ignored". It is also nonsense for an economist to say, "I'm interested in the pretense that people have well behaved utility functions, but I'm an instrumentalist, so I can ignore empirical evidence that they do not".

The other way of dealing with the lack of empirical evidence for the theory of individual choice is to interpret the theory as being about *ideal* rational behavior and not at all about real individuals, except insofar as their behavior approaches the ideal. This a prioristic interpretation has the merit of possessing foundations that are not in need of empirical verification. It says the theory can be verified by appeal to our well-considered, introspective intuitions about what rational agents would ideally do in ideal situations. The principal objection to this approach is that it severs the connection to real economic phenomena; the theory becomes unanswerable to the data. A priorism will not appeal to economists who do economics to further our understanding of actual human behavior and human societies.

Since instrumentalism and a priorism are unsatisfactory remedies for the Empirical Problem, let us now proceed to the examination of the analogy with reducing thermodynamics. Since facts about averages are to play a crucial role, let us first set aside some unacceptable construals of the averages involved. It is common in economic analysis to make use of a construct called a "representative individual", who is supposed to be representative of consumers (or firms in a parallel analysis) in the sense that his demands are given by

$$\bar{q}^j = f(p^j, \bar{y}) \quad (4)$$

where $\bar{y}$ is the mean income (expenditure) of all the individuals and

$$Q^j = n\bar{q}^j \qquad (5)$$

In light of the Empirical Problem, it might be tempting to think of such a representative consumer as some kind of quasi-real individual, an average individual, and to construe the theory as being about that individual or, perhaps, about n such individuals. If that were so, then (4) with its parameters econometrically estimated from market data would provide precisely what is required to confirm the reducing theory for the theory of demand. This temptation must be resisted. The representative consumer is not a real individual at all; his mathematical origin makes this clear. In general, talk about a representative is simply a convenient means for writing shorthand about the aggregate from which he arises. Any attempt to use information about representatives to satisfy the Empirical Condition on reduction would indeed be viciously circular. It would also be unhelpful to recall the a prioristic interpretation by maintaining that the representative possessed the relevant properties of an ideally rational agent. The reason is the same; it is likely that no actual agents are ideally rational, so it is unclear how such a representative can constitute a theory of *any* of them. And if it is not a theory of any of them, it is again unclear how it can be a theory of all of them or most of them.

Setting aside this and related misuses of representatives, there remains a way in which facts about aggregates that are summarized in the form of averages[9] can be relevant to the confirmation of hypotheses about actual individuals. Consider an imaginary example. A previously undiscovered asteroid of the type called Trojan is found and it is important to know what its mass is. The best way to find out is to observe the perturbations in its orbit for an entire period, but that takes too long. On the basis of preliminary observations, astronomers guess that its mass is X. Astronomers know from earlier results that the average mass of Trojan asteroids is very nearly X. This additional piece of information might count as very strong evidence that the mass of the newly discovered asteroid is about X. The strength of the evidence clearly depends on how the masses of Trojan asteroids are distributed. If half of them are about 2X and the other half are nearly massless, then the average is virtually worthless as evidence for the hypothesis about the new asteroid. The average will, however, be very strong evidence if the distribution of masses is normal with mean X and a very small standard deviation. In fact, it seems possible to specify the conditions under which information about an average can provide good evidence for hypotheses about actual individuals. These "Distribution Conditions" are: 1) The distribution of the individuals with respect to the property in question must be such that most individuals are clustered together near the mean of the distribution; and 2) The property of the particular individual in question must be near the mean.[10] The idea underlying these conditions is that their satisfaction points towards a systematic physical mechanism that generates the probability distribution.

We can conclude that relying on averages to solve the Empirical Problem requires showing that the relevant properties of individual economic agents have the right kind of probability distributions. Before considering the economic case, it is helpful to see what can be said about the probability distributions of the properties of molecules that figure in the reduction of thermodynamics. When deriving macroscopically observable properties from what is microscopic, the kinetic energy, which is equal to one half of the total mass of the molecules times the square of their mean velocity, is an important quantity. If, for example, one hypothesizes that the temperature of a gas is proportional to the mean kinetic energy of its molecules, it is possible to derive the macroscopic Boyle-Charles Law from laws governing the molecules.

Is Nagel's Empirical Condition for reduction met in this case? It is quite impossible to determine the velocity of every individual molecule in a sample of gas. In this respect the physicist is in a worse situation than the economist; it is at least *possible*, in some sense, to determine the preferences and income of particular individual people. So the question arises whether use of the quantity $\bar{E}$ (mean kinetic energy) has some independent warrant instead of its being tricked up solely to serve in a mathematical derivation of some other quantities that are of physical interest. In the latter case, there would be no theoretical reduction and no microphysical foundation for thermodynamics. There are, fortunately enough, at least three kinds of convincing indirect evidence.

First, there is the fact that kinetic energy is a useful and easily determined quantity for macroscopic hunks of matter. As Isaac Newton noted, there is a strong inductive argument from the fact that every directly observed hunk of matter, no matter how large or small has had kinetic energy equal to one half its mass times the square of its velocity ($1/2\ mv^2$) to the conclusion that unobservable particles of matter also have kinetic energy equal to $1/2\ mv^2$. Quantum effects aside, there is no good reason to suppose that unobservable particles are different from observable hunks of matter except for their unobservability. Furthermore, if we are convinced that kinetic energies are equal to $1/2\ mv^2$ for each individual, then we will not be worried about the legitimacy of the average either. Here the economist is at a disadvantage in holding up his end of the analogy. There are no "large", easily observable individuals whose properties are more readily determined than those of people and firms.[11]

A second kind of independent evidence concerning the behavior of individual molecules is that the hypothesis that temperature is proportional to $\bar{E}$ permits the derivation of a wide variety of important theoretical results that are experimentally confirmed, as any textbook on statistical mechanics reveals. It is questionable whether economic assumptions about individuals produce the same variety of theoretical results and whether these results have been, or can be, experimentally tested. We cannot consider this here. It is the third kind of indirect evidence that is most interesting in the present context.

I have mentioned how information about aggregates can provide evidence for hypotheses about individuals when there is also information about relevant probability distributions concerning the individuals. A review of the physics, which I shall provide shortly, shows that direct measurements of temperature (that is, of $\bar{E}$) do provide some probabilistic information about individual molecules. Similarly it could be the case that information about Q^j (that is, about $Q^j = \sum_{i=1}^{n} q_i^j$) could provide some degree of evidence about individual economic agents. Let us proceed to investigate whether this analogy holds up.

$E = 1/2\ mv^2$ for every particle of a gas, so it is mass and velocity that we wish to know something about. Mass turns out to be easy because the masses of molecules of given atomic compositions have well established values. Velocity is more difficult; the gas molecules in a sample at a fixed temperature have very different velocities. It is possible, however, to deduce by purely theoretical means the probability that a given molecule has a velocity falling within a certain interval. This relation, called the Maxwell distribution, can be written for one dimension as[12]

$$f(v) = \text{constant x } \exp(-mv^2/2KT) \qquad (6)$$

(K is the Boltzmann constant and T is temperature) This distribution function is nice and smooth with a gentle maximum representing the most probable speed. The distribution also has a fairly small variance for low temperatures, so the Distribution Conditions mentioned above are likely to be met for particular individual molecules.

This is certainly an impressive result, but it does not solve the Empirical Problem by itself. It would still be all too easy to get caught in a vicious circle by starting with a determination of the value of T, using this to get the value of $\overline{E}$, and then stipulating that since there is a reductive, formal derivation of T from $\overline{E}$, the individual molecules' speeds must be, or are very likely to be, distributed according to (6). It is fortunate that (6) does place a substantive restriction on the classical model of a gas, a restriction that has the potential to help solve the Empirical Problem. If there were some argument that the molecules did not have the Maxwell distribution, the model would be refuted. But if there were some further independent evidence that the molecules' speeds were distributed as required by the theory, then Nagel's Empirical Condition could be taken to be at least partially satisfied and the reduction could be successful. One of the beauties of this physical theory is that it is possible to get a direct *experimental* confirmation of the one-dimensional Maxwell distribution.

One method involves directing a pulsed beam of molecules (silver atoms in the original experiment) from a gas in equilibrium towards a rotating hollow drum with a slit in it. On the inside of the drum and opposite the slit one places a glass plate that collects the molecules. Since the molecules only reach the glass plate by passing through the slit and the drum continues to rotate while the molecules are inside it, the slowest molecules will be deposited on one end of the glass plate, the fastest at the other end, with all the others in between according to their speeds. The thickness of the layer of deposited molecules can be measured all along the glass plate. The results of these measurements clearly represent a speed distribution—the shape of the clumped molecules literally form a picture of the distribution. Of course, the distributions obtained in this experiment turn out to agree closely with the Maxwell distribution.[13]

So in the part of physics we have considered, the Empirical Problem is partially solved in two steps. Initially, the theory itself is used to produce restrictions on the shape of some probability distributions. These restrictions are then used to make predictions that can be elegantly confirmed by experiment. In economics, it is easy to see that theorists have been very successful in using facts about markets (the downward slope of demand curves for instance) or facts about the entire economy (the dependence of aggregate consumption on aggregate income, for instance) to place restrictions on the theory of the representative individual. For example, if (1), (2), (4), and (5) are to hold, then (3) cannot hold generally and must be restricted to

$$q_i^j = A_i^j(p^j) + B^j(p^j)y_i \qquad (7)$$

where $A_i^j(p^j)$ and $B^j(p^j)$ are linear homogeneous functions.[14] But these results are inadequate for present purposes. We need more fine grained results; we need to know how properties of individuals are dispersed around the properties of the representative.

Recently, W. Hildenbrand has shown (1983) that under the assumption that all consumers have the same preferences (or demand function), if the distribution of income levels has a continuous non-increasing density, then the aggregate partial demand curves will slope downward—the "Law of Demand" will hold. This is a good example because the Law of Demand has been well confirmed at the market level. Hildenbrand writes, "The strong assumption of the distribution of individual expenditure is *necessary* to obtain the law of demand since we made no restriction, other than $f(p,0) = 0$, on the form of the individual demand function..." (1983, 1001). In other words, if the observed market phenomenon of downward sloping partial demands is to be reductively derived from a choice theoretic foundation, then the individuals' income must have a special distribution.[15] This is undoubtedly an important result, but in the context of the Empirical Problem it is severely limited by the assumption that all consumers have the same individual demand function. Perhaps the most distinctive thing about individual demand behavior is that different consumers consume different things even when their income is the same. A much more convincing result would require saying something interesting about how the preferences that underlie individual demand functions must be distributed.

This too has been done; the most impressive results are in the work of J-M. Grandmont (1987). Grandmont begins by making precise a way of describing probability distributions of preferences. He then finds a class of distributions (defined in this special way) that, along with other standard assumptions, ensure that the Law of Demand holds. In other words, he shows that in the absence of any other special assumptions about consumers' preferences or incomes, the preferences must be distributed as stipulated to guarantee the validity of the Law of Demand. This result for preferences is comparable in importance for the Empirical Problem to that of the Maxwell distribution for velocities, if I may be permitted to stretch the analogy a bit. The latter enables us, in conjunction with an empirically determined value for $\bar{E}$, to make probabilistic inferences about particular molecules. The former makes it sometimes possible to make probabilistic inferences about particular consumers when we have empirical information about the market demand curve. I say "sometimes possible" because the class of distributions that Grandmont obtains is quite large and some of the permissible distributions do not have shapes that are in good accord with the Distribution Conditions. The Maxwell distribution, in contrast, satisfies these Conditions for all but extremely high temperatures. I shall return to this point.

In this discussion of thermodynamics, I said that part of the reduction's success was due to a two-stage solution of the Empirical Problem. The first stage was the placing of theoretical restrictions on distributions of properties of the individuals. We have just seen that the corresponding first stage for the economic case has been fairly well completed. What of the second stage? Have economists been able to test the empirical validity of the theoretically obtained distributions in a way that corresponds to physical tests of the Maxwell distribution?

Hildenbrand checked his restriction on income distribution against a "Family Expenditure Survey" for the United Kingdom in 1977. He seemed to think the results inconclusive because of missing evidence concerning Engel curves for unaggregated commodities (1983, 1000-1002), but the investigation of income distributions has some real potential because of the ready availability of family budget data. Nevertheless, the approach by itself is inherently limited as a solution to the Empirical Problem for the reason given above. The assumption that all individuals have the same preferences is much too strong. It idealizes away most of what is definitive of economic agents in the first place. This idealization is not at all akin to physical *approximations* such as setting intermolecular attractive forces equal to zero.[16] People do not have "approximately" the same preferences in any well-defined and interesting sense.

Evidently, the entire weight of the Empirical Problem in economics has been made to fall on experimental confirmation of results like Grandmont's on the distribution of preferences. The current empirical record here is not encouraging. The bad news is not that extensive experimental studies of individual preferences reveal that the distributions predicted by the theory are incorrect. That would be bad news indeed. Instead, the current situation is that very little relevant data exists. In order to break out of the chain of circular reasoning that threatens attempts to solve the Empirical Problem, it is necessary to have direct evidence about the probability distributions. It will not do to use econometrics to show that market demand functions are *consistent* with the theoretical distributions; we already know that. The most direct verification would come, of course, from determining the preferences of a large sample of individuals and simply looking to see what the probability distribution was. This sort of test has not been performed. Part of the explanation for the lack of the right kind of experimental results comes from the existence of inherent barriers to developing good experimental techniques for use on humans. The rest of the explanation can be found in prevalent misinterpretations of the significance for empirical work of revealed preference theory. These misinterpretations can lead to unreasonably strong instrumentalistic attitudes towards preferences. We can hope that future economists will overcome these obstacles. Scientists in other disciplines, such as psychology, have developed reliable experimental evidence for theories about various kinds of individual human behavior. And recent interest in microfoundational analyses has led to a growing appreciation of the importance of the behavior of actual individuals for both macro- and microeconomics.

It is also possible that more traditional econometric techniques can be of some use here. The Maxwell distribution was not verified by identifying individual molecules and their speeds (though it is physically possible to do so for many gases, a significant point). Instead, clumps of molecules were identified such that each clump consisted of molecules with the same definite speed. This suggests the procedure of finding aggregate demand functions (or representative preferences) for "clumps" of consumers. If there are enough clumps, then each clump could be treated as if it were an individual and the distribution of (representative) preferences for the clumps could be determined. This possibility is difficult to evaluate. We can begin by noting two disanalogies with the experimental procedure for verifying the Maxwell distribution. First, each clump of molecules on the collection plate contains individuals of almost exactly the same speed, but the groups of consumers may consist of individuals with extremely different preferences. This problem *might* be overcome to a satisfactory degree by getting a very large number of very small groups. The second disanalogy is that the clumps of molecules are collected from a gas in equilibrium and, therefore, constitute a virtually perfect random sample. It is hard to imagine being able to group together suitably randomized consumers. Naturally found groups will most likely be objectionably homogeneous in one or more of geographical location, income, age, sex, etc.. These biases might cast doubt on the evidential strength of empirically obtained distributions of group preferences. One might think that there could be enough information about individuals to avoid bias by randomizing their assignments to groups. It is hard to see how this information could be obtained without direct observation of particular individuals, however, and as already suggested, having this much information would make it possible to avoid using statistics and to directly determine the probability distributions.

I think that we are not yet in a position to speculate about whether the kinds of research programs just suggested will produce results that solve the Empirical Problem in economics. I have tried to make it clear that it is very important to find out. Fundamental questions about the theory of individual choice, GET, and the relationship between the two depend on the outcome. Perhaps the most basic goal of modern economic theory is to support the compelling principle that rational individual choice is the source of all economic behavior. Unless economists are to adopt a strong and implausible philosophical doctrine, such as an ad hoc version of instrumentalism or a priorism, the best way and maybe the only way to achieve this goal is through the kind of scientific inquiry I have described.[17] It is, therefore, still possible to hope that economic theory will find experimental foundations resembling those of parts of physical theory.[18] If such foundations are not forthcoming, then we must be prepared to accept the conclusion that economic science is fundamentally and profoundly different from physical sciences in ways that go beyond subject matter.

NOTES

1. At this point, I am using the term "reduction" in a general sense in which it is uncontroversial that reduction takes place. There is much controversy about how to *model* the kind of reduction that these historical cases exemplify.

2. Some traditional problems about aggregation can also be profitably examined in this way. For example, much of the work that has been done on the so-called Problem of Aggregation is related to the project of providing reductive microfoundations in a suprisingly complex way. Many of the mathematical results on aggregation are not directly relevant to reductive microfoundations, as will become evident in what follows. Also see Nelson (1984) for discussion and a review of some of the most important literature.

3. To simplify the discussion, I shall consider explicitly only the theory of the consumer. The theory of the firm, also required for complete reduction of GET, poses some slightly different problems for which there is no space here.

4. E. R. Weintraub (1979) has conceived microfoundations as the project of finding a suitable relationship between a macroeconomic theory and a full blown GET.

5. I shall loosely follow the treatment given by J. Fodor (1974).

6. It takes considerable discussion to fully motivate this claim. See Fodor (1974) and Nelson (1985).

7. This claim is argued for and explored more fully in Nelson (1986). Interest in experimental results for laboratory economic markets is steadily increasing. Some attention has also been given to the body of psychological results on individual choices among lotteries. For recent overviews see Roth (1986), Smith (1990), and Kahneman and Tversky (1982). For the most part, economic theorists do not yet seem to consider this empirical work as requiring the reevaluation of the basic assumptions of GET.

8. One might try to defend the position that individual humans need

not exist *in order for the theory of markets or GET to be scientifically valid*, their existence or non-existence is irrelevant. Those who adopt this position must explain to us, however, why there is any point at all in appealing to derivations from assumptions about individuals. There would not be much point in doing statistical mechanics if the existence of atoms and molecules were irrelevant to the theory. On the contrary, the early theoretical successes of statistical mechanics inspired experimental work to verify the atomic theory.

9. In what follows, "average" will always mean "mean."

10. Exactly what qualifies as "most" and "near" will depend on the details of the case in question and on the intentions of the scientist. For further discussion of these Distribution Conditions see Nelson (1988).

11. We cannot suppose that the whole market is a kind of easily observed individual whose properties reflect the properties of the smaller unobserved individuals. That would beg the very question at issue—whether or not they are the same.

12. So, this is, strictly speaking, a speed distribution and not a velocity distribution. The latter is easily obtainable from the former by symmetry considerations, but it will be simpler here to use the speed distribution.

13. For a fuller description, further references, and later experimental developments see Reif (1968).

14. For the economic details and additional examples and references see Deaton and Muellbauer (1980), Chapter 6, and Schafer and Sonnenschein (1982).

15. Hildenbrand gives some extensions of the result to simple GET models. They require some further simplifying assumptions that I do not discuss.

16. There is also a problem connected with the use of family incomes as opposed to incomes of individual persons. Unless one is going to swallow down whole a revealed preference interpretations or Becker's

interpretation of utility and preferences, it is individual persons and not households whose properties are important in choice theoretic contexts. For arguments to this effect see Nelson (1986).

17. Adopting alternatives, like regarding the theory as an elaborate academic game, would be prematurely desperate.

18. Colloquia based on this essay were held at the Economics and Philosophy Departments at Duke University. These were valuable in the preparation of the final version. Neil de Marchi provided helpful comments on an earlier draft.

REFERENCES

Deaton, A., and J. Muellbauer (1980), *Economics and Consumer Behavior*. Cambridge: Cambridge University Press.

Fodor, J. (1974), "Special Sciences: Or Disunity of Science as a Working Hypothesis," *Synthese*, 28, 97-115.

Grandmont, J-M. (1987), "Distributions of Preferences and the 'Law of Demand'," *Econometrica*, 55, 155-161.

Hildenbrand, W. (1983), "On the 'Law of Demand'," *Econometrica*, 51, 997-1019.

Hull, D. (1972), "Reduction in Genetics—Biology or Philosophy?" *Philosophy of Science*, 39, 491-499.

Kahneman, D., and A. Tversky (1982), "The Psychology of Preferences," *Scientific American*, 246, 160-173.

Nagel, E. (1961), *The Structure of Science*. New York: Harcourt, Brace, and World.

Nelson, A. (1984), "Some Issues Surrounding the Reduction of Macroeconomics to Microeconomics," *Philosophy of Science*, 51, 573-594.

__________________. (1985), "Physical Properties," *Pacific Philosophical Quarterly*, 66, 268-282.

__________________. (1986), "New Individualistic Foundations for Economics," *Nous*, 20, 469-490.

__________________. (1988), "Average Explanations," *Erkenntnis*, 30, 23-42.

Reif, F. (1965), *Statistical Physics*, New York: McGraw-Hill.

Roth, A. (1986), "Laboratory Experiments in Economics," *Economics and Philosophy*, 2, 245-273.

Schafer, W., and H. Sonnenschein (1982), "Market Demand and Excess Demand Functions," in *Handbook of Mathematical Economics*, Vol. II: 671-693, K. Arrow and M. Intriligator, eds. Amsterdam: North-Holland.

Smith, V. (1988), "Theory, Experiment and Economics," *The Journal of Economic Perspectives*, 8, 151-169.

Weintraub, E. R. (1979), *Microfoundations*. Cambridge: Cambridge University Press.

Wilson, M. (1985), "What Is This Thing Called Pain?—The Philosophy of Science Behind the Contemporary Debate," *Pacific Philosophical Quarterly*, 66, 227-267.

COMMENTARY BY BRUCE CALDWELL

I

Why is the "explanatory drive towards reduction" such a powerful urge among scientists, philosophers, and other members of the human species? Why is the reduction of appearances to the underlying reality that caused them often sufficient to satisfy the longing? Whatever answers we might give to these questions, the drive is so common that philosophers of science have developed a standard model of reduction in which the conditions for an adequate reductive explanation are specified. Unfortunately, most of the notable attempts at reduction within the physical sciences founder because of a failure to satisfy the translatability condition.

It is here that Alan Nelson introduces economics (in the form of general equilibrium theory) into the picture. For it seems that the theorems of general equilibrium theory can be derived from assumptions concerning the optimizing behavior of individual economic agents. Unlike the other sciences, this reduction in economics is accomplished without violating the translatability condition. There is a sticking point for economics, however. The standard model of reduction also requires that the reducing theory be supported by empirical evidence. What this empirical condition means for economics is that there should exist evidence that economic agents actually do optimize.

One of the major rationales for the existence of the field of economic methodology would be removed were it in fact true that agents optimize in the manner portrayed in our theories. They do not, and a large literature has arisen that attempts to respond to this dilemma. Nelson is not much interested in this methodological literature. He hurriedly reviews and even more quickly dismisses the instrumentalist and a priorist solutions to the problem. Nelson prefers instead an empirical (he calls it "scientific," which he contrasts with "methodological" or "philosophical") resolution of the issue. His gambit is to postulate an "average" or "representative" agent, and then seek evidence concerning whether and how such a construct might be considered to be optimizing.

The second half of his chapter is devoted to the careful examination of a number of issues raised by his proposed solution. For the use of an average to be acceptable, two distribution conditions should be met. The difficult question of how we might gain information concerning distributions of characteristics is handled by reviewing an analogous question and its solution in physics. The procedure involves placing theoretically derived restrictions on the distributions of properties, then testing to see if the distributions actually obtain. Economists have made some real progress in the former area, but despite the existence of revealed preference theory, virtually none in the latter. Nelson urges economists to undertake these empirical tests. He concludes his paper with the following words:

> Perhaps the most basic goal of modern economic theory is to support the compelling principle that rational individual choice is the source of all economic behavior. Unless economists are to adopt a strong and implausible philosophical doctrine, such as an ad hoc version of instrumentalism or a priorism, the best way and maybe the only way to achieve this goal is through the kind of scientific inquiry I have described. It is, therefore, still possible to hope that economic theory will find experimental foundations resembling those of parts of physical theory. (129)

In my comments, I will argue that Nelson misunderstands in a fundamental way the economic enterprise. He does not understand why economists ask the questions that they do.[1] In particular, he fails to recognize the purpose of economic methodology and of its contributions in dealing with the questions that he has chosen to explore. It is precisely these misunderstandings that make this a valuable chapter for economic methodologists to read. The chapter concretely demonstrates that though philosophers of science and economic methodologists are both interested in the interface between philosophy and economics, they often come to their tasks asking entirely different questions. This is no counsel of despair. Recognition of this fact is very nearly a necessary condition for the occurrence of interdisciplinary progress.

II

Nelson's first point is that the goal of economic theory is to show that rational choice is the source of all economic behavior. If one examines the models of economists, it is easy to understand how someone might get that impression. In the archetypal economic model, rationality is equated with consistency in choice over a well-ordered preference function, and it is assumed that optimizing agents have either perfect information or full information concerning whatever probability distributions might be relevant. These assumptions are made all the time by economists, and as Nelson correctly observes, perhaps the most impressive use of this approach is to be found in the elegant set of models known as general equilibrium theory.

But this brings us to a problem, and it is one of the core problems of economic methodology. It seems clear that these assumptions about the behavior and capabilities of economic agents are untrue. What are the implications of this? Why do economists use false assumptions? Does their falsity mean that the rest of economics is also untrue?

These are methodological questions, and the various answers that are given to them define a number of well-known methodological positions in economics. Nelson correctly identifies the three broad approaches to the problems posed by false assumptions: instrumentalism, a priorism, and empiricism, the last being what he calls "the scientific approach." (We will see that none of the labels is entirely satisfactory.) The first two are dismissed because they require one to embrace certain unacceptably "strong philosophical theses." Instrumentalism circumvents the problem of false assumptions by denying that agents exist, and a priorism accomplishes the same goal by turning agents into ideal types. Nelson's "scientific" alternative is to specify just what sort of "agent" (average, representative, or otherwise) is doing the choosing. His contribution is to establish the conditions that specifications of an "average agent" should meet.

Nelson does not do a good job in describing the versions of a priorism and instrumentalism that have developed in economics. But worse, he does not seem to understand why such apparently arcane doctrines might be invoked by economists. Though it is seldom articulated, the answer turns out to be rather simple. Economists know that their theories use false assumptions. They also know that economics is a tremendously useful social science. It permits us to make predictions about social behavior that are often remarkably accurate.[2] Even though our models are at best crude representations of reality, they help us to tell stories, important stories, about human behavior. If this were not true, economics would be little more than an elaborate game played by second rate mathematicians. It is this state of affairs that led economists to develop three different responses (empiricism, instrumentalism, and a priorism) to the problem of false assumptions. And each response when suitably interpreted helps us better to understand the discipline.

III

Nelson fits into the empiricist camp. Empiricists are those who propose operational definitions of the various assumptions, test whether agents actually choose rationally, and construct alternative theories to describe how agents actually choose. There is a rather long tradition here, most of it critical.[3]

Around the turn of the century institutionalists and other critics charged economics with assuming that humans behaved according to the dictates of hedonistic psychology. Economists responded by portraying their discipline as a "logic of choice," one whose behavioral assumptions are independent of any specific psychological theory (Coats, 1976). Next came the philosophically inspired contributions of T.W. Hutchison (1938) and Paul Samuelson (1938, 1947). Hutchison insisted that if economics were to be considered a real science, its assumptions would have to be testable. Writing in a different tradition and exhibiting the influence of physicist Percy Bridgman's work in his rhetoric, Paul Samuelson demonstrated how revealed preference theory could be used to "operationalize" economics. Most recently, a new interdisciplinary research area that has been dubbed "behavioral economics" has sprung up. Some studies in this tradition are critical, while others are supportive of neoclassical economics; all examine actual choice behavior (Gilad and Kaish, eds., 1986; Hogarth and Reder, eds., 1987; Earl, ed., 1988, and citations therein).

This work is useful because it sheds light on how agents actually choose. Unfortunately, in the past some economists have ridiculed such research because they feared it would undermine faith in economics. This is the dogmatic side of instrumentalism, but happily the attitude appears to be vanishing. The conference which led to the Hogarth-Reder volume was held at the University of Chicago, once widely perceived as a bastion of instrumentalist reaction.

It is significant that this specter did not haunt the creator of the revealed preference approach. Note how Paul Samuelson concludes his presentation of the theory in his *Foundations of Economic Analysis*:

> Many writers have held the utility analysis to be an integral and important part of economic theory. Some have even sought to employ its applicability as a test criterion by which economics might be separated from the other social sciences. Nevertheless, I wonder how much economic theory would be changed if either of the two conditions above [i.e., the two alternative statements of consumer behavior] were found to be empirically untrue. I suspect, very little (1947, 117).

Economists know that real consumers do not exhibit the kind of rationality that their models ascribe to them, and they know that, nonetheless economics is a useful and powerful social science. That is why most economists have not been very interested in pursuing Nelson's philosophically more attractive "scientific" route.

IV

Nelson defines instrumentalism as follows: "theories are to be considered no more than instruments for getting descriptive and predictive results. Instrumentalists do not take seriously any claims that the theoretical formalism is about actual existing things" (120). The economist whose methodological beliefs comes closest to instrumentalism is Fritz Machlup, though some parts of his approach do not fit the doctrine (Machlup, 1978). Machlup's methodology has not had much impact on the profession.

The same cannot be said for the ideas of Milton Friedman, whose 1953 essay is the most famous methodological article ever written. Friedman argues that the realism of a theory's assumptions does not matter in its assessment, and that the key criterion of theory appraisal is predictive adequacy. A number of writers have equated this position with instrumentalism, and there are elements of that doctrine to be found in his approach. However, his is not an instrumentalism that denies that theoretical terms make real reference. For Friedman, assumptions do refer: they are false. Their falsity does not matter, however, because theories are simply instruments used to make predictions. Friedman's instrumentalism, then, concerns the goals of science. The goal of science is to develop theories that are predictively adequate instruments that are helpful in the execution of policy. It is this doctrine that is of most importance in economics, and on which attention should be focused.[4]

Friedman's predictivist thesis can be interpreted in one of two ways. We have already alluded to the obstructionist aspects of the position: if prediction is all that matters, then investigations of actual choice behavior either can be ignored, or worse, should not be undertaken. This reactionary position is dangerous, untenable, and perhaps worst of all, uninteresting. The liberal interpretation of the predictivist thesis, on the other hand, is very interesting. It is liberal because it grants economists considerable latitude in their theory building. Economists are free to hypothesize at will, as long as the theories that they come up with meet the condition of predictive adequacy.

It is this liberal side of Friedman's variant of instrumentalism that permits economists to make policy even when they recognize that the assumptions of their models are false. If what I have been suggesting so far is right, that economists have something of value to say despite the fact that their models use false assumptions, then this is an absolutely essential methodological principle. In its absence, economists would be hard pressed to justify why anyone should listen to them. If we accept as a given that our assumptions are false, and as a given that economists have something of value to say, this principle permits us to act. The second given, of course, still needs to be established. But if it is accepted, then the poorly formulated version of instrumentalism that has emerged in the writings of economists is of inestimable value to the profession.

V

Two responses to the apparent falsity of the assumptions of economics have been examined so far. The empiricists would investigate actual choice behavior, while the instrumentalists would shift attention away from the assumptions to the predictions of the theory. The third alternative is to reformulate the assumptions in a way that would make them true. Often, introspection has been invoked as a guide to help in the reformulation.

The term that economists most often think of when this sort of approach is mentioned is "a priorism." A much better word is praxeology. That both terms are usually thought of together is primarily due to the influence of the Austrian Ludwig von Mises, author of *Human Action: A Treatise on Economics* (1949).

Mises defines praxeology as "the science of human action." Its fundamental axiom is that all human action is purposeful, goal-oriented, and aimed at improving the state of the agent. This emphasis on an active, choosing, purposeful agent is at the heart of praxeological reasoning. But Mises also wanted to insulate his doctrine from criticism. To do this, he claimed that the fundamental axioms of praxeology, though unverifiable and unfalsifiable, are known to be true a priori: they are "apodictically certain." Furthermore, a "verbal chain of logic" could be followed from the axioms to the conclusions of the theory, guaranteeing their truth as well. Mises' attempt at justificationism was never well received by economists. Even some of his fellow Austrians were put off by his a priorism.[5] The response of much of the rest of the profession was outright ridicule.

There are elements of the praxeological approach that make a good deal of sense. The idea that we might be able to discover general statements about human behavior based on the sort of distinctly human knowledge that introspection provides seems eminently reasonable, and would be problematical only for an unreconstructed behaviorist. Such general statements might not be testable in the usual senses of the word, and they might not qualify as true universal statements. But it is certainly possible that one might discover statements that are true in enough instances to provide a basis for policy, and that is an exciting possibility. It is only when one attempts to provide some kind of justificationist grounding for the statements, as Mises' misguided foray into a priorism was intended to do, that praxeology becomes an unreasonable position. Praxeologists should thus make explicit that their approach in no way depends upon a priorism. Mises' particular version of praxeology is best viewed as an historical oddity.

VI

In our cursory examination of the methodological literature we have discovered three ways in which economists have handled the "assumptions problem." The one advocated by Nelson involves defining the rationality assumption empirically, which seems straightforward enough. On any of a number of standard accounts of what constitutes legitimate scientific practice, however, neither of the other two are acceptable. Rather than directly confront the falsity of the assumptions of economic models with empirical work, instrumentalism (though empirical) ignores the falsity and praxeology (though seeking true statements) ignores empiricism. Yet, both of these positions have found more favor among economists than has the scientific one. It is no wonder that philosophers of science have such a hard time figuring economics out!

But there is a way to make sense of instrumentalism and praxeology in economics. *If* there were a general statement concerning human behavior that was true in enough instances that inferences could be drawn from it, and *if* those inferences were much the same as the ones economists draw from their presently used models, then both positions could be viewed as reasonable. Praxeology would be vindicated because the results of economics are actually based on a true understanding of some general aspects of human behavior. Instrumentalism would be vindicated because it directs us not to worry about the falsity of the assumptions of our formal models, since what counts is our true (but less formal) intuitions about human behavior. The sort of statement I am thinking of should be capable of capturing the most basic beliefs of economists, even if those beliefs are in most instances unarticulated.

VII

What is it that determines if one is an economist; what beliefs must one hold? When I sometimes ask this question of my students, the answer I give them, half-jokingly, is that an economist is someone who believes that demand curves slope downwards. To make it less of a joke, we then discuss what a downward sloping demand curve is generally taken to imply about human behavior: that agents try to make themselves better off, and that in doing so, those at the margin will respond to changes in prices by substituting among goods, and that this occurs sufficiently often that economists feel warranted in making inferences concerning human behavior. An even more general statement of this thesis would eliminate the focus on prices and goods, or interpret these constructs metaphorically. Then the thesis would read: *humans have goals, and in pursuing them will respond to perceived changes in constraints.* I submit that this simple statement is the basis of most of what is true, not only in the standard theories of economics, but in certain of the other areas of social science, and in particular in behavioral psychology.

Some qualifications should be added, but by putting things so baldly, I am hoping to draw attention to what is *not* included in my definition of what the study of economics is all about. In particular, what is not included is any commitment to the two mathematical artifacts that Nelson chose to emphasize, the rationality assumption and the set of models known as general equilibrium theory.

The standard definition of rationality encountered in the models of economists is consistency in choice over a well-ordered preference function. In the definition offered above, it is not assumed that agents have full information or well-formed preferences. As a result, agents are not always consistent in the choices they make. They learn by doing. They guess. They make mistakes. Their actions are based on their perceptions, but these perceptions can be wrong. There are substantial differences between this sort of agent and the perfectly informed, effortlessly consistent agent of neoclassical theory.

Most economists encounter general equilibrium models at some point in their training, but I suspect that few would wish to base their commitment to economics on a belief in the veracity of those models. General equilibrium theory (almost by definition) holds a central position in the discipline in relation to the partial equilibrium models economists employ. General equilibrium theory is, well, more general than partial equilibrium theory. One hopes that this is all that E. Roy Weintraub meant when he described general equilibrium theory as the "hard core" of economics (Weintraub, 1985, 1988). But this is very different from thinking that such models should play any significant role in determining one's beliefs about the truth or usefulness of economics. General equilibrium theory asks some interesting questions and solves them for a theoretical world. But aside from reminding us of the truism of market interdependence, it has little to say to us about our own world. It would be easy to understand how an outside observer, or, for that matter, even an economist whose education consisted solely in the construction of general equilibrium models, might be misled. The point nonetheless remains: our opinions about the (false) standard definition of rationality and about the (false) elegant theories of general equilibrium have absolutely no bearing on the truth and usefulness of economics. Nelson's recommendation that economists empirically investigate these constructs misses the point by a mile.

VIII

Humans have goals, and in pursuing them will respond to perceived changes in constraints. This statement, or something very much like it, provides the basis for most of the predictions economists make about human behavior. The actual process of choice engaged in by humans is exceedingly complex and cannot be easily captured in formal models. So, instead, economists use simplified (false) representations of the choice setting. This is warranted because in enough circumstances the predictions that such false models yield are correct. And the reason we often get predictions that are good enough from our false models is because the above true statement is the real basis of our predictions.

No attempt has been made to justify the italicized statement, and there is no discussion of its logical status. I would rather use the brief space that remains in speculating about the implications of this view, were it to turn out to be correct. I must confess that my thinking here is not very far advanced. But it seems that there may be a number of important implications, some of which are rather provocative.

If the statement above is the true source of the insights that economics provides, our evaluation of the development of contemporary economic theory would change. Certain episodes that had previously been viewed as paradigmatic examples of disciplinary progress would be subject to critical reassessment.[6] To use Nelson's example of theoretical exercises to determine the existence, uniqueness, and stability of general equilibrium in a particular formal model would no longer be viewed as very interesting. Other questions would become important, and scientists whose work shed light on them would be rehabilitated. Thus Hayek's formulation of "the coordination problem," game theoretic analyses of institution formation, and the work of systems theorists on feedback loops might all gain in prominence, since all (though in very different ways) investigate mechanisms that serve to coordinate the perceptions, knowledge, and behavior of agents.

Various positions in economic methodology would need to be reconsidered. For decades, critics of neoclassical theory have attacked the rationality assumption as "unrealistic." The presumption was that if the assumptions of neoclassical theory could be shown to be false, the rest of the theory could also be discounted. These criticisms must now be viewed as misguided.

The thesis about human behavior offered above is perfectly general. It could be used by a market economist in describing the response of consumers to changes in price. It could be used by a socialist intent on redesigning institutions to enhance the possibility of equality of outcomes. And indeed, it could be used by a psychologist who wished to extinguish certain behaviors and reinforce others. The implications here are truly dramatic. If the statement is true, then differences among various schools in economics (and possibly among the various social sciences) are due less to alternative views of human behavior than they are to differences over such things as which aspects of behavior are studied or which social outcomes are viewed ultimately as most desireable. This is not to say that either interdisciplinary or intradisciplinary pluralism need be abandoned. Rather, the unity at one level of analysis would allow for a clearer statement of the differences existing at the others. The potential for progress in methodological discourse would grow.

A final implication concerns the relationship between the philosophy of science and economics. Alan Nelson's chapter exemplifies all too well the path taken by many philosophers who would study the dismal science. Philosophers are interested in economics because it is a particular instance of a science. It can, therefore, be used to "test" the models that philosophers have developed about science in general. For reasons that should by now be clear, economics does not conform to any of the existing philosophical models. Though philosophers have recently paid much lip service to the idea that science is not all of a piece, this finding usually leads them to deprecate economics. The reason why philosophers have had such a hard time with economics is that they have focused attention on our false but impressive mathematical models instead of on the true but innocuous general statements that actually account for both our discipline's glowing successes and its most outrageous failures. The sorts of explanations that these statements are capable of generating appear to be categorically different from those that philosophers have thus far emphasized. Such a topic is worthy of their attention.

NOTES

1. This is not to say that economists always understand why they ask the questions that they do. To the contrary, economics is a discipline in which the absence of methodological self-consciousness is considered a virtue. For evidence supporting this claim, see Colander and Klamer (1987).

2. The three great questions of economic methodology concern assumptions, prediction, and values. The chapter focuses on the first question; the undefended statement in the text involves the second. Perhaps the best defense is to invite the reader to recall trying to explain the effects of various types of price-fixing to a noneconomist. It is at the Economics 101 level that the predictions of economists are most impressive, and except to an economist, the predictions are nonobvious.

3..The idea that that the falsity of the rationality assumption implies that neoclassical economics should be rejected is ubiquitous among critics of neoclassicism. This is why such diverse groups as the Marxists, Austrians, Post-Keynesians, and Institutionalists all end up sounding alike when they criticize "the mainstream." This is also why neoclassical economists have not been interested in testing their assumptions. Why test a claim that one acknowledges is false from the outset?

4. Critics of neoclassicism often think that Friedman's methodological position provides a framework for defending general equilibrium theory. This is exactly wrong, as Friedman's words on the subject demonstrate:

> One effect of the difficulty of testing substantive economic hypotheses has been to foster a retreat into purely formal or tautological analysis.... But economics must be more than a structure of tautologies if it is to be able to predict and not merely describe the consequences of action; if it is to be something different from disguised mathematics (1953, 11-12).

A considerable amount of work has been done recently to clarify Friedman's position. See, for example, the recent book by Hirsch and de Marchi (1990) and the symposium on Friedman, instrumentalism and scientific realism forthcoming in *Research in the History of Economic Thought and Methodology.*

5. For example, although Friedrich von Hayek occasionally uses the term "a priori," he never imbues it with the power it contains in Mises' system. His famous 1937 paper, "Economics and Knowledge," in many ways marks his break with Mises. Hayek specifies there that "the coordination problem" is the central problem for the social sciences to solve. His formulation challenges the Misesian notion that one can move smoothly via the verbal chain of logic from individual behavior to group behavior. Aspects of Austrian methodology are discussed in more detail in Caldwell (1984, 1986, 1988a, 1988b, forthcoming).

6. A recent revisionist history that complements my thesis is Philip Mirowski's *More Heat Than Light* (1989). Mirowski argues that most of the developments in economic theory since the Marginal Revolution derive from the misappropriation of a mathematical metaphor from the energy physics of the mid-nineteenth century. The metaphor was borrowed in an attempt to make economics more scientific, an urge so prevalent among economists that Mirowski describes it as a kind of disease; he dubs it "physics envy."

REFERENCES

Caldwell, Bruce (1984), "Praxeology and Its Critics: An Appraisal," *History of Political Economy*, 16 (Fall), 363-79.

________________ (1986), "Towards a Broader Conception of

Criticism," *History of Political Economy*, 18 (Winter), 675-81.

__________________ (1988a), "Hayek's Transformation," *History of Political Economy*, 20 (Winter), 513-41.

__________________ (1988b), "La Methodologie de Hayek: Description, Evaluation et Interrogations," *Politique et Economie*, 9, 71-85.

__________________ "Hayek the Falsificationist? A Refutation," *Research in the History of Economic Thought and Methodology*, forthcoming.

Coats, A. W., (1976), "Economics and Psychology: The Death and Resurrection of a Research Program," in Spiro Latsis, ed., *Method and Appraisal in Economics*. Cambridge: Cambridge University Press, 43-64.

Colander, David, and Arjo Klamer (1987), "The Making of an Economist," *Journal of Economic Perspectives*, 1 (Fall), 95-111.

Earl, Peter, ed. (1988), *Psychological Economics*. Boston: Kluwer Academic Publishers.

Friedman, Milton (1953), "The Methodology of Positive Economics," in *Essays in Positive Economics*. Chicago: University of Chicago Press, 3-43.

Gilad, Benjamin and Stanley Kaish, eds. (1986), *Handbook of Behavioral Economics*. Greenwich, CT.: JAI Press.

von Hayek, Friedrich A. (1937), "Economics and Knowledge," *Economica*, 4, 33-54.

Hirsch, Abraham and Neil de Marchi (1990), *Milton Friedman: Economics in Theory and Practice*. Ann Arbor: University of Michigan Press.

Hogarth, Robin and Melvin Reder, eds. (1987), *Rational Choice: The Contrast between Economics and Psychology*. Chicago: University of Chicago Press.

Hutchison, T. W. (1938), *The Significance and Basic Postulates of Economic Theory.* Reprint edition. New York: Augustus Kelley, 1960.

Machlup, Fritz (1978), *Methodology of Economics and Other Social Sciences.* New York: Academic Press.

Mirowski, Philip (1989), *More Heat Than Light.* Cambridge: Cambridge University Press.

von Mises, Ludwig (1949), *Human Action: A Treatise on Economics,* 1949. 3rd revised edition, Chicago: Henry Regnery, (1966).

Samuelson, Paul (1938), "A Note on the Pure Theory of Consumer's Behavior," *Economica,* 5 (Feb), 51-61.

__________________ (1947), *Foundations of Economic Analysis.* (Cambridge: Harvard University Press).

Weintraub, E. Roy (1985), *General Equilibrium Analysis: Studies in Appraisal.* Cambridge: Cambridge University Press.

__________________ (1988), "The NeoWalrasian Program Is Empirically Progressive," in Neil de Marchi, ed., *The Popperian Legacy in Economics.* Cambridge: Cambridge University Press, 213-27.

REPLY BY ALAN NELSON

Bruce Caldwell criticizes my chapter at a rather abstract level since he thinks that while purporting to be a contribution to "methodology," it in fact shows that I "misunderstand the economic enterprise" and "fail to recognize the purpose of economic methodology." This is not a good way of expressing our disagreement because we both agree about the nature of the economic enterprise and the primary purpose of methodology. Economics is for understanding and explaining the economic world and for using this understanding to predict and control it for social good. Methodology is for helping us understand the successes and failures of economic theory and also, perhaps, to contribute to progress in economics by clarifying what is involved in doing it successfully. I think that our disagreements are substantive ones about how to understand the foundations of economic theory. I shall briefly discuss two of these disagreements.

First, Caldwell sees economic methodology as divided into three basic "camps": the instrumentalist, the a priorist, and the empiricist. He thinks that well-formulated versions of the first two are very good, but that empiricism is not much good, at least for economics, and that I have made the mistake of falling into this camp. One consideration he mentions in this connection is a kind of argument from authority: "most economists have not been very interested in pursuing Nelson's philosophically more attractive 'scientific' route" (139) and, "both of these positions [instrumentalism and a priorism] have found more favor among economists than has the scientific one" (142). I think that these statements are false; *most* economists are not in any kind of methodological camp. Most do economics in blissful ignorance of self-conscious methodology. Moreover, I think that most economists, if asked, would say that what they are doing is science and that their methods are very similar to those of physical scientists except for regrettable difficulties in performing controlled experiments. (This is why I was reluctant to characterize my approach as falling into a methodological camp; it is more like doing away with special philosophico-methodological justifications for economics). Whether these economists are being laudably optimistic about the future, or whether they have miserable cases of "physics envy," only time will tell, but either way my approach ought to be more attractive to most economists than instrumentalism or a priorism. It generates hypothesis that are directly testable, unlike the traditional methodologies.

I also disagree with Caldwell about the intrinsic merits of these methodologies.[1] He thinks that empiricist interpretations of economics are based on misunderstandings about economic knowledge; instrumentalism and a priorism (or "praxeology"), however, he supposes to capture important insights about economics. Concerning instrumentalism he writes,

> *If* there were a general statement concerning human behavior that was true in enough instances that inferences could be drawn from it, and *if* those inferences were much the same as the ones economists draw from their presently used models, then both positions [instrumentalism and a priorism] could be viewed as reasonable. (142)

But consider the following familiar sort of argument. Suppose that in the year 1600 there was a general statement about planetary behavior that was "true in enough instances that inferences could be drawn from it"; for example, Jupiter moves through the sky more quickly than Saturn. These inferences would have been much the same as the ones astronomers drew from their (then) presently used Ptolemaic model. Would this make "reasonable" methodological defenses of the Ptolemaic model against "empiricist" objections from advocates of the Copernican model? Plainly not. Scientists ought to pursue true models (or laws or theories or statements, etc.), not models that simply give the same results as true models. If we follow Caldwell and accept it as given that economics has "something of value to say" and that this valuable something is accurate and useful predictions, then it is still a mystery that they should issue from false assumptions.

Praxeology impresses Caldwell because he thinks it may be possible to use this method to produce a true principle of economic action. If this came to pass, then old interpretations of economic models would need to be reevaluated. The project of reevaluation that Caldwell describes in his Sections VI through VIII deserves some sympathy, but his candidate for the true basis of all accurate economic predictions is too general. Before it can be of any use in guiding economic research, it will have to be toughened up into something more specific and, like the rationality principle, probably false. If a more specific version is false, of course the project collapses. In fact, in plain English, Caldwell's stated principle, *Humans have goals, and in pursuing them will respond to perceived changes in constraints*, amounts simply to this: *If someone wants something they will try to do what they think will get it for them.* It is notorious that this is suspiciously close to being a tautology. If economic science really rests on this, then we should not expect any more from it than we get from the judicious application of common sense.

Finally, I want to indicate one way in which the orientation of my essay could be reconciled with one more congenial to Caldwell. Suppose again that economics has something of value to say, but drop the assumption that the value lies primarily in predictive power. Suppose that economics has intrinsic value as a body of substantial discourse subject to an appropriate Sprachethik. Suppose further that nonpractitioners respect this discourse and look to its practitioners for various sorts of edification and guidance. If these suppositions are true, then my own essay can be thought of as an exercise in rhetorical analysis. Economic discourse is full of talk of individualism, aggregation, and reduction. I have argued that the significance of this talk is not to make the kinds of empirical claims that physicists make with similar talk. This serves to unmask the actual rhetorical function of such language in economics; it is to persuade the reader of the legitimacy of economic models by falsely insinuating that they are constructed in accordance with methods that closely resemble those used in the physical sciences.

NOTES

1. Recall that there are important differences between respectable instrumentalism as it is applied to physical sciences and the decidedly unscientific economic instrumentalisms that have been proposed. There is some justice to Caldwell's complaint that I describe and

dismiss instrumentalism and a priorism somewhat hastily in my chapter, but I still think that I clearly identified their crucial faults. There are more detailed studies available. See, for example, Nelson (1990) and the references cited therein.

REFERENCES

Nelson, A. (1990), "Are Economic Kinds Natural?" *Minnesota Studies in the Philosophy of Science*, XIV, 101-135.

CHAPTER 4

TWO KINDS OF RATIONALITY

Cristina Bicchieri

INTRODUCTION

The concept of rational behavior plays an important role in economics, as well as in politics, sociology, ethics and political philosophy. Rationality has both a normative content, in that it points to what one should do in order to attain a given end, and positive applications, as it is used to describe, explain and predict human behavior. It is customary in rational choice theory to distinguish between normative and descriptive functions, together with their respective justifications. Normative theories of rationality are justified by appeal to intuition; optimizing behavior can be thought of as an extremely idealized version of something we experience in a less accurate, more approximate way. We constantly interpret and understand our own and other people's behavior as goal oriented. Individuals have aims and beliefs, are able to reflect upon them and are capable of devising and directing means toward the attainment of their desires. We keep choosing and evaluating the outcomes of our choices and the means adopted, trying to achieve what we deem to be the best for us. A normative theory of rationality makes this rough process of maximization explicit, and in so doing, it filters out all the impurities, such as ill-defined goals, lack of motivation, inability to calculate or to store information, as well as many other human failings that plague our deliberative processes. What an actor should do—if perfectly rational and optimally informed—has been long recognized to be quite distant from what common exemplars of *homo sapiens* in fact do, and which often falls well below the high standards set by normative theory.[1]

Questions of empirical relevance do not arise only in connection with descriptive models. It is important, even in a normative context, to ask whether a definition of rationality is appropriate, in the sense of being a reasonable approximation of human behavior. If we observe systematic deviations from rational behavior, the rationality of the hypothesis itself might be called into question.[2] Violations of rational behavior are even more relevant to explanations of actual behavior. The aim of positive rational choice theory is to show that observed choices can be rationalized by a theory of optimization, and this is done by postulating their internal consistency. Experimental results obtained by psychologists and experimental economists are convincing evidence that optimization is often a poor model for how people choose.[3] Besides the occurrence of intransitivities, there are many other occasions on which even the simplest notion of rationality fails, as when there is an incomplete preference ordering. In such cases, there is no optimal action, and rationality cannot fulfill its positive aim.[4]

Yet, I believe the main deficiency does not lie in rational choice theory *per se*. As a descriptive tool, it is adequate for a large number of applications, especially in economics, that are characterized by completely ordered and stable preferences. In such cases, the choice environment is not new, either because it is often repeated, or because it is sufficiently similar to another well-known choice situation. This suggests that rationality can be thought of as a steady state of an adaptive process, in which repeated exposure to the same environment has allowed the actors to learn how to improve outcomes.[5] This sets limits to the applicability of rational choice models, but in no way makes them trivial or irrelevant for the description of social phenomena. What kind of social situation can be described in terms of rational choice models, and to what extent, remains an empirical question to be answered, case by case.

Economics, like other social sciences, studies group phenomena and the behavior of social systems. Individual actions are important insofar as they contribute to system behavior, but what is wanting is precisely the description of the passage from individual choices to system behavior. This transition is never immediate. Rational choice needs supplementing; specific auxiliary hypotheses must be added in order to derive system-level behavior. These additional assumptions may refer to the way agents interact, or they may specify the environment within which interaction takes place. While economics, as well as political science and sociology, need *ad hoc*, local assumptions to model different phenomena, game theory takes a more general approach to social institutions. It tries to explain the endogenous emergence of social structure, how institutions such as markets, prices, committees, voting systems, legal systems or social norms came about. The starting point is never a given institution, but a set of rational individuals endowed with a given amount of information and a physical description of the situation within which they interact. Since it shows how institutions are the outcome of multiperson strategic interactions, game theory encompasses all social sciences, insofar as they take the rational viewpoint as their frame of analysis.

A description of the passage from individual rational choices to social structure is most important whenever social structure is modeled as the outcome of rational choices. An important feature of strategic interaction is the presence of endogenous uncertainty. Each individual is uncertain about the possible actions of other individuals, and since the outcome of one's choice depends upon other individuals' choices, what it is rational to do is determined by what one expects others to do. Each individual has to assess a subjective probability distribution over every other individual's actions, and each is aware that every other individual is similarly conjecturing what others might do. The solution to each individual's decision problem depends upon the solution to the other individuals' decision problems. Since choices are interdependent, individuals cannot just maximize as if facing a static physical background, and maximization of subjective expected utility is possible only if the other individuals' decisions can be specified.

Given a game, we ask what outcome (that is, what combination of payoffs) to expect. Different classes of games are associated with different outcomes, and a *solution concept* is a function that associates outcomes with games. A solution concept applied to almost every area of economic theory, as well as to social choice, political science, sociology, biology, ethics and computer science, is that of *Nash equilibrium*.[6] A Nash equilibrium is a combination of actions, one for each player, such that each player's action is a best reply to the other players' actions, if taken as given. Each individual, that is, maximizes his/her expected utility under the constraint represented by other individuals' choices.

Typically, the argument for Nash equilibrium assumes that each player can find out the other players' strategies and make a best reply. Although Nash equilibrium expresses individual rationality, in too many cases it is far from clear how rational agents would reason to an equilibrium. Even if, in some particular games, the players know what the single optimal choice for each player is, the amount of information needed to infer another player's strategy generally goes well beyond the information contained in the payoff matrix, as was originally assumed by von Neumann and Morgenstern.[7] In most games, that a particular combination of strategies is a Nash equilibrium is a necessary, but not a sufficient condition, for one to be able to predict it as the choice of rational players.

Unless further hypotheses about players' knowledge and beliefs are specified, the assumption that players can find out each other's strategies is groundless, and rationality cannot fulfill its explanatory and predictive functions, nor its normative role. Indeed, in the case of strategic interaction, descriptive and normative spheres cannot be distinguished. Normative game theory prescribes actions that will bring about an equilibrium, which means providing each player with a unique rational recommendation on how to play. But the unique rational action recommended to each player depends upon correctly predicting the other players' behavior, since what it is rational to do is a function of the other players' expected choices. In this sense, what one *should* do cannot be determined independently of what others *will* do.

As in rational choice theory, each player performs a practical inference that takes the individual's beliefs and desires as premises and concludes in favor of choosing a particular action.[8] Since a game-theoretic solution is the outcome of independent choices, to every such solution is attached a 'social' practical inference that concludes in favor of the players acting so as to realize that solution. Each component individual action, in turn, is the outcome of a process of practical reasoning that leads to the conclusion that one should do his part in realizing the solution. But how is this conclusion reached? If joint collective acting requires that all individual practical inferences are interconnected, in that each agent's choice is *conditional* upon what other agents are expected to do, successful coordination of actions requires that agents' beliefs be somewhat 'coordinated', too.

A property generally required of beliefs is that they are rational, that is, consistent. In the single-agent case, this means that one cannot believe that P and not P at the same time, or that one cannot believe that P but disbelieve what P entails. In a multi-agent environment, beliefs are about other people's actions, and the beliefs that lead them to act in one way or another. For example, one cannot consistently believe that a player is rational and does not choose his best reply, given the putative beliefs about other players' choices one attributes to him. Thus defined, consistency is an internal matter: a player's beliefs about other players can be consistent and yet wrong.

The consistency criterion of belief rationality is adequate if the aim is that of justifying a strategy choice on the part of a player. If instead, one wants to predict what a player will choose, that criterion is seldom useful. Hence, even if an equilibrium configuration of actions can be rationalized as the outcome of a social practical inference, it may be impossible to predict whether the players will aim at it. Justifying equilibrium play involves much more than internal consistency of beliefs. Typically, the beliefs supporting an equilibrium are self-fulfilling, in that each player's beliefs are consistent with the actual beliefs held by the other players. Yet, knowledge that some beliefs are self-fulfilling, while others are not, does not help in specifying how agents come to hold beliefs of the self-fulfilling type.

The *problem of justifying equilibrium play* is often compounded by the existence of multiple equilibria, some of which may be intuitively unreasonable. This difficulty has given rise to a vast literature on refinements of Nash equilibrium that aims at finding criteria that rule out those Nash equilibria that involve irrational (though not inconsistent) expectations on the part of the players.[9] The multiplicity of refinements suggests that there is no agreement upon a unique set of criteria for belief rationality, and this might be due to the fact that none of the proposed refinements has been successful in eliminating all but one equilibrium in large classes of games.

The games discussed here are described in *normal form*, that is, the game is played only once, and the players choose their strategies simultaneously and independently of each other, so that one player's change of strategy cannot cause a change by any other player. An alternative description is the *extensive form*, which makes explicit the causal structure of the sequence of decisions and the information available to each player at each decision point. Von Neumann and Morgenstern argued that any extensive form game can in principle be reduced to an equivalent normal form; this reduction is possible if we assume that each player can plan all of his actions in all possible contingencies before the game begins. The equivalence of normal and extensive form representations has been questioned recently, since the normal form description may omit information relevant to the solution of the game. But for the purpose of the present analysis, this problem need not be tackled.

The normal form representation of a game lends itself quite naturally to the questions of why and under what conditions the players might be expected to play a Nash equilibrium. Since choices are conditional upon expectations and players' expectations might be 'uncoordinated', a rational choice and an equilibrium choice need not coincide.

My aim is not to provide a solution that fills the gap between individual rationality assumptions and collective outcomes. Rather, a case is made for reconsideration of this gap and of its consequences for explanation and prediction of social outcomes. Since descriptive game theory is ubiquitous in the social sciences, it is important to understand that practical inferences from rationality premises only tend to eliminate some outcomes, and that prediction of particular configurations of actions requires additional assumptions about players' knowledge and beliefs.

SINGLE-AGENT CHOICE

The paradigmatic case of practical reasoning from rationality premises is that of an isolated agent who has certain knowledge of his/her environment. Rational choice arguments typically deduce the action that an agent will choose, or has chosen, from a premise of optimization, plus a specification of the agent's objectives and environmental constraints. It is seldom noticed that in order to get a prediction (or to explain), two quite different arguments must be made.

The first argument (A1) specifies a means-end model of behavior: it tells the actor's goal and the optimal means to attain it. It is, furthermore, assumed that the chosen action will depend on what the agent believes about the relationship between actions and outcomes, and that this belief is arrived at *by way of an argument*. For example, a firm whose pricing decision is being predicted may be depicted as involved in a practical argument whose conclusion is the statement that a particular price will lead to maximum profit. This argument is by no means purely analytical, depending as it does on empirical evidence about the market as well as on the application of general economic principles. The empirical argument must be a good one, in the sense that the evidence considered does in fact support the conclusion; in other words, the conclusion must be a *rational belief*. A1 then specifies an optimal action, given some goal and constraints.

The second argument (A2) consists in attributing the above argument to the agent, and concluding that the agent will or did act accordingly. This is by no means a surprising step, provided that the goal is to explain or predict actual behavior. This new argument is made of two premises, a general and a special one, which I introduce in reverse order of generality:

(1) The agent acts rationally—that is, agent x does p in the belief that by doing p, he or she will attain q, and q is the desired outcome;

(2) the belief that p leads to q is grounded on the correct assessment of the available evidence.

(3) The correct assessment of the available evidence leads to the conclusion that, in order to achieve q, one has to do p.

From premises (1,2)-(3) the conclusion that x did or will do such and such thing follows. Premise (3) is the general one, and perhaps the most questionable. It can be rephrased as a universal statement to the effect that everyone, if put in the agent's circumstances, will arrive at those conclusions, provided that the agent argues correctly. The agent's available evidence need not be the same as our's, but we must at least be able to correctly reconstruct the evidence available to the agent at a given time. Furthermore, the agent whose action we try to explain is supposed to use the same rules of inference we use, as well as to adopt reasonable modes of data processing. Indeed, if one were uncertain as to what sort of rules of inference and ways of data processing agents use, or how much and what kind of information they have collected, it would be erroneous to argue from what one concludes to what others would conclude. More generally, to make sense of an action an observer has to find reasons for it, and impose rationality and consistency conditions upon desires and beliefs.

If we go back to premise (1,2), we see that it states that x argues correctly, and therefore is an application of (3) to the special case at hand. Premise (1,2) also says that the agent is rational, and in so doing it makes a twofold claim. The first is an attribution of *practical rationality*: it has to do with the optimality of one's action, given one's desires and beliefs. Thus, if agent x desires q and believes that action p will secure q, the agent is practically rational in choosing p. How the agent came to believe that p leads to q is not relevant, nor is it relevant that the agent's belief might be unfounded or patently false. For practical rationality to hold, no assumption about belief formation is needed. The agent might have come to form a belief by consulting an astrologer, tossing a coin, or by careful research: what matters is the relation between desire, belief and action.

The second claim attributes *epistemic rationality* to the actor; here rationality is an attribute of belief, and consists in recognizing its correctness, given the evidence at one's disposal. In argument A2, both forms of rationality have been imputed to the agent, who has to be practically rational, otherwise it would be impossible to predict the action. Given the belief (however obtained) that p is the required action, one must be assured that x will act in conformity with the agent's belief. To assume practical rationality is thus indispensable for predicting what actors will do, even if we know their beliefs; in this sense, practical rationality is far from being a trivial assumption. The need for epistemic rationality arises when it is impossible or impractical to assess beliefs directly. Then, one could not infer an agent's beliefs from the evidence at her/his disposal, unless the assumption were made that those beliefs are coherent and grounded upon that evidence.

Of course, finding reasons for action and imposing rationality conditions does not lead to the immediate conclusion that they have produced or will produce a given action. Reasons and action must be causally connected, in the sense that the imputed motives must be efficacious in producing that action. I may know your reasons for doing q, but my explanation of your doing q for those reasons may be wrong. Or you may have the intention of doing the right thing and fail to act because of weakness of the will. So, when one postulates a desire and a belief that a given action will satisfy it, it is implicitly assumed that the right conditions for action obtain.[10]

Is it necessary to impose a double rationality requirement in order to explain and predict behavior? Isn't practical rationality enough? Traditional price-theoretic models are good examples of the possibility of doing without epistemic rationality, since here the agent has perfect knowledge of the certain outcomes of the alternatives open to him/her, can identify the best of them, and choose it on that account. What needs to be assumed is that individual preferences satisfy certain consistency and continuity conditions; whenever they do, they can be represented by a well-defined utility function. Rationality can then be identified with constrained utility maximization and, in order to determine an agent's choice, all one needs to know are the agent's preferences.

But perfect knowledge is not the most common, nor the most interesting case. A common case in which practical rationality is too thin a requirement is that of choice under risk or uncertainty. If one chooses among actions whose outcomes cannot be uniquely predicted, the desirability of a possible outcome is only one factor; the other relevant factor is one's beliefs about the possible states of the world, which are expressed in the probabilities assigned to the states. In the case of *risk*, there exist objective probabilities associated with all possible outcomes, while in the case of *uncertainty* objective probabilities are undefined, and the assigned probabilities only represent the decision maker's private information about the states. In both cases, the assignment of utilities to the outcomes and of probabilities to the states allows the decision maker to compute the expected utilities of the different acts by weighting the value of each outcome by the probability of its occurrence. Assuming practical rationality here means expecting the individual to choose that action that yields maximal expected utility. Since maximization of expected utility is itself the consequence of certain constraints imposed upon behavior, practical rationality reduces to a set of consistency and continuity axioms concerning the decision maker's ordering of probability distributions over outcomes.

In order to reconstruct an individual's practical argument to conclude in favor of a given action, something more than expected utility maximization needs to be assumed. The individual's beliefs, too, have to be specified, something that—short of the case in which they are directly available—requires assuming epistemic rationality on the individual's part. In the case of risk, the decision maker can be expected to learn the relevant probabilities, but what if the probabilities are undefined? The decision maker in this case must assign subjective probabilities to the possible states, and all that can be required is that the axioms of probability calculus are obeyed.

This criterion of belief rationality is extremely weak and obviously does not allow one to infer an actor's choice. It is always possible to reconstruct *ex post* more than one configuration of beliefs and utilities that makes a choice rational with respect to them. In this case, we have indeterminacy of explanation. *Ex ante*, it may prove extremely difficult to decide which beliefs a rational agent would entertain when faced with uncertainty. Provided the decision maker's beliefs are rational, in that they satisfy the laws of probability, any arbitrary probability assignment is admissible.

Suppose, however, that an individual has been exposed to the same environment over and over and has had the chance of observing or 'experimenting' with the environment, so as to obtain new information. In time, subjective probability distribution will converge toward that of any other observer who has been exposed to the same environment long enough to learn what the world is like.[11] In this case, we would be able to tell which beliefs a rational agent should have, if we think the agent is intelligent enough to be capable of learning from experience. This point is important since it says that when the environment is sufficiently stable and the choice situation is familiar, *rationality can be a predictive tool.* It becomes even more important because we may not be able to reach the same conclusion when the environment is not a natural but a social one.

MULTI-AGENT CHOICE

It might be interesting to predict whether Smith will spend his holidays at the beach or in the country, given this year's uncertain weather, but this is hardly an interesting question for the social theorist. What concerns the theorist is rather the interaction of individuals whose actions affect one another, and the outcome of such interactions. Microexplanations of social institutions, for example, typically aim at showing how the institution in question results from multiperson interactions. A price system, a legal system, a social norm, as well as a social contract, a political organization or an international treaty can all be 'reconstructed' as configurations of individual choices. These explanations require a further step, an argument that deduces those collective outcomes from the solutions to the decision problems of isolated agents.

This second step proceeds by assuming that the collective outcome will be a state of *equilibrium.* By this is meant, as described earlier, a situation in which no agent would have any reason to change his/her action, if accepting the actions chosen by other agents as given. Given knowledge of what each agent would choose under each possible set of environmental constraints (that is, each possible configuration of actions on the part of other agents), it is possible to deduce which joint actions, if any, would constitute equilibria. Prediction and explanation become more problematic in the case of this second step—an argument from the assumed existence of equilibrium—than in the case of a simple argument from rationality on the part of an agent facing exogenous constraints.

One might wonder why there needs to be any difficulty here. After all, the only difference between a natural environment and a social environment is just the presence of other people. Isn't rational choice the same in both cases? Imagine Robinson Crusoe, alone on his island, deciding whether to spend the afternoon cutting wood, or allowing himself to be lazy, taking a bath, napping and eating bananas later on. He would prefer the second alternative, but worries that tomorrow it might rain, in which case he would be better off under a roof built with the wood he would have cut today. To be uncertain about the rain simply means assigning subjective probabilities to the possible states of tomorrow's weather, and to be rational means to maximize expected utility with respect to this probabilistic assessment.

Now imagine a different scenario. Robinson has met Friday, so his environment is now quite different; there is nature with all its uncertainties, but Robinson has got a friend. He still faces a choice between industry and laziness, with an important difference. If Friday were to cut the wood, Robinson could be lazy without worrying. Too bad Friday is on the other side of the island and Robinson cannot communicate with him until tonight. They did not coordinate their plans before, but Robinson knows Friday is facing the same dilemma. Both know one of four things can happen: either one cuts the wood and the other rests, both cut the wood, or both rest.

Since Robinson is uncertain as to what Friday is going to do, he should assign a subjective probability to each of Friday's possible actions. Then, if Robinson is rational, he will proceed to maximize his expected utility. And were Friday a reliable automaton, he would indeed succeed. But Friday is a human being, and as such, capable of reasoning and forming expectations. In order to assign probabilities to his possible actions, Robinson needs to have a theory (however rudimentary) of Friday's behavior, and since Friday's choice will be guided by his beliefs and desires, Robinson will first need to form some ideas about them.

Our story can be simplified by having Robinson know that Friday, besides facing the same options, has the same preferences he has, in that each prefers to be idle if the other works, but each prefers to work rather than risking to remain unsheltered in a rainy day. Putting L for 'lazy' and I for 'industrious', Friday's preference ranking can be thus expressed:

L,I	(Friday rests and Robinson works)
I,I	(both work)
I,L	(Friday works and Robinson rests)
L,L	(both give way to laziness).

The top of the list is Friday's most preferred option, followed by the other options in a decreasing order of preference. Ordering preferences by means of numbers, Robinson may couple each alternative with a number representing its (ordinal) utility, thus L,I = 4; I,I = 3; I,L = 2; L,L = 1. This ranking would have little meaning without a further assumption: Friday is rational, hence he will try to get as much as he can out of the circumstances. Since he is not acting under certainty (remember: *Robinson* is now part of his environment), for him to be rational means trying to maximize his expected utility.

In order to decide whether Robinson (R) can infer Friday's (F) behavior from what he knows about him, let us review Robinson's knowledge:

(1) R knows F is rational,
(2) R knows all of F's possible actions,
(3) R knows F's utilities of outcomes.

Well, what Robinson knows makes him predict that Friday would certainly allow himself to be lazy just in case he *expects* Robinson to cut the wood. But propositions (1)-(3) tell Robinson nothing about Friday's expectations. Propositions (1)-(3) do not permit Robinson to infer anything specific about Friday, unless he makes some assumption about Friday's knowledge, or the evidence from which he reasons about Robinson. Were Friday ignorant about Robinson's possible choices, utilities, or rationality, he would be at a loss in trying to imagine what Robinson could possibly do. In either case, Friday's inability to predict Robinson's choice would make Robinson unable to predict Friday's choice. Thus, a few more assumptions are needed to proceed towards predictability, that is:

(4) F knows that R is rational,
(5) F knows all of R's possible actions,
(6) F knows R's utilities of outcomes.

Now suppose Robinson knows (4)-(6). Is he better off in terms of predictive capability? Well, now Friday faces the same predicament that Robinson faced before since he, too, is trying to predict Robinson's choice. But, from (4)-(6) alone, he cannot infer what Robinson's choice will be, since he has no way to tell Robinson's predictions about him. For example, if Friday does not know that Robinson knows that he is rational, his actions will be based on a calculation that would not exclude the case where Robinson does not know that Friday is rational. Since Friday is including this case in his calculation, so must Robinson. So, both may still have to analyze what would happen if Friday were not rational. To avoid this, Friday must be endowed with further knowledge; in particular, he will have to know propositions (1)-(3). A further assumption is thus added:

(7) Both F and R know (1)-(6).

Does (7) make a relevant difference? Note that (7) only says that each knows (1)-(6), but no assumption has been made to the effect that each knows that the other knows (1)-(6). Put yourself in Friday's place and just try to infer what you can from your knowledge of Robinson. Friday knows Robinson is rational (by (4)) and also knows that Robinson knows that he is rational (by (1)). But does Friday know that Robinson knows that Friday knows that Robinson is rational? The question is not vacuous. Indeed, were the answer to be negative, Friday could never be sure of Robinson's capability to predict his choice. Since Friday does not know that Robinson knows (4), his actions will be based as in the preceding case, on a calculation including the case in which Robinson does not know (4). Since Friday is including this case in his calculation, so must Robinson. Thus, both may have to analyze what would happen were Robinson not to know (4). The same reasoning applies to Robinson, since he does not know that Friday knows (1).

It can be verified that endowing both of them with knowledge of (7) does not solve the problem that reappears at higher levels of knowledge. For example, with iterated mutual knowledge of *n*th degree of each other's rationality, it would still be the case that each would be uncertain as to the other's *n*-th level knowledge of his rationality, thus requiring the addition of a *n*+1th degree of mutual knowledge of rationality. For each of them to be put in a position to predict the other's behavior, *common knowledge* of (7) must be assumed, that is:

(8) (7) is common knowledge among F and R.

Simply stated, common knowledge of p among a group G means that each member of G knows p, and each knows that each knows p,... and so on ad infinitum.[12] Common knowledge of each other's rationality, utilities and strategies is a precondition for predictability, but does not guarantee its attainment. How does one reason from the above assumptions to a 'solution' to the Robinson/Friday predicament? Given propositions (1)-(8), what Robinson now knows is that Friday will cut wood only if he expects Robinson not to, since in this case to cut wood will be Friday's best reply to Robinson's choice. That is, were Friday to assign probability 1 to the event that Robinson chooses to rest, he would maximize his expected utility by working. If it were obvious that Robinson would choose to be lazy, then it would be obvious what Friday's response would be, since Friday's rationality, options and utilities are by assumption common knowledge. Since a truly obvious mode of behavior must be obvious to both parties, each will assign probability 1 to the other doing the obvious thing. In this case, a solution would be reached.

Alas, Robinson's choice is anything but obvious. Indeed, Friday can predict that Robinson will be lazy only if he can predict that Robinson expects him to be industrious. And why should he? After all, what each does depends on what each believes the other is expecting him to do, and what each expects the other to do depends on what each expects the other to expect him to expect the other to expect in an infinite regress of expectations. A person may be unpredictable, like the weather, but for different reasons. Someone is unpredictable, not because that person chooses randomly, or is incapable of forming a plan and sticking to it, but because that person's rational choice depends on what that person expects you to choose, which in turn depends on what you expect that person to choose. When rational choice depends upon beliefs about other agents' beliefs, what it is rational to do may remain undefined because of the indeterminacy of those beliefs.

GAME-THEORETIC REASONING

The Robinson/Friday story is an example of game-theoretic reasoning, and an especially difficult one, since there are multiple solutions and no way to discriminate among them. The situation can be put in strategic (normal) form as follows:

G1

		Friday L	Friday I
Robinson	L	1, 1	4, 2
	I	2, 4	3, 3

The two *pure strategies* available to each player are L (to be lazy) and I (to be industrious).[13] Each combination of strategies results in a pair of utility outcomes (payoffs), one for each player. For each pair of payoffs, the first is the payoff of Robinson, the second is Friday's. Payoffs are expressed in terms of *ordinal* utilities, hence they only show the preference ranking of the alternatives for each player, not how much, or with what intensity, a player enjoys a particular option.

This normal form game is completely defined by the number of players, the strategies available to each player, and the payoffs (utilities) each player can expect from any combination of his and the other's strategies. The players choose simultaneously: each picks a strategy independently and without communicating with the other. If there is some reason to discriminate among strategies, this reason must be embodied in the structure of the game; for example, if a player's strategy is obviously better than any other strategy that might be chosen, independently of the other players' possible choices, this fact must be reflected in his payoffs. This means that only an endogenous rationality argument (for example, an argument whose premises concern only the structure of the game) can induce a player to discriminate among strategies, while it allows other players to see what the player's obvious rational choice is.

We have also assumed the players to have common knowledge of their mutual rationality, payoffs and strategies. While these assumptions are necessary in the game we are discussing, there are many games in which they are not needed. An example is the following modification of game G1:

G2

		Friday	
		L	I
Robinson	L	1, 1	4, 2
	I	2, 4	4, 3

Here Robinson is indifferent between being lazy, while Friday is industrious and also being industrious himself, maybe because he does not dislike working, but finds the effort useless if he is sure that somebody else is doing the job. On the other hand, the other's idleness irritates him, thus detracting from the pleasure of cutting wood (the combination (I, L) gets Robinson a payoff of 2). If we look at Robinson's strategies, we see that—whatever Friday does—Robinson is never worse off by choosing strategy I. If Friday plays L, I is a bet-ter reply than L for Robinson. If Friday plays I, Robinson does as well playing I as L. We call I a *weakly dominant* strategy for Robinson.

In this case, I is the 'obvious course of action' for Robinson. For rational Robinson to reach this conclusion, he has no need to know that Friday is rational, nor to know Friday's payoffs. Friday, on the contrary, needs to know Robinson's rationality and payoffs in order to infer Robinson's obvious choice. Then Friday's 'obvious' response is L, which is the best he can do given Robinson's choice. Indeed, (I, L) is the only logical solution to this game, and we have reasoned to it from rationality assumptions alone.

Note, that the above reasoning, which involves eliminating weakly dominated actions, does not always result in an appealing outcome. In the following game, Column player (Col), if rational, will always choose Right, which guarantees a higher payoff than Left if Row plays Top, and the same payoff as Left if Row plays Bottom. Knowing this, Row will always play Top, which is his best reply to Right. Top-Right is the only 'logical solution', unequivocally proceeding from the players' rationality, but it is clearly worse for both players, in that both would be better off by playing Bottom-Left (which is an equilibrium, too).

G3

		Column L	Column R
Row	T	1, 1	2, 2
Row	B	4, 4	0, 4

If we go back to game G1, it is easy to verify that there is no weakly dominant strategy for either player, hence there is no 'obvious course of action' for the players to follow. In this case, rationality cannot recommend any strategy; a player's initial expectation about the other's likely strategy choice is completely arbitrary, and therefore, unpredictable. Since the players have to choose anyway, and given that any conjecture about the other's choice is admissible, it is possible that the joint outcome will turn out to be an unpleasant surprise for both. For example, Robinson may believe that Friday plays I with probability 1, and therefore, respond with L, which guarantees him the highest expected utility. In turn, if Friday believes that Robinson will play I with probability 1, he will pick L, too. But (L,L) is the worst outcome for both, since both refraining from work exposes them to the likely injuries of rain the following day.

It has been argued that, in cases such as this, other choice rules (for example, *maximin utility*, *minimax loss*, *Hurwicz* α, and others) that avoid using subjective probabilities are more suitable.[14] For example, if Robinson were prudent, he would choose the strategy that minimizes the maximum possible loss; the maximin strategy is I (since by playing I the worst payoff he can get is 2, which is better than 1, the worst possible outcome of L).

Even if each of the alternative choice rules gives a definite recommendation on how to play, none of them enjoys a privileged rational status, and some of them are known to lead to irrational decisions in practical situations. An example is the following: suppose both players in G1 are using the maximin utility criterion, and each knows that the other is a maximin player. Then each player, expecting the other to choose I, would have an incentive to deviate from his maximin strategy and play L; the result would be (L,L), which is the worst possible outcome for both.

Had there been the possibility of communicating *before* each went his own way, would Robinson and Friday have been better off in terms of knowing what to do? We may think of them discussing until they reach an agreement to follow a certain course of action (that is, to play a given pair of strategies). Afterwards, they leave one another and communication is no longer possible between them; next, each one chooses his strategy in complete ignorance of the other's choice. The agreement, we must add, is *not binding*: there is no moral or material sanction for betraying it, and each has the choice of betraying the agreement or being faithful to it.

There are non binding agreements that have the following property: if one assumes the other party to be loyal, then one has every reason to be loyal. In other words, the agreement is *self-enforcing*. Can one envisage such agreements for game G1? It is easy to verify that if one of the players were to agree to cut the wood while the other rests, then it would not be reasonable for either one to defect unilaterally. In fact, (I, L) and (L,I) are the only two pairs of strategies that are self-enforcing in the above sense.

The above is an example of *equilibrium analysis*. Each player is supposed to think 'as if' unaware of strategic interdependence; considering a combination of other players' strategies as exogenously given, each must seek to maximize his/her own expected utility over all conceivable switches of one's own strategies. To put it differently, to decide whether a combination of one's own and the others' strategies is an equilibrium, a player must reason hypothetically and ask whether the fact that the other players play their part in that combination would induce one to modify one's own choice. For example, the combination (I,I) of game G1 is not an equilibrium in that, were any of the two players to expect the other to play I, the player would do better by playing L instead of I. In this sense an agreement to play (I,I) would never be self-enforcing.

CONDITIONAL AND UNCONDITIONAL RATIONALITY

The notion of equilibrium embodies the idea of individual rationality in interactive contexts, since everybody acts simultaneously to maximize expected utility. An equilibrium strategy is always a best reply, but only *insofar as the other players' strategies are kept constant*; hence, it is a rational choice only conditionally upon considering the other players' strategies as exogenously given. It represents, in other words, a form of *conditional rationality*. The difference between conditional and unconditional rationality needs to be stressed, since only the latter has predictive power. Moreover, conditional and unconditional rationality may disagree in that an action that is rational conditionally upon a given set of expectations may be unconditionally irrational (if the expectations themselves are irrational).

Unconditional rationality says that whenever a player i has to perform one of two mutually exclusive actions a_{i1} and a_{i2}, such that a_{i1} leads to a payoff p_{i1} and a_{i2} leads to a payoff p_{i2}, and $p_{i2} \geq p_{i1}$, the player will choose a_{i2}. Formally, let us interpret the following symbols as follows:

a_{ij} : player i chooses action j
p_{ij} : action j's payoff to player i

Then unconditional rationality can be formally expressed as follows:[15]

(UR) $[(a_{i1} \vee a_{i2}) \; \& \; \sim(a_{i1} \; \& \; a_{i2}) \; \& \; (p_{i2} \geq p_{i1})] \dashrightarrow a_{i2}$.

In game theory, a decision is unconditionally rational only in very special cases, like the one depicted in game G2. In that game, what Robinson chooses is *independent* of his conjecture about Friday's choice. Indeed, Robinson chooses as if he were alone. It would be misleading, however, to assume that UR obtains only when expectations do not matter. If mutual expectations were common knowledge, for example, then a player's choice would be unconditionally rational, too. This case is discussed in the last section of the chapter.

In most circumstances, though, a player has to conjecture other players' choices, and this cannot be done without taking into account the players' expectations about each other's behavior. As it has been pointed out, an infinite regress of expectations may leave unconditional rationality undefined. This explains why, in games like G1, being an equilibrium is no guarantee of being a 'logical solution' to the game.

Conditional rationality says that whenever a player i takes the actions of all other players as given and has to perform one of two mutually exclusive actions a_{i1} and a_{i2}, such that a_{i1} leads to a payoff p_{i1} and a_{i2} leads to a payoff p_{i2}, and $p_{i2} \geq p_{i1}$, the player will choose

a_{i2}. Formally, let us interpret the following symbols as follows:

a_{-i} :	a combination of actions of all players except i
$p_{ij}(a_{-i})$:	action j's payoff to player i, given a_{-i}

Then conditional rationality can be formally expressed as follows:

$$\text{(CR)}\ [a_{-i} \ \&\ (a_{i1} \vee a_{i2}) \ \&\ \sim(a_{i1} \ \&\ a_{i2}) \ \&\ (p_{i2}(a_{-i}) \geq p_{i1}(a_{-i}))] \dashrightarrow a_{i2}.$$

CR and UR coincide whenever the rational solution to an individual's decision problem is independent of the solution to the other individuals' decision problems. Without such independence, individual rationality (plus a specification of the game and the common knowledge assumption) is not sufficient to infer the behavior of the players in a normal form game. Individual rationality says that a player will follow the principle of expected utility maximization, but if UR is not defined, CR alone cannot predict which joint outcome will result from players' choices.

To predict the occurrence of a particular equilibrium, we need a theory of the individuals that, interacting, aim at it. Unless we can explain by decision theoretic principles alone, that is, by a theory of individual decision making processes, why an equilibrium strategy is chosen, we cannot be certain that an equilibrium, when it exists, will be attained by the players. Conditional rationality guarantees that, whenever there is a solution to a game, that solution will be an equilibrium; this is because the solution is a strategy combination that the players can rationally use and expect others to use. But unless some constraints are set on players' expectations, the existence of an equilibrium is only necessary, not sufficient, to infer the behavior of rational players.

RATIONALIZABLE CHOICES

What does it mean to say that UR is not defined? There are several ways in which this can happen. A player may not know the payoffs, or be uncertain as to the possible strategies to choose. The case of interest here, however, is another: when the expected payoff of a given action depends upon the choice of another player, and this choice is unpredictable, expected utility maximization involves arbitrary choices. In the previous examples, weak (and strict) dominance enabled the players to infer each other's expectations (or to do away with them), while its absence led them into an infinite regress of expectations and to an arbitrary choice.

Two objections might be raised to this account. One is to claim that in all those cases in which there is a *unique* equilibrium, playing the equilibrium strategy is the 'logical' mode of behavior for a rational player. Another objection argues that there might be other ways—besides dominance—to get to infer other players' beliefs and thus their choices. I shall consider this second objection first.

It has been argued that—even when multiple equilibria are present—there is no need of a dominance criterion to decide that one of them is 'more logical' than the others. Criteria such as *Pareto optimality* and *salience* would be sufficient to isolate one equilibrium as 'the obvious choice' for both players. Consider the next two games; both have multiple equilibria that embody those criteria and are generally thought to have a solution that is 'more logical' than the others. But in both cases, since unconditional rationality is undefined, the players cannot predict each other's behavior. Consequently, there is no good reason to favor one equilibrium strategy over the others.

G4

		Col	
		L	R
Row	T	9,9	0,8
	B	8,0	8,8

Of the two pure strategy equilibria, Bottom-Right and Top-Left (T,L) is the most attractive for both players, since it guarantees each of them a payoff of 9, which is better than (8, 8). Since (T,L) is Pareto optimal, should the players expect one another to play it? In order to answer, let us follow the reasoning of Row (which is symmetrical to that of Col), remembering that both the structure of the game and their mutual rationality are common knowledge among the players.

Row may thus reason: "Since Col is rational, she will want to maximize her expected utility, given her beliefs about my strategy choice. She knows that I am equally rational, so she certainly expects me to choose the strategy that maximizes my expected utility, given my beliefs about her choice. She will choose Left only if she expects me to choose Top, but the only reason why I would choose Top is my expectation that she will choose Left. How can I be sure she will play Left? How can she be sure I will play Top?" That (T,L) is the equilibrium with greater payoffs for both players does not make it individually rational to choose it, unless one is sure enough the other player is playing it, too. Unconditional rationality is undefined, since one cannot find an *independent reason* for the other player to pick a given strategy.

This reasoning may seem counterintuitive, since in game G4 one would expect the players to have no trouble in coordinating their expectations at the best equilibrium point (T,L). To be of any use, this intuition should be captured by the formal model of the game as a description of the knowledge possessed by the players. If it were common knowledge that equilibrium points with greater payoffs for all players are preferred in equilibrium selection, then coordination of expectations would follow.

Another reason for the common knowledge specification is that in games like G4 other reasonable conjectures are possible. For example, an equilibrium may have better payoffs for both players, but be riskier than another equilibrium.[16] Indeed, the equilibrium (B,R) risk-dominates (T,L), in that for either player to choose the strategy associated with equilibrium (T,L) is a much riskier choice than to choose the strategy associated with equilibrium (B,R). For in choosing Top (respectively, Left) a player risks obtaining a zero payoff; while if the player chooses Bottom (respectively, Right) he/she player cannot obtain less than 8. There is then good reason to expect the players to lend some weight to this factor in forming their subjective probabilities on the other player's behavior. Since the game is symmetrical, we may just consider the reasoning of Row.

First, Row has to consider the losses incurred if he deviates from either equilibrium point. In Row's case, a deviation from (T,L) involves a loss of 1 (9 - 8), and a deviation from (B,R) involves a loss of 8 (8 - 0). Let us call these losses, respectively, a and b. Row will choose Top if the probability p of Col playing Left is such that $9p \geq 8p + 8(1 - p)$. If instead p is such that $8p + 8(1 - p) \geq 9p$, he will select Bottom; then Bottom is a best reply if Row thinks that Col may shift to Right with probability greater than 1/9, and Top is a best reply if he thinks that Col may shift to Left with a probability larger than 8/9. Col can easily replicate Row's reasoning, but all he knows as to the value of p is that it must be equal or greater than b/(a + b) for Row to play Top. Unless Row's and Col's probability assignments are common knowledge among them, there is no reason to expect coordination of expectations and convergence to an equilibrium.

Pareto optimality can be thought of as a special case of salience. Simply stated, anything focussing the players' attention on one particular equilibrium may create a situation in which all players expect this equilibrium to occur and thus implement it.[17] Qualitative features that make an equilibrium unique, symmetry or equity considerations are all examples of salience. The following is a typical case where a salience argument would be used to predict the choice of an equilibrium:

G5		Col L	Col C	Col R
	T	2,2	0,0	0,0
Row	M	0,0	1,1	0,0
	B	0,0	0,0	2,2

Among the three equilibria Top-Left, Medium-Center, and Bottom-Right, only (M, C) calls itself to our attention, by virtue of being different from the others. Experimental evidence shows that if this type of game is repeated over and over by the same players, there will be convergence to one of the equilibria (not necessarily MediumCenter), plausibly due to learning and adaptation.[18] But if the game is one-shot, nothing in its structure gives us reason to expect the players to see (M, C) as a 'focal point'. Even if Row sees (M, C) as salient, he has no reason to believe Col to think likewise. And even if he knew that Col considers equilibrium (M, C) special, this would not be a sufficient reason to play it, since unless common knowledge that both players consider (M, C) salient is assumed, one cannot be sure that the other player expects him to do his part in that equilibrium.

What about games that have a *unique* solution? In this case, it may seem that the equilibrium solution is the only logical outcome, and that this fact is so obvious to the players as to induce them to choose it. But consider the following game:

G6

		Col		
		L	C	R
	T	10,4	4,-1	4,-1
Row	M	2,1	5,-2	2,2
	B	2,1	3,2	5,0

Here, a dominance argument cannot be used, since there is no strictly or weakly dominant strategy for any of the players. Note that Top-Left is the unique equilibrium in pure strategies, and has the attractive feature of being the outcome that guarantees each player the highest payoff in the game. How are the players reasoning to that solution? If Row were to expect Col to choose Left with probability 1, then her best reply would be Top, and vice versa if Col were to expect Row to pick Top with probability 1, then his best reply would be Left. This only establishes that (T, L) is a Nash equilibrium; it does not tell why a player should assign probability 1 to the other's equilibrium strategy.

A further element in players' reasoning needs emphasizing: if Row assigns a probability equal (or very close) to 1 to Left being played, one way to justify her belief is to show it is not inconsistent with a putative belief of Col that justifies his choice of Left. Then, if Row believes that Col will play Left with probability 1, Row must also believe that Col expects Row to play Top with probability 1 (since, by assumption, Col is rational), and believe that Col believes that Row expects Col to play Left with probability 1 and so on. One's beliefs about the other player's choice and the beliefs supporting it must be *consistent* with each other.

Is belief consistency a feature characteristic of the solution only? Note that belief consistency does not refer to the players' *actual* beliefs, but only to the players' beliefs as they are *conjectured* by another player. For example, suppose that in game G6, Row believes that Col will play C with probability 1. Then, she must also believe that Col assigns probability 1 to Row choosing B, since C is only a best reply to B, and Col is known to be rational. But Col must then also believe that Row expects R to be chosen with probability 1, since B is only a best reply to R, and Row is known to be rational. Then, Col also believes that Row believes R is played with probability 1, because Row believes that Col expects her to choose M with probability 1, a choice in turn justified by Row's belief that Col plays C with probability 1.

The original conjecture of Row is perfectly consistent with the beliefs she attributes to Col in order to justify her expectation that Col picks C. More generally, an *internally consistent* conjecture can be defined as follows: if player i has a belief about player j, then he must believe his belief is among the possible beliefs which j has about i himself.[19] But a consistency criterion of belief rationality, though necessary, is not sufficient to select an equilibrium, in that it allows one to 'rationalize' choices that are not equilibrium ones.[20] In the above example, Row will end up choosing M, which is not an equilibrium strategy.

Thus far, we have established that conditional and unconditional rationality need not coincide. When they do not, a game may have one or even multiple equilibria, yet have no 'logical solution'. The weakness of a notion of conditional rationality becomes even more apparent when an action that is conditionally rational turns out to be unconditionally irrational. This means that an equilibrium strategy may involve an irrational move on the part of a player.

Consider again game G2. In this game, since Robinson has a weakly dominant strategy I, he will surely choose it, since I guarantees him a payoff of 2 (which is better than 1) in case Friday plays L, and if Friday chooses I instead, I guarantees Robinson as much as L. For Friday, in turn, it is enough to know that Robinson is rational to expect him to choose I with probability 1. Therefore Friday will always choose L. The combination of strategies (I, L) is the 'obvious' solution to the game, but it is not the unique equilibrium. Another equilibrium is (L, I), since if Friday believes that Robinson will choose L, then Friday's best reply is I, while if Robinson believes that Friday will choose I, then he will be indifferent between L and I, and so L is a best reply.

Is (L, I) a credible solution? Since it is always better for Robinson to choose I instead of L, there is no ambiguity over what each player *should expect* the other to do. It is irrational for Friday to expect Robinson to pick strategy L, since Robinson has no reason to believe that Friday expects him to play L and every reason to believe otherwise, and this should be obvious to both. Since conditional rationality only requires that the players' beliefs be consistent, both Nash equilibria in G2 are rationalizable, provided that a player's choice is a best reply to the other player's expected choice.

In order to identify and eliminate unreasonable equilibria, several refinements of the Nash equilibrium concept have been proposed. For example, it can be assumed that there is always a small probability that a player will make a mistake, which has the consequence that every strategy can be chosen with a positive probability. Then a Nash equilibrium is also a *perfect equilibrium* if it is stable with respect to small perturbations in the players' strategies, that is, if each player's equilibrium strategy is a best reply to the opponent's strategy and to some slight perturbation of that strategy.[21] Consider again game G2. Assume that for some unspecified reason the players have agreed to play equilibrium (L,I); if Robinson has a small doubt that Friday plays L (for example, even if Friday wants to pick I, his hand may 'tremble' with probability $\epsilon > 0$, so that he chooses L instead), then it is better for Robinson to switch to I. Since the same reasoning applies to Friday, neither of them will expect the other to keep the original agreement to play (L,I). Indeed, the only stable (perfect) equilibrium is (I,L).

The concept of perfect equilibrium, however, does not eliminate all intuitively unreasonable equilibria. Consider next an enlarged version of game G2, where each player has a further, strictly dominated strategy (D) available:

G2*

		Friday L	Friday I	Friday D
Robinson	L	1,1	4,2	-3,-3
Robinson	I	2,4	4,3	-5,-5
Robinson	D	-6,-6	-5,-5	-8,-8

There are still two Nash equilibria: (L,I) and (I,L). If the players agree to play equilibrium (L,I) and both expect mistake D to occur with greater probability than mistake I (respectively, L), then *also* (L,I) is a perfect equilibrium. But it seems odd that an equilibrium that is unreasonable under a set of circumstances becomes reasonable (perfect) when something as irrelevant as dominated strategies are added to the game. The problem seems to lie in the mistake probabilities. In game G2*, (L,I) is a perfect equilibrium only if the probability of mistake D is greater than the probability of another mistake. If the players are rational, however, they should try hard to prevent costly mistakes, and consequently they should never expect mistake D to occur with a greater probability than mistake L (respectively, I). The idea that rational players will make a more costly mistake with a smaller probability than a less costly one underlies the idea of *proper equilibrium.*[22] In the above game, if the players make mistakes in a rational way (I,L) is the only proper equilibrium.

Perfect and proper equilibrium are only two among several refinements of Nash equilibrium. In both cases, 'unreasonable' equilibria are ruled out by extending the definition of rationality to include the acknowledgment of possible mistakes and their costs. Note that both notions of perfect and proper equilibrium assume the players to have *common knowledge* of the appropriate definition of rationality, and to use this knowledge in selecting their equilibrium strategies.

In some games, common knowledge of perfectness or properness criteria entails common knowledge of beliefs on the part of the players. If beliefs are common knowledge, then it is common knowledge which strategies the players will follow, and unconditionally rational choices will be well defined. In other games multiplicity persists, pointing to the ad hoc nature of the refinements. Indeed, it might be questioned why a player who incurs costs in preventing costly mistakes would not altogether try to avoid mistakes, and whether an assumption of rationality is compatible with allowing the players to make mistakes.

SOCIAL PRACTICAL INFERENCES

Conditional rationality may thus involve irrational or indeterminate beliefs. In terms of predictability, the consequences are dismal. Since mutual beliefs are determinate only when conditional rationality is coupled with unconditional rationality, there are relatively few cases in which game theory can predict that a particular equilibrium will be played by rational players. To understand why prediction and justification need not coincide, let us replicate the practical syllogism that provides a player with a decisive reason for choosing a strategy.

For simplicity, the example is that of a two-person game, but the same reasoning can be easily extended to an n-person game. Also, the beliefs considered are non probabilistic, as admitting probabilistic beliefs would considerably complicate the picture.
Let us interpret the following symbols as follows:

(i) $a_{i1} \mid B_i b_{j2}$: i plays a_1 given the belief that j plays b_2

(ii) $B_i b_{j1}$: i believes that j plays b_1

(iii) $B_i (b_{j1} \mid B_j a_{i2})$: i believes that j plays b_1 given that j believes that i plays a_2

(iv) $B_i B_j a_{i1}$: i believes that j believes that i plays a_1 (loop belief).

Consider next the following game:

		j	
		b_1	b_2
i	a_1	1, 1	3, 2
	a_2	2, 3	2, 2

Each player has two strategies (a_1 and a_2 for player i, and b_1 and b_2 for player j). By assumption, the structure of the game and their mutual rationality are common knowledge among the players. A combination of strategies can be rationalized by reconstructing each player's practical inference which concludes in favor of doing his part in that strategy combination. For example, the equilibrium ($a_1 b_2$) can be rationalized as the outcome of a social practical inference whose components are the independent practical inferences of players i and j.

Player i's practical argument (Ai) can be thus depicted:

p_{i1} : $a_{i1} \mid B_i b_{j2}$ and $a_{i2} \mid B_i b_{j1}$ [i's conditional rationality]

p_{i2} : i knows $b_{j1} \mid B_j a_{i2}$ and $b_{j2} \mid B_j a_{i1}$ [j's conditional rationality]

p_{i3} : $B_i B_j a_{i1}$

---

c_i : i plays a_1

Similarly, j's practical argument (A_j) is the following:

p_{j1} : $b_{j1} \mid B_j a_{i2}$ and $b_{j2} \mid B_j a_{i1}$ [j's conditional rationality]

p_{j2} : j knows that $a_{i1} \mid B_i b_{j2}$ and $a_{i2} \mid B_i b_{j1}$ [i's conditional rationality]

p_{j3} : $B_j B_i b_{j2}$

---

c_j : j plays b_2

Since by assumption, players' rationality is common knowledge among them, premises p_{i1}, p_{i2}, p_{j1}, p_{j2} are common knowledge, too. A crucial premise in both arguments is each player's belief about the other player's conjecture about his own choice. Take player i's belief that j believes that i plays a_1. Since i knows that j is rational, he expects him to pick b_2, which is a best reply to a_1. $B_i B_j\ a_{i1}$ and $b_{j2} \mid B_j\ a_{i1}$ jointly entail $B_i b_{j2}$, which makes i conclude in favor of choosing strategy a_1

How are the *loop beliefs* that appear in premises p_{i3} and p_{j3} justified? The consistency criterion of belief rationality only requires that if one expects a player to choose a given strategy, one must not assign to that player beliefs incompatible with that choice. Thus, if $B_i B_j\ a_{i1}$, belief rationality requires that player i also believes that $B_j B_i\ b_{j2}$, and believes that $B_j B_i B_j\ a_{i1}$, and so on up to higher and higher levels of beliefs. Every new loop belief is justified both by common knowledge of rationality and by a further, higher level loop belief. But an infinite iteration of loop beliefs *can only rationalize the original loop belief*, hence, a player's choice, which may remain arbitrary and unpredictable as the original loop belief.

Indeed, suppose that, instead of p_{j3}, player j has a different loop belief p_{j3*}, namely $B_j B_i\ b_{j1}$. If so, player j's choice will be to play b_1, which is a rationalizable choice but *not* an equilibrium choice, since by assumption player i still believes $B_j\ a_{i1}$. Players' expectations are internally consistent, but they do not 'coordinate' in the right way, so their expectations about each other's behavior turn out to be wrong. The practical arguments A_i and A_j can jointly rationalize the equilibrium (a_1,b_2), but cannot by themselves allow one to predict that it will be attained.

Note that the practical inferences underlying an equilibrium are both *interconnected*, because each player's choice is conditional upon his expectation about the other players' choices, and *self-fulfilling*. In other words, an equilibrium is supported by a configuration of consistent and self-fulfilling expectations.

This suggests a *stability condition* that beliefs must satisfy in order to support an equilibrium:

(C) If a player were to know the beliefs of the other players, he would have no reason to change his beliefs.

Condition C is not satisfied by the beliefs appearing in premises p_{j3*} and p_{i3}. If each player were to know the belief of the other, he would have reason to revise his conjecture. Premises p_{j3*} and p_{i3}, however, are in no way 'irrational', since the rationality criterion commonly assumed in game theory does not impose any constraint upon beliefs besides consistency.

Game theory takes expectations to be endogenous, in that they are based on factors internal to the game. In the normal form description, common knowledge of the structure of the game and of their mutual rationality on the part of the players does not entail beliefs satisfying condition C. A solution consists in assuming the beliefs sup-porting a particular equilibrium are *common knowledge* among the players.[23] An assumption of common knowledge of beliefs, however, begs the question, since what needs to be explained is precisely *how* common knowledge of their mutual beliefs can arise among rational players.

Is common knowledge of beliefs always sufficient to predict equilibrium play? Consider the following game:[24]

		Col L	Col R
Row	T	0,0	0,-1
Row	B	1,0	-1,3

This game has a unique Nash equilibrium in mixed strategies. The equilibrium strategy of Col is (1/2 Left, 1/2 Right), and the equilibrium strategy of Row is (3/4 Top, 1/4 Bottom). The equilibrium yields both players a payoff of zero. If the prior beliefs are common knowledge, each player knows that, no matter what he does, he receives a payoff of zero. This means that it is common knowledge that no player has an incentive to play his equilibrium strategy, and consequently no player can predict what the other player will do.

What does all this mean for the plausibility of the Nash equilibrium concept? So far, we have established that in most normal form games, common knowledge of the structure of the game and of their mutual rationality does not allow the players to predict each other's strategy choices. Mutual beliefs play a crucial role, but a criterion of belief consistency can seldom lead to a prediction about the outcome of the game. The beliefs supporting an equilibrium are both internally consistent and self-fulfilling, but the information contained in the normal form description of a game does not tell how the players come to form such beliefs. It would be wrong, however, to conclude that the gap between individual rationality and collective outcomes is unbridgeable. The limitations of the normal form representation point to the importance of beliefs and the inadequacy of a consistency criterion of belief rationality. Stronger criteria of belief rationality may have to specify the ways in which players form and change their beliefs, and the natural environment for this analysis is the extensive form representation that describes players' knowledge and beliefs at every stage of the game.[25] Whether the extensive form description answers some of the problems presented here and, thus, provides a firmer foundation for Nash equilibrium is a subject that deserves further investigation.

NOTES

1. For an illuminating discussion of different kinds of irrationality, see A. Sen, "Rationality and Uncertainty", in L. Daboni et al. (eds.), *Recent Developments in the Foundations of Utility and Risk Theory* (Reidel, 1986), 3-25.

2. A well known experimental result that is inconsistent with rational choice theory is the preference reversal phenomenon. For a discussion of experimental evidence, see D. Grether and C. Plott, "Economic

Theory of Choice and the Preference Reversal Phenomenon," *American Economic Review* 69 (1979): 623-38.

3. At present, alternative models of choice are being developed and applied to different choice situations, but it is too early to tell the direction and magnitude of their implications for research in the social sciences. For a survey of alternative models of behavior toward risk, see M. Machina, "The Economic Theory of Individual Behavior toward Risk: Theory, Evidence and New Directions", Institute for Mathematical Studies in the Social Sciences Technical Report no. 433 (Stanford University, October 1983).

4. Jon Elster has discussed these and other cases of failures of rational choice models to yield unique predictions in his Introduction to J. Elster (ed.) *Rational Choice* (Blackwell, 1986).

5. This thesis has been expounded by Robert Lucas in "Adaptive Behavior and Economic Theory", in R. Hogarth and M. Reder (eds.) *Rational Choice. The Contrast between Economics and Psychology* (The University of Chicago Press, 1986).

6. Cf. J. Nash, "Non-cooperative Games," *Annals of Mathematics* 54 (1951): 286-295.

7. Cf. J. von Neumann and O. Morgenstern, *Theory of Games and Economic Behavior* (Princeton University Press, 1944).

8. It would be more correct to say that the conclusion of a practical syllogism is the intention to perform a given action, and not the action itself. In what follows, I equate intending to act with acting, assuming that there are no external or internal impediments to realizing one's intentions.

9. A good survey of the literature on refinements up to 1983 is E. van Damme, *Refinements of the Nash Equilibrium Concept* (Springer-Verlag, 1983).

10. On this point, see D. Davidson, *Essays on Actions and Events* (Oxford University Press, 1980).

11. Cf. B. de Finetti, "La prevision: ses lois logiques, ses sources subjectives," *Annales de l'Institut Henri Poincare* 7 (1937).

12. The iterated definition of common knowledge is due to David Lewis. Cf. D. Lewis, *Convention* (Harvard University Press, 1969).

13. For simplicity, I only consider pure strategies. Mixed strategies are randomizations over pure strategies, i.e., each pure strategy is played with a given probability.

14. For a discussion of these alternative choice criteria, cf. R. D. Luce and H. Raiffa, *Games and Decisions* (Wiley, 1957, ch. 13). Also, R. Radner and J. Marschak, A Note on Some Proposed Decision Criteria", in R. M. Thrall et al., *Decision Processes* (Wiley, 1954, 61-68).

15. The symbols 'v', '&', '~', ' ----->' read 'or', 'and', 'not', 'implies' respectively.

16. For a definition of risk dominance, see J. Harsanyi and R. Selten, *A General Theory of Equilibrium Selection in Games* (The MIT Press, 1988, ch. 3).

17. This has been called the 'focal point effect' by Thomas Schelling. Cf. T. C. Schelling, *The Strategy of Conflict* (Oxford University Press, 1960).

18. For experimental evidence on focal point equilibria in bargaining games, cf. A. Roth and F. Schoumaker, "Expectations and reputations in bargaining: an experimental study," *American Economic Review* 73 (1983): 362-72.

19. Cf. T. Tan and S. Werlang, "The Bayesian Foundations of Solution Concepts of Games," Working Paper 86-34 (University of Chicago, 1986).

20. The idea that beliefs can be consistent without being common knowledge is embodied in the concept of 'rationalizability' developed by David Pearce and Douglas Bernheim. Cf. D. Pearce, "Rationalizable Strategic Behavior and the Problem of Perfection", *Econometrica* 52 (1984): 1029-50. Also D. Bernheim, "Rationalizable Strategic

Behavior," *Econometrica* 52 (1984): 1007-28.

21. Cf. R. Selten, "Re-examination of the perfectness concept for equilibrium points in extensive games," *International Journal of Game Theory* 4 (1975): 25-55.

22. Cf. R. Myerson, "Refinements of the Nash equilibrium concept," *International Journal of Game Theory* 7 (1978): 73-80.

23. This solution has been proposed by Aumann, who assumes the prior subjective probability distributions are common knowledge among the players. Cf. R. Aumann, "Agreeing to Disagree," *The Annals of Statistics* 4 (1976): 1236-39, and "Correlated Equilibrium as an Expression of Bayesian Rationality," *Econometrica* 55 (1987): 1-18.

24. Cf. R. Aumann and M. Maschler, "Some thoughts on the minimax principle," *Management Science* 18 (1972): 54-63.

25. Stronger criteria of belief-rationality are introduced in C. Bicchieri, "Strategic Behavior and Counterfactuals", *Synthese* 7 (1988): 135-169. See also my "Counterfactuals and Backward Induction," *Philosophica* 44 (1989): 101-118.

COMMENTARY BY ALEX ROSENBERG

Bicchieri's chapter is an illuminating tour through some arresting puzzles in game theory. But it is sometimes difficult to keep in touch with the fundamental methodological position to which she is committed. In this commentary I grant the technical details and attempt to identify and focus for discussion the fundamental themes of her chapter. For it turns out that the methodological claims it makes need argument, at least within the philosophy of science, though they represent the accepted mores of economics and game theory.

Economics, Bicchieri tells us, "studies group phenomena and the behavior of social systems. Individual actions are important insofar as they contribute to system behavior."[1] This claim follows a hallowed tradition that goes back explicitly to the late 1930s, but no further.[2] For a discipline interested in individual behavior merely as a stepping stone to the study of systems, economics has certainly been unshakable in its claims about individuals, remarkably narrow minded in the sort of claims about choice that it will countenance, and endlessly inventive in its attempts to reconcile the existence of collective institutions with claims about individual behavior that apparently make these institutions inexplicable or at least surprising. Bicchieri's claim makes economic theory's interest in individual behavior inexplicable. If economic theory were interested in rational choice only as a "stepping stone," it would have long ago surrendered it as a stumbling block to theoretical advance.

A more plausible explanation for economic theory's fixation on rationality is that economists are, or ought to be, very seriously interested in individual behavior as well as system behavior. One obvious reason for this interest is that descriptions of individual behavior will not explain system behavior at all unless it has some claim to be accurate, correct, or true, at least to a reasonable approximation.

In fact, if this were not so, Bicchieri's concern with the problem of common knowledge would itself be groundless, or at any rate, little more than a curiosity for economists. After all, the common knowledge assumption is a claim about the epistemic status of each rational agent: For some proposition p, each agent knows that p, knows that each agent knows that p, knows that each agent knows that each agent knows that p. On the one hand, this assumption is patently false and even less defensible than other assumptions made about individual rationality. Transitivity and completeness of preference rankings are merely implausible claims about many individuals in many cases. Common knowledge is a false assumption about every one in all cases. On the other hand, if Bicchieri is correct, this uniformly false assumption is essential in the explanation of many different institutions "insofar as they take the rational point of view as their frame of analysis" (157).

Bicchieri's point seems to be that in spite of the dependence of explanation on individual rationality, there is a "gap between individual rationality assumptions and collective outcomes . . . [such] that *prediction* of particular configurations of actions requires additional assumptions about player's knowledge and beliefs" (160, emphasis added). The gap exists apparently because "prediction" requires that most collective outcomes be equilibria, and Nash equilibria at that: "In most games, that a particular combination of strategies is a Nash equilibrium is a necessary but not a sufficient condition for one to be able to predict it as the choice of rational agents" (158). One might cavil here at the incautiously chosen word "prediction"; by and large economic theorists who take Nash equilibrium seriously as an adequacy condition for the existence of a collective outcome, are interested in mathematical derivation, not empirical prediction.

In particular the additional assumption that she identifies as crucial to equilibrium derivations and thus to "predictions" are those that reflect common knowledge. "Common knowledge of each other's rationality . . . is a precondition for predictability . . ." (168).

Bicchieri writes of "additional premises." "Additional premises" here cannot mean above and beyond the assumption of perfect information under pure competition, since there is no ignorance presumed and so no scope for additional assumptions about further bits of knowledge. In pure competition, that is, markets with so many traders that no individual can affect the supply or the price by his own action, and in which there is perfect information, common knowledge is already available and is also gratuitous: the individuals act only as price takers and so need give no thought to the stratagems of others. Bicchieri, and others who have concerned themselves with common knowledge, may well note that it is just because the assumption of common knowledge is either superfluous, or implicitly covered in the complete information condition of the derivation of general equilibrium under perfect competition, that economic theory has been blind to it for so long.

On the other hand, economic theory has not been blind to other substantial departures from reality that perfect competition and perfect information make. And yet, it has remained confident of the relevance of its idealizations to reality in spite of these facts. Perhaps common knowledge is no more significant an omission for its purposes than other assumptions. Indeed, there is prima facie reason to think it is less serious an omission. One has only to introspect to know that we not only do not satisfy the common knowledge assumption, but the question of what other agents know about our own knowledge does not even occur to us, even when it should. By and large, individuals treat their economic choices as games against nature—par-ametric games—not strategic ones.

As such, the common knowledge assumption plays a rather anomalous role in the "explanation" of social outcomes. If Bicchieri is right, common knowledge is (a) essential to proving equilibrium in many cases, and (b) completely groundless as a claim about peoples' actual beliefs. The questions (a) and (b) raise are what sort of explanation game theory provides and how the goal of game-theoretical prediction can be attained, if an *essential* feature of each is an assumption known to be impossible of satisfaction. It's not just that predictions and explanations that appeal to rational choice by individuals, in fact, trade on false assumptions: all successful predictions and explanations in science presumably do so—science is fallible. But it turns out on Bicchieri's view that if we are going to explain and predict collective outcomes on the basis of rational choice, most of the time we must use an additional assumption about individuals that we know they cannot satisfy, even in principle. NO one can hold an infinite number of explicit occurrent beliefs.

The only way this argument could work, I think, is if we add as a *necessary* feature of *any* explanation or prediction of collective outcomes by game theory that it proceed by deriving an *equilibrium.* The reason is that the common knowledge assumption is itself only indispensable when the object of the theoretical investigation is to establish an equilibrium and perhaps also show that it is unique and stable. Much of Bicchieri's chapter is devoted to showing the trouble an absence of common knowledge makes for the derivation of equilibria, and in particular, Nash equilibria. Bicchieri comes close to saying that equilibria demonstrations are essential for prediction and explanation, though she does not realize that her view requires a stronger conclusion than she gives: "A solution concept applied to almost every area of economic theory, as well as to social choice, political science, sociology, biology, ethics and computer science, is that of *Nash equilibrium*" (157). No wonder this "solution concept" is ubiquitous. On her view it's methodologically required for explanation and prediction of the collective outcomes of rational choice.

So, there is a more important claim in Bicchieri's chapter than the claim that the common knowledge assumption is often required. There seems to be also the implicit claim that explaining and predicting collective outcomes, given rational choices, must always proceed via derivations of equilibrium. These are strong claims: on the one hand that rational choice explanation and prediction usually require common knowledge, on the other, that such explanations must always be equilibrium ones.

Are these claims too strong? I suspect that they are. To begin with, when proving equilibrium is not deemed to be necessary for explanation and prediction, it is pretty clear that common knowledge may not be required either. How much scope there is for explanations in economics, which do not involve equilibrium, is a controversial question. Those of us who hold that, in fact, the economy and collective institutions generally are not characterized by equilibrium have little need for the common knowledge assumption in any case.

But assume that equilibrium is essential to explanation and prediction and consider the requirement of common knowledge. As we know, the efficiency of many markets, competitive and otherwise, is often the product of rational choices by only a few traders. While the vast majority operate with what are misleadingly called "adaptive expectations"—that is, the expectation that the near term future will be more like the near term past than anything else—some few individuals employ "rational expectations." These are the ones that explicitly include some beliefs about the beliefs and principles of choice of others (but not indefinitely many iterations of these beliefs). By capitalizing on rational expectations, these individuals move markets in the directions that common knowledge would move them, albeit more slowly and fitfully. Here common knowledge does not obtain, though something like it and less widespread does among the arbitragers. And yet there are equilibria solutions, or at any rate, explanations and predictions that appeal to such solutions.

It is only in markets with a finite number of agents—small markets, ones characterized by oligopoly, for example, that beliefs about the beliefs of others, and their beliefs about ones' own knowledge, enters with devastating results for the derivation of unique stable equilibria. Now, this is a well-known problem, long ago diagnosed as due to problems of common knowledge, and it has long been acknowledged that economics has little to say about price and output strategy among oligopolists just because there is no Nash equilibrium strategy for the game in which they engage.

But is it reasonable to demand that rational choice explanation and prediction of collective outcomes proceed via the derivation of an equilibrium? One cheap argument for this conclusion is simply to define rational choice explanations and predictions as ones that proceed by deriving equilibria. Aside from the fact that it would beg some interesting questions, it is something of an embarrassment to this cheap argument that few, if any, predictions can be confidently credited to such derivations. Even the explanations are controversial; they are, in part at least, because they trade on the derivation of equilibrium. That is, at least some schools of economic methodology reject the requirement that we derive equilibria. They reject the existence of equilibria and yet claim to proceed from assumptions of rationality while purporting to explain economic phenomena. The most obvious example of such a view is the Austrian school. I hold no brief for this movement in economics, but its skepticism about the existence of equilibria is probably worth taking seriously. This, of course, naturally raises skeptical questions about the obligatory role of equilibrium derivations in economic explanations. In fact, Bicchieri may have inadvertently given the opponents of equilibrium a new and more powerful argument against the demand that economic explanation must advert to it, for her claim about the importance of a common knowledge assumption amounts almost to an impossibility proof against the existence of equilibria. For consider, in any market with finite numbers of agents, attaining equilibrium requires that each must take into account the strategies of others, up to the level of infinitely iterated common knowledge. Since this number of occurrent beliefs is impossible for any individual to attain, it follows that no stable equilibria are attainable either.

A comment on Bicchieri's chatper is not the occasion for a general inquiry into the role of equilibrium in economic theory, but this is the direction that her claims about the importance of common knowledge in the rational explanation and prediction of collective outcomes must lead her.

NOTES

1. "Two Kinds of Rationality." All page numbers in the text refer to this chapter.

2. See Sir John Hicks, *Value and Capital* (Oxford University Press, 1939, 76). Compare Wicksteed, *The Common Sense of Political Economy* (MacMillan, 1910), who insists that the domain of economic theory explicitly includes individual choice and its aggregate consequences.

COMMENTARY BY MAARTEN C. W. JANSSEN

Economics studies behaviour both at the individual (micro) level and at the system (macro) level. Textbook theories in economics, however, do not specify how the passage from individual to system behaviour is made. The problem is easily illustrated by considering a single market on which producers and consumers are acting. The agents on both sides of the market independently make choices of what to supply and demand. At this point the problem arises. Economic theory specifies the market (system) outcome only in the case where the individual choices are compatible. In textbook theories it remains unclear what happens at the system level when the individual choices are incompatible. The methodology of game theory requires, as Bicchieri rightly points out, that the system outcomes are specified for all the actions the individual agents can possibly take. It is from this perspective that I will comment on Bicchieri's chapter. I will take a simple example to illustrate more general observations about how rationality and equilibrium notions are used in game theory to construct a bridge over the gap between the individual and the system level.

AN EXAMPLE[1]

Let there be a single homogeneous market in which two firms set prices so as to maximize their profits. The price of firm *i* will be denoted by p_i. The firms have identical costs, which are given by a quadratic cost function, $c(q_i)=q_i^2$, where q_i is the production level of firm i. It is assumed that consumers buy the goods from the firm that is charging the lowest price. Should both firms charge the same price, they will sell the same number of products. The market price p, i.e., the price at which the goods are sold, is thus equal to the minimum of p_1 and p_2. Demand is given by $d(p)=8-p$.

The game is played as follows. The two firms simultaneously quote a price. To keep the game as simple as possible, it is assumed that firms can only choose a price of 4, 5, or 6 per unit. The minimum of those prices is determined and the demand for the goods follows. A firm has to satisfy all the demand for the product it is producing. Individual and total profits can then be calculated. The strategic form of the game is as follows:

		Firm 2		
		$p_2=4$	$p_2=5$	$p_2=6$
	pl=4	4, 4	0, 0	0, 0
Firm 1	$p_1=5$	0, 0	$5\frac{1}{4}$, $5\frac{1}{4}$	6, 0
	$p_1=6$	0, 0	0, 6	5, 5

One can see that there are two Nash equilibria in this game, namely (4,4) and (5,5), and that the strategy $p_i=6$ is weakly dominated by $p_i=5$, i=1,2. It is also clear that the system outcomes (market prices) are specified for all the actions the individual agents can possibly take and not only for equilibrium actions.

Questions I will focus on in the rest of this comment are some of the questions Bicchieri also discusses in her chapter, namely, can we explain and/or predict the market price (a system outcome) in this game, and if so, what is the structure of such an explanation or prediction? What is the role of rationality and equilibrium notions?

EXOGENOUS AND ENDOGENOUS INSTITUTIONS

Bicchieri claims that game theory "tries to explain the endogenous emergence of social structure, how institutions such as markets, prices . . . came about. The starting-point is never a given institution, but a set of rational individuals endowed with a given amount of information and a physical description of the situation in which they interact" (157)[2]. Let us consider this claim in the light of the above example.

How, in the example above, does a system outcome, such as the market price, come about? We have said that the firms simultaneously choose a price and that, subsequently, consumers buy from the firm that is charging the lowest price. If the firms charge the same price, demand is split up equally over the firms. These rules of the game are the setting in which firms have to make a decision. If we are able to predict which decision a firm takes, or if we are able to explain why a firm takes a certain decision, then we are also able to predict and/or explain the market price that emerges. This is so because the firms' decisions about their prices, together with the rules of the game, determine the market price. A discussion of the reasons a firm might have to quote a particular price is given in the next section. The question we have to consider in this section then is whether the rules of the game have to be interpreted as a physical description of the situation in which individual agents (firms) interact as Bicchieri thinks, whether they are the result of the decisions taken by individual agents, or whether they are exogenous institutions.

I think that a rule of the game can be any of the three possibilities given. The assumption that the firms have to decide simultaneously can be interpreted as a "physical description"; that consumers buy from the firm that is charging the lowest price can be interpreted as a consequence of consumers' rationality (although this step is not explicitly presented in the simple example above). However, the assumption that demand is split up equally over the two firms, if it happens that they charge the same price, should be regarded as an institutional assumption. It is not a "physical description," and with the assumptions we have made, it is also hard to interpret it as a consequence of rational behaviour on the part of the consumers.

So, I agree with Bicchieri when she says that some institutions are endogenously explained in a particular game. I disagree with her when she says that institutions are never among the exogenous variables (the givens) of a particular game. In fact, in game theory individual agents act in an institutional environment and together they produce (other) institutions. We have the following situation:

macro level institutions ↘ … ↗ other institutions

micro level individual behaviour

Coleman, a leading exponent of the rational choice school in sociology, has used a scheme like this to discuss the tenets of *methodological individualism* (MI).[3] MI does allow for "institutions as exogenous variables, what it does not allow is that "institutions explain institutions" without intervening individual behaviour. In fact, MI is at the core of game theory.

If one concentrates on the pure structure of the game (players, strategies, payoffs), as Bicchieri basically does, one easily neglects that individuals behave in an institutional environment. In the pure structure of the game, individual choices *seem* to be connected with the payoffs without interference of any rule. Looking at the example's story on which the normal form description is based, reveals, however, that the individual payoffs (profits) can only be determined in an indirect way in which the rules of the game play an important role.

RATIONALITY

In this section I deal with the reasons a firm might have for charging a particular price. In economics (and also in game theory) individual behaviour is understood in terms of the rationality notion. Bicchieri rightly makes a distinction between practical (or instrumental) and epistemic (or cognitive) rationality, because the issues involved are quite different.

Agents choose an action that is practically rational if that action is the best they can do given a certain expectation about the action the opponents will take. In the example, firm i is practically rational if it quotes a price of 4 when it expects the opponent to do the same and it quotes a price of 5 when it expects the opponent to quote a price of either 5 or 6. Implicitly, this assumes that firms know how the individual price quotes are transformed into market prices. Otherwise, how can the firms know their individual payoffs?

So, a practically rational firm chooses a price of either 4 or 5. Which price it actually chooses depends on its expectation of the price the other firm chooses. Epistemic rationality requires that an expectation about the other firm's behaviour is consistent with what the firm knows about the other firm. So, a firm can expect the other firm to choose a particular price only if that firm knows something about the other firm. In the example, however, the firms cannot figure out whether the other firm will choose a price of 4 or 5 even if they have common knowledge of the game and each other's practical rationality. So, even if we make strong assumptions about the knowledge firms possess, we cannot rule out either of the prices 4 or 5 on the basis of the imputation of practical and epistemic rationality to firms. Thus, there are four possible outcomes of the example: they both quote a price of 4 or 5, or one quotes a price of 4 and the other quotes a price of 5.

EQUILIBRIUM

What about Nash equilibrium? Is there any reasons to believe that one of the two Nash equilibria results in the example? I think there is none. To put it more plainly, I think that if there is reason to believe that a game (not only the example above, but any game) results in a Nash equilibrium, then it is *not* because it is a Nash equilibrium, but instead because of other properties that this Nash equilibrium (accidentally) possesses. Let us consider what Bicchieri has to say on the use of Nash equilibrium in game theory. There are two issues I want to focus upon: (1) the use of the Nash equilibrium notion to bridge the gap between individual choices and collective outcomes, and (2) the relation between Nash equilibrium and individual rationality.

Bicchieri argues that the way collective outcomes are deduced from the solutions to the decision problems of isolated agents "proceeds by assuming that the collective outcome will be a state of *equilibrium*" (164). My analysis of exogenous and endogenous institutions above is very different from this view. Collective outcomes, such as the market price in the example) are determined for every pair of individual choices. Individuals act in an institutional environment and usually it is assumed that they know this environment (see the previous section). An institution, and not the Nash equilibrium notion, transforms individual outcomes to collective outcomes. Instead, the Nash equilibrium notion is used to try to give a more determinate solution to the decision problems of the individual agents. (In the example, there are only two Nash equilibria, whereas there are four outcomes that are consistent with practical and epistemic rationality.) A Nash equilibrium is a particular configuration of individual choices. Even if we require that individual choices form a Nash equilibrium, there is still the problem of how the individual decisions are transformed into a collective outcome. In short, unlike Bicchieri I think that the Nash equilibrium does *not* bridge the gap between individual choices and collective outcomes.

The second issue is whether there is any rationale for focusing on Nash equilibria as the solution to the individual decision problems. Bicchieri is ambivalent on this issue. She says "the notion of equilibrium embodies the idea of individual rationality in an interactive context" (172), but also "unless we can explain by decision theoretic principles alone . . . why an equilibrium strategy is chosen, we cannot be certain that an equilibrium, when it exists, will be aimed at by the players" (174). I do not see what is meant by "embodies" in the first quote, but I do not want to quarrel about words. The issue can be put in a more simple way as follows. Either the structure of the game is such that the Nash equilibrium coincides with the solution of the individual decision problems or the Nash equilibrium imposes additional restrictions. In the first case, there is reason to believe that the game results in a Nash equilibrium, but it is because the Nash equilibrium is the solution to the individual decision problems and *not* because of some sacred properties of the Nash equilibrium notion itself. In the second case, there is no reason to believe that the game results in a Nash equilibrium and the additional restrictions are unjustified.

As a straightforward consequence of the above argument, there is no reason to look at the refinements of Nash equilibrium literature as closely as Bicchieri does. Of course, some Nash equilibria are patently unreasonable, but that is because the strategies that support these equilibria are unreasonable. A strategy is the outcome of the individual decision problem and an unreasonable strategy will not be chose by a rational agent. Accordingly, a strategy should be the basic notion in game theory and not Nash equilibrium.

PATTERN PREDICTION

This brings me to the last issue I want to discuss, which is whether game theory is able to yield explanations and/or predictions. In the previous section I have argued that a strategy should be the basic notion in game theory. Taking reasonable strategies, instead of equilibria as the basic notion, considerably weakens the predictive power of game theory (if there is any at all). In the example above we have seen that four outcomes are consistent with the imputation of practical and epistemic rationality to firms, whereas there are only two Nash equilibria. Nevertheless, I think that if there are two agents playing the game described in the example that we can predict that one of the four outcomes in the upper left corner will result.[4] No common knowledge assumption is needed to reach this conclusion.

The fact that in most games more than one outcome can result is due to the fact that the agents who play the game are often not able to figure out precisely what their opponents will do. The better that individual agents can predict the behaviour of their opponents, the more determinate the theorist's prediction can be. So, the more assumptions the theorist makes about the knowledge with which the agents in his game are endowed, the narrower the range of possible outcomes. The desire to give a unique prediction about the outcome of a certain game can lead to the imputation of knowledge agents usually do not possess. In a game, it is not important what the theorist knows, but instead it is important what *the agents who play the game know*. This requires a certain realism in the assumptions made. For example, an assumption about knowledge of rationality of other agents cannot be effective unless agents, in fact, *do* know that the others are rational. At the moment, the state of the art in game theory is such that most games (as the example given) are too abstract a representation of reality to satisfy this requirement. In this sense, game theory does not yield any empirical prediction.

NOTES

1. The example I will use throughout this comment is taken from M.C.W. Janssen, "The Alleged Necessity of Microfoundations," *Journal of Macroeconomics* 13 (1991): 619-39.

2. All page numbers in the text refer to Bicchieri's chapter, "Two Kinds of Rationality".

3. See, e.g., J. Coleman, "Social Theory, Social Research and a Theory of Action," *American Journal of Sociology* 91 (1986): 1309-35.

4. This can be regarded as a kind of pattern prediction in the sense of Hayek.

REPLY BY CRISTINA BICCHIERI

The individualistic paradigm in the social sciences amounts to a constraint on the explanation of collective phenomena. Explaining a social phenomenon means showing that it is the outcome of intentional actions, and that these actions are understandable in the light of the actors' circumstances. Within the individualistic paradigm, a central intellectual task is to account for the passage from the individual level to the systemic level. The perfectly competitive market of neoclassical economics is a good example of a successful transition. It starts with individuals endowed with utility functions, a set of goods, and a behavior principle stating that a person will act so as to maximize her expected utility under the constraint represented by her initial resources. The final outcome is a set of market-clearing prices. In order to derive an equilibrium, the theory has to assume that there are no externalities in production or consumption, that information flows freely, that there are no transaction costs, and that resources and commodities are perfectly mobile. These are institutional assumptions, and they are essential in deriving system behavior. Specification of the institutional environment is similarly essential in political and sociological derivations of collective outcomes: an election outcome, for example, is constrained by the decision rule adopted, as much as wage bargaining is constrained by custom and law. The individualistic paradigm does not deny the importance of specifying the institutional environment within which actions are performed. A given exogenous institution, however, acts as a constraint on choice and not as an explanatory variable in accounting for the emergence of social patterns or other institutions.

Whenever the outcome of an individual's action depends as much on him as on the actions of other individuals with whom he interacts, their activities display a strategic component, and thus fall within the definition of a game. Chess, elections, wage bargaining, market transactions, the arms race, and international negotiations are but a few examples of games. They differ in many respects, but are also similar in that all possess a strategic component. Once we strip away the details, we see that the agents involved face an abstract decision problem whose general structure does not change with the kind of interaction we study. What we call the 'structure of the game' specifies some set of constraints within which interaction takes place. I can easily agree with Janssen's claim that payoffs are determined "in an indirect way in which the rules of the game play an important role". This, however, does not mean that a player's choice is not directly determined by the expected payoffs. Take as an example the prisoners' dilemma. I think we all agree on the following: were the players allowed to enter into binding agreements, or if they shared a common honor code, their payoffs (and the outcome of the game) would be very different. In this case, too, the rules of the game can be interpreted as institutional assumptions that shape players' payoffs. Here it seems that Janssen is confusing two different points. If one asks why the players have such and such payoffs, where do they come from, then of course it makes sense to look at a host of things that may not be specified in the game structure. But the game theorist asks an altogether different question. Game theorists are interested in what a rational chooser should do given the constraints specified by the structure of the game. Within the specified environment, individual choices are a function of the payoffs and the expectations of a player, and the way in which payoffs are determined plays no direct role in those choices.

Contrary to what Janssen claims, I do not find puzzling how individual choices can produce a collective outcome in a game. In his example, a given market price is the result of players' rational calculations and a particular configuration of beliefs. But we have to be careful in distinguishing between a collective outcome, that is, the joint result of the individual choices of the players, and a solution to the game. When the firms make a choice, they generate a collective outcome that includes the quantity supplied, the market price and the firms' profits. Now suppose you are one of the two firms. At first, there are six possible outcomes available, but since you are rational and know your opponent is rational, too, you rule out $p_i = 6$. You are left with four outcomes, only two of which you are really interested in. They are (4,4) and (5.25,5.25). Your goal is not just that of choosing in a rational manner; you want your choice to 'coordinate' in the right way with that of the other firm so that you can make a profit. You want to make a very good guess as to the other's choice, and know that your opponent is likewise trying hard to figure you out. In this sense a solution to one's strategic problem is always a mutual solution, since none of the parties can solve his strategic problem without solving the other's at the same time. Evidently one's guess may be wrong, but in this case we cannot say that a solution to the strategic problem has been achieved.

Is there a pair of expectations regarding each other's choice that leads each player to act in such a way that the resulting pair of strategies confirms those expectations? Yes, if firm 1 expects the other to set the price at 4, firm 1 will choose $p_1 = 4$, too, and if firm 2 expects 1 to set the price at 4, its choice will be $p_2 = 4$. The same can be said for the pair of expectations 'firm 1 chooses $p_1 = 5$, firm 2 chooses $p_2 = 5$'. In both cases, the joint outcome will satisfy both players. So Janssen's game has two solutions, or two Nash equilibria, which are combinations of actions that have the property that if both players make their corresponding choices—each expecting the other to do so—each has behaved correctly in accordance with his expectations and each has confirmed the opponent's expectations. In this sense, I say that Nash equilibrium embodies the idea of individual rationality: in equilibrium, a player's strategy maximizes her expected utility against the opponent's choice and, furthermore, she is not misperceiving the situation she is in since her expectations are correct. Short of assuming that players come to the game with correct expectations about the opponent's play, one has to figure out what goes on in the mind of the other players. This involves modeling the deliberative process that leads a player to play a Nash strategy. In this light—and since the basic condition for Nash equilibrium is that players are quite certain of how opponents will act—an important question becomes whether the information available to each player is sufficient to form correct expectations. I must hasten to add that there are lots of circumstances that resolve strategic uncertainty: preplay negotiation is one, another is past experience with the same game or some similar one, yet another is the existence of social conventions that make one equilibrium particularly conspicuous.

Game theorists are accustomed to identify, in any given game, a Nash equilibrium as the solution and to predict that the players will do their part in that equilibrium. But then they are implicitly assuming that there is an 'obvious' way to play the game; as I have made clear in my paper, this practice is not always justified, at least in the normal form. In Janssen's example many game theorists would argue that since one of the equilibria is Pareto-efficient, the players can be expected to play it. I can see how, in a real economic setting, the parties may have come to expect each other to play their part in the best equilibrium, either because of repeated interaction with the same party, or because each knows how the opponent has behaved in the past in similar circumstances. But if we stick to the normal form representation, we have a one-shot game without past or future, and the information provided by the model is not enough to infer that setting the price equal to 5 is the predictable choice.

I believe that a complete theory of the game should provide a purely logical deduction of equilibria from endogeneous, explicitly formulated premises. But for many normal form games, the usual rationality and knowledge assumptions are not strong enough to reason to an equilibrium in a rigorous way. Aside from those cases in which players have dominant strategies, often, there is no 'obvious' way to play the game. In these circumstances, Nash equilibrium may not have any particular claim on us, but the situation is reversed if we allow retrospection, repetition, or preplay communication. Dominance, preplay communications and focal points are but different ways to ground players' beliefs on some piece of mutual evidence. Of the three strategies, only dominance relies on information provided by the game, whereas the other two depend upon factors such as communication and shared perceptions of what appears to be conspicuous in a given setting, that lay outside the scope of game theory. An alternative way of bridging the gap between Nash equilibrium and the usual game-theoretic premises is to modify those premises and the notion of rationality in particular. For example, if a rational player, besides being an expected utility maximizer, is also understood to be a cautious player, then he should avoid playing weakly dominated strategies and, consequently, should not be believed to play them by an opponent who knows he is rational in the appropriate sense. This broader definition of rationality serves as evidence in forming players' expectations about what rational opponents will do, so players' beliefs are further constrained by the requirement that they cohere with a more encompassing view of how rational players act. This, I believe, is the rationale behind much of the refinement literature. A good reason to take it seriously is that it is a serious attempt to state what kind of endogenous evidence a player may plausibly have that elicits the right kind of belief. To summarize: in Janssen's example, a given outcome is the result of the firms' rational calculations and beliefs. In this sense, I see no gap between individual choices and collective outcomes. Where the gap may lie is between individual choices and Nash equilibria. The important question thus becomes whether it makes sense always to expect players to play a Nash equilibrium, and we have seen that the answer depends on the circumstances of play.

In spite of setting up a straw man, Rosenberg's commentary calls attention to similar difficulties with the justification of Nash equilibrium. The straw man he sets up is a single, undifferentiated game theory; whereas, distinctions should be made concerning the representational form of the game, whether the game is one-shot or repeated, and the informational constraints one wishes to set up. For example, the common knowledge requirement is not always necessary to infer a Nash equilibrium, and there are games—such as finitely repeated games of perfect and complete information—where the classical backward induction solution depends upon assuming only limited knowledge on the part of the players. Furthermore, even in normal form games of complete information, common knowledge is not necessary to *prove* that there exists a Nash equilibrium. Throughout his commentary, Rosenberg keeps confusing existence and occurrence of Nash equilibrium: Nash equilibrium is a well defined object that always exists in finite games with mixed strategies. Another question is whether the players in any particular game will converge to a Nash equilibrium; only in this respect may common knowledge may be necessary.

The issue of convergence—and the deliberative process that leads a player to play a Nash strategy—is only important if one is interested in the predictive significance of equilibrium points, something that Rosenberg has doubts about. Equilibrium analysis is not always relevant. There are games such as chess in which it is impossible to compute the Nash equilibria, others in which there is no evident way to play, others yet in which the strategy space behaves so badly as to make equilibrium analysis useless. Yet, there are many other areas, such as monopolistic behavior, entry deterrence, oligopolistic markets and arms races, to name a few, in which game theory is successful at modeling real phenomena and equilibrium analysis provides qualitative predictions. In general, equilibrium analysis works best when there is reason to believe that evolution or education have 'rationalized' the parties. Thus, an interesting question to ask is how do players behave when equilibrium analysis is misplaced. For example, how should one model players that start out with 'wrong' expectations and learn from experience? How should one represent agents that are only boundedly rational and have limited computational capabilities? These are important and challenging questions, and much of the recent literature on game theory is devoted to answering them. One should not conclude, however, that the idealizations of perfect rationality, unlimited calculation capability, common knowledge, and the like, are useless burdens that should be promptly abandoned in favor of more realistic pictures of agents' behavior. If used with care, they can help us understand the behavior of real people. The proper test of those 'unrealistic' models is whether the economic/social/political analyses that use game theory as an analytical tool do improve our understanding of the phenomena under scrutiny. And this is an empirical, not a philosophical question.

III. Discourse, Gender and Doing

CHAPTER 5

DECONSTRUCTION, RHETORIC, AND ECONOMICS

Jane Rossetti

DECONSTRUCTION, RHETORIC, AND ECONOMICS

Some economists have recently started paying attention to the way we write and talk about economics. With this shift has come either a de-emphasis, or rejection, of economics as "scientific" or "objective". This in turn has other economists dismayed, at best, and uncertain what this means for the discipline. This chapter will explain one literary approach (deconstruction) to reading economics, compare it to externalist readings of the history of economics and to McCloskey's rhetorical approach, and draw out some implications for how we do the history of economic thought.

What is deconstruction? It is a poststructuralist, or antifoundationalist school of literary theory, that argues that "objective" or "true" foundations of knowledge are impossible to attain (thus the label, antifoundationalist). This argument is rooted in an understanding of language and the meaning it conveys as being completely and unavoidably context-dependent. We are always trapped within some context; we can never step outside of it to attain an objective basis for our thought and our models.

This way of thinking is opposed to transcendental phenomenology wherein language contains some (recoverable) objective meaning.[1] There, the individual consciousness is seen as the center of meaning. Meaning has at its base an intentional or ideal object, formed without, and prior to, language. The individual intends his world, creates it, and communicates it via language that is an expression of this true inner meaning. Language fixes meaning, which is independent of the language.

Consider an example. You contemplate a rock whose physical existence you do not doubt. It has a set of qualities. It is an inanimate, mineral, hard object. These are attributes the rock owns in the sense that they are not *ascribed* to the rock, but they *are* the rock, its essence or its presence. This presence, the essence of rockness, is experienced in an unadulterated, pure, almost transcendental form, unmediated by language or thought.

At some point, language becomes necessary; we want to talk about a rock without having to point at it. So we develop a sign to stand in for the actual rock. The word "rock" captures, with no distortion, the presence of the rock and is what Jacques Derrida will later call the "deferred presence" of the object. The substitution of the word for the object is secondary to the original presence of the object. This means that when "rock" appears in a text, its meaning is self-evident, self-contained. The context is irrelevant. The rock's essence is immutable; therefore the meaning of the sign is fixed. The same argument is extended to concepts. They have an essence that is conveyed by language. The meaning is in the word and is context-independent. Thus, words and language are capable of conveying meanings that do not require any interpretation on the part of the reader. Words have a literal meaning, and texts[2] contain true discoverable, stable meaning. The meaning of the literary work, written or spoken, is fixed and identical to "the mental object the author had in mind." (Eagleton, 1983, 67) Thus, the meaning[3] of a literary work is identical to the author's intent at the time of its writing.

The philosophical attacks on transcendental phenomenology and authorial intent are rooted in the work of Heidegger and Wittgenstein, among others. These works argue that

> meaning is not simply something 'expressed' or 'reflected' in language: it is actually *produced* by it. It is not as though we have meanings, or experiences, which we then proceed to cloak with words; we can only have the meanings and experiences in the first place because we have a language to have them in. (Eagleton, 60)[4]

The theory of language as a pure representation of intended meaning was also being attacked from the linguistic camp by Ferdinand de Saussure. He argued that signifiers (words) had meaning not because they somehow produced a sign for an essence or intent (the signified), but only because they differed from all other signifiers. He conceived of language as a systematic differing between signs, one with a "neat symmetrical unity between one signifier and one signified" (Eagleton, 127) so that the system is stable in its set of differences.

Structuralism emerged from Saussurean linguistics and semiotics, the systematic study of signs. With Saussure's idea of language as a synchronic (self-contained or "autonomous")[5] system, texts could be analyzed without reference to the intent of the writer or to its own context. The signs are disconnected from the world outside their text and gain meaning only from their relationship with the other signs within the text.

The structuralist critics of the late 1950s and 1960s believed that the relationships between individual signs[6] reflected the objective laws governing their use and impact. The signs could be categorized, relationships typified, and the laws governing the building of meaningless blocks into meaningful sentences and narratives discovered. By assumption, the system is stable, and the rules held to be unchangeable, universal, 'embedded in a collective mind which transcended any particular culture...'(Eagleton, 109) Structuralists tried to formulate a purely objective reading of works (criticism) based on identifying and articulating the relationships among signs. It was scientific, objective, and based on universal laws. Structuralism came under criticism from several quarters,[7] but with Derrida the criticisms coalesced into a new school of thought: poststructuralism.

DERRIDA AND POSTSTRUCTURALISM

Derrida's fundamental extension of Saussurean linguistics was to break the connection Saussure had retained between the signifier and the signified. Does a rock have an unmediated presence, a meaning before language? No, says Saussure, and Derrida agrees. It only has a set of characteristics ascribed to it. There is nothing everlasting about these descriptions. A rock need not always be conceptualized as inanimate. "Inanimate" makes sense only when we are working within a system of categories that differentiates between animate and inanimate; this system need not always exist.[8] What, then, is the essence of a rock? Is it an object? Is it inanimate? Is it dead? Its characteristics change across space, time and culture. It has no qualities that transcend all cultural (contextual) changes. It no longer has an essence, no longer has an unmediated presence. If an object has no presence, then a word cannot convey it. Only within some context would "rock" inform you of its deadness, it inanimateness, or its worth.

Derrida pushes the argument further. "Inanimate," like "rock," has no essence. Since it has no essence, no particular attribute that is always and everywhere understood, the word cannot tell us what "inanimate" is. Within contexts, it may have as many meanings as there are contexts. Within a particular context, "inanimate" is able to convey meaning, for it can tell us what it is *not*. It is not (for us) living or dead. Within a particular context, we can understand "inanimate" not because we grasp a true unalterable meaning, but because we understand what it is not, how "inanimate" differs from all other categories.

Derrida puts this idea as follows:

> The signified concept is never present in itself, in an adequate presence that would refer only to itself. Every concept is necessarily and essentially inscribed in a chain or a system, within which it refers to another and to other concepts, by the systematic play of differences.[9]

Meaning lies between all the words in their sum, in their negative sums, and cannot be finally and fully pinned down.[10] A word is the sum of a context-dependent set of negative qualities (differences), qualities it does not possess. The qualities themselves are not essences but are sums of yet other negative qualities. Meaning differs from other sets of differences. Words can have meaning only within a giant web of differences that connects and defines each word.

This can only occur in a social context wherein we can understand the other concepts from which they differ. But just what *do* they differ from? They do not differ from a core of meaning, from a steady stable meaning. There is no core, no presence, no benchmark, no absolute from which they could vary.

Meaning is now completely context-dependent. It is only within the context that we know which differences are being called on, given importance. A word needs to be interpreted, placed inside its context, before its meaning can be grasped. As the context changes, the interpretation changes. New meaning is created by rearranging sets of differences. Meanings are dynamic. However, some ordering has to be brought to this continuously differentiating system. The ordering is done through the construction of categories (animate, living) that will recognize and codify specific differences. The categories are socially constructed, grouped around *chosen* characteristics that themselves are differences.

Derrida argues that in the construction of categories, some set of categories (natural, male, rational) is privileged over the others. These serve as referents. Other categories (artificial, female, emotional) serve as supplements, derivatives. A hierarchy is established. The world is organized and understood around the primary, the so-called "privileged" categories, so that, for example, what is natural or rational is considered the norm, the original or prior category. However, we know that the privileged categories have no absolute basis on which to claim privilege.

Once constructed, the categories appear to be organic to those living within the same context. This is not because they *are* organic categories, but because they reflect the world that they themselves have organized and created, the order imposed on the other groupings of differences. The hierarchy arranges sets of meanings, it categorizes and organizes our knowledge, and so our world and ourselves. Subsequently, the concepts appear to be basic to all life, everywhere. If we had built different categories, the organization of our knowledge, our world and ourselves would be quite different.

Deconstruction identifies the primitive organizing concepts and the hierarchy that relates them. It "locates not truth, but only the place where it was thought to be but cannot be." (Berman, 1988, 211) It levels the hierarchy by showing in the text that the primary categories necessarily refer to and contain the secondary (supplemental) categories and so cannot logically be considered prior to, or apart from, them. This must be the case, as the categories are only groupings of differences that necessarily refer to each and all other sets. The privilege previously attached to these "primary" characteristics or concepts, consequently, are revoked.

So, for example, the distinction natural/unnatural is shown to be an arbitrary, not prior, division of objects. "Natural" contains meaning only when it can represent differences from other states, when it can be compared to "unnatural." "Natural" could not be a concept prior to "unnatural" but can have meaning only symbiotically. This levels the hierarchy. The categories can exist only side by side.

Deconstructing the constructed hierarchies and categories reveals the intellectual and social frameworks within which the author works (and which is part of the author—see below). It reveals the categories and hierarchies the author employs and so reveals the system of values underlying the work. Although some words may appear to have a literal or absolute meaning, that illusion exists only because the context is so widely shared as to be unobservable. "Rock" may seem to *be* hard, inanimate, but such a thought misses the mark, by taking the context for granted. Outside such a context, "inanimate" cannot convey those distinctions, and what we considered its essence would evaporate. The concept itself, as well as the word that conveys that concept, are context-dependent, no matter how transparent that context may be.[11]

Deconstructive thought denies the possibility of independent consciousness. We have no available means of considering ourselves without recourse to language and its relative categories and differences. We are 'selves' only by virtue of the fact that we differ from others, who in their differing from us, define us. In this way we are created by our context, as we create it.

An author's thought and self are created by the differences and hierarchies in which she works, even as she helps create and define new categories. An author can not step outside the system of differences in order to choose the ones she prefers to employ. "Choice" is made within the significant constraints of the existing perceived sets of differences. The choices made will, perhaps, shift the web slightly, realigning or redefining some of the categories, but they cannot be made outside of the system.

Since our selves exist only within a certain structure, we cannot step outside of it to evaluate or judge its content, whether or not it is True. Its content defines us, is us; we cannot leave it behind to judge objectively or comprehend Truth. If somehow we were able (which we aren't) to disentangle our selves from this web, with each broken thread we would lose part of our being and ultimately cease to be. There is no space outside the differences from which we can objectively view the world.

Although there can be no essential self (no self outside some social context), the same does not hold for essential Truth. There may be Truth or God existing outside of and prior to the system of language and thought, absolute, complete in itself, free of the need for context. However, if this Truth does exist, it is not accessible by any of us via rational inquiry. We are barred from approaching or attaining this objective, unbiased, encompassing Truth precisely because we are unable to be objective.

Our Western notions of truth are tied up in its objectivity, that true statements are always and everywhere correct, that truth is complete explanation. We carry the notion that truth by its nature lies outside any perspectival bias. But once we begin to talk or think about truth, it necessarily is dragged into a relative discourse, losing its objective status. We cannot talk about truth without perverting what we consider its most important attribute. We do not have a meta-language in which we can talk about truth the way we desire.[12]

For the same reason that deconstruction denies essential selves, it denies the possibility of a definitive deconstruction. The process cannot logically ever end, because there is no available definiteness, no absolute. The deconstruction itself is presented in language, and hence carries within it the same troubles. Any deconstruction is by its very nature another construction. The critic cannot "claim the privilege of a critical meta-language." (Berman, 211) One text's categories are revealed only by implicitly comparing them to a different set of categories, those held by the deconstructor. The deconstructor is permanently lodged within the system albeit at a different place. Deconstructors have no choice but to bring their own interpretational angle to their work. A deconstruction is as legitimate to deconstruct as is any other text. The process has no logical end point.

To see how this approach differs from both externalist[13] histories of thought and from rhetorical analyses,[14] and what insights into the history of economic thought it may contribute, we look first at W.C. Mitchell's externalist histories of economics and identify the differences and similarities between them and deconstructive work, and then at McCloskey's work on rhetoric in economics to see what his method shares with deconstruction, where the analyses part company, and what deconstruction adds for the history of economic thought.

W.C. MITCHELL

In "On the Study of the Economic Classics," the first chapter of *Types of Economic Theory*,[15] Wesley Clair Mitchell argues that the course of development of economic theory is determined externally, that is, by forces outside the theoretical arena of the discipline. His basic argument is rather straightforward.

Economists are creatures of time, space, and particular contexts. They see problems particular to their situations. New problems are created by changes in economic organization and economic behavior of men. These changes in the world are the impetus for economists to change the focus of their attentions, to select and attempt to solve new problems, both by using old economic theories in new situations, and by developing new theories and techniques. Consequently the development of economic theory is essentially reactive and externally driven.

By looking back in time, we can trace how changes in context have resulted in changes in the approaches and conceptualizations of economics. From this standpoint, interest lies in

> the type of problems the man attacks, his way of formulating them, what materials he had to work with, the general method he employed, the things he took for granted without inquiry, the grounds for the confidence he felt in his results, what use he put these results to, their acceptance or rejection by his contemporaries and the reaction of his scientific work upon social processes. (Mitchell, 1967, 6-7)

That is, we must keep in mind the influence of the world around us. Study of the broader history of economic thought may bring forth other benefits as well:

> It should give us clearer insight into the conditions which promote or retard the progress of knowledge in the social sciences. Perhaps some at least among these conditions will prove to be amenable to control. Thus we may win knowledge which will help us to promote the growth of the social sciences. (Mitchell, 7)

That is, the history of economic thought can serve as a laboratory[16] in which we may be able to isolate and control certain conditions in order to promote its current development. This implies an ability to separate the discipline from its historical and political surroundings. This is at odds with the initial argument he makes that such a separation is not possible or desirable. He addresses the history-as-laboratory issue from a different tack when he speaks of the need to study economic history in order to "guard against accepting wrong forecasts." (Mitchell, 9) Mitchell's use of history as a method of testing theories is accompanied by a belief in the progress of economics and of its scientific nature.

Mitchell repeatedly turns to the theme of scientific progress and development of the discipline as a response to the externally posed problems. His representation of economics as a science in early stages of development, his defense of its progress, his hopes for its future (see esp. pages 9-12) are made, initially, without reference to external conditions. The solutions to the externally given problems at times appear to be internal, the stuff of which scientific progress is made. "What the world needs seems to be a development of the social sciences comparable to that of the natural sciences" (Mitchell, 12).

> The scientific worker accepts the principles of today as working hypotheses, which help toward making discoveries - discoveries which may lead to radical modifications of the principles and so to inquiries in new directions of which nobody dreams today. (12)

Economists-as-scientists

> will need to know accurately what their predecessors have done, how the subject stands today. They will need various technical skills in handling the tools of analyses. But they will accept all of this in a skeptical spirit - provisionally. And the skepticism will be nourished as an aid to constructive work. (12-13)

This is not the tone of a scientist understanding the relative and subjective nature of his work, only of a scientist being humbled by the acceptance that his beliefs are only hypotheses, not yet proved, but able to be proved.

Mitchell's argument shifts back and forth between an externalist and an internalist approach. He is struggling with the problem of retaining the scientific (objective) nature that he believed economics possessed, and was valuable, while underscoring the social (subjective) origins of the theory and science itself. The tension exists because to Mitchell "scientific" meant "objective," which is difficult to reconcile with the importance of context. The continued emphasis on science and scientific thinking, conflicting with the acknowledgment of the social nature of man and knowledge, persists through this chapter in Mitchell (see, for example, 29 -30). Two brief examples should make this tension apparent.

The solutions of the classical economists, for instance, contained definite conclusions and definite laws. The classical economists used externally generated problems to build and extend scientific, internal models. The response to the external problems is portrayed as being purely an internal, scientific development. And yet Mitchell is not comfortable with this separation. He warns us that:

> it must never be forgotten that the development of the social sciences [including economics] is still a social process. Recognition of that view...leads one to study these sciences.. [as] ..the product not merely of sober thinking but also subconscious wishing. (25-26)

His resolution, as far as it goes, is to acknowledge that these two strands "cannot be presented separately without falsification" (27), because the external conditions shed light on the direction of movement of the subject.

The difficulty reconciling objective science with social context is even more apparent in Mitchell's section on the marginal revolution. When the form of economics comes to resemble science more than philosophy, his analysis, too, comes to lean almost exclusively on 'scientific' and not social or philosophical developments. This chapter focuses on the biographies of the three central characters (Jevons, Menger, and Walras), the content of Jevons' theory, and the differences between Jevons, and Menger, and Walras. In discussing their works, he makes no mention of the advances in physics, of the burgeoning of the other natural sciences, of the appeal of 'scientificness', or of liberal philosophies. He traces the development of some of Jevons' ideas in earlier writers but makes almost no mention of any changes in the political or social or intellectual climate between their time and Jevons'.[17] Mitchell falls back to the internalist explanations that come so much more easily once the neoclassical period is reached.

Mitchell does not address directly, nor resolve, the contradictions involved in 'scientific thinking' being directed by political or cultural context. He has no resolution, except to incorporate knowledge of the history of economics back into economics, to accept external influences as important on the direction of scientific development and its usefulness both in providing valuable lessons in framing questions and in convincing economists to remain humble, not doctrinaire, in their work.

In comparison, a poststructuralist history might provide an argument about why economics is impossible to separate from the rest of the world, beyond observing that economists are indeed part of an external world and so, necessarily, influenced by it. Deconstruction is not telling externalist histories. It is an argument for why those are the only kind we could possibly tell. Deconstruction goes beyond externalist histories by showing that even within a text or theory externally situated, the theoretical basis can not claim an "objective" ground. It is an examination of the works themselves to reveal the influence of the world around the author in his theorizing, in his preconceptions, his structure of thought and the logic on which the framework of theory and practice is built. Mitchell is only seeing the most blatant kind of external influence, (the Corn Laws, population theory) not the subtler infusions, the changing presuppositions, definitions and methods of practice.

And, importantly, such a treatment would resolve Mitchell's quandary. Deconstruction does not provide space for any thinking or theorizing outside that resulting from one's immersion in all facets of life; it does not acknowledge 'scientific' thinking as being somehow pure and uninfected by social or philosophical beliefs. Deconstruction is not tied to finding a way to view economics as objective while continuing to claim importance for its social context. Here it offers a consistent approach to telling stories that incorporate science and context at the same time and remains unseduced by the apparent scientific and internal course of development which others have traced out from the 1870s, at least until Keynes. The internal/external contradiction is resolved by deconstruction. It is also resolved by McCloskey, albeit in a different manner, to which we now turn.

McCLOSKEY

McCloskey approaches several of the issues important in deconstruction in *The Rhetoric of Economics*. He identifies the failure of modernism as a methodology; he addresses the social nature of language; and he argues that the actual work of economists is one of persuasion, not proof. He argues for a rhetorical approach to evaluating economic theory on the basis that it is an "opening up" of the scope of arguments used in an effort to persuade.

In the chapters and sections that discuss methodology McCloskey treads a fine line around the question of the possibility of an objective social science. On one side he states explicitly "The much-discussed question of whether there can be a value-free social science will not be much discussed here. (5, fn.)" On the other he concludes:

> Modernism promises knowledge free from doubt, free from metaphysics, morals and personal convictions. What it is able to deliver...(is) the economic scientist's metaphysics, morals, and personal convictions. (16)

McCloskey leaves room for the reader to continue to believe in some sort of objectivity being possible, while arguing it is not important because it is not in fact what we do. What economists, among others, do is believe in a theory and then test it for support, not falsification, so that "the 'objectivity' of economics is exaggerated and what is more important, overrated." (36) McCloskey is either being very shrewd or just very pragmatic. He is willing to leave certain issues unresolved and unexamined. Objectivity is 'overrated'; not non-existent, or impossible. It just doesn't have relevance for what we do.

Once modernism is set aside, McCloskey turns to argue that following any one particular methodology is a rather foolish approach to research and knowledge.

> Methodology claims prescience in scientific affairs. The difficulty with prescience is that it is exactly 'pre-science'—that is, knowing things before they are known, contradicting itself. Methodology entails this contradiction. It pretends to know how to achieve knowledge before the knowledge to be achieved is in place. Life is not so easy. (53)

Therefore we should not limit ourselves to any one method but open ourselves up to good conversation. McCloskey rejects strict and dogmatic adherence to any one methodology as being 'blindered' (41), 'uniform though narrowing' (39). In any methodology's place he would put rhetoric, which he calls an antimethodology.

> Rhetoric does not claim to provide a new methodology, and therefore does not provide formulas for scientific advance. It does not believe that science advances by formula. It believes that science advances by healthy conversation, not adherence to a methodology. (174)

McCloskey also puts himself in an agnostic position vis-a-vis Truth. Whether or not Truth exists or is attainable is not a question McCloskey is interested in pursuing, since theories are not judged by their truth, but by whether or not they are "persuasive, interesting, useful, reasonable, appealing, acceptable." (47) Their truth is irrelevant, unimportant. This is again a pragmatic solution. McCloskey's stance isn't that we couldn't find truth if we wanted to, but that it is not what we want to do. We need not preoccupy ourselves with it.

Having separated research and argumentation from the search for truth, having shelved the issue of objectivity, and having posited research in a conversational, rhetorical setting, McCloskey can, and does, (see p. 51) separate himself and his rhetorical approach from an alliance with Foucault, Rorty and the literary critics, the anti-modernists. This done, he opens up what most economists (among others) regard as a can of worms, the question of appraisal.

How does one know when there is progress in the conversation? "One recognizes with ease when a conversation in one's own field is working well." (27) The standard of conversation comes from the practitioners within the field, including "editors, referees, and members of research panels." (28) McCloskey cites Mark Perlman's statement: "The essential methodological question is what does it take to convince oneself or others of the validity of an idea?" (35) It isn't the truth of the statement, but its validity that is in question, where validity is judged by the other practitioners.

McCloskey then shows how economists try to convince others of the validity of their work. He analyzes various economic writings to reveal the strategies, consciously or unconsciously used by a variety of authors, to persuade us to their point of view. In each case, he focuses on some strategy of persuasion, picks it out of the text, and traces through the work the technique of persuasion applied. Some of the emphasis is to show that despite the authors' words to the contrary, the argument being made is not in fact a modernist one but rather a persuasive one.

In analyzing significance tests, for instance, McCloskey points out that while standards for statistical significance are clear, standards for their economic significance or underlying norms are neither clear nor mentioned by the authors. The point is that looking at these tests with an eye to their rhetorical purpose, instead of a modernist mind, will lead us to consider and ask other questions. This is an example of the 'opening up' brought by rhetoric.

McCloskey hopes that by showing the strategies of persuasion, we will learn not to be led astray by modernist talk. We will be able to view the metaphors and significance tests as matters of persuasion, not science, opening up the field to other questions and issues that need to be addressed before we can be fully persuaded to accept the theory in question.

RHETORIC AND DECONSTRUCTION

Much of McCloskey's approach is quite similar to deconstruction. One similarity is the emphasis on the social nature of language and of categories. In the "Exordium," McCloskey tells us "the language used is a social object, and using language is a social act." (xvii) The emphasis on persuasion is an emphasis on the external context of the work, of language calling up images that help to persuade the reader. Throughout the book, McCloskey alludes to the social construction of categories[18] and the importance of discussion in establishing them. Categories are created and can be dismantled or redefined, as a post-structuralist would agree.

While the rejection of modernism is an obvious point of agreement, the reasoning behind the rejection is quite different. McCloskey's call is to reject modernism because it is not what we do, and further, to reject any methodology because it cannot guarantee success in constructing more persuasive accounts or models. His conviction that persuasion is the endpoint of research leaves him to observe that to drag Truth into the discussion serves no purpose. With persuasion the goal, the volume focusses on economists' literary techniques of persuasion, the methods and arguments marshalled to persuade us (the readers) to change or form our opinions, to accept the writer's point of view and conclusions. Since McCloskey's primary concern is with discourse, not ontology or epistemology, he is content to let the issue of whether or not we could ever do anything but persuade remain moot. McCloskey takes all his steps in a deconstructive direction but doesn't follow the road to the end, preferring to adopt a pragmatic and somewhat pluralist stance.

Poststructuralism takes the arguments further, maintaining that truth and objectivity are irrelevant because they are unattainable, and therefore, persuasion is all there ever could be. While this results in a stance similar to McCloskey's, the argument is quite different. The differences in the views of truth and rationality are reflected in the different goal of analyzing the texts. Deconstruction looks not for the techniques of persuasion but for the underlying premises on which the work is based.

McCloskey doesn't analyze why certain techniques are persuasive, a step Mirowski[19] takes. Mirowski not only examines economics in terms of physics' metaphors but comments on why such a metaphor is seen to be persuasive, why it worked. McCloskey's work pushes us in this direction, without convincingly arguing that it is the only way to understand the content and direction of progress of the (or any) discipline. McCloskey doesn't peer beneath them to analyze the fundamental categories to which the writers are trying to win us over. This is the point and the goal of deconstructive work and the major difference with respect to McCloskey's argument. Deconstruction looks beneath the text, yet further, to find what the major or privileged categories are, how they are ordered, what is the view of the world, and the chain of values that underlays and inhabits the work itself. What is the basic set (a basic set) of orderings, of contrasts and comparisons being made? These are issues that McCloskey does not address, which deconstruction does.

Deconstruction offers a wider framework, a different context, in which to understand McCloskey's work. While McCloskey argues that we are all, forever and always, engaged in conversation and so ought to pay attention to the forms the conversation takes, deconstructive thought reminds us that the conversation is, always and forever, a construction of beliefs and values, of a particular understanding of the world we create.

WHAT DOES THIS MEAN FOR ECONOMICS?

Viewing economics from a poststructuralist framework is a large change of viewpoint for most economists. The ramifications can at first seem overwhelming and threatening. The implications for economics and other disciplines rest primarily on the loss of any objective foundation for knowledge. For some, this is a great loss. First, it means that economic research is not progressing in any fashion, linear or otherwise, towards an Objective or True Understanding or Explanation of how the economy works, or even what the economy is. Such an understanding is unattainable because objectivity as well as Truth are unattainable (at least by rational means).

We also lose the notion of practicing "objective" economics. We construct theories and models from within a certain context we all share and which shapes us. Our models are drawn from a particular, although malleable, perspective. We create our economy and our understanding of it from within our social context. From that place we interpret and explain. Theories and models are judged and accepted on the basis of, as McCloskey puts it, how persuasive they are.

The idea that we judge theories on the grounds of their persuasiveness annoys most economists. We like to think of our work as scientific and as containing or at least promising, movement towards a more refined understanding of the economy. To say this movement depends on persuasiveness, on rhetoric, not scientific accomplishment, is unsettling.

But persuasiveness is not simply a question of which advocates have a stronger vocabulary or more compelling metaphors. Persuasiveness comes from the pervasiveness of the interpretational vision of the theorists; of how well their points of view accord with the existing stable, social perceptions and intellectual organization; of how well they represent institutional assumptions; or how cleverly they redefine, redraw, reinterpret (within strict limits) those assumptions. The cleverness or lucidity will be evaluated, as always, by the communities that share these institutions, vocabulary, and assumptions—what Stanley Fish calls "the interpretive community," and what Imre Lakatos refers to as "the scientific community." What we, as a group, find compelling and acceptable is viewed as progress.

This is not inviting chaos to rule over the discipline. Rather, this is recognizing that the control of method, content, and style that any discipline imposes upon itself is sociological, not the unavoidable result of that discipline's "true content." We all share fundamental categories and differences, structures and ways of thought, or we could never talk meaningfully to each other. Theories that do not incorporate the basic assumptions will have no impact, they may not be communicable, and they would not be acceptable. These are models that aren't "good." The community develops the standards and then is developed by way of those standards until a new view or value or measure develops.[20]

Deconstruction warns us against pursuing apparently internal, scientific or objective histories of economic thought. By deconstructing particular texts, we see that "internal forces" are merely "external" ones in disguise. It is no longer a question of whether we "believe," "think," or "conceive" (Mitchell's words) that external forces are important. We see that those forces are inseparable from and necessarily inhabit the very texts and theories. Their self-contained nature is illusory when the context is so shared as to be transparent. One strength of deconstruction is that it reveals this as illusion. Since deconstruction obliterates the logic of the in/external division, it also removes the ground for arguments over which was more important.

Deconstructive analyses incorporate both the belief that forces "external" to the theories themselves matter, and that language and persuasion are important in our academic/scientific undertakings. By removing the idea of an 'objective' language, deconstruction generally supports various types of literary analyses, including rhetoric and persuasion. Deconstruction, ironically, provides a foundation that is otherwise lacking for these arguments. While the arguments of Mitchell and McCloskey are consistent with a poststructuralist approach, the latter takes the argument further. An emphasis on language isn't only pragmatic (we currently persuade, but truth seeking and objectivity may be possible), it is all there ever could be (we are stuck in a social framework).

Deconstruction is a logical connection between "externalist" theories and rhetorical analysis. Language, investigated by rhetoricians, lies at the center of the structures of thought and theory, and is necessarily connected to all external, historical, and social conditions. But deconstruction does more than provide grounding for external and literary analysis; it differs from these approaches in its focus, even as it supports the general direction of their undertakings. Deconstructive work helps unearth the social and historical perspectives attached to the language and theory, predating the language and tying it to the external world.

This suggests that one ought not view economics as a science progressing towards a fixed point. It might encourage one to undertake the sort of work of which Foucault's *The Order of Things*[21] is an example, to look for fundamental categories, concepts and relationships organizing economic and other knowledge across time. The categories Foucault unearths (the subtitle of the book is *An Archeology of the Human Sciences*), are precisely the kinds of categories and groupings on which the deconstructionists focus. Of course, even then, Foucault's (as well as anyone else's) is only one story among many possible. Deconstruction gives us a different way to try and make sense of changes in economic theories and categories, methods of inquiry and types of models, as reflecting changes in the intellectual and social world. It gives us a new (albeit ever shifting) framework in which to view economics, one which can only be subjective but cannot be faulted for that. It puts economics back into the social world and out of what we would like to consider the "scientific" one. Since no deconstruction is ever final, it also provides us with the opportunity for ongoing, ever-changing, intriguing research and discourse.

NOTES

This chapter was written while the author was a Visiting Assistant Professor at Williams College. The author thanks E. Roy Weintraub, N. de Marchi, D. McCloskey, C. Goodwin for suggestions, for corrections and comments on earlier drafts, and acknowledges all remaining misstatements as purely her own.

1. For a more detailed discussion of the philosophical ideas and lineages, see Terry Eagleton, *Literary Theory: An Introduction* (University of Minnesota Press, 1983).

2. "Texts" should be understood to refer to both written and spoken communications; "talk" to include "write"; "word" to include both the written and spoken sign.

3. Hirsch differentiates the 'meaning' of a work, from its 'significance'. The meaning is identical to authorial intent and is fixed for all time, providing a bound to any interpretation. However, the

significance of the work, what people across time and space glean from it, may change. But this is not to be confused with its true meaning.

4. Gadamer recognized the implication that textual meanings change across time and cultures, that there was no sense in seeking to understand the text as it is, for it is created endlessly by particular interpretations of it. He, however, drew back from the extreme of allowing the meaning to remain so ephemeral by tying it to its place in the existing literary tradition. This conception lies behind hermeneutical emphasis on tradition, an emphasis that post-structuralist thought does not share.

5. See Art Berman, *From the New Criticism to Deconstruction* (University of Illinois Press, 1988, 116-23).

6. These relations may include similarities, oppositions, graphical, metrical, and phonological systems.

7. Bakhtin (who argued that language was caught up in 'definite social relationships' (Eagleton 1983, 122)) and Austin and Searle (who argued that language is, indeed, used to bring about certain effects, that is, intentions matter) among others.

8. Imagine a culture in which any naturally occurring form has a Spirit within; or one in which there is no distinction between dead and inanimate; or one, on an isolated sandy island, where rocks are used as a store of value.

9. Derrida, J. "Differance," translated by Alan Bass. In *Margins of Philosophy* (University of Chicago Press, 1982, 1-27, 11).

10. There is a further element of instability, a temporal aspect. Since meaning is not contained within a word, but only in its interplay with all other words, meaning is suspended or deferred, depending on what is to come and what has come before. This is what Derrida means by the *trace*. Each element (sign) "retains the mark of a past element and already lets itself be hollowed out by the mark of its relation to a future element." (Derrida, "Differance," 14). Or, in Eagleton's less opaque prose : "[F]or the words to compose some relatively coherent

meaning at all, each one of them must, so to speak, contain the trace of the ones which have gone before, and hold itself open to the trace of those which are coming after." (128)

11. To some extent, even physical objects are drawn into this relative morass. Physical reality may have an existence of its own, outside our thinking about it, but the way in which we think about it structures its meaning for us, its inhabitants. A tree that has a physical reality of its own has no independent meaning for us, for our understanding of the tree is colored by our social, religious, and economic, among other, beliefs. The same tree is something different for a lumberman than it is for a Shinto worshipper. While the tree has a physical existence of its own, its relationship to the human beings around it is context dependent. In this sense, the meaning of physical reality is relative and context dependent.

12. Truth can retain a possibility of existing outside this framework, unlike self, because we think of it as lying outside and prior to any prejudice or bias or perspective, of having an existence prior to language and context. This differs from the self in hermeneutical phenomenology, which is only called into being through language. Self could retain a prior status only by recourse to the existential phenomenology, which has a different philosophical lineage.

13. In presenting the works of those authors who discuss 'external' versus 'internal' histories, I will drop the quotation marks from around the words, only for ease of exposition. It should be borne in mind, however, that deconstruction does not recognize the distinction being drawn by these authors in the use of the words, and that my use of them without quotation marks is not to be interpreted as granting the idea legitimacy.

14. The differences between a deconstructive reading and an internalist (logic of development) presentation of the history of economic thought should be apparent. We will focus here on the externalist and rhetorical approaches.

15. Mitchell, W.C. *Types of Economic Theory.* Joseph Dorfman, ed. (Augustus M. Kelley Publishers, 1967). Two volumes.

16. Abraham Hirsch, in his dissertation, argued that Mitchell's work was grounded in a Deweyan pragmatism that suggested not only the importance of understanding "the practical context of the everyday experience *in which their thoughts developed*" (Hirsch, 9), but also in the belief that progress in any field required "a continuous process of ever new observation and the experimental test of ideas." (Hirsch, 9) The first chapter of *Types of Economic Theory* incorporates these two themes: the importance of social conditions and the use of history to test hypotheses.

17. The single contextual comment he makes is that "[Jevons' theory] came at a time when hedonistic psychology was being superseded by changed conceptions of human nature." (Mitchell, 84) This is further notable because he later goes on to explain that Jevons' theory was, in fact, based on hedonistic psychology, and as such, was discredited. The one reference to context here does not, in fact, help to explain the success of Jevons' theory, although it might shed some light on its origins.

18. See especially chapter 8.

19. Mirowski, (1987).

20. See Arjo Klamer's *Conversations with Economists* for instances of noncommunication between dissimilar contexts.

21. Foucault, M. *The Order of Things* (Random House, 1970).

REFERENCES

Azariadis, C. (1981), "A Reexamination of Natural Rate Theory," *American Economic Review*, 71 (December), 946-960.

Berman, A. (1988), *From the New Criticism to Deconstruction.* Urbana: University of Illinois Press.

Blaug, M. (1986), *Economic History and the History of Economics.* New York: New York University Press.

____________________. (1985), *Economic Theory in Retrospect.* Fourth Edition. New York: Cambridge University Press.

____________________. (1980), *The Methodology of Economics.* New York: Cambridge University Press.

Brunner, K., Cukierman, A. and Meltzer, A. (1980), "Stagflation, Persistent Unemployment and the Permanence of Economic Shocks," *Journal of Monetary Economics*, 6, 467-92.

Cherry, R., Clawson, P., and Dean, J. W. (1982), "Microfoundations of Macrorational Expectations Models," *Journal of Post-Keynesian Economics* 4 (Winter), 214-230.

Colander, D. C. and Guthrie, R. S. (1981), "Great Expectations: What the Dickens Do 'Rational Expectations' Mean?" *Journal of Post-Keynesian Economics*, 3 (Winter), 219-34.

Davidson, P. (1978), *Money and the Real World.* Second Edition. New York: MacMillan Press.

DeCanio, S. J. (1979), "Rational Expectations and Learning from Experience," *Quarterly Journal of Economics*, 93, 47-57.

Eagleton, T. (1983), *Literary Theory: An Introduction.* Minneapolis: University of Minnesota Press.

Foucault, M. (1970), *The Order of Things.* New York: Random House.

Frazer, W. J., Jr. (1978), "Evolutionary Economics, Rational Expectations, and Monetary Policy," *Journal of Economic Issues*, 12 (June), 343-72.

Garraty, J. A. (1978), *Unemployment in History*, New York: Harper and Row.

Hirsch, A., *Reconstruction in Economics; the Work of Wesley Claire Mitchell*, unpublished dissertation, Library of Congress, microfilm AC-1, no 58.2536.

Kantor, B. (1979), "Rational Expectations and Economic Thought," *Journal of Economic Literature*, 4 (December) 1422-41.

Klamer, A. (1983), *Conversations with Economists*. Totowa: Rowman and Allanheld.

___________________. (1984), "Levels of Discourse in New Classical Economics," *History of Political Economy*, 16(2) (Summer), 263-290.

Lowenberg, A. D. (1982), "A Critical Assessment of the Macro Rational Expectations Paradigm," *The South African Journal of Economics*, 50 (September), 208-24.

Maddock, R. and Carter, M. (1982), "A Child's Guide to Rational Expectations," *Journal of Economic Literature*, 20 (March), 39-51.

McCloskey, D. N. (1983), "The Rhetoric of Economics," *Journal of Economic Literature*, 21, 481-517.

___________________. (1985), *The Rhetoric of Economics*. Madison: The University of Wisconsin Press.

Mirowski, P. (1987), "Shall I Compare Thee to...," *Economics and Philosophy*, 3, 335-58.

Mitchell, W. C. (1967), *Types of Economic Theory*, Joseph Dorfman, ed., two volumes. New York: Augustus M. Kelley Publishers.

Nelson, J. S., Megill, A., and McCloskey, D. (1987), *The Rhetoric of the Human Sciences*. Madison: The University of Wisconsin Press.

Rogers, C. (1982), "Rational Expectations and Neo-Classical Economics: The Methodology of the New Classical Macro Economics," *South African Journal of Economics*, 50 (December), 318-339.

Santomero, A. M. and Seater, J. J. (1978), "The Inflation-Unemployment Trade-Off: A Critique of the Literature," *Journal of Economic Literature*, 16 (June), 499-544.

Shiller, R. J. (1978), "Rational Expectations and the Dynamic Structure of Macroeconomic Models" A Critical Review," *Journal of Monetary Economics*, 4, 1-44.

Struthers, J. J. (1984), "Rational Expectations: A Promising Research Program or a Case of Monetariest Fundamentalism?" *Journal of Economic Issues*, 18 (December), 1133-54.

Tobin, J. (1982), "Are New Classical Models Plausible Enough to Guide Policy?" *Journal of Money, Credit and Banking*, 12 (November), Part 2, 788-799.

Weintraub, R. (1988), "On the Brittleness of the Orange Equilibrium," in Klamer, A., McCloskey, D. N., and Solow, R. M. (eds.) *The Consequences of Economic Rhetoric*, Cambridge: Cambridge University Press, 1988, 146-62.

Woglom, G. (1979), "Rational Expectations and monetary policy in a simple macroeconomic model," *Quarterly Journal of Economics*, 93 (February), 91-106.

CHAPTER 6

THREE VIGNETTES ON THE STATE OF ECONOMIC RHETORIC

Philip Mirowski

PROLOGUE

A funny thing happened to Rhetoric on its way to being recruited as the lastest in a long line of defenses of the legitimacy of neoclassical economics. What began as an attempt to import considerations from recent developments in the history of science, hermeneutics, literary theory, and other postmodern pursuits (McCloskey, 1983; 1985) provoked such an outcry of pollution taboo from economists, that it appears now to have evolved into a simple castigation of any citation of philosophy of science or methodology in the context of an economic argument (McCloskey, 1988).[1] This palpable degeneration of what began as a laudable call for greater self-consciousness in economic discourse was perhaps a predictable outcome, given that any attempt to renounce the scientism of economic discourse, while maintaining the scientistic explanatory structure of neoclassical economic theory, was an inherently self-contradictory procedure (Mirowski, 1987; 1990).[2] A postmodern neoclassical theory would be rather like an a-political Paul de Man: looks good on paper, but the suspicion lingers that the denial of a world outside the text is in the last analysis motivated by a fervent desire to keep the skeletons locked in the closet.

Nevertheless, I would like to argue that the lessons of rhetoric have not yet been exhausted in the economic context. In particular, the topoi of the present text is chiasmus, or the inversion of the second of two parallel statements. If McCloskey insists that rhetoric reveals that methodological discussion is fruitless, Mirowski will hereby counter that methodological discussion could and should also be subject to rhetorical analysis and appraisal. Putting it somewhat differently, the perennial complaint that "Those who can, do; those who can't, pontificate on method" is simply false, but serves a particular set of rhetorical functions within the economics profession. These functions are all rooted in concepts of order: hierarchical order within the profession, as well as, within the larger culture; notions of orderly academic discourse; and reified notions of orderly exchange within economic activity. The simple truth is that every sentient economist engages in some form or another of methodological discourse at some juncture in their career. But for the most part that discourse is not located in contexts of sanctioned "scientific" outlets or in formal venues; instead, it appears in contexts that are inevitably identified as "personal": in biographical reminiscences, in teaching situations, referee reports, book reviews for popular newspapers, in correspondence, or in verbal debate. Hence, the problem of this chapter is to understand why method-talk is asserted to be taboo in economics, when in fact it is surpassed in its ubiquity only by discussion of other people's salaries.

To that end, I would like to draw the attention of the reader to a profound article entitled "Why is There No Hermeneutics of Natural Science?" (Markus, 1987). In it, the author asks why even hermeneutic philosophers, such as Hans Georg Gadamer, think that modern natural scientific sign systems, amongst all other forms of discourse, seem privileged. In hermeneutics, as in much of postmodern philosophy, one is enjoined to recognize that meaning is constantly negotiated by both sender and receiver, and that appeals to the nature of logic, of mind, the external world, and so forth, are just so many more attempts to negotiate a stable ground of discourse[3]; and yet, contary to this precept, almost every advocate of hermeneutics sees natural science texts as somehow different. Gadamer calls these texts "monologic" in the sense that the subject matter entirely determines the content of the text. If it were the case that natural science texts were somehow univocal, magically self-sufficient, unambiguously clear to any reader with adequate preparation and competence, then, indeed, the natural sciences would be superior to the "soft" social sciences and their kissing cousins, the humanities.

Markus argues, contrary to this incongruous conviction, that the natural sciences maintain their seeming superiority over the social sciences and the humanities by means of essentially rhetorical figures and tropes, particularly with respect to the standard format of the "scientific paper". As he notes, "Contemporary natural science (as a cultural genre) is characterized by the extreme *paucity* of its accepted literary genres or forms" (Markus, 1987, 12). This should sound familiar to those who have been following McCloskey's complaints about modern economists. They refuse to recognize the vast range of types of discourse in their writing and speaking, opting for cliched forms in a nonreflexive manner. But Markus argues that this is precisely the key to an understanding of the supposed superiority of the scientific paper. "Science" in the modern world has come to mean the depersonalization of the author within its literary manifestation, all the while restricting personality to the sphere of oral discourse (or perhaps personal letters in the days before the telephone and the jet-setting academic). The purpose of such a separation is to create the impression that knowledge exists independenly of the knower, that content can be transmitted independent of the vehicle.

The characterization of the standard format "scientific paper" will be recognized by anyone who has read the *Journal of Political Economy*, the *American Economic Review*, or *Econometrica*:

> The existence of the Abstract posits that it is possible to summarize its essential 'content', ie. that the latter is independent from the exposition's literary form and argumentative context. The distinction between Introduction and Discussion on the one hand, and Methods and Results, on the other, implies the possibility to divorce 'interpretation' from 'description', while the division between Methods and Results indicate a similar possibility of separating the ways of investigation from its 'findings' (Markus, 1987, 12).

One can see why anyone enamored of the sciences could believe in an abstract all-encompassing "method". The style of the scientific paper shrinks the author to the vanishing point, replacing him with tubs of Lego blocks marked "Review of the Literature," "Description of the Data," "Corrections to the Standard Linear Regression Model" and so on. Yet Markus points out a tension here: If its all just a matter of snapping together prefabricated bits, why should the author get all the credit, particularly for "originality"? This tension gives rise to the irreconcilable difference between written and oral discourse. The author must present a paper persona to the world of inscriptions as a humble, faceless, and indifferently expendible worker quarrying preexistent veins of knowledge in ploddingly predictable but intrinsically inevitable ways (Latour, 1987). But in actual social interactions within the discipline, one is allowed (and perhaps even encouraged) to give vent to personal peccadillos, deploy arguments *ad hominem*, appeal to inaccessible evidence, raise parochial concerns, and indeed, to engage in the many and varied forms of persuasion generally analyzed by hermeneutics and rhetoric.

This tension and the disjunction between what economists write and how they talk accounts for the impact of Arjo Klamer's book *Conversations with Economists* (Klamer, 1983; Klamer in Klamer et al., 1988). To "hear" the advocates and detractors of the rational expectations movement in macroeconomics give their impressions of how the change in thought had happened and what it meant for them was a shock precisely because it violated the format of the scientific paper, a rhetoric that the rational expectations group used to great effect in their inscribed texts. One began to suspect that personality made a difference in the evolution of economic thought and that the meaning and intention of the seminal papers was not so very transparent as it may have initially appeared. Ultimately, it also, of course, raised that great taboo, the question of whether economics should be considered a science.

Method-talk, philosophy, metaphysics and what-have-you are indeed ubiquitous in economics, but they are exiled to the margins of discourse largely by means of a rhetorical device, namely, the literary format of the scientific paper. But in economics, as opposed to physics, economists face a further contradiction in their quest to quarantine the process of investigation from its legitimation.

Economists, after all, do on occasion claim to be social theorists. Neoclassical economists, in particular, have a theory about the structure and meaning of social coordination achieved through the instrumentality of something they call "the market", which is patterned upon equilibrium within a field of potential energy (Mirowski, 1989). In this metaphor, insofar as market transactors are portrayed at all, they are regarded as humble, faceless, and indifferently expendable. (Think of Walrasian general equilibrium.) The family resemblance between the paper persona of the scientist and the neoclassical economic man (Mirowski, 1987b) has suggested to many neoclassicals that their idea of market coordination is identical to that embodied in the rhetoric of the standard scientific paper, to the extent that one might infer there was a virtual "market" in ideas that coordinates the world of thought. In this rhetorical trope, which is a very common figure of speech amongst economists, just as a perfectly competitive market guarantees a Pareto optimum in economic affairs, the scientific paper guarantees a Pareto optimum in the "marketplace of ideas".

The problem with this folk wisdom among economists is that the scientific paper embodies one account or implicit theory of social order, while the neoclassical economic theory embodies another. The former, as we have observed, attempts to deny the existence of human personality in the course of the negotiation of knowledge, whereas the latter has no explanation for who might bring the equilibrium about. The latter negates rationality by rendering the outcome in a completely mechanical manner, while the former postulates a supremely confident rationality without fixed character available to all. These theories are not the same, nor do they agree on the meaning of societal order in all respects. Therefore, method-talk is doubly repressed in modern economics by asserting, without any justification, that the market metaphor can be legitimately projected upon the scientific process, particularly on occasions when personality and process threaten to violate the boundaries of orderly discourse. The tactic of appeal to a "free market of ideas" is eminently rhetorical, given that few would ever seriously take the time to evaluate the metaphor. What precisely is being "sold" in this market? What is the means of "payment"? Is the "commodity" invariant through the process of exchange? Just because you buy a person or their screed, it doesn't always follow that you have bought his ideas (Leff, 1988). And finally, why does this kind of "competition" have any relationship to the tortured history of the word in economics (Dennis, 1977)?

I would like to claim that the market metaphor, with its attendant prohibition of method-talk in the scientific paper, is an inadequate vehicle to understand the nature of neoclassical economic discourse, but that it is, nonetheless, necessary, because of the clash of the radical individualism of neoclassical theory with the palpable social control of economic discourse exercised by the orthodoxy in myriad ways, ranging from the bland and smug homogeneity of the major journals to the conscious control of access to jobs and research funds. This problem of how to conceptualize social order in scientific discourse dates back at least three centuries, as observed by Shapin & Schaffer (1985, 78) in their profound book on the dispute between Hobbes and Boyle on the significance of experiment:

> Radical individualism—the state in which each individual set himself up as the ultimate judge of knowledge—would destroy the conventional basis of proper knowledge, while the disciplined collective social structure of the experimental form of life would create and sustain that factual basis... Legitimate knowledge was warranted as objective insofar as it was produced by the collective, and agreed to voluntarily by those who comprised the collective... Human coercion was to have no visible place in the experimental form of life.

The neoclassicals have never been able to avail themselves of the full panoply of the "experimental form of life," and worse, espouse a theory that presumes a form of radical methodological individualism. Hence, they have been ever hard-pressed to justify their imitation of the "scientific" procedures of their brethren the physicists (Mirowski, 1989). The interim solution has taken the format of a form of repression of both method-talk, as the province of those not capable of scientific thought, combined with an intolerance for deviate conceptions of economics. The dissonance between social control and the praise of individualism is papered over by the market metaphor, for in neoclassical theory, it is the market that putatively reconciles the self-seeking behavior of the individual with the social dictates of systemic coherence.

Let us see how economists deal on a day-to-day basis with these contradictions in their stance towards method in three instances taken from very recent history. These will be presented in the format of "vignettes," since this narrative has no pretense of aspiring to be a standard scientific paper.

THE FREE MARKET OF IDEAS

The place: a National Bureau of Economic Research (NBER) Conference on Macroeconomics, Cambridge, Massachusetts. The time: March 13, 1987. The context: an annual conference sponsored by the National Bureau for Economic Research to codify the "New Macroeconomics," or to say it another way, to put a nonchalant face on the mess that has been made of Keynesian economics by repeated attempts to force it to conform to neoclassical general equilibrium, standard econometrics, the rational expectations postulate, etc. The cast of characters: by invitation only, the best and brightest as judged by the advocates of this new macroeconomics, including Benjamin Friedman, Robert Barro, Bennett McCallum, Olivier Blanchard, and a cast of thousands. The setting: an invited paper by Lawrence Summers, professor at Harvard University, intriguingly entitled "The Scientific Illusion in Macroeconomics."

The talk closely followed the conference paper, from which I will quote. The primary argument of the paper was summarized in three theses:

> First, only a small part of our lack of knowledge results from our ignorance of taste and technology parameters. It instead involves other matters having ultimately to do with information problems... Second, to the very limited extent that our inability to account for events does stem from ignorance of tastes and technology, the construction of more elaborate models is unlikely to be successful... Third, idealized research with its focus on the estimation of fully developed models is unlikely to contribute much to the process of theory creation and elaboration (Summers, 1987, 6).

The paper began with an endorsement of Donald McCloskey's *Rhetoric of Economics* as a "provocative and largely on-target book," one that "argued that economic science has progressed largely through a process of persuasion and argument unaided and at times hampered by the trappings of rigorous science."

> Motivated by an analogy to hard sciences like physics macroeconomists increasingly insist that theories be built up from first principles and that hypotheses be rigorously formulated and subjected to allegedly definitive statistical tests. They reject as outmoded and ad-hoc theories built up inductively from empirical observation, dismiss as foolish predictions not generated from optimizing models, and deny the evidence of the eyes as a source of empirical knowledge (1).

It should be understood that the practices putatively denounced by the modern macroeconomist are those by which Summers would apparently characterize his own work. Yet, how could it be that "economic science" has been "hampered by the trappings of rigorous science"? Is the coloratura hampered by the trappings of the opera? And what precisely provoked those troublesome analogies with physics in the first place? In what sense do econometric practices diverge from "evidence of the eyes"? And as one finds oneself from time to time in conversations bringing it down to the level of personalities, how was it that Lawrence Summers came to be considered one of the best and brightest if his work was so thoroughly scorned by the epigones of modern macroeconomics? While the hiring practices of the Harvard Economics Department have so far resisted econometric modelling, it would seem perverse to suggest that they went looking for a wide-eyed Baconian empiricist who rejected neoclassical theory.

As we can see, Summers was violating the tenets of orderly discourse within economics. It was not simply that he was engaging in method-talk—we shall see his audience also doing this shortly—but rather that he was allowing the margins of discourse to encroach upon an occasion predicated upon the presumptions of the standard scientific paper. As the audience squirmed, Summers continued to confound the expectations of his audience. "It is difficult to think of many empirical studies from more than a decade ago whose bottom line was a parameter estimate or the acceptance or rejection of a hypothesis." (Summers, 1987, 14) "Probably the most important problem with formal work directed at identifying deep structural parameters is that there are none to be found" (1987, 15): These, of course, are questions of the greatest import; ontological questions, questions concerning what it is there is to know. What can we, as economists, claim to know? Summers dodged any such direct query, instead, proffering for the consideration of his esteemed audience "empirical work that has had a durable impact on our view of how the economy operates. I think of Friedman and Modigliani's treatments of the consumption function and Mitchell's work on business cycles as obvious examples." (1987, 19)

These claims illustrate a set of practices encouraged (though certainly not created) by the McCloskeyan conception of rhetoric. There typically is an oblique reference to some community standards of excellence in economic analysis, neither specifying the standards nor the community of reference. Further, there is a lack of attention to actual historical inquiry. In this instance, while obeisence must be paid to the first research director of the NBER at an NBER sponsored conference, it really seems odd in 1987 to claim that Mitchell's *Business Cycles* has had a durable impact upon "our" understanding, given that every single member of the audience was most assuredly unfamiliar with it; more than that, it was necessarily the case since the capture of the NBER by Martin Feldstein had as one consequence the banishment of all vestigial influences of Mitchell's Institutionalist School from the premises. (We shall leave the "durability" of the contributions of the other mentioned figures to the reader's own judgment.) Summers here was violating conventional scientific discourse. For, as Markus says, natural science has 'seminal' and 'normal science' texts, but does not possess 'classic' texts: "those literary products of the (usually more remote) past to which the present cultural practice ascribes an 'atemporal' (or at least epochal) validity: an ability to shed light on the questions of any age, even if it is realized that they were born out of a specific cultural context." (Markus, 1987, 31)

Up to this point, Summers was trying to use McCloskey's text to justify some reorientation in the practices of macroeconomists, while guilelessly ignoring the dissonance of such a reorientation with his own previously published works. The relationship between McCloskey's program of rhetorical analysis and Summers' own vision of an alternative praxis was tenuous, but this was largely irrelevant for his audience, as we shall shortly observe. That there was a severe divergence between Summers' previous authorial practices and his conference persona was only mildly disconcerting, for as Markus has observed, that is the fate of all who write the scientific paper. But then, Summers proceeded to enmesh his discourse with yet a third rhetorical problem, one we identified in our prolog above, one which is especially characteristic of economic discourse and McCloskey's rhetorical program.

"But any economist should ask a natural question—why doesn't laissez faire direct science properly?" His answer, as in nearly every response to this question by every neoclassical economist, appealed to a direct analogy with neoclassical theory: "First, the commission of papers like this is part of the process by which a scientific community sets its priorities. Second, there is at least the possibility that systematic forces could lead to misplaced research priorities. Certainly there is no general theorem holding that Nash equilibria are Pareto optimal... I believe that the process of peer evaluation in economic research reinforces what might be called the 'technical imperative'" (Summers, 1987, 27-28).

Unlike his brethren in the physical sciences, the neoclassical economist is caught in a peculiar rhetorical bind in that he simultaneously advocates two incompatible theories of social order. One theory is described by Markus and enshrined in the very style of the scientific paper:

> The boundary limiting and enclosing natural science discourse is not pre-given, but actively maintained. The layman and the non-specialist are posited in the natural sciences as ones whose interpretation of, and opinion about, the works of science ought not to intrude into the relevant discussions at all. Their views are culturally fixed as being in principle irrational (1987, 22).

The other notion of order is encapsulated into the very tradition of mechanistic natural order that gave rise to neoclassicism from its inception (Mirowski, 1989): impersonal, irreducably individualist, inexorable, beyond the realm of social construction. The appeal to a "free market of ideas" exacerbates the contradiction because the governing metaphor of the standard scientific paper is not that of the neoclassical version of free exchange or perfect competition (Knorr-Cetina, 1982); rather, it is predicated upon the premise that the author and his desires are irrelevant, as are his clientele and the vehicle of dissemination of his ideas. McCloskey also encounters the same problem in his advocacy of rhetorical analysis. As I asked in Mirowski (1987; 1990), why isn't the theory of social order in rhetoric congruent with the notions of social order in neoclassical theory? To put it another way: If people in general are neoclassical optimizers, and if economists are people, then don't economists maximize over a set of personal objectives that are contrary to the pursuit of open and honest conversations? If there is a conscious and concerted maintenance of order in the sphere of economic discourse, why shouldn't there also be a conscious and concerted social imposition of order in the market as well?

We shall return to this troublesome, yet reflex, reference to a neoclassical metaphor of science as a market of ideas: it is the common theme in all three of our vignettes. But first, we must observe the response to this rather unexpected performance on March 13. Academics are a preternaturally excitable bunch when it comes to controversy and calumny, but the hubbub on this occasion was second only to that which would have occurred if Summers had chanted Alan Ginsburg's "Howl" with accompaniment on bongos. Alan Blinder, the designated discussant of Summers' paper, appeared at a loss as to how to begin, even though he had written prepared comments. "The real trouble," he said, "is that we have patterned ourselves after mathematics and perhaps mathematical physics. We would have done better to have patterned ourselves after medicine, or biology, or even the less theoretical branches of physics." Of course, no reasons were tendered as to why such alternative patterns are, were, or should have been attractive, much less the slightest evidence of historical awareness that such options had indeed been entertained in both the distant and the recent past of economic thought.[4]

No matter, because then Blinder launched into an anecdote, the gist of which was that he, Blinder, was envious of the successes of modern physics and thought economists should be emulating them. "I'll skip the assumption of optimizing behavior; I guess that's what distinguishes us from the lower social sciences."[5] On the other hand, "Medical science—and I am not talking about practicing physicians and dentists here—is profoundly empirical and inductive. It's first concern is with what works, not with developing grandiose theories... Can you imagine an academic economist achieving fame and fortune with a vita like that?"

The response from the floor was even better; here we can only give a sample of the gamut of responses. Christopher Sims suggested that he agreed with Summers that there was too much of a tendency to adhere to the "sadomasochistic" school of methodology, namely, that theories are attractive because they provide discipline. But, he demurred, one cannot forget that the public does not regard the economics profession as akin to dentists, but rather as second cousins to snake oil salesmen. The only way to overcome this suspicion, he insisted, was to "get some common ground" in method. Robert Lucas warned that if Summers were taken seriously, the whole review process for allocation of research funds might be overturned. One should expect that the economist, above all other considerations, would worry where that next paycheck was coming from. Herschel Grossman opined that you can't trust everyone with an informal empiricist approach. Consider, he said, a representative piece of work done by an economist who has not been trained in the state of the art techniques; what you get is garbage. One can just compare the recent evolution of economics in Europe versus America. In Europe, the

Keynesian methodology of being a wise person who has clever insights is taken seriously, and as a result, most of the important work in economics happened in the United States, where "we" followed a different research strategy. Martin Bailey suggested externality problems in research, playing upon the market metaphor.

There was more indignation from the floor, most of it in the same vein. Summers nevertheless stuck to his guns, venturing a prediction that any empirical studies in economics, remembered fifteen years from now, will not have relied in any essential way on complex statistics. This echoed the conclusion of his paper that "persuasive economic work is so rarely self-consciously scientific" (Summers, 1987, 29).

On the simplest possible level, this incident is an illustration of the extreme divergence between the image of knowledge presented in the scientific paper and that prevalent in convocations of actual personalities in social situations. Where the rhetoric of the scientific paper guarantees that the nature of science cannot be included in the text by its very construction, it is, however, the subject of interminable (and might we add, naive and unsophisticated?) dispute in personal interactions by people who do not identify themselves as "methodologists." Hence, the persistent scorn of "methodology" is itself a rhetorical tactic; the message is that one should not mix personal negotiations with inscribed texts. This separation must be maintained at all costs. Witness the fact that Summers' conference paper was later denied publication in the second NBER macroeconomics annual, something that had not happened before in the brief history of those convocations.

On a bit more subtle level, one observes the tension between the formal rhetoric of the scientific paper, which is seemingly accessible to all competent parties, and the actual praxis of a science, where the main social structures exist to exclude unwanted participants from the ongoing conversation (Markus, 1987, 24). The comments from the floor illustrate this tension, particularly Lucas' concern that this not get out to the funding agencies. And attendance at the conference, we repeat, was by invitation only; further, the Summers paper was denied inclusion in the published conference volume. When the meaning of "competence" in discourse is itself contentious, then it becomes all the more imperative to erect strong demarcations between "inside" and "outside." Insiders must present a unified face to the outside world, which means strong prohibitions against the ubiquitous method-talk from going public. Outsiders, on the other hand, regularly violate these prohibitions, primarily because they have little to lose and few resources with which to attract adherents. Summers, after all, did not go out to find a different outlet for his paper.

And then there is the deeper problem, the bankruptcy of the metaphor of intellectual endeavor as resembling a "free market". No one other than the select few could "buy" access to Summers' ruminations on McCloskey and scientism in economics, since they were denied access. Martin Bailey suggested that the market of ideas had imperfections, but the implications of that statement were not followed up. Lucas wanted to censor Summers' remarks to prevent the *emptor* from experiencing some profound *caveats*. Better to let sleeping dogs lie.

THE SCARAB OF REPLICATION

Among the many other interesting observations made by Markus are some particularly incisive ruminations on the role that the ideal of replicability plays in the supposed banishment of intersubjectivity in the scientific paper:

> In the case of 'research reports' this claim of strict intersubjectivity takes on the form of the well-known postulate of the replicability of experimental results. This postulate has a paradoxical character. Those features of scientific texts which allow such a claim to be made also exclude its fulfillment in any 'literal' or ordinary sense... the text's mere focusing on particular-local, non-recurrent aspects of the laboratory events would immediately situate its author in a position of a privileged, exceptionally placed observer (Markus, 1987, 25).

This tension or contradiction in the very structure of the scientific paper was recently stumbled upon in, of all places, the *American Economic Review*, in the article by (Dewald, Thursby & Anderson, 1986). In a prodigious undertaking (funded by the National Science Foundation, to see what it was getting for its money in the free market of ideas), those authors requested the computer programs and data sets from the authors of all of the empirical articles published in the *Journal of Money, Credit and Banking* (*JMCB*) in order to rerun all of their econometric exercises. These materials were broken into two subsets: (1) those published from 1980 to June 1982, prior to the initiation of the replication project; and (2) from July 1982 onwards, all articles submitted to the *JMCB* or under review. The results were noteworthy, both for NSF and from our present vantage point.

First, 66 percent of authors falling in class (1) were unable or unwilling to comply with requests for programs and data tapes, whereas 28 percent of class (2) authors likewise did not comply. Second, of the 54 instances where the requested materials were supplied, only 8 of the submissions were in a sufficiently problem-free state to permit an attempt at replication. Third, and finally, only two out of those eight articles were found to be susceptible to replication of econometric results in their entirety. This final number represents an overall global replication success rate of 1.3 percent. Although the authors did not say so in so many words, this estimate is well outside the bounds of any confidence intervals around the conventional norm of replication. What is of special note is how the investigators tried to explain this rather poor showing. As in our previous vignette, when in a pickle and confronted with the problematic nature of their scientific rhetoric, neoclassical economists resort to thinking of science using their market metaphor. Their findings revealed "market failure," they said, suggesting that the "benefits of reduced frequency of errors in empirical articles share many of the characteristics of public goods" (Dewald et al., 1986, 589).

The public goods argument is a non-starter for a whole gamut of reasons. In a loose sense, it was probably intended to evoke some divergence between social and private valuations of "errors" in econometric reportage, but upon reflection, all the interesting issues are concealed in the unstated premises concerning the meaning of "errors," the constitution of "value," the purposes of the investigators, and so forth. First, it simply takes for granted that the metaphor of a market is an adequate framework to describe intellectual discourse, an idea that runs into trouble wherever it is broached and entertained with any seriousness, as indicated in the previous vignette. Second, a case may be made that the very concept of a "public good" is incompatible with the core of neoclassical value theory (Mirowski, 1989, chap. 5), but since that is not our interest here, we shall pass over that argument lightly. Third, consider the definition of the public good from Rosen (1985, 99): "A public good has two characteristics: (1) Once it is provided, the additional resource cost of consuming the good is zero—consumption is nonrival. (2) To prevent anyone from consuming the good is either very expensive or impossible—consumption is nonexcludable." (See also Cornes & Sandler, 1986, 6-7.)

We embark upon thin ice here because one can rarely pin down an advocate of the free market of ideas on what precisely the commodity is in his scheme; but let us at least try to participate in his language game. The *JMCB* group seems to be thinking of "correct information" as the commodity. Less than the optimal amount is being "produced" because the "producer" can't monitor use and payment or exclude access to the benefits of meticulous econometrics. But is this really the case? We have argued at greater length in Mirowski & Sklivas (1991) that the cost of use of the information is precisely nonzero: there are costs of familiarizing oneself with the tacit background knowledge; costs of access to the relevant scientific community; and costs involved in familiarizing oneself with the character and reliability of the reported results. Moreover, the "benefits" of empirical endeavor should not be characterized as some generic "knowledge," but rather as the direct benefits that accrue to a scientist located at a particular social nexus—primarily, whether the researcher can claim the identity of a supporter or challenger of a particular research program. Further, the whole process of negotiation over the publication and promulgation is one of "rivalry" and "exclusion." In Mirowski & Sklivas (1991), we argue that the key variable in a model of the replication process is the control of the originator of a novel result over the extent to which he will provide legitimation and documentation for any further elaboration of "his" result. The reason the *JMCB* group does not engage in the further elaboration of their "public good" metaphor is that it would lead them into discussions of the social structure of their science, something they undoubtedly view as a distasteful and unscientific prospect. Better to blame the problem on the "thing," the "information," than on the person. Who wants to become embroiled in a disputation about morality? One cannot freely admit to rivalry and exclusion in the standard scientific paper.

A more promising line of inquiry into replication in the sciences has been initiated by Harry Collins (1985) and can be found in the work of such historians of science as Shapin & Schaffer (1985, chap. 6), Galison (1987;1988) and Latour (1987). The indispensible prerequisite for any description of the replication process is an appreciation of just how difficult it is, even under the best of circumstances, to achieve "perfect replication." Absolute perfect replication would dictate that every conceivable aspect of the exercise be reproduced; this is, of course, simply impossible. No one can achieve the same space/time coordinates, the same attitudes and behaviors as the experimenter, the same apparatus, and so on. Moreover, no one would ever want to achieve absolute perfect replication, because it would be meaningless: it would add nothing to what was already known. Therefore, replication activity is a highly qualified phenomenon, hedged about by numerous heuristics that define "asymptotically satisfactory replication." These *might* encompass time invariance of the experiment, independence of seemingly irrelevant alternatives, near-identical tacit background knowledge, and a condition at the heart of scientific rhetoric: independence of outcome from the personality of the investigator. It is important to see that these are all matters for *negotiation*. There is no way that all the conditions can be guaranteed met in any *a priori* manner. Another way of putting this is that the attempt to replicate an experiment or trial is simultaneously a struggle to define what will count as an asymptotically identical experiment within a certain research community. The "identity" of any given phenomenon is not an ontological attribute, but rather is intrinsically relative to "our" purposes.

Let us draw some examples from (Dewald et al, 1986) to illustrate this problem. One might naively expect that once the data and programs were provided by the original investigators to the *JMCB* project, the definition of successful replication would have been straightforward: the exact numerical reproduction of the estimated regression coefficients, t-statistics, R-squareds, and so on. But, as the *JMCB* researchers found to their dismay, at one time or another all simple heuristics of "asymptotically satisfactory replication" were violated. Time invariance was compromised by the updating and revision of data sets by data source providers, rendering the exact figures used in the original studies nearly impossible to recover. Independence of results from the personality of the experimenter was also a vexed problem for the *JMCB* project. They repeatedly had to go outside of the printed text, querying the original authors as to their research tactics, most of which were only implicit, trying to discover and understand the possible sources of divergence of the *JCMB* regression equations from those reported in the texts (Dewald et al., 1986, 593). The professional location and status of the authors, far from being irrelevant, in many cases created insuperable difficulties for the *JCMB* project, such as their failure to reproduce the Harvard-MPS model on Ohio State University's IBM (Dewald et al., 1986, 596-7). The independence of seemingly irrelevant alternatives was violated by such "minor" considerations as variations in computer hardware and software, such as differences in the precision of rounding in algorithms and subroutines, even within purportedly the "same" statistical package (Dewald et al., 1986, 594fn). Questions of the "correct" use of statistical procedures relegates the subject to an infinite regress of potential revisions.

As Collins shows, these particular obstacles are no different from those encountered in the search for gravity waves, quarks, and the fully functioning gas laser. The problem of all scientific research is to constitute a sufficient degree of identity "in the phenomena" so that results become stabilized for a particular scientific community. This is where the impersonal stylistic format of the scientific paper comes into play: it is written as if it were a neutral "report" where results present themselves with no temporal dependence, no intrusion of investigator persona, no soul-searching about tacit knowledge residing in an unproblematic shared "literature." The average scientific paper must be written as if "interpretation" could be entirely divorced from "description," indeed, as if any competent reader could have performed the same experiment, run the same regressions: No dissension, no competing interests, no social structures, no historical context, just the immobile impassive world and the calm dispassionate free floating Eye. While, from many points of view, this ideal of democracy in the laboratory (or the computer center?) is laudable, that does not belie the fact that it is simply false. While replication is an ideal image of science, replication activity rarely occurs in actual history, as Collins and others have shown. The reason why the Ideal can remain the Idol is not that it exists, but rather the stylistic requirements of the scholarly journal foster the impression that it is so.

The reaction of the *American Economic Review* (*AER*) editors to the *JMCB* project article is as important to this story as the article itself. After all, the article could have prompted a profound reevaluation of the entire social structure of academic journals, as well as the predispositions of economists to remain in conformity with the standard scientific paper format. However, the editors of the *AER* merely appended a preface to Dewald et al. (1986) suggesting that the solution was to "get tough." They said that they would from that time forward institute a "policy" that would require that "the data used in the analysis are clearly and precisely documented, [and] are readily available to any researcher for purposes of replication, and where details of computations sufficient to permit replications are provided."

The resemblance of this statement to "jawboning" in incidents of macroeconomic policy are a little too close for comfort. It would appear that the editors had no intention of changing any of their practices, and indeed, in the interim, there has been no substantial change in submission behavior, because as one source suggested to this author, the costs of storage and routing of such documentation would be much too high. Futher, there has been no encouragement of replication behavior in the sense of soliciting articles whose primary purpose was attempted replications of already published articles. I was told later that the AER was not interested in prolonging a protracted controversy on this issue by publishing further discussions of the Dewald et al. paper. After all, who wants to contemplate the possibility that all of econometrics is itself just another rhetorical device, one whose primary purpose is to further obscure the role of the personality of the author in the process of the social construction of facts and their interpretations? Instead, better to let sleeping dogs lie.

"BOURGEOIS LIBERAL THAT I AM, I WANT TO LET A THOUSAND FLOWERS BLOOM"[6]

There is another perspective to be gained on the rhetoric of the standard format of the scientific paper; it is achieved by watching what a scientist says when forced to direct his discourse not to his profession, but rather to the general intelligent layperson. As we shall see, this too involves a certain range of tensions, of incompatible objectives. On the one hand, a certain modicum of personality is allowed, even encouraged to shine through the prose, for that is one way to make the subject interesting. But, counterposed to that, one must maintain the facade that portrays science as impersonal, definitive, a-social, and uncontroversial. Some of the best popularizers of science have transcended the conflict by directly confronting the myth of the asocial character of science: one thinks of Ruben Hersh and Philip Davis in mathematics, Stephen J. Gould in biology, and James Gleick in physics. Economics, sadly, has yet to find their peer.

Nevertheless, the publication of *The New Palgrave*, a dictionary of economics edited by John Eatwell, Murray Milgate, and Peter

Newman signaled a different sort of attack on the problem. The original *Palgrave's Dictionary of Political Economy* appeared in three volumes in 1894, 1896 and 1899; essentially, it was patterned upon a lexicon and written by a comparatively few authors representing the orthodoxy of the incipient economics profession. For instance, Francis Ysidro Edgeworth's rococo prose graces 126 entries in the old *Palgrave*, while James Bonar was responsible for 78 entries. By and large, it was an attempt to consolidate the tyro economics profession around some stabilized referents, and indeed, it performed that function well.

The New Palgrave is an entirely different kettle of fish. One of the modern editors has suggested that what he liked about the old *Palgrave* is that "there was none of the artificial politeness which has crept into academic writing today" (Eatwell, 1987, 16). Whether or not this is a fair characterization of the Victorian work, it certainly captures some of the motivation behind the modern version. The purpose of *The New Palgrave*, whatever else it might be, is not to stabilize a coherent profession around a shared lexicon. Indeed, while not actually discussing the nature and rhetoric of science directly, it does manage to achieve a novel approach to addressing the layperson through active recruitment of an extremely diverse collection of authors to write on a vast array of entries, all of which were predicated on the presumption that there *did not* exist any single unified paradigm or framework that subsumed all entries. As one editor has suggested, "Economics is in a great flux, a massive transition. While I was impressed by the solidarity of the profession, there is no apparent solidarity of ideas" (Eatwell, 1987, 17).

Perhaps this sounds antithetical to the whole idea of a dictionary, but I believe that is entirely the point of this vast exercise. One way to faithfully present the range and scope of such a motley entity as "economics" is to subvert a literary form dedicated to standardization and conformity, teaching the reader that their expectations of faceless monolithic answers is destined to come to grief. It is true that the tyro should be warned of this fact at some point in their confrontation with *The New Palgrave*, but with some luck, how this happens could enhance the learning experience. In any event, for the working economist these volumes are great fun. Strange and unfamiliar entries like "meaningfulness and invariance" jostle for our attention with old standbys like "supply and demand." Emile Burns snuggles up against Arthur Burns, and of all things, there is an entry for "relativity, principle of, in political economy" by John Neville Keynes, reprinted from the original *Palgrave*. You can practically imagine the editors winking at you with that one! It doesn't happen very often in economics, but here is the real thing, a masterpiece of rhetoric in form and content.[7]

If anything, one of the subtle effects of *The New Palgrave* is to exacerbate the tensions inherent in the older rhetoric of the standard scientific paper and its adherents. The depth of this effect can be gauged in the reviews of the *The New Palgrave*, particularly the one by Robert Solow in the *New York Times Book Review* (Solow, 1988).[8] Solow is often praised for his facility in addressing the layperson, and so we do not have to confront the awkward fumblings with language that seem so common in the economics profession. Moreover, Solow had just won the Nobel Prize in economics prior to writing the review and so was apparently taking seriously his charge to come forward as a responsible spokesperson for the orthodox majority, the "real" profession.

Solow prefaced his review by saying he had not read the entire dictionary: "You could write about the Interstate highway system without having driven every last mile of it." He then began, as should every discreet reviewer, by saying something nice about the volumes at hand: "The best things in 'The New Palgrave' are the technical articles." The editors, as part of their plan, had sought out reputable neoclassical mathematical economists to write some of the entries. Many of these articles were written in nearly impenetrable prose (when you could find the prose), but no matter, Solow thought these were just the trick for a dictionary that would serve as a reference for the general public. The reason for his opinion was that, "At any moment there is a state of the art. A master can describe his or her special corner of it to anyone with an adequate general training. Even where there is controversy . . . the technically adept will be able to communicate. No doubt that is why the technical [read: mathematical—P.M.] articles are so successful."

Then Solow came to his main objection: *The New Palgrave* did not "keep the various 'paradigms' in proportion." For instance, one discovered quite a number of Marxist entries, but "most serious English-speaking economists regard Marxist economics as an irrelevant dead end. . . . It is rather as if a medical dictionary were to intersperse articles on mainstream orthopedics, written by orthopedists, with articles on osteopathy, written by osteopaths, and were to leave it at that." Of course, that was the idea. No one comes out On Top because of the rhetorical structure of the volume rather than the more conventional tropes of attack and defense—not the Marxists, not the Austrians, not the Post-Keynesians, not the Institutionalists, and certainly not the neoclassicals. But what Solow found most offensive was not that this or that doctrinal point might be disputed—after all, the beauty of the thing is that it is over four thousand pages long, and to want to fight with it makes you feel what it is like to want to fight with the entire economics profession—no, it was that *The New Palgrave* violated the very thing that the Massachusetts Institute of Technology stood for, the Standard Scientific Format. "The editors seem to have asked each author to provide a personal account of the assigned subject, not a neutral survey."

Here, as in each of our other vignettes, is the deep transgression, the mortal sin of scientific discourse: they let their individual personalities shine through. (Even the mathematicians!) In this case, atrocity was compounded with outrage, because it was done with the complicity of venerable names (other Nobel winners, for instance), and it was done for an *audience of outsiders.* And herein lay the major lesson that Solow wished to draw from *The New Palgrave*: "Economics is no longer a fit conversation piece for ladies and gentleman. It has become a technical subject. Like any other technical subject it attracts some people who are more interested in the technique than the subject. That is too bad, but it may be inevitable." So tremble, ye heathen, and beware the juggernaught of Science, lest ye be crushed beneath the wheel.

So whatever happened to the free market of ideas?

> Suppose someone sits down where you are sitting right now and announces to me that he is Napoleon Bonaparte. The last thing I want to do with him is get involved in a technical discussion of cavalry tactics at the battle of Austerlitz... Since I find that fundamental framework ludicrous, I respond by treating it as ludicrous—that is, by laughing at it—so as no to fall into the trap of taking it seriously and passing on to matters of technique (Solow in Klamer, 1983, 146).

Better to let sleeping dogs lie.

NOTES

This chapter was written with the help of a grant from the National Endowment for the Humanities. The author has benefitted tremendously from an ongoing discussion with Arjo Klamer that has only been partially curtailed due to the exegencies of academic survival, as well as from avowedly avuncular comments by Neil de Marchi. I also want to thank Don McCloskey for kindly supplying copies of the various reviews and reactions to his book on rhetoric, and would hope someday to learn the knack of his tolerance for critique and diverse opinions.

1. For other examples of this prohibition of method talk under the influence of postmodernism, see Weintraub (1990).

2. "Philip Mirowski, among others, accuses me of 'inconsistency' for advocating a rhetorical view of economics along with a Chicago neoclassical view of the economy. He wants to argue that a rhetorical approach must overturn neoclassical economics. I don't think so, at least if the word neoclassical is not used ahistorically" (McCloskey in Klamer, et al., 1988, 290). The problem I have with McCloskey's preferences in economic theory, as opposed to those in rhetoric, is his unjustified adherence to the Marshallian line that one can effortlessly violate most of the analytical structures of the neoclassical physics metaphor and still maintain that one is operating within the logical bounds of that tradition. I elaborate upon this problem in "Smooth Operator: How Marshall's Curves of Demand and Supply Rendered Neoclassicism Safe for Public Consumption but Unfit for Science," in Rita Tullberg, ed., *Alfred Marshall in Retrospect*, (Aldershot: Edward Elgar, 1990).

3. An excellent introduction to postmodern philosophy may be found in (Baynes, Bohman & McCarthy, 1986), especially the chapters by Rorty, Foucault, Gadamer, Ricoeur, and Blumenberg.

4. For some consideration of the long-standing attempts to pattern economic thought upon biological theory, see the Winter 1988 special issue of the journal, *Social Concept*, on biological analogies in economics.

5. Indeed, constrained optimization is the core of the imitation of physics by neoclassical economics. On this issue, see (Mirowski, 1989, chap. 5).

6. Direct quotation, letter from Robert Solow to Arjo Klamer, dated May 13, 1987.

7. Perhaps the reader will be better able to situate my opinion in the larger context if they are informed that I was not asked to contribute any entries to *The New Palgrave.*

8. Other reviews by neoclassicals appear essentially to recapitulate Solow's complaints. See, for instance, (Stigler, 1988) and (Blaug, 1988).

REFERENCES

Baynes, K., Bohman, J., and McCarthy, T., eds. (1986), *After Philosophy: End or Transformation?* Cambridge: MIT Press.

Blaug, M. (1988), *Economics Through the Looking Glass.* London: IEA Occasional Paper no. 78.

Collins, H. (1985), *Changing Order.* London: Sage.

Cornes, R., and Sandler, T. (1986), *The Theory of Externalities, Club Goods and Public Goods.* New York: Cambridge University Press.

Dennis, K. (1977), *Competition in the History of Economic Thought.* New York: Arno.

Dewald, W. G., Thursby, J. G., and Anderson, R. G. (1986), "Replication in Empirical Economics," *American Economic Review*, 76, 587-603.

Eatwell, J. (1988), "Interview on the New Palgrave," *Challenge*, 16-22.

Furner, M. (1975), *Advocacy and Objectivity.* Lexington: University of Kentucky Press.

Galison, P. (1987), *How Experiments End*. Chicago: University of Chicago Press.

__________________ (1988), "History, Philosophy and the Central Metaphor," *Science in Context*, 2, 197-212.

Heelan, P. (1989), "Yes! There is a Hermeneutics of Natural Science," *Science in Context*, 3, 477-488.

Klamer, A. (1983), *Conversations With Economists*. Totawa: Rowman & Allenheld.

__________________, McCloskey, D. and Solow, R. (1988), *The Consequences of Economic Rhetoric*. New York: Cambridge University Press.

Knorr-Cetina, K. (1982), "Scientific Communities or Transepistemic Arenas of Research? A Critique of Quasi-Economic Models of Science," *Social Studies of Science*, 12, 101-130.

Latour, B. (1987), *Science in Action*. Cambridge: Harvard University Press.

Leff, N. (1988), "Policy Research for Improved Organizational Performance," *Journal of Economic Behavior and Organization*, 9, 393-403.

Markus, G. (1987), "Why is There No Hermeneutics of Natural Sciences?" *Science in Context*, 1, 5-51.

McCloskey, D. (1983), "The Rhetoric of Economics," *Journal of Economic Literature*, 21, 481-517.

__________________ (1985), *The Rhetoric of Economics*. Madison: University of Wisconsin Press.

__________________ (1988), "Two Replies and a Dialogue on the Rhetoric of Economics," *Economics and Philosophy*, 4, 150-166.

Mirowski, P. (1987a), "Shall I Compare Thee to a Minkowski-Ricardo-Leontief-Metzler Matrix of the Mosak-Hicks Type?" *Economics and Philosophy*, 3, 67-96.

__________________ (1987b), "The Philosophical Basis of Institutionalist Economics," *Journal of Economic Issues*, 1001-1038.

__________________ (1989), *More Heat Than Light: Economics as Social Physics, Physics as Nature's Economics*. New York: Cambridge University Press.

__________________ (1990), "The rhetoric of Economics," *History of the Human Sciences*, 3, 243-257.

__________________, and S. Sklivas (1991), "Why Economists Don't Replicate (Although They Do Reproduce)," *Review of Political Economy*,

Rosen, H. (1985), *Public Finance*. Homewood: Irwin.

Solow, R. (1988), "The Wide, Wide World of Wealth" [review of *The New Palgrave*, edited by John Eatwell, Murray Milgate and Peter Newman], *The New York Times Book Review*, March 20: 3, 25.

Shapin, S. and Schaffer, S. (1985), *Leviathan and the Air-Pump*. Princeton: Princeton University Press.

Stigler, G. (1988), "Palgrave's Dictionary of Economics," *Journal of Economic Literature*, 26, 1729-1736.

Summers, L. (1987), "The Scientific Illusion in Macroeconomics," unpublished paper presented to the NBER Conference on Macroeconomics, March 13; the Charles Hotel, Cambridge, Mass.

Weintraub, E. R. (1989). "Methodology Doesn't Matter, But the History of Thought Might," *Scandinavian Journal of Economics*, 91, 477-93.

COMMENTARY BY DONALD N. McCLOSKEY

Economics, thank the Lord, is starting to look at itself with a richer theory of discourse than the received view in the philosophy of science. Economists believe they follow the received view, but of course they do not. No one does. Three decades of work in the philosophy, history, sociology, and now the rhetoric of science has shown that the self-descriptions of the natives are not to be listened to uncritically. As the psychologist David Baken remarked early in the work, "The common rhetorical form 'science is this' and 'science is that' is hardly ever backed up with empirical observations on the scientific enterprise itself" (1967, 140). The chapters by Jane Rossetti and Philip Mirowski identify new places from which to observe what economists actually do.

I have only minor disagreements, therefore, with their chapters and programs. We agree that paying attention to words differs from claiming that economics is not scientific. To suppose that being literary about economics is a denial of the scientific character of economics is to fall into the dichotomy of modernism,that you are either a Dr. Strangelove scientist or a Santa Monica touchie-feelie. Rossetti, Mirowski, and I—with a small but growing number of other economists who have woken from the long sleep of modernism—believe that you can be a scientist (small s) yet still be conscious of your rhetoric. Newton was; Darwin was; it is time that economic scientists became so.

My main disagreement with Rossetti is unfair to her excellent chapter. She and I note that the job in literary criticism is to read texts; the job in economics is to read the economy and to read the texts of economists about the economy. The jobs are similar, we agree, and therefore, economists can learn from literary critics. But if someone looked at her chapter alone, and had not dipped into the other literary criticism of economics by Arjo Klamer, or Roy Weintraub, or a few others, he might come away with the impression that literary criticism consists of deconstruction.

In the 1950s, an older man who had studied economics at college in his youth asked Bob Solow to recommend to him a book to freshen his knowledge. Bob told him that a good elementary book, which any lay person could handle, was "Samuelson," by which he meant *Economics*. A month later the man bumped into Solow again and said, "My word, economics has become mathematical! I couldn't make head nor tail of that book by Samuelson you recommended." It developed that the fellow had got hold of *Foundations of Economic Analysis* instead of *Economics*. No wonder he found it hard going. I worry that Rossetti's emphasis on deconstruction, which is the *Foundations* of literary criticism though not its foundation, will have the same effect.

Rossetti is serious about the use of literary theory in reading economics (she has taken the unusual step of actually learning something about literary theory; by contrast, the opponents of a literary approach have so far reckoned they can get along without knowing what they oppose). Certainly anyone who is serious, pro or con, ought to know something about deconstruction. But to recommend it as necessary for a literary reading of economics would be like recommending Tom Sargent's latest book as necessary for a nonliterary reading of economics. Both French deconstruction and freshwater macroeconomics (which have more than a few similarities) are good to know about and sometimes useful. But anyone who viewed them as the whole of literary criticism or the whole of economic science would be making a big mistake. You could frighten someone away from modern economics by telling them that math-proud economics was its essence. Likewise, you could frighten someone away from modern criticism by telling them that French leftwing criticism was its essence. I worry that focusing on something so terrifying as deconstruction will give economists a cheap excuse to go on ignoring the other half of their intellectual culture.

Deconstruction, for all the calls to arms from intellectually conservative publications like *The New York Times*, constitutes only a tiny part of criticism. It is not even the most *recent* of literary theories (feminism and new historicism are). It is merely one of a score of partially overlapping ways to do literary criticism. A partial list in historical order would contain: rhetorical, philological, belles lettristic, historical, new critical, psychoanalytic, Marxist, reader-response, deconstructive, feminist, and new historicist. In the same way you could divide up economics into Good Old Chicago School, eclectic econometric macro, nouvelle Chicago, highbrow general equilibrium, policy oriented micro, and so forth.

The reason I have to make the point is that people have a way of seeing a novelty such as literary approaches to economics through the strangest version with which they imagine they are familiar. Thus, outsiders to economics think they can reject a modest version of supply side economics by attacking what they imagine are the opinions of Arthur Laffer. The reason people do this is that they are naturally conservative, intellectually speaking, and would rather avoid investing in a new set of thinking tools if they can get away with it. You cannot blame journalists and other people outside the thinking racket for taking evasive action when they are presented with a new idea, but you *can* blame the professors. Contrary to what one might suppose, professors are especially inflexible about new ideas because they are paid large sums to know things already. As Harry Truman put it, "An expert is someone who doesn't want to learn anything new, because then he wouldn't be an expert." The professors reckon they know a thing or two about literary criticism if they had a college English course, or about economics if they took macroeconomics twenty years ago.

I myself have two objections to deconstruction (I *do* know a thing or two about it: some of my best friends are deconstructionists). The first is that as the *Times* has cleverly discerned, deconstruction does combine politics with literature. I don't like the combination any better than does the *Times*. No one could deny that the two are connected, but the deconstructionists (and, by the way, Philip Mirowski) think they are indissoluble. They want to make every literary question into a political question. The literary critic Gerald Graff argues persuasively against such a move. He wishes to "get beyond the whole dubious project on attaching specific political implications to [literary] theories independent of the way they operate in concrete social practice. A theory such as interpretive objectivism doesn't 'imply' any single politics. . . . Making political judgments and classifications of theories requires an analysis of social practices. Is there any reason to think current literary critics possess such an analysis?" (1983, 604f).

My second objection is that deconstruction seems stuck on a problem that I do not regard as a problem. Jacques Derrida's problem is that he is vexed with his inability to found his beliefs on bedrock. Unlike American pragmatists, he cares. After all, he and the other deconstructionists are French, schooled from childhood in Cartesian foundationalism; French people find American pragmatism or British eclecticism irritatingly casual about foundations. Deconstruction freezes itself in the anguished moment of disillusion, repeating over and over the mantra of lost illusions—"Seek not foundations for language." The American economist admits it is so, gives a sympathetic smile, and then gets back to work.

In this connection, on the matter of grounded Truth, I need to make only one adjustment to Rossetti's accurate and equitable summary of my own views. She writes, "McCloskey's stance isn't that we couldn't find truth if we wanted to, but that it is not what we want to do." I would say rather that we would not know Truth even if we found it since we do not have a path to God's understanding, and that in any case we do not want Truth—we want truth, small t, which is the practical knowledge we have of crossing the street or detecting electrons.

And yet the deconstructionists can help in literary work, as Rossetti's paper argues well. One insight that I think Derrida and company is properly to be credited with is the notion of verbal "hierarchy." Economists need help in "deprivileging," as the professors of literature would put it, the superior term in pairs like "microfoundations/macroeconomics" or "general/partial" or "rigorous/informal."

Rossetti does not deliver a deconstructionist account of the work of W. C. Mitchell or of other economists. She is writing about deconstruction, not showing it in action. The action can be shown easily. Look back for an example at the passage from Mitchell about "subconscious wishing" that Rossetti quotes (p. 220). It contains at least these half-spoken hierarchies ready for liberating deconstruction (reading back to front, the terms in square brackets being those implied but not mentioned): sober/subconscious, thought/wishing, product/[mere ephemera], sciences/[mere humanities], study/[beach reading], one/[you personally], leads/[compels], view/[grounded conviction], sciences/[mere] processes, development/[mere chaotic change], must/[can]. The first term of each is the privileged one—except that in the pairs leads/[compels] and view/[grounded conviction] they are in fact polite self-deprecation, with ironic force: Mitchell is on the contrary claiming the commanding heights of compelling and grounded conviction, not the soft valleys of mere gently leading views.

That's quite a haul for two sentences, and suggests that Derrida and his followers might be of some use to the economic reader, if she can figure out what in hell he is saying (no easy task, I assure you). In the vernacular, the economist Mitchell is playing all kinds of mind games on us readers, and we'd better watch out. Mitchell, of course, is not special. We all do it, both you and I. It is nothing to be ashamed about because as Rossetti stresses, the "economics is impossible to separate from the rest of the world." I would only add that the rest of the world we cannot be separated from is rhetoric.

Rossetti does well to remind us of that Wesley Clair Mitchell. American economists need to know about this surprisingly influential man, as influential in shaping American economics as was Paul Samuelson a generation later. He helped create the American enthusiasm for social engineering, writing for example in 1924 that "In economics as in other sciences we desire knowledge mainly as an instrument of control. Control means the alluring possibility of shaping the evolution of economic life to fit the developing purposes of the race" (quoted in Adelstein, 1990, 13). The erotic fascism of such ambitions for science was ravishing in the 1920s and 1930s. We still have not entirely gotten over it.

Rossetti's analysis of Mitchell's influence, I repeat, is not particularly deconstructionist. The social construction of knowledge is no invention of the deconstructionists. It has been a commonplace from Protagoras of Abdera to the present. When Mitchell himself speaks of sciences as "the product not merely of sober thinking but also of subconscious wishing," he is doing nothing more avant garde than reinscribing Francis Bacon's idols (with a Freudian fillip). And when Rossetti discusses Mitchell she is doing nothing more avant garde than reinscribing Protagoras: man is the measure of all things. But whether the point is entirely novel or not, Rossetti and I basically agree on it.

When I turn to Mirowski, I have more disagreement. Rossetti may be a little stuck on deconstruction, but Mirowski has not yet read literary criticism, deconstructive or rhetorical, or reader response, or new critical or whatever. Until he does his homework on literary criticism, it is going to be hard to take his literary criticism seriously. Mirowski, as I have remarked, believes in a dubious sociology of knowledge that there is an intimate connection between philosophies and practices. It is like saying that free verse and free love go together. (Such a view written out on the final exam is what would come from not turning in one's homework.)

This is my main problem with Mirowski and with other less sympathetic critics of a rhetorical approach. In a nutshell, they do not know what they are talking about and seem to be pleased that they do not. Their attitude reminds me of a reply that John Searle, the American analytic philosopher, gave me once when I asked him if he had read Hegel. "I have never read a page of Hegel; and furthermore, I propose never to do so." The reply evoked gales of laughter from the philosophy graduate students gathered around the great man, who thus exhibited his disdain for the considered judgment of half his culture.

But let me admit that even though Mirowski has not done his homework, he is so bright that he gets a pretty good grade on the McCloskey exam anyway. I agree with him, for example, that economists engage in methodology even while attacking it. Paul Samuelson and George Stigler are good examples: most papers these two have written contain methodological ukases mixed with lofty sneering at the very idea of thinking about thinking. Contrast James Buchanan, say, or Gordon Tullock, who have never apologized for making methodological points and have realized when they are doing it, since both are more than economists.

Mirowski and I agree, too, that the scientific paper is a literary device. If Mirowski must come to this realization through recent philosophy and sociology, I guess I should not object. At least he gets the point. True, it is vexing when he does not understand that the philosopher Markus's point is a commonplace of criticism, and has been since the Greeks. That the scientific paper in economics is a literary genre has been, of course, the main point of my tiny little ten-year contribution to the stream. But anyway, he comes to the same conclusion, which we agree is crucial for a reformed economics.

And the substantive stories he tells are excellent. I was shocked at the story about Larry Summers's travail at the NBER conference. Maybe "shocked" is not quite the right word; "depressed," rather, for it has been some time since intellectual thuggery has surprised me. Virginia Woolf deplored the philological wars of earlier times, "the extraordinary spectacle of men of learning and genius, of authority and divinity, . . . calling each other names for all the world like bookies on a racecourse or washerwomen in a back street" (1925 (1953), 198-99). Modern times witness the extraordinary spectacle of men and women of science behaving for all the world like *mafiosi* in conference or Chicago aldermen trying to keep the newspapers in the dark. Professors will do almost anything to prevent the calling of their rhetorical bluff. Mirowski instances the study of replication. I would add statistical significance (Bakan 1967, Chapter 1; Denton 1988). Economists go on using statistical significance even though the alert among them know that it cannot do what it is claimed to do—namely, tell an economist whether a coefficient is large enough to be scientifically interesting.

The biggest disagreement between Mirowski and me is over the word "neoclassical." Like a lot of people, he makes his scorn for mainstream, neoclassical economics much simpler by characterizing neoclassical economics in its silliest possible terms. Recall the problem with highlighting deconstruction. Similarly, the enemies of institutionalist, or Marxist, or Austrian economics make their life simpler by characterizing each as so idiotic as to be self-refuting.

Mirowski has in mind the formalism that identifies economic science with certain routines of constrained maximization. I do not deny that there exist terminally silly neoclassical economists who espouse such a model for economics, and who are often people with little experience of life. "The neoclassicals," says Mirowski, "have never been able to avail themselves of the full panoply of the 'experimental form of life,' and worse, espouse a theory which presumes a form of radical methodological individualism." But his characterization does not fit most neoclassicals. Marshall was a neoclassical economist; Keynes was a neoclassical economist; Theodore Schultz is a neoclassical economist; Robert Solow is a neoclassical economist; Ronald Coase is a neoclassical economists; and to descend quite a few notches, I am a neoclassical economist.

So it is wrong, to give an instance, for Mirowski to claim that neoclassical economics "has no explanation for how equilibrium is achieved." In partial equilibrium terms, the story is simple and convincing. It is no less an explanation than institutionalist explanations for how institutions are achieved, or Marxist explanations for how class dominance is achieved. Maybe general equilibrium with continuous traders in Banach space and other Monty Python versions of economic science have "no explanation" for what they see before them, but the same is not true of most neoclassical economics, working in the here and now.

Mirowski's basic notion in disagreement with me is that there is something inconsistent between using neoclassical economics, as I do in economic history, and yet being self-conscious about rhetoric, as I claim to be: to "renounce the scientism of economic discourse while maintaining the scientistic explanatory structure was inherently self-contradictory." He is repeating a claim he made at some length a few years ago in his urbane but ignorant reaction to *The Rhetoric of Economics* (1987 (1988)). He has repeated the notion since on many occasions and seems satisfied to stop his thinking there. I admit that I still don't get it. I still don't see why "the theory of social order in Rhetoric [is not] congruent with the notions of social order in neoclassical theory." And I still don't see why it matters if it is not.

Anyway, in my kind of neoclassicism, order of the economy is the same as the order of the speech. My kind is Keynes's kind, and Coase's kind, and the kind of many other neoclassicals. My kind reverses the metaphor: the market itself is a conversation, to be negotiated, driven by rules of talk. Think of Keynes's animal spirits and Coase's transaction costs. Advertising of consumers' goods is the obvious and easy example. Notice how much sellers and buyers of producers' goods talk to each other, filling airplanes with talkers on their way to conversations. Again, Larry Summers would, I think, agree with Arjo Klamer and me that the stockmarket is a conversation of humankind, most of whose motion cannot be attributed to "objective" events (and even these are read through language). As Klamer and Metin Cosgel have argued recently, still again, the entrepreneur is above all a rhetor, a persuader of bankers and workers and customers. The market lives on the lips of men and women, not in some place or on some graph. No neoclassical economist who thinks with something other than his engineering math book (and even not all of them) would deny such notions.

The neoclassical economists who have grasped the literary approach have mainly agreed with it: I would instance Robert Lucas, Theodore Schultz, Robert Solow, and Frank Hahn. They are not agreeing to anything very shocking. Mirowski himself joins me in noting that even the formalism depends on, as Nietzsche put it, "a movable host of metaphors, metonymies, and anthropomorphisms: in short, a sum of human relations which have been poetically and rhetorically intensified, transferred, and embellished, and which, after long usage, seem to a people to be fixed, canonical, and binding" (1870 (1979), 84).

The analysis of a language game—deconstruction, among others, if you wish—is not the same as advocating its destruction. The deconstructionists themselves often commit this error, being sometimes of a nihilist and usually of a radical hue, so it is not surprising that deconstruction has come to be associated with radicalism (root-and-branch). But as the literary critic Stanley Fish is fond of saying when he is trying to make the same point, nothing is implied by analysis. In particular, realizing that a language game is being played with certain elaborate rules, does not imply that one wants to stop the game or even change its direction. One realizes in baseball that there is an explicit, if complicated rule, called the infield fly rule. One realizes also that there is an implicit, if simple rule, that a player can cheat in certain ways (hide the ball as a first baseman in an attempt to catch the runner off base) and that, if not caught, the player is not held up for opprobrium. Realizing that such rules are in force does not imply a criticism of baseball in the nonacademic sense of "criticism." It does not imply that one disapproves of the sanctioned cheating, for example; it does not imply that a game in which the players realize that the infield fly rule is in operation will be paralyzed in an attitude of self-regard or filled with doubt that baseball has adequate foundations.

A lack of understanding of the rules is conservative because it leads to an uncritical following of whatever rules happen to be going at the moment: "That's the way we do it; don't ask me why, or even very closely, what." The corresponding attitude in literary criticism is a seat-of-the-pants belles lettrism, such as most educated people evince, fiercely but uncritically devoted, say, to a traditional canon of great works which they never read. (I am not denying that a belles lettristic attitude can be argued seriously; I am merely saying that often it is not.)

It does not follow, however, that understanding of the rules is necessarily radical. My radical friends, such as Mirowski, cannot get this straight. That conservatives do X does not mean that radicals necessarily do not-X. I admit that the sense of identity that motivates so much political and academic dispute tends to drive people into such absurdities as "Conservatives are polite in controversy [supposing for the sake of argument that they are; in my experience, actually, they are not]; therefore to be a proper radical I must be abusively impolite in controversy." It reminds me of a remark of E. A. G. Robinson, in an obituary on Keynes. The man himself did not believe "that nonsense syllogism that has so much bemused economics in recent years: I want to be a great man; Lord Keynes is a great man; Lord

Keynes always says something that appears to be paradoxical nonsense; therefore I must discover something that is paradoxical nonsense and say it. Truth is too delicate a fabric to be best produced as a by-product of intellectual vanity" [1947, 26]. Truth (small t, mind you) is too delicate a fabric to be best produced as from a superficial equation of verbal methods and political position.

In other words, it does not follow, *contra* Mirowski and Rossetti, that because I claim to have noted some of the rules of economic discourse that I am committed to overthrowing them. One can admire the economic game, as I do, and yet look into its rules, even with a notion of improving them. Come to think of it, the infield fly rule needs some work.

Yet Rossetti and Mirowski have made fine beginnings. Whatever minor differences I have with them, we entirely agree that economics needs to be looked at honestly, in a way that does not merely reproduce the official picture of economics. Incidentally, recent work on the history of econometrics has been disappointing on this score. Someone could do a serious history of econometrics that did not swallow its methodological pretenses by focusing on how the arguments were in fact sustained.

Talking in Rossetti's, or Mirowski's, or my way about the social construction of economics or other sciences is not to fall into dread Relativism. The Johnsonians among philosophers need not commence kicking rocks and pounding tables to show that the world is more than socially constructed. The world is still there, but we are still constructing it. It is like fishing. The fish are there by God's command, but humans make the nets. To catch fish we need both. It is unhelpful to argue that the caught fish are "really" social or "really" objective. They had better be both, or we are not going to eat on Fridays.

Mirowski's opening story of a literary criticism of economics degenerating to Methodology bashing is behindtimes, and arises again from his lamentable ignorance of literary criticism. Klamer, Weintraub, and as you can see, Rossetti, have in fact gone on to more detailed analyses in a literary vein. It is no longer just a proposal to be rejected on merely speculative grounds. The conversational methodology in economics, which seems frozen around 1965, has not so much been rejected as by-passed by literary approaches to economics. If someone wants to continue ruminating endlessly on Friedman's article of 1953, like a neurotic washing his hands fifty times a day, I suppose nothing can be done. But people who want a pointed and, yes, even a radical criticism of economics will be in the market for something else. Rhetoric, believe me, is what they are looking for.

REFERENCES

Adelstein, R. P. (1989), "'The Nation as an Economic Unit'. Keynes, Roosevelt and the Managerial Ideal." Department of Economics, Wesleyan University, unpublished manuscript.

Bakan, D. (1967), *David Bakan on Method: Toward a Reconstruction of Psychological Investigation.* San Francisco: Jossey-Bass.

Denton, F. T. (1988), "The Significance of Significance: Rhetorical Aspects of Statistical Hypothesis Testing in Economics," in Klamer, A. McCloskey, D. N. and Solow, R. M., eds., *The Consequences of Rhetoric.* Cambridge: Cambridge University Press, 163-183.

Graff, G. (1983), "The Pseudo-Politics of Interpretation," *Critical Inquiry*, 9 (March), 597-610.

Mirowski, P. (1987 [1988]), "Shall I Compare Thee to a Minkowski-Ricardo-Leontief-Metzler Matrix?" *Economics and Philosophy*, 3 (April), 67-96, reprinted in Klamer, McCloskey and Solow, eds., *The Consequences of Rhetoric*, 117-145.

Nietzsche, F. W. (1870 [1976]), *Philosophy and Truth: Selections from Nietzsche's Notebooks of the Early 1870s.* Atlantic Highlands, N.J.: Harvester Press.

Robinson, E. A. G. (1947), "John Maynard Keynes 1883-1946," *Economic Journal*, 57 (March), 1-68.

Woolf, V. (1925 [1953]), *The Common Reader.* New York: Harcourt Brace Jovanovich.

CHAPTER 7

GENDER AND ECONOMIC RESEARCH

Janet A. Seiz

> What types of knowledge do you want to disqualify in the very instant of your demand: "Is it a science?" Which speaking, discoursing subjects—which subjects of experience and knowledge—do you then want to "diminish" when you say: "I who conduct this discourse am conducting a scientific discourse, and I am a scientist"?
>
> —Foucault (1980, 85)

INTRODUCTION

Economists have long aspired to have their work accorded the status of science, and toward that end they have appropriated (or adapted) the positivist/empiricist methodologies of the natural sciences, including the ideal of value-free inquiry.[1] Though philosophers have in recent decades drastically pruned the epistemic authority associated with science, scientists' prestige and power in the world outside philosophy departments shows no signs of diminishing. Writing on economic methodology has become much more voluminous and philosophically sophisticated, so economists are increasingly likely to have heard the news that "positivism is dead."[2] But they seem little inclined to alter their practice—and there is little agreement among methodologists as to just how economic practice should be affected.

I wish here to add to the chorus of voices calling for change in economics, drawing upon what has become a substantial literature by feminist critics of the natural and social sciences.[3] This literature in many ways parallels other work on science and epistemology discussed in this volume. It shares the post-Kuhnian emphasis on the *social* nature of scientific activity, and it confronts the vexing and now-familiar conflicts between objectivism and relativism, but its focus on the "genderedness" of scientific work gives its critique unique elements. The first part of this chapter will identify some key questions raised and arguments advanced in this literature thus far, as applied to broad categories of science or the sciences rather than to specific disciplines or projects. I expect that readers of this part will have varying views of the relevance of these critiques to economics. In the second part of the chapter, I shall discuss the as yet rather limited literature addressing the question of the genderedness of economic discourse and present my own views of the implications of the feminist science critiques for the practice of economics.

FEMINIST CRITIQUES OF THE SCIENCES

> Feminist scholars have studied women, men, and social relations between the genders within, across, and insistently against the conceptual frameworks of the disciplines. In each area we have come to understand that what we took to be humanly inclusive problematics, concepts, theories, objective methodologies, and transcendental truths are in fact less than that. Instead, these products of thought bear the mark of their collective and individual creators, and the creators in turn have been distinctively marked as to gender, class, race and culture.
>
> —Harding (1986), 15

Feminist work on science began by addressing two problems that came to be seen as closely related: women's experiences, interests, and potentials have often been *misrepresented* in scientific accounts of natural and social reality; and women are *underrepresented* in the ranks of practitioners of science.

Many of the achievements of the sciences have led to improvements in women's well being, but scientists have often either neglected women's concerns relative to men's, as if women's lives were of little interest, or worse, scientists have done work that served to legitimate the oppression of women. Natural and social scientists have in numerous instances portrayed the male power and privilege observed in their societies as "natural" or "functional" or (in economists' case) the product of women's own choices. In the biological sciences, one thinks of the nineteenth century arguments that women should not receive education because this intellectual activity would damage female reproductive organs, and the great effort devoted to measuring skulls and weighing brains in hopes of finding physical explanations for the presumed intellectual inferiority of white women and women and men of color. In contemporary biological discourse, targets of feminist criticism include sociobiologists who affirm the naturalness of the gender division of labor, war, rape, and racial conflict; endocrinologists and neurobiologists who claim to offer biological explanations for presumed innate differences in men's and women's aggressiveness and mathematical (or visuospatial) abilities; and primatologists who tell stories of human evolution that focus so intently on the activities of man-the-hunter that it appears that only men have evolved, while women's natures and tasks have changed but little. Social scientists have often built upon notions of innate gender differences to argue that the gender division of labor—including the exclusion of women from positions of political, economic, religious and intellectual authority—is both in accord with women's natures and essential to social stability.[4]

Examining episodes such as these, feminists have challenged the pretense that objectivity sharply distinguishes the sciences from other sorts of inquiry (the view that scientific knowledge merely "mirrors what is," without invoking values or the subjectivity of the inquirer) and argued that the sciences, like other disciplines, are vulnerable to charges of androcentrism and ethnocentrism. The degree to which disciplines are vulnerable to charges of gender bias will obviously vary: the social and biological sciences, which deal explicitly with gender, are most suspect, but many feminists would argue that even sciences such as chemistry and physics are challengeable at some levels.

Knowledge and Identity

One plausible (if only partial) explanation of the sciences' misrepresentations of women and gender relations focuses upon the underrepresentation of women in scientific professions. In the sciences, as in other fields, the male near-monopoly on knowledge production means that the disciplines' notions of the good and the true (as well as the interesting) are notions that *men* find appealing.

Feminist scholars have taken on two tasks regarding the role of women in the sciences: they have documented the lives and contributions of numerous women scientists whose work was ignored or underrated in previous histories; and they have asked why there have been and are now so few women active in scientific inquiry. Their studies show that women have been excluded from scientific work and constrained as scientists in a multitude of ways.[5] Investigations of conditions both past and present have detailed the enormous obstacles placed in the paths of would-be and practicing women scientists by those who control access to scientific credentials, employment, research facilities, funds, and publication opportunities. These external obstacles are complemented by internal ones: women's socialization by families, educational and religious institutions, and the media has persuaded many that they lack the logical and quantitative abilities required for careers in science, or that such work in unwomanly. Finally, scientific careers (like many others) are structured so that it is quite difficult to reconcile the demands of work and family; in fact, it could be argued that it is difficult to achieve more than moderate success without the supportive labor of a "wife."

Though some scientists probably have consciously set out to use their work to strengthen male (and/or white and western) privilege and power, feminists do not argue that the androcentrism of science is a matter of conscious intent.[6] Rather, in common with many other science critics, they emphasize that scientific inquiry takes place in a world structured by relations of power and privilege based on class, race, gender, and geography, and those relations shape scientists' work in at least two important ways: first, and most obviously, scientists must pursue the agendas of those who fund their research, and it is likely to be the privileged and powerful who control such funding. Second, scientists as individuals themselves occupy positions in these social structures and one's position is associated with a set of *experiences* that affect what one is likely to see and to wonder about, and with a set of *interests* that afffect what one hopes to be true.[7]

The identity of the knowledge seeker is clearly operative in the context of discovery. As Harding notes, "there is no such thing as a problem without a person (or groups of them) who have this problem: a problem is always a problem *for* someone or other" (1987a,6). But subjectivity may operate as well in the context of justification. The sciences' justificatory practices do, of course, often lead to the discrediting of theories, and so, scientific ideology presents "the scientific method" as "the protector against rampant subjectivities and the guarantor of the objectivity and validity of scientific knowledge" (Bleier, 1986, 3). But scientists are unlikely to devote much effort to attempting to falsify theories that they find plausible and useful; and even if they did, there are, strictly speaking, no "crucial tests." Thus, the lack of diversity in the scientific community produces a commonality of interests and of limitations of vision; androcentric and enthnocentric theories are not rooted out, and better explanations are not advanced, because those who might challenge the prevailing arguments lack numbers and influence. The pretense that scientists are merely neutral and objective observers of reality, then, serves both psychological and political functions:

> By draping their scientific activities in claims of neutrality, detachment, and objectivity, scientists augment the perceived importance of their views, absolve themselves of social responsibility for the applications of their work, and leave their (unconscious) minds wide open to political and cultural assumptions. Such hidden influences and biases are particularly insidious in science because the cultural heritage of the practitioners is so uniform as to make these influences very difficult to detect and unlikely to be brought to light or counterbalanced by the work of other scientists with different attitudes. Instead, the biases themselves become part of a stifling science-culture, while scientists firmly believe that as long as they are not conscious of any bias or political agenda, they are neutral and objective, when in fact they are only unconscious (Namenwirth 1986, 29).

If knowledge is indeed importantly shaped by the social identity of the inquirers, a large-scale influx of women into the scientific professions might be expected to improve scientific knowledge.[8] Women scientists might ask new questions, obtain new observations, suggest new explanations, and uncover and correct the flaws produced by androcentric bias. Thus, having more women practicing science may be seen as not merely a question of fairness (equal opportunity), but also one of truth. Making the community of knowledge seekers more diverse might yield new, more reliable knowledge, providing more adequate pictures of the natural and social worlds.

It is here that the really difficult part of the discussion begins. The argument that "were more women to engage in science, a different science might emerge" is, as Evelyn Fox Keller notes, in sharp conflict with "the formal view of science as being uniquely determined by its own logical and empirical methodology" (1985, 76). If feminists are in agreement (and in good company) in challenging this received view, they are far from agreed as to just how different science should be. What might feminist sciences look like? What would it take to eliminate androcentric bias from the sciences? How extensive a transformation should feminists hope for and demand? Harding (1986, 1987a) identifies three basic stances taken by feminist science critics on these questions, which she calls feminist empiricism, feminist standpoint epistemology, and feminist postmodernism.

The most moderate position, "*feminist empiricism*," accepts the basic positivist/empiricist methodologies and forms of argument of the sciences and suggests that what is needed is simply a correction of the bias-produced flaws in scientists' claims and research procedures. This position, Harding says, "appears to challenge mainly the incomplete way empiricism has been practiced, not the norms of empiricism themselves"—its argument is that "mainstream inquiry has not rigorously adhered to its own norms" (1987a,183). In this scenario, new work done by scientists, who are unhampered by the blinders of androcentric bias, will increase the objectivity of scientific knowledge in accordance with existing standards of "good science."

Proponents of what Harding calls "*feminist standpoint epistemology*" argue that the transformation of scientific claims and practices must be considerably more extensive. Women and men, in this view, have very different standpoints on, or ways of knowing, natural and social reality. Thus, the new (nonandrocentric) sciences' arguments may differ from the old in *form* as well as *content*, and may be reached and even justified, by quite different methods. Here, it is expected not merely that women scientists might offer different accounts of matters concerning gender and gender relations; women might actually change science in much more fundamental ways, including the relationship posited between the inquirer and the object of knowledge.

Two rather different versions of feminist standpoint epistemology have been advanced. One, most closely associated with the work of Keller, takes an essentially psychological approach, tracing the dissimilarity of male and female standpoints and values to divergences in early childhood development. The other, associated with Hilary Rose, Nancy Hartsock, and Dorothy Smith, is more sociological, resembling the stance of some Marxists: the inquirer's standpoint—what one can "see" and how one "knows"—is determined by one's experience of work and one's place in the society's hierarchies of rulers and ruled.[9] The two approaches will be considered here in this order.

Keller argues that to understand the history of science, one must recognize not only "that science has been produced by a particular subset of the human race—that is, almost entirely by white, middle-class men," but also that science "has evolved under the formative influence of a *particular ideal of masculinity*" (1985, 7; emphasis added). One must not merely argue that, since all scientific work is value-laden, scientists' claim to objectivity is a false one; one should go further, and ask how far the prevailing notion of scientific objectivity is itself a product of the genderedness of science.

The association of scientific inquiry with masculinity appears in the most basic categories of Western thought and has been present from the very beginning of modern science. Western thought, including scientific thought, is pervaded by dualisms—mind/body, reason/emotion, culture/nature, objectivity/subjectivity—in which the first of each pair is associated with the masculine and the second with the feminine, and for centuries the project of civilization has been said to require the dominance of the former over the latter.[10] The persona of the autonomous, emotionally detached, impersonal inquirer, and the related notion that the purpose of knowledge is to obtain control over the object of study, are in this view themselves androcentric, embodying what many feminists consider an undesirable stance toward natural and social reality.

Keller (1985) suggests that the masculine scientific persona originates in males' psychological needs for emotional distance, personal autonomy, and control, all of which are core aspects of masculinity as constructed in modern Western culture. She draws upon object relations theory to describe how these psychological needs develop as part of the formation of gender identity in male children.[11] Females, according to object relations theory, are socialized to value relationship and reciprocity over autonomy and control; thus, a science less determined to exclude the "feminine" might approach the object of knowledge quite differently. Keller calls for a scientific attitude she calls "dynamic objectivity," which would resemble "empathy," building upon the inquirer's "kinship" with the object of study and making use of "subjective experience" (1985, chs. 6,9).[12]

The more sociological approach focuses upon differences in men's and women's adult experiences, particularly upon the gender division of labor. Rose (1986) and Hartsock (1983a) emphasize women's "caring labor" in the family, which they see as at once manual, intellectual, and affective, and thus different from most of the work roles occupied by men. Rose argues that "women's labor constitutes a material reality that structures a distinctive understanding of the social and natural worlds" and calls for the development of a feminist epistemology that "transcends dichotomies, insists on the scientific validity of the subjective, on the need to unite cognitive and affective domains," and "emphasises holism, harmony and complexity rather than reductionism, domination, and linearity" (1986, 72). Rose, like Keller, is thinking primarily of the natural sciences. Hartsock makes a similar gender-division-of-labor analysis of social inquiry, and calls for the development of a feminist historical materialism.

Dorothy Smith, writing about sociology, emphasizes that inquirers' standpoints are determined by their positions in both gender and class structures. It is the demands of "ruling" that have shaped the direction of sociological inquiry and the voice in which sociological knowledge is transmitted (the reader may wish to try substituting "economics" for "sociology"): "Sociology is part of the practice by which we are all governed and that practice establishes its relevances. . . . The relevances of sociology are organized in terms of a perspective on the world which is a view from the top. . . . Issues are formulated as issues which have become administratively relevant, not as they are significant first in the experience of those who live them" (1974, 8). Sociology's agenda "is grounded in the working worlds and relations of men, whose experience and interests arise in the course of . . . participation in the ruling apparatus of this society" (1987, 62). Women are largely excluded from such participation, and "women's questions" are not pursued. Evading the fact that "our kind of society is known and experienced rather differently from different positions within it," sociology acts to confer scientific authority on this view of society from the top, delegitimating accounts of society as it looks from below (1974, 12).

Smith proposes "to make a sociology from the standpoint of women," one which "would make it possible for us to look at any or all aspects of a society from where we are actually located, embodied, in the local historicity and particularities of our lived worlds" (1987, 8). Examined from women's standpoint, the structure and problems of a society may appear quite different.

Arguments that men and women have distinct standpoints as knowers have a number of disturbing implications that will be discussed at some length below. One of the largest problems is that of the apparent incommensurability of knowledge claims, to the extent that they are based upon distinct male and female experiences. This would seem to offer little hope for achieving consensus about the way the world works. Among feminist science critics, there are some—whom Harding calls "*feminist postmodernists*"—who appear willing, at least at some moments, to embrace the relativism toward which standpoint epistemology seems ultimately to point. These writers, influenced by the declarations of epistemological crisis in recent philosophy and in postmodernist literary and cultural studies, reject science itself as an enterprise. They argue that all accounts of reality are necessarily partial, and that it is, therefore, fruitless to search for a single account of a phenomenon that would be universally acknowledged as adequate. Rather than claiming that one has uncovered the truth, it would be preferable simply to allow that there are many truths. As Jane Flax puts it, "Perhaps reality can have 'a' structure only from the falsely universalizing perspective of the dominant group. That is, only to the extent that one person or group can dominate the whole, will reality appear to be governed by one set of rules or be constituted by one priviledged set of social relations" (1987, 634).[13]

Feminism and Knowledge

The three groups identified by Harding take different positions on fundamental questions concerning the existence of, and most fruitful approach to, truth. These epistemological questions are ones that feminists share with all contemporary commentators on science. If feminists have not been able to resolve (or, more modestly, to reach consensus on) them, neither have other scholars, and it is likely that no consensus will ever be reached.

The work that seems to me most promising does not fit easily into any of the three categories discussed above. This work rejects both the old-fashioned positivist faith Harding attributes to her feminist empiricists and the relativism of the postmodernists. And though it makes much of the importance of points of view to inquiry, those points of view are characterized as "feminist" and "nonfeminist" rather than "female" and "male."

The argument that one's questions, beliefs and values are shaped by one's experience, which is in turn shaped by one's social location, is an appealing one. It may well be that women and men differ, on average, in their questions, beliefs, styles of inquiry, and ways of justifying claims, and that scientific communities have tended to adopt conventions that conformed to the masculine style and to eschew approaches that might be thought of as feminine. Still, it would seem a mistake for feminists to frame their objectives as a call for a more "feminine" science. There are several serious problems with arguments that there is, as Longino (1987, 52) puts it, a specific "female sensibility or cognitive temperament" that a "female" or "feminist" science would express.

1. Even if consciousness could be said to be reliably determined by social location, there would have to be many different "women's standpoints," since women are of different races, nationalities, classes, religions, sexual/affectional orientations, etc. There is increasing recognition in feminist theory that such differences do not merely constitute "additions" to what all women experience in common "as women"; rather, the meaning of being a woman (or man) is likely to vary with these other aspects of social location. So to posit a unitary women's standpoint is to engage in the same sort of false universalization that feminists have deplored in androcentric discourse.[14] And women with like social locations do not in fact all see the world similarly; in particular, they hold varied views on gender issues. Thus, "standpoint epistemologies must either develop complicated explanations of why some women see the truth and others do not, a strategy that threatens to undermine the very notion of a 'women's standpoint,' or collapse into a trivial and potentially contradictory pluralism that conceives of truth as simply the sum of all women's partial and incompatible views." (Hawkesworth, 1989, 546).

2. Even though feminists generally emphasize that it is experience and not biology that makes women's standpoints differ from men's, emphasizing gender difference has dangers. To many listeners, an acknowledgment that gender differences exist (that the distributions of some traits and attitudes among men and women are different, though overlapping) is easily taken for a proposition that those differences are universal, inevitable, and perhaps even innate.

3. Feminists should not seek to valorize every characteristic

associated with women; such efforts, Longino observes, conflate "feminine with feminist. While it is important to reject the traditional derogation of the virtues assigned to women, it is also important to remember that women are *constructed* to occupy positions of social subordinates. We should not uncritically embrace the feminine." (1987, 52-53).

4. Finally, there are the discomfiting questions mentioned earlier that such arguments raise about the status of feminist claims about reality. If women's standpoints are so different from men's, what hope is there of reaching scientific agreement? Must female scientists aim their work only at female audiences, or can they also hope to persuade men of the validity of their claims?[15]

It would be better to replace the question "how would *women* change science," with "what difference would a *feminist perspective* make to the sciences?" This would avoid a deterministic overemphasis on the social identity of the inquirer, without denying the importance of subjectivity. One would expect that women would be more likely to adopt feminist perspectives than would men, because of the interests involved, but one would not expect all women inquirers to be feminists, nor rule out the possibility of feminist work being done by men. The epistemological and methodological tasks facing feminists then center on defining the role of values in the search for knowledge and developing standards for assessing knowledge claims and research methods in varied fields. How can feminists acknowledge the value-ladenness of inquiry and the fallibility of knowledge without embracing relativism or seeming to assess claims principally by their consistency with the political goals of feminism, disregarding other criteria? Longino (1987, 1990) argues that the difficulties are not insurmountable. She pictures feminist inquirers consciously choosing, in many cases, to work with analytical frameworks or assumptions that differ significantly from those of their nonfeminist colleagues. Feminist biologists looking at human sex differences, for example, might well reject a model that assumes "a direct one-way causal relationship between pre- or post-natal hormone levels and later behavior or cognitive performance," and develop instead a more complex model that "allows not only for the interaction of physiological and environmental factors but also for the interaction of these with a continuously self-modifying, self-representational (and self-organizing) central processing system." (1987, 58) They will thus be rejecting a narrow biological determinist account of sex differences, emphasizing instead that we humans have the capacity to change our concepts of self and our behavior. Both models will be subject to criticism and testing; since empirical investigation may never establish decisively which model is more "true," the scientific community's choice between them will necessarily also be guided by values.

This scenario, in which one of the criteria for theory appraisal is consistency with feminist goals, may sound like a dangerous sort of instrumentalism to those who are not used to thinking of inquiry as properly "political." But feminists might respond, first, by emphasizing that feminist inquiry should be pursued with integrity—inquirers should be open to criticism, to confrontation with evidence, and to persuasion; and second, by insisting that all inquiry is guided by values, and making those values explicit, should facilitate (not hinder) inquiry and theory-assessment. The value freedom and infallibility that this scenario abandons hope of attaining are phenomena more characteristic of scientific ideology than of scientific practice. As Longino notes, "a consequence of embracing the social character of knowledge is the abandonment of the ideals of certainty and of the permanence of knowledge. Since no epistemological theory has been able to guarantee the attainment of those ideals, this seems a minor loss." (1990, 232)

Feminist scholars will not all agree on how to develop "feminist-consistent" research methods, analytical frameworks, and fundamental assumptions for use in (and across) individual disciplines; they will certainly not all agree on particular claims made in specific areas of inquiry; and they may not often succeed in totally displacing the arguments of nonfeminist opponents. But "the accretion of such interventions, of science done by feminists as feminists, and by members of other disenfranchised groups, has the potential, nevertheless, ultimately to transform the character of scientific discourse." (Longino 1987, 62)

ECONOMICS AND THE FEMINIST CRITIQUES

As the most male dominated of the social sciences, economics would seem a likely target for feminist critique. While I have argued above that one should not overemphasize the degree to which inquirers' social identities shape their intellectual work, a discipline that is neither hospitable nor attractive to women inquirers should be suspected of androcentrism. Thus, I shall begin by discussing the representation of women in the economics profession. Feminists have been highly critical of the ways in which mainstream economists explain women's experiences and gender relations, and I shall discuss their principal criticisms. Considerably less has been written thus far on the question of androcentrism in economic method, and the final section of the chapter will explore whether the fundamental analytical frameworks employed in neoclassical economics might themselves be viewed as gender-biased.[16]

Women in Economics

Women are poorly represented in the economics profession. In the late 1970's, only 8 percent of Ph.D.'s in economics were being received by women; by 1988, the figure had risen only to 19 percent, still far lower than the proportions in other social sciences. Many departments of economics have no female faculty members, and women economists are distributed very unevenly among fields.[17]

Strikingly little research has been done on what prevents women from achieving greater numbers and influence in economics. As with other scientific disciplines, one must suspect that a variety of obstacles play a part. The profession appears to be far from free of bias against women. When the University of Chicago Press established its *Journal of Labor Economics*—labor economics being the field where gender issues are most likely to be addressed—it created a furor by having no women economists on the journal's editorial board. Alice Rivlin, the 1987 President of the American Economic Association, was the first woman to hold that position in a hundred years of the organization's existence. The AEA is the only major social science professional organization that has not initiated a project to address the treatment of gender issues in teaching.[18] Economics is the only discipline in the social sciences besides anthropology that does not have a journal specifically devoted to work on women and gender.[19] And a small sample study of economics journals found that when journals used "double-blind" reviewing procedures, the acceptance rates for articles authored or coauthored by women were higher than those for articles authored by men alone, but women's work had lower acceptance rates than men's when reviewers were given the names of the authors (Ferber and Tieman, 1981).

It may be that the way economics is taught makes it particularly unappealing to women students. Introductory economics textbooks, according to one feminist study, give little attention to gender issues, tend to reinforce gender stereotypes, minimize the importance of discrimination as a factor in gender inequality and undermine arguments for social change by insisting that (in general) greater equality can only be achieved at the cost of reduced efficiency (Feiner and Morgan, 1987). And economics, even at the undergraduate level, is more and more a quantitative discipline. If, as many believe, female students learn to be frightened of, or averse to mathematics, they may be deterred from becoming economists.[20]

Economics on Women and Gender Relations

One sometimes finds in feminist economists' work, particularly work written for multidisciplinary audiences, broad indictments of the treatment of gender issues in economic discourse. Feminists have noted that women's lives and concerns were long ignored in economic literature. Until very recently, economists

> showed little interest in those segments of the economy that have been largely the domain of women, namely household production and volunteer work. They also generally ignored the extent to which women were involved in the rest of the economy and the ways in which behavior, their problems and their accomplishments differed from those of men. While no justification for this neglect was offered, it was presumably caused by the view that the importance of market work was secondary for women, destined to be wives and mothers, and that the importance of women's market work was secondary to the economy (Ferber and Teiman, 1981, 128; see also Barrett, 1981).

The exclusion of women's unpaid work from measures of national income reflects the social undervaluation of such work, as well as the measurement problems involved. And discussions of economic policies regarding, for example, taxation, government expenditure, economic development, and international trade only rarely ask what effects policy choices will have on women and on gender relations.

Feminists have offered some harsh characterizations—some might say caricatures—of the ways in which neoclassical economics explains women's lives.[21] There has been particularly strong criticism of "Chicago school" work on discrimination, human capital, and the economics of the household. Gary Becker's work on the family, Barbara Bergmann argues, "explains, justifies, and even glorifies role differentiation by sex. . . . To say that the 'new home economists' are not feminist in their orientation would be as much of an understatement as to say that Bengal tigers are not vegetarians" (1987, 132-33). "Neoclassical economics," says Ester Boserup, explains economic inequality between men and women "as a result of free and rational choice, based upon the biological differences between the sexes," and has "helped to make the principle [of male superiority] acceptable. Since the theory assumes that differentials in wages equal differentials in marginal productivity of labor, the lower wage rates for women could be taken as a confirmation of the general assumption of female inferiority" (1987, 824-25). And Marianne Ferber and Michele Teiman assert that "The new tools developed for the economic analysis of the family . . . have to a considerable extent been used to tacitly endorse the status quo" (1981, 131).

Other criticisms offered by feminist economists include (but are not limited to) the following:

1. Neoclassical economics has tended to reproduce gender stereotypes by portraying behavior in the marketplace (seen as men's domain) as guided by the rational pursuit of self-interest, and behavior in the household (seen as women's sphere) as guided by altruism (Folbre and Hartman, 1988).[22]

2. Economic models which posit a unitary household utility function or assign family decision-making power to a benevolent despot abstract from conflict among family members concerning the allocation of individuals' time and the use of income (Folbre, 1984, 1986, Hartmann, 1981b, McCrate, 1987).

3. Economic theory rationalizes the gender division of labor. Women are said to specialize in work in the home, and men in market work, as rational responses to their respective comparative advantage. Such accounts fail to capture the extent to which childrearing and housework are tasks "whose social imposition is one manifestation of gender hierarchy" (Ciancanelli and Berch, 1987, 245). Far from being the result of simple mutual interest, "both in the household and in the labor market, the division of labor by gender tends to benefit men" (Hartmann, 1987, 114).

4. Theories explaining women's occupations and earnings similarly rationalize women's economic disadvantage. Women are said to choose occupations that are most compatible with "their family responsibilities," which require little investment in human capital, are

relatively easy to leave and reenter, offer hours that do not disrupt childcare, etc. This presents a view of "the inferior labor market position of women as something women have freely chosen, as a normal and generally benign adaptation to 'their responsibilities' for housework and childrearing. Low-wage work is seen as appropriate for people who behave as they do. The laws against discrimination and the apparatus designed to enforce them are, in this view, superfluous or of minor value" (Bergmann 1989, 43). The situation that feminists decry as unjust is portrayed in such accounts as a vicious circle of women's own making: "women specialize in housework because they earn less in labor market, and they earn less in the labor market because they specialize in housework" (Ferber and Birnbaum 1977, 20).

5. Women's economic activity and contributions have been consistently underestimated by economists and statisticians, who employ definitions of work that are modeled on the work experiences of men (Ciancanelli and Berch, 1987). And economists have lately underpredicted women's labor force participation rates because they have tended "to assume that women only react to changing economic conditions and ignore the impact of changing attitudes and ideologies brought about by the new feminist movement" (Ferber and Teiman, 1981, 133). The methodological rule that one should assume constant preferences, adopted to prevent economists from advancing ad hoc and untestable arguments, has here impeded understanding, blocking from view a widespread change in social consciousness.[23]

6. Too many economists, ostensibly because they are unpersuaded that labor market discrimination is consistent with profit maximization in competitive markets, simply deny the importance of discrimination. Much too much weight is placed on supply factors and much too little on demand in explaining earnings inequality.[24]

A complete feminist critique of economic discourse on gender might: 1) explain what is wrong with arguments such as those criticized above, and provide alternative accounts of women's and men's economic experiences; 2) explain how androcentrism is implicated in the origins and acceptance of flawed arguments; and 3) argue either that the arguments' weaknesses are inextricably linked to the methods of inquiry that produced them, or that the same methods can be used to develop, present, and justify adequate arguments. I shall concentrate here on parts (2) and (3) of this agenda.

The Need for Feminist Histories of Economic Discourse

It is easy enough to see how it is in the interest of male (or antifeminist) economists to believe theories that portray existing gender relations as inevitable or as the product of women's own choices. But this in itself neither establishes that androcentric bias exists in economics nor constitutes an explanation of how such bias might operate. There are thus far no detailed accounts of exactly where and how androcentric bias enters economic research, and why "bad" arguments are not eliminated over time.

Feminists should be providing close studies of particular economic texts and research programs along these lines.[25] Models for such studies exist; they build upon two crucial insights:

1. Elaborating a theoretical argument, developing and testing a hypothesis, and interpreting empirical results require the researcher to make a number of choices. Though reports of scientific work rarely acknowledge those choices (much less indicate the researcher's motivation in making them), it is often possible to identify "roads not taken." Choices are made again as the scientific community appraises arguments, and one can inquire as to how warranted was the reception a particular argument received, given the community's conventions regarding assessment.[26]

2. Scientific writings can be analyzed as *texts*. Scholars of scientific discourse can utilize literary theory and rhetoric to explore scientists' strategies for persuasion, including the tacit assumptions and silences in their writings. Here it is important to recognize the indeterminancy of language and the active role the reader plays in investing a text with meaning.

One model for feminist histories of economic discourse might be Longino and Doell (1983), which applied the first of these insights in a study of endocrinological and primatological research. They examined the "chains of scientific reasoning" in the two fields, seeking to identify the points at which researchers' decisions might be most vulnerable to "external" (psychological, cultural or institutional) influences. They emphasized four such points: 1) the choice of problems (of phenomena which require explanation); 2) the choice of language to describe the problems; 3) the choice of theories to be considered as possible explanations; and 4) the choice to characterize certain facts as evidence for a particular hypothesis, which involves positing a more or less extensive structure of auxiliary assumptions.

Scientists' choices may reflect a variety of interests or values, some disciplinary and some extrascientific—for example, the history and aspirations of a research program may produce methodological constraints.[27] And since theories in different fields of research have different logical structures and different degrees of "distance" between hypotheses and data, the precise ways in which androcentric bias and other values enter research can differ considerably from one line of inquiry to another.

One will of course not "prove" from such investigations that it was androcentric bias that determined any particular choice by a researcher or a professional audience. But I expect that as feminists look closely at economic literature, we will see many instances in which gender ideology seems to have strongly influenced (and to be reproduced in) economic research. In some cases, such research may be judged "bad science" by conventional standards, and those instances are important to uncover. But in other cases, the arguments will not have appeared unsound or poorly supported at the time they were advanced and accepted. At any rate, the goal of such feminist historical inquiries should not be to convict particular economists of having been biased, but rather to reveal the operation and weaken the authority of gender ideology in economic discourse.

The second insight, which has begun to influence discussions of economics due to the work of Arjo Klamer and Donald McCloskey,[28] involves exploring the generation of meanings in scientific texts. Questions concerning meanings and the interpretive role of the reader have been little explored by scholars of economic discourse. Most discussions focus on models and tests, the parts of economic discourse that best conform to positivist/empiricist views of science and neglect other types of economic argumentation. This narrowness is encouraged by the influential "predictionist-instrumentalist" argument, that economic models should be viewed not as (simplified) representations of reality, but rather as devices for generating predictions (Friedman, 1953). But it is impossible to fully understand the operation of gender ideology in economics if we focus exclusively on models and tests. And the predictionist-instrumentalist view, because it evades the issues of representation raised by feminist (and other) critics of neoclassical economics, is an important obstacle to the feminist project.

Meanings are present in economic models and economic language and in the examples and analogies economists offer when they discuss theoretical propositions. A model presents a "story" about the behavior of decision makers in particular situations and implies that correlations should be found among certain variables. Observed correlations may be consistent with a number of conflicting stories that contain very different meanings. Predictionist instrumentalists discourage discussion of these meanings by insisting that the story a model tells is unimportant: all that matters, they say, is whether economic outcomes occur in reality "as if" the story were accurate.[29]

But economists devising and appraising models do so in the context of a larger public discourse that offers its own narratives explaining gender relations. And the degree to which economists' models are congruent with those popular stories must surely influence how models are read and judged. Bleier noted the importance of context in a study of biological sex difference research. Examining the language used to present claims, she concluded that "the scientists whose work I quote stop just short of making assertions that their data cannot defensibly support. But they can rely upon their readers—other scientists, science writers, and the science-reading public—to supply the (intended) relevant cultural meaning to their text; for example, that women are innately inferior in visuospatial and mathematical skills" (1986, 10). Feminist analyses should take account of this interplay, and ask what messages readers are likely to extract from an economic text. The work of Chicago school economists, for example, need not contain explicit statements that (in Bergmann's words, quoted above) "the inferior labor market position of women" is "something women have freely chosen," and thus is "benign." Those texts, nevertheless, are often read (by both supporters and opponents) as embodying that view.

Economic discourse, it should be noted, encompasses more than economists' academic writing. Feminists should examine not just what economists write for their professional peers, but also work directed to broader audiences. Investigation of androcentrism in economics should also encompass inquiry into the sociology of knowledge production in economics. Feminist historical/literary/sociological analyses of economics will undoubtedly meet resistance, but they may over time contribute substantially to the reduction of gender bias in economic discourse.

Gender and Economic Methodology

Though very little has been written about whether the methods of economics are androcentric, one can find some glimmers of the "feminist empiricist" and "standpoint epistemology" stances discussed in the first part of this chapter.

Some feminist economists clearly believe that feminists can and should develop, articulate, and justify their arguments in accordance with the mainstream conventions of constrained optimization modeling and econometric testing. Ferber and Teiman, after arguing that "the new tools developed for the economic analysis of the family" have largely been used "to tacitly endorse the status quo," go on to suggest that "the same tools have the potential for being used constructively" (1981, 131). Lloyd and Niemi criticize the "dominant approach to labor market analysis" for assuming "that roughly the same wide array of choices lies before each individual" and for assigning the demand side of the labor market "an essentially passive role in the determination of sex differentials" (1979, 2-4). But they do not call for any fundamental changes in economic method for addressing gender issues; rather, they suggest economists use "the concepts of segmented labor markets and discrimination . . . to broaden, rather than to replace, the orthodox theory" (1979, 5). These "feminist empiricists" in economics would have women/feminists pose new questions, obtain new data, propose new explanations, and devise new tests, to produce within the neoclassical framework more adequate representations of the interests, perceived options, and actions of women and men.

Some might argue, in fact, that most of the feminist criticisms of economic theories on gender listed above are already being addressed within the broad confines of neoclassical economics. The problem of conflict in the household, for example, is being analyzed in interesting ways using game theory and a transactions cost approach, and work continues on theories of discrimination and searches for evidence of its importance.[30]

The "standpoint epistemology" stance is (so far) best represented by Donald McCloskey's "Some Consequences of a Feminine Economics." Here McCloskey characterizes conventional "modernist" economics, which he criticized at length in his *Rhetoric of Economics* (1985a), as a "masculine" enterprise, and suggests that a "feminine" economics would be quite different. Women, he believes, have interests, values, perceptions and communication styles that differ from those of men; thus, women should tend to approach economics in general (not just the analysis of gender issues) very differently than men do. "Looking at the economy with feminine eyes . . . is made more difficult than it has to be by certain masculine rules of methodology" (1985b,13). For example, he suggests that women economists, being more willing than men to allow the objects of inquiry to speak for themselves, would make more use of qualitative survey research and place less emphasis on mathematical modeling:

> The implicit rule against surveys arises from a peculiarly masculine view of inquiry: "If you ask someone what they are doing they will tell you lies." . . . The hostility to the survey among men, and their eagerness to reduce it to numbers, probably arises from their well-known lack of practice in talking [or, one might note, listening?] (1985b, 13).
>
> The favored epistemological status of mathematical proof favors men, who believe it more readily. . . . The notion that one can prove or disprove a great social truth by standing at a blackboard is a peculiarly masculine delusion. . . . Men . . . can believe any crazy abstraction about society, and indeed stand ready to impose the abstraction on others by force of arms, because they do not know what a "society" is. . . . The plan to reduce all science to True Theorems and Non-Falsified Predictions reflects a masculine view of the simplicity of life (1985b, 16-17, 21).

These arguments, certainly provocative, merit further discussion. But they are subject to all the criticisms of standpoint epistemology outlined earlier. There is no cognitive temperament or view of economic reality that is common to all women. To suggest that there is constitutes false universalization and reinforces false notions of inevitable (or even innate) gender differences. Approaches to inquiry that may be more favored by women than by men do need to be explored, but they should not be embraced simply because of their association with femaleness. Women may indeed be less attracted to mathematical reasoning than are men, but that is by no means a sufficient reason for feminists to reject the language of mathematics; and one need hardly be female to appreciate the usefulness of surveys and qualitative research.

A more persuasive call for transformation would not rest upon a "way of knowing" unique to women, but upon an argument that the reality of gender relations cannot be adequately represented within the individual optimization framework. In this view, economists must develop new analytical approaches in order to fully understand the experiences of women. They may then find that those new concepts and techniques are useful for analyzing other problems as well (Nelson 1987). The call here is for the adoption in economics of a *feminist* standpoint, not a *feminine* one.

Thomas Kuhn observes that one of the functions of a scientific paradigm is to help scientists choose problems

> that, while the paradigm is taken for granted, can be assumed to have solutions. To a great extent these are the only problems that the community will admit as scientific or encourage its members to undertake. Other problems . . . are rejected as metaphysical, as the concern of another discipline, or sometimes as just too problematic to be worth the time . . . A paradigm can . . . even insulate the community from those socially important problems that are not reducible to the puzzle form, because they cannot be stated in terms of the conceptual and instrumental tools the paradigm supplies (1970, 37).

One of the central tasks of feminist scholars has been to investigate the extent to which the conceptual frameworks and analytical techniques employed in particular disciplines impede recognition and critical examination of women's oppression. I would like here to explore ways in which the primary theoretical method of neoclassical economics—individual optimization and market equilibrium modeling—limits our ability to understand gender relations.

There are three principal features of neoclassical analytical method which are problematic from a feminist point of view:

1. its conceptions of rationality and of human motivations;
2. its insistence on emphasizing individual choice; and
3. its inability to deal with power relations.

In each case, the problems that must be examined are twofold: there are the meanings and normative messages conveyed by the simplest presentations of neoclassical analysis, such as those in textbooks; and there are the analytical shortcomings that characterize even sophisticated neoclassical work.[31]

Rationality and Motivation

Might one view individual optimization modeling as itself a product of the genderedness of economics? Feminist historians and philosophers have argued persuasively that modern Western concepts of "rationality" and "individuality" have been fashioned to conform with the particular emotional needs and self-images of men (or more precisely, of men who are privileged by class and race as well as gender): "Rationality has been conceived as transcendence of the feminine; and the 'feminine' itself has been partly constituted by its occurrence within this structure" (Lloyd, 1984, 104; see also Bordo, 1986).

Economists' notion of rationality is of course a specialized one. The rational actor in economics need not be detached from his emotions. His preference ordering is defined as rational if it is consistent, whether or not it represents his "true" welfare as judged by some set of outside criteria, and his behavior is said to be rational so long as his actions bring about the outcome he most prefers among the set of possible outcomes open to him. While these definitions do not seem to embody any gender bias, there are other ways in which *Homo Economicus*, as traditionally presented, might be seen as a distinctively *male* persona. Recall the earlier discussion of Keller's work on the formation of gender identity in male and female children. The psychological theory that she utilized argues that male selves are constructed as "separative," with strong desires for autonomy and control, while female selves are constructed as "connective," with strong values placed on interpersonal relationships and empathy. Several feminist scholars have observed that *Homo Economicus* fits the image of the (masculine) "separative" persona rather well: "The conception of human nature underlying neoclassical economics is of an individual human as radically separate from other humans and from nature; the emphasis is on separation, distance, demarcation, autonomy, independence of self. . . . The environment has no effect on him, but rather is merely the passive material, presented as 'constraints,' over which his rationality has play" (Nelson, 1990, 14; see also England, 1989). A feminist analysis would view this as a seriously distorted portrayal of human actors because it neglects the imbeddedness of individuals (both female and male) in social relationships that shape both our actions and our wants.

This distortion can be reduced by reframing the notion of rationality so that it does not imply either selfishness or immunity to social influence. Neoclassical economists have incorporated altruistic behavior into their analyses by constructing an individual's utility function so that it includes the well being of certain others. And they have explored the notion that an individual might make efforts to change his or her tastes in order to become the sort of person who, say, appreciates certain sorts of art, or behaves responsibly toward others even when that behavior is costly (Stigler and Becker, 1977; see also Elster, 1989). If human motivation is conceived in this more nuanced way, then I believe that rational actor theory can have an important place in a feminist economics. Whether women's and men's preferences differ systematically is an empirical question that deserves more attention than it receives from economists, but both women and men can usefully be depicted as choosing actions that serve their objectives.

The difficulty, of course, is that more complicated representations of human motivations cause economic models to lose some of their tractability and determinacy. If people must be shown (realistically) as behaving sometimes selfishly and sometimes altruistically, predictions will be much more difficult to make. There will, therefore, be a tendency to opt in practice for the simpler representation—the selfish agent with given and unchanging wants (England, 1989). While the distortions resulting from this simplification may be negligible for many of the problems with which economists are concerned, they are likely to be significant for many questions concerning gender relations where caring for others and defining one's personal identity may be important determinants of individual actions.

The Emphasis on Choice

Optimization analysis, an ostensibly value-neutral technique, is often seen to embody normative messages. Since optimization models portray economic phenomena as the results of rational individual choice, they may appear to justify those phenomena. The economist's conclusion that the outcome of rational choice in competitive markets is "optimal" may be read as a broad endorsement of existing conditions—"we get what we choose"—rather than as a restricted and contingent assessment of situations that may on ethical grounds be judged deplorable. These normative messages may be explicit (as they often are in textbook presentations), or they may be extracted (incorrectly but understandably) by the unwary reader when a text fails to emphasize the very limited extent to which welfare judgments can be made from economic models.

These problems are not eliminated altogether when the analysis and the audience are more sophisticated. Recall Bergmann's complaint about economists who "view the inferior labor market position of women as something women have freely chosen" (1989, 43). What does it mean for feminist economists to say that women's occupational status and pay are *not* "freely chosen"?

One might argue that the options facing women are so limited, and so different from those faced by men, that to put the emphasis on "choice" is extremely misleading. Though it is true that "choice" is involved whenever more than a single alternative is available, in some instances constraints are so restrictive that the choice problem becomes relatively trivial. In such cases, the important question is what social factors are responsible for the existence of systematic differences in individuals' choice sets. An early paper by Marxist economist John Roemer (1978) uses this sort of reasoning to argue that neoclassical analysis emanates from a particular class standpoint: constrained individual optimization, he suggests, characterizes economic life as it is seen by the petit bourgeoisie, but it misrepresents the situations of both the bourgeoisie proper (those who control large capitals, and are often able to take individual or collective action to alter the constraints facing them) and the proletariat (who do not have substantial choices to make regarding large areas of their economic lives).

Alternatively one might emphasize that the preferences guiding choice are the products of socialization and social pressure: people are constructed to be the sorts of people who will "choose" to behave in certain ways. As Roemer notes in a later work, what people choose is not always what they prefer, nor is what they prefer always what leads to their welfare since "their preferences have been formed under conditions of inadequate opportunity, have been warped, more generally, by capitalist [or, a feminist would say, patriarchal] society. [Thus] we cannot easily draw welfare conclusions from observing individual choice" (1986, 193-94).

These issues are particularly salient when the phenomenon one wishes to explain is the gender division of household labor. "Tradition" assigns the bulk of this labor to women. Gender identities are constructed such that women feel more responsibility for childcare and housework than men do, and there are social sanctions (ranging from ridicule to economic and legal penalties) for violating gender norms. Under these circumstances, choice and optimality must be viewed as having very restricted meanings.[32]

Representing Power

Marxists have long criticized neoclassical economic theory for abstracting from power relations, and many feminist economists argue that Marxist political economy provides a more useful framework than the neoclassical one, though Marxist analysis must itself undergo some transformation if it is to be applied to gender and race.[33] Marxist analysis focuses on conflictual and exploitative relationships, where neoclassical models center upon market transactions that are mutually beneficial. Actors in Marxist theory are members of distinct groups tied to each other via structural class relations, while in neoclassical theory, individuals (or households) are relatively undifferentiated and unrelated except as buyers and sellers. In neoclassical work, in Rhonda Williams' words, "labor markets are apolitical exchange relations, and earnings inequality is simply the outcome of market-determined efficiency." Marxist political economy argues, in opposition to those representations, that "market life distributes income according to relative power" and "the distribution of work and wages result from and create conflict between unequally empowered political agents" (Williams 1988, 3).

Neoclassical general-equilibrium analysis also conveys a sense of inevitability that feminists may find undesirable: given preferences, technology, and endowments, there is a unique production and distribution equilibrium which must simply be identified and actualized by the Walrasian auctioneer. A Marxist-feminist analysis, in contrast, views race and gender differentials as the results of complex historical processes of conflict, the outcomes of which were by no means inevitable. These processes may involve interactions among organized groups as well as between individual buyers and sellers, the state may be an important actor; interactions are not limited to transactions on markets; and struggles over beliefs about economic reality and about justice may be of crucial importance. As Feiner and Roberts put it, neoclassical general-equilibrium analysis "effectively obliterates history by admitting it only in the form of exogenously given preferences, endowments, and institutional imperfections. In a curious way, history comes to look like destiny, since equilibrium concepts obscure the open-ended historical process" in which earnings and entitlements are determined (1990, 176).

But how does one talk about "power"? Individual optimization and market equilibrium models can only identify differences in choice sets, and something more than that is called for here, something that has to do with relations between agents. Marxist have often opted for "structural-functional" explanations—explaining a phenomenon not in terms of the intentions of those whose behavior directly causes it, but in terms of the benefits it produces for a dominant group. Employers are said to benefit from racial antagonism among employees if that antagonism prevents workers from uniting to demand better wages, or male workers are said to benefit from employers' discrimination against women, since it keeps men's wages higher than they would otherwise be and makes women more likely to perform domestic labor at home for men. While such arguments provide valuable insights, they are analytically incomplete, since they do not explain just how the phenomena in question are established and maintained. Thus, while neoclassical models tend to overemphasize individual choice, abstracting from the inequalities among individuals built into the social structure, Marxist accounts sometimes seem to obliterate individual agency.

Recently, proponents of "rational choice Marxism" have urged Marxists to abandon structural-functional analysis and join neoclassical economists in explaining phenomena with reference to individual intentions. They suggest that the power relations and conflictual interactions central to Marxist analysis can be captured by game theory. How satisfactorily this translation can be effected remains to be seen. While Marxist-feminist economists have for some time been doing very promising work on gender relations using a broad bargaining framework, the usefulness of formal game-theoretic models appears limited.[34] My own expectation is that while methodological-individualist frameworks will be fruitfully employed to tell particular stories about class, race and gender, Marxist and Marxist-feminist economists will continue to find structural-functional theory (and institutions and historical investigations) essential to their projects.

CONCLUSION

Feminist scholars argue that the natural and social sciences are androcentric, that they have paid insufficient attention to women's experiences and needs, and have often misrepresented women's situations, desires, and capacities in ways that served to legitimate male privilege and power. I have sought here to extend this critique to neoclassical economics, exploring the extent to which androcentrism might be implicated in some of the discipline's claims and analytical methods. The neoclassical framework, I have suggested, does not enable us to adequately understand and accurately represent the economic lives of women. As Nelson argues, "analyzing phenomena fraught with connection to others (e.g., responsibility for children), tradition (e.g., the division of household tasks) and relations of domination (e.g., labor market discrimination) with only the language of individual agency, markets and choice is very likely to create a feeling of distortion, a feeling that what is most important has been left out" (1990, 17). These problems are by no means peculiar to gender issues. The existence of systematic differences in individuals' choice sets, the social construction of preferences and the phenomena associated with power and conflictual group interactions are central as well to understanding issues of race and class.

I suspect, then, that eliminating gender, race, and class bias from economics will require changes in the form of economic arguments as well as in their content—that, as black feminist poet Audre Lorde says, "the master's tools will never dismantle the master's house" (1984, 110). But discussion of these issues is just beginning. Much more evidence will have to be amassed before arguments about the relative merits for feminist purposes of individual optimization, game theory, structural-functional and historical methods will even become clear. And those arguments will never be "resolved," since methodological choice always values, whether those be political, aesthetic, or career-driven pragmatic ones.

Two characteristics of feminist inquiry, according to Harding, are: 1) that it focuses on gender, conceived as "a systematic social construction of masculinity and femininity that is little, if at all, constrained by biology," and "takes a critical stance toward gender" (1987b, 29); and 2) it "generates its problematics from the perspective of women's experiences," that have been neglected or distorted by androcentric inquiry (1987b, 30). We can hope to see a wealth of innovative work along these lines by feminist economists both within and outside neoclassical economics. Some feminists will feel that neoclassical techniques are quite adequate for feminist purposes. Those who do not share Marxists' critical view of capitalism (or Marxist-feminists' strong critique of gender relations) will not wish to employ Marxist language or methods. And aside from truth, there are practical reasons to remain in the mainstream: to suggest that feminist economists forsake neoclassical work is, given the profession's current structure and values, to demand that they jeopardize their careers and abandon hope of reaching audiences unwilling or unable to hear arguments framed in different languages.

Whatever their methodological leanings, all economists should be attending to feminist questions and utilizing the vantage points of women's experiences. Economists' teaching and writing on state policies, economic fluctuations, development, technological change, etc. should ask about the impact of those events on men, women, and gender relations.[35]

Though economists need to make predictions, predictionist instrumentalism, in which all that matters for appraising a theory is its empirical implications, is not helpful to the pursuit of social change. Certainly, it is important to establish whether a theory has novel empirical content, but economists should not be indifferent between conflicting theoretical representations whose "reduced forms" are identical. Theories are representations of human actors and the relations between them. The meanings produced by these representations matter a great deal; they are part of how we understand and assess social reality and explain it to others. If economists wish not to support the dissemination of falsehoods that impede progress toward a more just world, they (like other scientists) will have to become more responsible about the stories they contribute to society's discourse on social relations.

No one should be surprised that economic discourse is a prime terrain for political struggle. The theoretical, empirical, and methodological questions being sparked in economics, as a result of political conflicts outside the discipline, present exciting challenges for all economists, and the consequences of these debates will be far-reaching. We might see the renewal of analytical approaches, such as institutionalism and Marxist political economy, that have been marginalized in the profession. We may hope to see a greater pluralism and methodological openness in the discipline as a whole. Some of us will be members of the intellectual "rainbow coalition" that leads the struggle for such changes, but the changes themselves will benefit a far larger community of economic inquirers.

NOTES

For encouragement and helpful criticism, I am very grateful to Bina Agarwal, Rhonda Cobham-Sander, Nona Glazer, Gail Hornstein, Susan Kellogg, Helen Longino, Julie Nelson, and Sandra Zagarell.

1. Though, there have always been some who opposed this emulation,

and many question how well economists practice what they preach. See Marr and Raj (1983) for a selection of essays on economics as science.

2. Among the most prominent contributions are Blaug (1980), Boland (1982), Caldwell (1982), de Marchi (1988), Klamer (1984) and (1988), McCloskey (1985), and Mirowski (1989).

3. The best introduction to this literature is Harding (1986); three anthologies of important articles are Bleier (1986), Harding and O'Barr (1987), and Tuana (1989). Jaggar (1983) usefully explores several important issues that I am unable to treat in this chapter: she defines three very distinct types of feminism (liberal, radical, and socialist), and argues that each is associated with a particular epistemology. I shall be speaking of "feminism" in this chapter without elaborating just what set of claims and objectives I take "feminism" to encompass.

4. The literature of critiques of particular disciplines is large. Farnham (1987) and Spender (1981) are collections covering a wide range of disciplines. For the biological sciences, see Bleier (1984), Fausto-Sterling (1985), and Hubbard et al. (1982). Russett (1989) provides a fascinating account of science and gender in the nineteenth century. For the social sciences, see the works collected in Harding (1987a) and Hess and Ferree (1987), along with Stacey and Thorne (1985) and Westkott (1979). And see Gould (1981), Ladner (1971 and 1973), and Reid (1987) for forceful arguments about racial bias in the natural and social sciences.

5. See Rossiter (1982) and Gornick (1983); Schiebinger (1989) gives additional references.

6. Though scientists encountering feminist criticism often react as though this is what they *hear*: and since they often feel sure that they hold no such malice or prejudice, they feel excused from listening further, and suspect that their critics are simply mean-spirited or ignorant.

7. Feminists are far from alone in asserting the importance of personal, cultural and political factors in the generation and acceptance of scientific claims. That assertion, though resisted intensely by

most scientists, is consistent with many of the "social studies of science" that have followed the work of Kuhn (though interestingly, that literature has almost entirely ignored gender) with some important work in the philosophy of science and with the work of other science critics concerned about science's support for racism, militarism and environmental destruction.

8. The influx of just a few individual women into a discipline cannot be expected to make any difference. Surrounded by skepticism about their ability as scientists, such women will be under intense pressure to conform with current conventions, even if they would like to pursue unconventional approaches (which of course they might not).

9. See Lukacs (1971) for an influential statement of Marxist epistemology. Mepham and Ruben (1979) and Resnick and Wolff (1987) present stimulating and sophisticated Marxist treatments of epistemological questions. There is disagreement among both Marxists and feminist standpoint epistemologists as to whether the knowledge acquired from the standpoint of oppressed groups is *superior* to, or merely *different* from, that gained from the standpoint of dominant groups. Hartsock (1983a,b) clearly privileges women's knowledge, arguing that women's perspective permits a "less distorted" understanding of gender relations.

10. On these dualisms and the history of science, see Bordo (1986), Fee (1986) and Merchant (1980).

11. See also Flax (1983). Note that it is by no means established that such needs are universal across racial/ethnic and class groups: see Fee (1986) and Spelman (1988).

12. Keller has written a good deal on the work of geneticist Barbara McClintock, whom she sees as an exemplar of this sort of scientific practice—see Keller (1983; 1985, ch. 9; and 1987). Her argument, it must be emphasized, is not that this "empathic" approach would *necessarily* be preferred by all women scientists or avoided by all men. Rather, the "masculine" orientation of the sciences has discouraged practitioners from developing approaches that call upon attitudes and experiences considered (socially constructed as) "feminine."

13. An excellent collection of essays on feminism and postmodernism is Nicholson (1990). Since discrediting sexist and racist views is an important part of the struggle to transform gender and race relations, the postmodernist stance is quite problematic. As Donna Haraway notes, "An epistemology that justifies not taking a stand on the nature of things is of little use to women trying to build a shared politics." (1981, 480).

14. On false universalization in feminist theory, see Lugones and Spelman (1983, Mohanty (1985), and Spelman (1988).

15. An additional question is this one: what should one make of the fact that very similar critiques of science are being advanced from quite different quarters, that some of the aspects of science feminists identify as "masculinist" are being called "Eurocentric" by Third World and African-American critics? See Fee (1986) and Harding (1986).

16. My discussion will focus upon mainstream or neoclassical economics, and I shall give references to feminist critiques of Marxist political economy. How far my criticisms and suggestions are relevant to other approaches to economics—Austrian, institutionalist, and post-Keynesian, for example—is a matter for later investigation.

17. See Chapman (1975), CSWEP (1989), Reagan (1975), Strober (1975), and Strober and Reagan (1976.

18. Such a project has been announced recently, but it does not have AEA sponsorship: see CSWEP Newsletter, Feb. 1988, 9.

19. The situations of the two disciplines are very different. Gender has always been a subject of considerable interest in anthropology, and feminist scholarship has had a substantial (if not sufficient) impact in the discipline; thus, feminist scholarship on women and gender is likely to be published in a variety of anthropology journals.

20. This argument would seem to be undermined by the fact that women receive a higher proportion of undergraduate and graduate degress in mathematics than in economics.

21. In addition to the works referred to in the following section of the text, feminist critical surveys of the treatment of gender in economics

include Bergmann (1986), Blau (1987), Blau and Ferber (1986), Brown (1989), Humphries (1987), Humphries and Rubery (1984), Lloyd and Niemi (1979), Rubery (1987), and, from a Black feminist perspective, Williams (1984 and 1988).

22. Folbre and Hartmann argue that to recast explanations of household behavior in terms of "selfishness" is not a sufficient solution; economists should recognize that there is in fact a complex mixture of both types of motivation in both spheres of activity.

23. See Becker (1976) for a defense of the rule of assuming constant preferences.

24. See Bergmann (1989) for criticism of the argument that competition will eliminate discriminating firms.

25. An excellent example of feminist history of economic thought is Folbre and Hartmann (1988). See also Pujol (1984).

26. Whether those conventions are themselves androcentric is discussed later in the section on method.

27. Thus, in looking at, for example, the work of the "Chicago School" on gender, one would want to identify important values other than gender ideology that may be shaping the research—e.g. judgments that government intervention is undesirable, and a strong desire to demonstrate the virtuosity of neoclassical economic modelling. See Seiz (1990b).

28. See Klamer (1984, 1987, 1988), McCloskey (1985a), and Klamer, McCloskey and Solow (1988). The rhetoric approach to economic discourse, as developed by McCloskey and Klamer, has a great deal to offer feminist scholars of economics: it has opened a space in which many sorts of criticism of economic discourse may be pursued and provided a framework for investigations of how claims in economics are presented and assessed. See Seiz (1990a).

29. This question about the meanings of (in) models is, to me, the most interesting issue raised in the debates over Friedman's "Methodology of Positive Economics" (see the documents collected in Caldwell (1984). I believe one can only say that all that matters is prediction, if

the sole goal of inquiry is "control"—which suggests that predictionist instrumentalism, like the sociology discussed by Smith, may often emanate from a "standpoint of ruling."

30. Game-theoretic work includes Manser and Brown (1979) and McElroy and Horney (1981). On transactions-cost work, see Pollak (1985). For surveys of discrimination theories, see Blau (1984), Lundahl and Wadensjo (1984), and Marshall (1974).

31. The broad issues treated here concerning structure and agency are also prominent in Marxist critiques of neoclassical economics and are at the center of a current debate among Marxists over "analytical" or "rational choice" Marxism. For an introduction to "rational choice Marxism," see Elster (1985) and Roemer (1986). Useful commentaries are Carling (1986), Hodgson (1986) and Wood (1989).

32. These issues about women's choices (or the relative importance of constraints and preferences in explaining occupational differences between women and men) were the focus of the recent EEOC v. Sears case. The EEOC charged Sears with excluding women from lucrative commission sales jobs. Each side employed a feminist historian as expert witness. Alice Kessler-Harris, testifying for the EEOC, argued that women have tended to move readily into higher paying "men's jobs" when they have been permitted to do so. Rosalind Rosenberg, for Sears, argued that women's occupational preferences differed from men's, both because women accepted more responsibility for childcare and housework and because women were less competitive and less income-focused than men. The judge ruled in favor of Sears. See the material on the case in *Signs* 11:4 (Summer (1986): 751-779, and Milkman (1986).

33. The literature of Marxist-feminism is large. Good introductions to the issues include Barrett (1988, Beechey (1987, Vogel (1983, Walby (1986, and the recent special issues of the Review of Radical Political Economics (published in 1977, 1980, and 1984) on the Political Economy of Women. Important works by Marxist-feminist economists include those of Nancy Folbre (1982, 1983, 1986), Heidi Hartmann (1976, 1981a, b, 1987), and Elaine McCrate (1987, 1988).

34. I noted earlier that neoclassical feminist economists such as

McElroy and Horney have begun to apply game theory to the analysis of household behavior; feminist work with the broader bargaining approach includes Agarwal (1990), Folbre (1983, 1984, and 1986), and Hartmann (1981b). Sen (1985 and 1990) provide insightful discussions of the usefulness of bargaining frameworks for the analysis of gender issues. Mirowski (1986) expresses skepticism about game theory's potential for the analysis of conflict, coercion and historical change. I discuss both game theory and bargaining frameworks in Seiz (1990c).

35. Feiner and Morgan (1987) offers very useful concrete suggestions for improving the treatment of gender and race in both research and teaching.

REFERENCES

Agarwal, B. (1990), "Social Security and the Family: Coping with Seasonality and Calamity in Rural India." *Journal of Peasant Studies* 17(3), 341-412.

Barrett, M. (1988), *Woman's Oppression Today: Problems in Marxist Feminist Analysis*. Second edition. London: Verso.

Barrett, N. S. (1983). "How the Study of Women Has Restructured the Discipline of Economics." In Elizabeth Langland and Walter Gove, eds. *A Feminist Perspective in the Academy: The Difference It Makes*. Chicago: University of Chicago Press.

Becker, G. S. (1976), *The Economic Approach to Human Behavior*. Chicago: University of Chicago Press.

Beechey, V. (1987), *Unequal Work*. London: Verso.

Bergmann, B. (1986), *The Economic Emergence of Women*. New York: Basic Books.

__________________. (1987), "The Task of a Feminist Economics: A More Equitable Future." In Christie Farnham, ed. *The Impact of Feminist Research in the Academy*. Bloomington: Indiana University Press.

__________. (1989), "Does the Market for Women's Labor Need Fixing?" *Journal of Economic Perspectives*, 3 (Winter), 43-60.

Blau, F. D. (1984), "Discrimination Against Women: Theory and Evidence." In William Darity, Jr., ed. *Labor Economics: Modern Views*. Boston: Kluwer Nijhoff.

__________. (1987), "Gender." In John Eatwell, Murray Milgate and Peter Newman, eds., *The New Palgrave: A Dictionary of Economic Theory*, 4 vols. New York: The Stockton Press.

Blau, F. D. and Ferber, M. (1986), *The Economics of Women, Men and Work*. Englewood Cliffs, NJ: Prentice-Hall.

Blaug, M. (1980), *The Methodology of Economics*. New York: Cambridge University Press.

Bleier, R. (1984), *Science and Gender: A Critique of Biology and Its Theories on Women*. New York: Pergamon Press.

__________, ed. (1986), *Feminist Approaches to Science*. New York: Pergamon Press.

Boland, Lawrence A. (1982), *The Foundations of Economic Method*. Boston: Allen & Unwin.

Bordo, S. (1986), "The Cartesian Masculinization of Thought," *Signs: Journal of Women in Culture and Society*, 11 (Spring), 439-56. Reprinted in Harding and O'Barr, 1987.

Boserup, E. (1987), "Inequality Between the Sexes." In John Eatwell, Murray Milgate and Peter Newman, eds. *The New Palgrave: A Dictionary of Economics*. 4 vols. New York: The Stockton Press.

Brown, L. J. (1989), Gender and Economic Analysis: A Feminist Perspective. Paper presented at the American Economic Association annual meeting.

Caldwell, B. (1982), *Beyond Positivism: Economic Methodology in the*

Twentieth Century. Boston: Allen & Unwin.

____________________. (1984), *Appraisal and Criticism in Economics: A Book of Readings*. Boston: Allen & Unwin.

Carling, A. (1986), "Rational Choice Marxism," *New Left Review* 160: 24-62.

Chapman, J. R. (1975), "Review Essay: Economics," *Signs: Journal of Women in Culture and Society*, 1 (1) (Autumn), 139-46.

Ciancanelli, P. and Berch, B. (1987), "Gender and the GNP." In Beth B. Hess and Myra Marx Ferree, eds., *Analyzing Gender: A Handbook of Social Science Research*. Newbury Park: SAGE Publications.

CSWEP (Committee on the Status of Women in the Economics Profession). (1989), "Annual Report 1988." *American Economic Review*, 77 (May), 422-25.

de Marchi, N., ed. (1988), *The Popperian Legacy in Economics*. New York: Cambridge University Press.

Elster, J. (1985), *Making Sense of Marx*. New York: Cambridge University Press.

____________________. (1989), "Social Norms and Economic Theory," *Journal of Economic Perspectives*, 3 (4) (Fall), 99-117.

England, P. (1989), "A Feminist Critique of Rational Choice Theories: Implications for Sociology," *The American Sociologist*, 20 (Spring), 14-28.

Farnham, C., ed. (1987), *The Impact of Feminist Research in the Academy*. Bloomington: Indiana University Press.

Fausto-Sterling, A. (1985), *Myths of Gender: Biological Theories About Women and Men*. New York: Basic Books.

Fee, E. (1983), "Women's Nature and Scientific Objectivity." In

Marian Lowe and Ruth Hubbard, eds. *Woman's Nature: Rationalizations of Inequality*. New York: Pergamon Press.

_________________. (1986), "Critiques of Modern Science: The Relationship of Feminism to Other Radical Epistemologies." In Ruth Bleier, ed. *Feminist Approaches to Science*. New York: Pergamon Press.

Feiner, S. F. and Morgan. B. A. (1987), "Women and Minorities in Introductory Economics Textbooks: 1974 to 1984," *Journal of Economic Education*, 18 (Fall), 376-92.

_________________, and Roberts, B. B. (1990), "Hidden by the Invisible Hand: Neoclassical Economic Theory and the Textbook Treatment of Race and Gender," *Gender and Society*, 4 (June), 159-181.

Ferber, M. A. (1982), "Women and Work: Issues of the 1980's," *Signs: Journal of Women in Culture and Society*, 8 (Winter), 273-95.

_________________, and Birnbaum, B. G. (1977), "The 'New Home Economics:' Retrospects and Prospects," *Journal of Consumer Research*, (June), 19-28.

_________________, and Teiman, M. L. (1981), "The Oldest, the Most Established, the Most Quantitative of the Social Sciences—and the Most Dominated by Men: The Impact of Feminism on Economics." In Dale Spender, ed., *Men's Studies Modified: The Impact of Feminism on the Academic Disciplines.* New York: Pergamon Press.

Flax, J. (1983), "Political Philosophy and the Patriarchal Unconscious: A Psychoanalytic Perspective on Epistemology and Metaphysics." In Sandra Harding and Merrill B. Hintikka, eds. *Discovering Reality: Feminist Perspectives on Epistemology, Metaphysics, Methodology and Philosophy of Science.* Boston and Dordrecht: D. Reidel.

_________________. (1987), "Postmodernism and Gender Relations in Feminist Theory," *Signs: Journal of Women in Culture and*

Society, 12 (Summer), 621-43. Reprinted in Nicholson, 1990.

Folbre, N. (1982), "Exploitation Comes Home: A Critique of the Marxian Theory of Family Labor," *Cambridge Journal of Economics*, 317-329.

__________. (1983), "Of Patriarchy Born: The Political Economy of Fertility Decisions," *Feminist Studies*, 9 (Summer), 269-84.

__________. (1984), "Household Production in the Philippines: A Non-neoclassical Approach," *Economic Development and Cultural Change*, 32, 303-330.

__________. (1986), "Hearts and Spades: Paradigms of Household Economics," *World Development*, 14, 245-255.

__________, and Hartmann, H. (1988), "The Rhetoric of Self Interest and the Ideology of Gender." In Arjo Klamer, Donald N. McCloskey, and Robert M. Solow, eds. *The Consequences of Economic Rhetoric*. New York: Cambridge University Press.

Foucault, M. (1980), *Power/Knowledge: Selected Interviews and Other Writings 1972-77*. Edited by Colin Gordon. New York: Pantheon.

Friedman, M. (1953), "The Methodology of Positive Economics." In *Essays in Positive Economics*. Chicago: University of Chicago Press.

Gornick, V. (1983), *Women in Science: Portraits from a World in Transition*. New York: Simon & Schuster.

Gould, S. J. (1981), *The Mismeasure of Man*. New York: W.W. Norton.

Haraway, D. (1981), "In the Beginning Was the Word: The Genesis of Biological Theory," *Signs: Journal of Women in Culture and Society*, 6 (Spring), 469-82.

Harding, S. (1986), *The Science Question in Feminism*. Ithaca: Cornell University Press.

__________________, ed. (1987a), *Feminism and Methodology: Social Science Issues*. Bloomington: Indiana University Press.

__________________. (1987b), "The Method Question," *Hypatia*, 2 (Fall), 19-35. Reprinted in Tuana, 1989.

Harding, S. and O'Barr, J. F., eds. (1987), *Sex and Scientific Inquiry*. Chicago: University of Chicago Press.

Hartmann, H. (1976), "Capitalism, Patriarchy and Job Segregation by Sex," *Signs: Journal of Women in Culture and Society*, 1 (3 pt. 2) (Spring), 137-69.

__________________. (1981a), "The Unhappy Marriage of Marxism and Feminism." In Lydia Sargent, ed. *Women and Revolution*. Boston: South End Press.

__________________. (1981b), "The Family as the Locus of Gender, Class and Political Struggle: The Example of Housework," *Signs: Journal of Women in Culture and Society*, 6 (Spring), 366-94. Reprinted in Harding, 1987a.

__________________. (1987), "Changes in Women's Economic and Family Roles in Post-World War II United States." In Lourdes Beneria and Catharine R. Stimpson, eds. *Women, Households and the Economy*. New Brunswick: Rutgers University Press.

Hartsock, N. C. M. (1983a), "The Feminist Standpoint: Developing the Ground for a Specifically Feminist Historical Materialism." In Sandra Harding and Merrill B. Hintikka, eds. *Discovering Reality: Feminist Perspectives on Epistemology, Metaphysics, Methodology and Philosophy of Science*. Boston and Dordrecht: D. Reidel.

__________________. (1983b), *Money, Sex and Power: Toward a Feminist Historical Materialism*. New York: Longman.

Hawkesworth, M. E. (1989), "Knowers, Knowing, Known: Feminist Theory and Claims of Truth," *Signs: Journal of Women in Culture and Society*, 14 (Spring), 533-57.

Hess, B. and Ferree, M. M., eds. (1987), *Analyzing Gender: A Handbook of Social Science Research*. Newbury Park: SAGE Publications.

Hodgson, G. (1986), "Behind Methodological Individualism," *Cambridge Journal of Economics*, 10, 211-224.

Hubbard, R., Henifin, M. S., and Fried, B., eds. (1982), *Biological Woman: The Convenient Myth*. Cambridge: Schenkman.

Humphries, J. (1987), "Women and Work." In John Eatwell, Murray Milgate and Peter Newman, eds. *The New Palgrave: A Dictionary of Economic Theory*. 4 vols. New York: The Stockton Press.

________________, and Rubery, J. (1984), "The Reconstitution of the Supply Side of the Labour Market: The Relative Autonomy of Social Reproduction," *Cambridge Journal of Economics*, 8, 331-346.

Jaggar, A. (1983), *Feminist Politics and Human Nature*. Totowa, NJ: Rowman and Allenheld.

Keller, E. F. (1983), *A Feeling for the Organism: The Life and Work of Barbara McClintock*. San Francisco: W.H. Freeman & Co.

________________. (1985), *Reflections on Gender and Science*. New Haven: Yale University Press.

________________. (1987), "The Gender/Science System: or, Is Sex to Gender As Nature Is to Science?" *Hypatia*, 2 (Fall), 37-49. Reprinted in Tuana, 1989.

Klamer, A. (1984), *Conversations With Economists: New Classical Economists and Their Opponents Speak Out on the Current Controversy in Macroeconomics*. Totowa, NJ: Rowman & Allenheld.

________________. (1987), "As If Economists and Their Subjects Were Rational." In John S. Nelson, Allen Megill and Donald N. McCloskey, eds. *The Rhetoric of the Human Sciences: Language and Argument in Scholarship and Public Affairs*. Madison: University of Wisc

__________________. (1988), "Economics as Discourse." In Neil de Marchi, ed. *The Popperian Legacy in Economics*. New York: Cambridge University Press.

Kuhn, T. S. (1970), *The Structure of Scientific Revolutions*. Second edition. Chicago: University of Chicago Press.

Ladner, J. (1971), *Introduction to Tomorrow's Tomorrow: The Black Woman*. New York: Doubleday & Co. Reprinted in Harding 1987a.

__________________, ed. (1973), *The Death of White Sociology*. New York: Random House.

Lloyd, C. B. and Niemi, B. T. (1979), *The Economics of Sex Differentials*. New York: Columbia University Press.

Lloyd, G. (1984), *The Man of Reason: "Male" and "Female" in Western Philosophy*. Minneapolis: University of Minnesota Press.

Longino, H. E. (1987), "Can There Be A Feminist Science?" *Hypatia*, 2 (3) (Fall), 51-64. Reprinted in Tuana, 1989.

__________________. (1990), *Science as Social Knowledge: Values and Objectivity in Scientific Inquiry*. Princeton: Princeton University Press.

__________________, and Doell, R. (1983), "Body, Bias, and Behavior: A Comparative Analysis of Reasoning in Two Areas of Biological Science," *Signs: Journal of Women in Culture and Society*, 9 (Winter), 206-27. Reprinted in Harding and O'Barr, 1987.

Lugones, M. C. and Spelman. E. V. (1983), "Have We Got a Theory for You! Feminist Theory, Cultural Imperialism and the Demand for 'The Woman's Voice'," *Women's Studies International Forum*, 6, 573-81.

Lorde, A. (1984), *Sister Outsider*. Trumansburg, NY: The Crossing Press.

Lukacs, G. (1971), *History and Class Consciousness*. Trans. Rodney Livingstone. London: Merlin Press.

Lundahl, M. and Wadensjo, E. (1984), *Unequal Treatment: A Study in the Neo-Classical Theory of Discrimination*. New York: New York University Press.

Manser, M. and Brown, M. (1979), "Bargaining Analyses of Household Decisions." In Cynthia Lloyd, Emily Andrews and C. Gilroy, eds. *Women in the Labor Market*. New York: Columbia University Press.

Marr, W. L. and Raj, B., eds. (1983), *How Economists Explain: A Reader in Methodology*. Lanham: University Press of America.

Marshall, R. (1974), "The Economics of Racial Discrimination: A Survey," *Journal of Economic Literature*, 12, 849-71.

McCloskey, D. N. (1985a), *The Rhetoric of Economics*. Madison: University of Wisconsin Press.

__________________. (1985b), "Some Consequences of a Feminine Economics." Unpublished paper.

McCrate, E. (1987), "Trade, Merger and Employment: Economic Theory on Marriage," *Review of Radical Political Economics*, 19 (Spring), 73-89.

__________________. (1988), "Gender Difference: The Role of Endogenous Preferences and Collective Action," *American Economic Review*, 78 (May), 235-39.

McElroy, M. B. and Horney, M. J. (1981), "Nash-Bargained Household Decisions: Toward a Generalization of the Theory of Demand," *International Economic Review*, 22 (June), 333-49.

Mepham, J., and Ruben, D.-H., eds. (1979), *Issues in Marxist*

Philosophy. Vol. 3: Epistemology, Science, Ideology. Brighton: Harvester Press.

Merchant, C. (1980), *The Death of Nature: Women, Ecology, and the Scientific Revolution.* San Francisco: Harper & Row.

Milkman, R. (1986), "Women's History and the Sears Case," *Feminist Studies*, 12 (Summer), 375-400.

Mirowski, P. (1986), "Institutions as Solution Concepts in a Game Theory Context." In Philip Mirowski, ed. *The Reconstruction of Economic Theory.* Boston: Kluwer Nijhoff.

__________________. (1989), *More Heat Than Light.* New York: Cambridge University Press.

Mohanty, C. T. (1985), "Under Western Eyes: Feminist Scholarship and Colonial Discourses," *Boundary*, 2, 333-58.

Namenwirth, M. (1986), "Science Seen Through a Feminist Prism." In Ruth Bleier, ed. *Feminist Approaches to Science.* New York: Pergamon Press.

Nelson, J. A. (1987), "Gender and Economic Thought," *CSWEP Newsletter*, (Oct.), 2-6.

__________________. (1990), Gender, Metaphor, and the Definition of Economics. Working Paper, Department of Economics, University of California-Davis.

Nicholson, L. J., ed. (1990), *Feminism/Postmodernism.* New York: Routledge.

Pollak, R. A. (1985), "A Transaction Cost Approach to Families and Households," *Journal of Economic Literature*, 23 (June), 581-608.

Pujol, Michele. (1984), "Gender and Class in Marshall's Principles of Economics," *Cambridge Journal of Economics*, 8, 217-234.

Reagan, B. B. (1975), "Two Supply Curves for Economists? Implications of Mobility and Career Attachment of Women," *American Economic Review*, 65 (May), 100-07.

Resnick, S. A. and Wolff, R. D. (1987), *Knowledge and Class: A Marxian Critique of Political Economy*. Chicago: University of Chicago Press.

Roemer, J. E. (1978), "Neoclassicism, Marxism and Collective Action," *Journal of Economic Issues*, 12 (March), 147-61.

__________, ed. (1986), *Analytical Marxism*. New York: Cambridge University Press.

Rose, H. (1986), "Beyond Masculinist Realities: A Feminist Epistemology for the Sciences." In Ruth Bleier, ed. *Feminist Approaches to Science*. New York: Pergamon Press.

Rossiter, M. (1982), *Women Scientists in America: Struggles and Strategies to (1940*. Baltimore: Johns Hopkins University Press.

Rubery, J. (1987), "Women's Wages." In John Eatwell, Murray Milgate, and Peter Newman, eds. *The New Palgrave: A Dictionary of Economics*. 4 vols. New York: The Stockton Press.

Russett, C. E. (1989), *Sexual Science: The Victorian Construction of Womanhood*. Cambridge: Harvard University Press.

Schiebinger, L. (1989), *The Mind Has No Sex? Women in the Origins of Modern Science*. Cambridge: Harvard University Press.

Seiz, J. A. (1990a), "Comment [on Klamer]." In Warren J. Samuels, ed. *Economics as Discourse*. Boston: Kluwer-Nijhoff.

__________. (1990b), Economic Discourse on Race and Gender: The Work of the Chicago School. Paper presented at the Mary Ingraham Bunting Institute, Radcliffe College, Feb. 1990.

__________. (1990c), The Bargaining Approach and Feminist Methodology. Paper presented at the annual meeting of the Allied Social Science Association. Forthcoming in *Review of*

Radical Political Economics.

Sen, A. K. (1985), "Women, Technology and Sexual Divisions," *Trade and Development*, 6, 195-223.

__________________. (1990), "Gender and Cooperative Conflicts." In Irene Tinker, ed. *Persistent Inequalities: Women and World Development*. New York: Oxford University Press.

Smith, D. E. (1974), "Women's Perspective as a Radical Critique of Sociology," *Sociological Inquiry*, 44, 7-13.

__________________. (1987), *The Everyday World as Problematic: A Feminist Sociology*. Boston: Northeastern University Press.

Spelman, E. V. (1988), *The Inessential Woman: Problems of Exclusion in Feminist Thought*. Boston: Beacon Press.

Spender, D., ed. (1981), *Men's Studies Modified: The Impact of Feminism on the Academic Disciplines*. New York: Pergamon Press.

Stacey, J. and Thorne, B. (1985), "The Missing Feminist Revolution in Sociology," *Social Problems*, 32 (April), 301-316.

Stigler, G. and Becker, G. S. (1977), "De Gustibus Non Est Disputandum," *American Economic Review*, 67 (March), 76-90.

Strober, M. H. (1975), "Women Economists: Career Aspirations, Education and Training," *American Economic Review*, 65 (May), 92-99.

Strober, M. H. and Reagan, B. B. (1976), "Sex Differences in Economists' Fields of Specialization." *Signs: Journal of Women in Culture and Society*, 1 (3, part 2), 303-17.

Tuana, N., ed. (1989), *Feminism and Science*. Indianapolis: Indiana University Press.

Vogel, L. (1983), *Marxism and the Oppression of Women: Toward a*

Unitary Theory. New Brunswick: Rutgers University Press.

Walby, S. (1986), *Patriarchy at Work: Patriarchal and Capitalist Relations in Employment*. Minneapolis: University of Minnesota Press.

Westkott, M. (1979), "Feminist Criticism of the Social Sciences," *Harvard Educational Review*, 49 (Nov.), 422-430.

Williams, R. M. (1984), "The Methodology and Practice of Modern Labor Economics: A Critique." In William Darity, Jr., ed. *Modern Labor Economics*. Boston: Kluwer Nijhoff.

__________________. (1988), Beyond Human Capital: Black Women, Work and Wages. Wellesley Center for Research on Women, Working Paper no. 183.

COMMENTARY BY ARJO KLAMER

Feminism is with us, whether we like it or not. If by "us" is meant "academicians" (after all, the chance that a nonacademic glances at this page is pretty small), we experience the impact of feminism both in our personal lives and in the office. There is no need to elaborate on the arguments between spouses on the responsibilities for childcare, career priorities, and who follows whom in the next move: we academics talk about little else, at least in our personal lives. The discussions easily spill over into our working lives, where we talk about childcare facilities on campus, maternity and paternity leaves, sexual harassment, affirmative action, the small number of tenured women faculty, etc. Any academic who is conscious of life cannot ignore the issues that we tend to associate with feminism.

The discussions easily become heated, or end up in thorough confusion, at least they do in my admittedly limited experience. To sample some of the numerous occasions I recall the following:

In an interdisciplinary seminar, Donald McCloskey presented a paper on feminist economics (Seiz refers to this paper). Using Carol Gilligan's work as a source, McCloskey claimed there were distinct male and female experiences and suggested that economics privileged male experience. He concluded that economics as a discipline would improve if it were to take into account feminist concerns. Two female colleagues protested vehemently against his characterization of female and male experiences and argued that by asserting the differences McCloskey was reinforcing gender stereotypes. An intense debate ensued.

In another case, a class on postmodernism turned to the problem of defining feminism. One student stated that feminism was about the fight for sexual equality. Another saw in feminism the affirmation of differences between men and women and the celebration of feminine characteristics. A woman participant asserted that feminism eludes definitions, since there is a plurality of feminisms. The class was confused (and so was I).

In the preceding chapter, Seiz succeeds in clearing up much of the confusion. In the spirit of contemporary feminist scholarship, she presents gender as the issue, where gender denotes the system of social relationships that produces distinctions between males and females. Thus Seiz steers the discussion away from biological differences. That helps. Whatever opinions we may have about the implications of physical constitutions, we are warned that no feature or characteristic is innately male or female; that much, feminist research across time and cultures has shown. The proposal to focus on the social formation of gender roles is, therefore, fair and helpful.

The focus in Seiz's chapter is on the manifestations of gender in economics. Especially clarifying is her separation of the *political* issue (the position of women in economics) from the *substantive* issue (the treatment of women's issues by economists) and the *epistemological* issue (the consequence of gender for the way we know the world).

The political issue remains a nasty one. Gender continues to matter in hiring and tenure decisions. The numbers of female graduate students, assistant professors, and tenured professors continue to be relatively low. Publishing, seminars, committees, and conferences still appear to involve a gender politics of one sort or another. Seiz does not elaborate on the politics, assuming, quite rightly, that people already know.

Less obviously plausible are the feminist claims in the next domain that Seiz distinguishes, namely, the subject of economics. Here the main argument is that mostly male economists have overlooked the distinctive position and role of women in the economy. The resisters among the economic establishment may wonder whether ignoring women matters to their theoretical and empirical results. The willingness to include gender as a separate factor in theories will be limited, as the premise of neoclassical economic theory is that we do better to abstract from distinctive human features. Seiz makes clear that we still need to understand the economics of the phenomena in which women play a major role, such as family life, childcare and poverty. The purpose of feminist scholarship is to break the silence that mainstream economics has obeyed with respect to such phenomena. Who can object to that?

Seiz subsequently calls attention to the possible constraints that the language of mainstream economics imposes. She is careful on this count. She resists the common feminist argument that neoclassical economics, with the a-personal, a-psychological and a-social individual maximizer as its main analytical character, does not allow for a serious discussion of women in the economy. This argument prescribes dismissal of feminist research in the neoclassical mode. Seiz is not willing to go along.

Her caution turns out to be inspired by her position on the third domain that she distinguishes, namely epistemology. At stake is the theory that gender affects the knowledge process. Is science, economics included, androcentric, favoring a male way of knowing the world? If that were the case, then scientists and economists would have to give up their cherished cover of neutrality and detachment. Another implication is that there must be a female way of knowing, or an epistemology with feminine qualities. McCloskey suggests exactly that in his paper on feminine economics. Seiz demurs. She does not know and warns against the danger of feminists privileging such a feminine discourse.

According to standard practice, I should carry on the monologue now. But why should I, in this age of communication? So Seiz and I engaged, with the aid of electronics, in a dialogue on her chapter. Selections follow.

DIALOGUE, ARJO KLAMER/JANET A. SEIZ

AK In your paper, you express strong reservations toward the feminist "standpoint epistemology." You particularly doubt the existence of a distinctive female way of knowing, and critique my dear friend Donald McCloskey for asserting as much. I have known you as a feminist scholar and would have expected you to claim more.

JS I am sympathetic to many of the ideas of "standpoint epistemology," but I'm very wary of any strategy that emphasizes gender differences. I do think people's values, beliefs, and cognitive styles tend to be influenced by their social locations, including their gender identities. But there's a great deal of variation among women, and I don't want to see any particular trait or attitude defined as "feminine" and permanently identified with women or thought of as characterizing all women. And I don't want to accept any limitations on feminist inquiry. I don't want feminist inquirers to be constrained to employ methods that conform with some alleged female way of knowing. I do believe that scientific inquiry has been shaped in unfortunate ways by the notions of masculinity prevailing among the men who created the sciences. And I think the sorts of changes the "standpoint epistemologists" call for—away from reductionism, toward empathy, and so on—are good ones. But those should be argued on their own merits, rather than embraced because they conform with "female" ways of interacting with the world.

AK So you are willing to give feminists who do neoclassical economics the benefit of the doubt. Where does that leave you? On other occasions I have heard you be very critical of neoclassical economics.

JS There are many reasons why I don't find neoclassical stories very satisfying. Some of those I share with you, and some are due to my affinity with feminism and Marxism. But I'm not willing to reject neoclassical economics as a language for feminist economic inquiry. The questions concerning the relationship between the form of an argument and the meanings it conveys are open questions: We don't yet know what feminists and analytical Marxists will be able to do with individual optimization models or with game-theoretic models. There are other good reasons for pluralism. There are a number of different varieties of feminism (as the student in your postmodernism class pointed out), and it may well be that the language of individual choice captures some feminists' views of women's situations quite well. I might disagree with that type of feminism, but I would not deny that such work is feminist. Feminists have a lot of work to do, and I expect that we'll need a lot of languages to tell all our stories. I'll want to read historical work and institutional case studies and structural-functional analyses and bargaining models, as well as stories of individual optimization and equilibrium. I'm open to persuasion about the relative merits of these various frameworks. You could say mine is a pragmatic stance.

AK Now I understand. This is also the stance that the rhetorical perspective inspires. Absolutes are out. Epistemological foundations do not exist. Accordingly, any attempt to debunk male science from an epistemological point of view is doomed to fail. Likewise, any claim to a superior way of knowing is suspect.

JS I agree. I am an anti-foundationalist. I can't prove that a particular neoclassical claim is wrong or that the neoclassical framework is inadequate. But that doesn't mean that I don't passionately believe in my arguments on these matters. I reject relativism. This is the position the feminist science critics find themselves in: lacking the old-fashioned positivist faith in the certainty and objectivity of scientific knowledge, but at the same time urgently wishing to make claims about women and gender relations and to have those claims broadly accepted. Of course, feminists are not the only ones in this position of trying to define the grounds for belief when we know that knowledge is socially constructed, time-bound, and fallible. It's a quandary for everyone.

AK Yes. Stanley Fish clarified this anti-foundationalist-combined-with-anti-relativist stance very eloquently in the book I edited with McCloskey and Solow (Klamer, McCloskey and Solow 1988). Anti-foundationalism does not mean "live and let live." By the way, that reminds me: in your chapter, you mention rhetorical inquiry but you do not elaborate much. Why not? After all, such inquiry gets one to think about the ways in which meanings get produced through the use of metaphors, stories, and other rhetorical devices. Aren't you proposing such an inquiry yourself?

JS I may not have made it clear enough in the chapter, but I do find the rhetorical perspective extremely useful. The rhetorical approach treats economics as a text and encourages us to explore the meanings that are produced in that text. These aspects of economics have been invisible in conventional discussions of economic literature.

AK Precisely. And now, consider the meanings that neoclassical economics excludes. It fails to give expression to the experiences of pain and anger, of the dramas of life, the dramas of success, failure and deprivation, the realities of power, and the impact of culture. Neoclassical economics confines itself to the discourse of (property) right and choice and excludes meaningful connections with the social and spiritual dimensions of life. Even if it were to get close to economic truths, we still could passionately maintain that neoclassical discourse lacks meaning for the world that you and I are trying to understand. The rejection is not based on absolutes, on some kind of epistemological point, but on a rhetorical or interpretive assessment of the meanings that the discourse produces (See Klamer, 1988 and, for the interpretive approach to economics, Lavoie, 1991).

JS That seems right to me. Such a critique exposes the limitations of the language of constrained optimization. That language may be quite useful to interpret certain choices people make, but those choices may be only a small part of the whole picture.

AK At any rate, my point is, I think, that you as a female and I as a male can find a great deal in common. Your perspective appears to concur with the interpretive approach that I favor. Doesn't that support your doubts as to the existence of a specific female way of knowing?

JS Yes, definitely; although it's likely that you and I see things differently regarding gender issues, and I'd attribute that at least in part to our different experiences and gender interests. But on the epistemological and methodological issues, there's indeed a lot of common ground, and I'm much indebted to you and McCloskey for your deconstructions of economic methodological rhetoric.

AK You're too kind. But that at least gives me the chance to say that this chapter of yours has helped me a great deal in recognizing gender in economics.

REFERENCES

Klamer, A. (1987), "As If Economists and Their Subjects Were Rational." In John S. Nelson, Allan Megill, and Donald N. McCloskey, eds. *The Rhetoric of the Human Sciences: Language and Argument in Scholarship and Public Affairs.* Madison: University of Wisconsin Press.

____________, McCloskey, D. N. and Solow, R. M., eds. (1988), *The Consequences of Economic Rhetoric.* New York: Cambridge University Press.

Lavoie, D., ed. (1991), *Economics and Hermeneutics.* New York: Routledge.

CHAPTER 8

LEARNING ECONOMIC METHOD FROM THE INVENTION OF VINTAGE MODELS

Bert Hamminga

This study is a specimen of work done with an extremely narrow conception of economic methodology. In a wider conception, methodology's aim is to arrive at well-founded opinions on how to do economics: how to build theories, what to pretend with theories, how to interpret them, how to test them, on what grounds to accept them or "believe" in them (if this is what "acceptance" means), how to decide for working at one line of research rather then at another. There is no general agreement among economic methodologists about the precise subset of the above mentioned items that should be placed on the agenda of economic methodology.

My narrow conception consists of believing it not in the interest of the profession of economic methodology to place any of these items on the agenda. This is my argument: if you claim that today's eminent economists are certified to do what they do, then you are likely to be considered a bore. If you claim they are not, you will be found funny at best.

Accordingly, there is no other task for methodology than to contribute to the growth of empirical knowledge about what the professionally successful economists of the real world actually do and how they do it. These questions are defying and intriguing, for instance, at times when the answers are not in harmony with the established opinions of the economic profession (if you show that economists do not do what they say they do, you are neither funny nor

boring). But it is also useful to add some details consistent with the global picture of economics prevailing among professional economists. I think this is rewarding enough and usually the best result that methodological study can attain.

We do not know as much about what economists do as is often believed. Some methods for the analysis of economic theories and research lines have been discovered, such as the method of identifying and measuring "empirical content" (Popper (1934), Lakatos (1970)), "structural" analysis (Sneed, 1971), and Nowak's method of analysis, (Nowak, 1980). But the general tendency of the methodological profession is—or at least has been for too long a time—to make a normative or evaluative "philosophy" out of these methods of analysis, rather than to use them to formulate working hypotheses that can be tested against relevant facts in the history of economics.

Economic methodology cannot, I hold, be more than a branch of the history of economics. It is the branch that seeks answers to methodological questions in case histories that tries to generalize these answers into empirical theories, that tries to test the resulting generalisations by digging out new case histories, and so on and so forth. It is the method that so many economic methodologists have preached to economists, and that, fortunately, a rising number of them are now starting to practice themselves, though, I admit, this often is done with a wider conception of "methodology" than the one I wish to maintain.

This essay reports on an empirical exercise that, I hope, satisfies the standards that I set for myself. It concerns an historical case study into the invention of vintage models at the end of the 1950s. It seems particularly interesting for economic methodology, because Johansen, Salter and Solow worked at the idea simultaneously and independently,[1] publishing their respective papers in 1959. This means that we have both a case of multiple discovery and multiple testability of existing views on economic method.

These are the questions: what exactly suggested the vintage idea to the three economists? Which theoretical intentions did they have with the idea? Which problem did they want to solve? What rôle did "empirical observation" play in the process? We are especially interested in the role of econometrics, which is often considered to be a technique for testing economic theories. We shall learn that in two of the cases the vintage idea emerges in a context of econometric research but that in none of the three cases did econometrics itself play any role as a means for detecting the solution, or as a means for testing the validity of the idea.

JOHANSEN'S SURVEY OF THE GROWTH THEORY OF THE 1950S

The 1950s can safely be characterized as a period of full employment with output growing faster than labour supply. In 1953, Joan Robinson writes: "The student of economic theory is taught to write O = f(L, C), where L is a quantity of labour, C a quantity of capital and O a rate of output of commodities" (Robinson, 1953, 81). This student, about whom, it should be mentioned, Solow replied that "this is neither the student's first nor last course in economic theory" (Solow, 1955, 101), has only three opportunities to explain growth of O: (1) growth of C ("the stock of capital"), (2) the shifting of f, and (3) some combination of both. The remaining logically-possible factor: growth of labour input, had no central significance for explaining growth as it was in the 1950s, and this was the natural task of the economics of the time. Growth theory was the hot item, and labour input as a determinant of growth was largely out of consideration. Writing "f" meant thinking about production technique, and writing "C" meant thinking about machines, buildings, and stocks of goods, and these two were the promising items for explaining growth of the type that the world was experiencing.

Before presenting, in his article of 1959, his own invention for explaining growth, Leif Johansen surveys the growth theory of the preceding years. He distinguishes: "(a) Models with a given capital coefficient, where the labour input does not enter the analysis explicitly, but is treated rather vaguely in supplementary comments. The models of R.F. Harrod (1939), Hans Brems (1957), Robert Eisner (1952) and Ingvar Svennilson (1956) exemplify this class. (b) Models with fixed production coefficients for labour input as well as for the capital stock, or some other kind of strict complementarity. As examples one might mention the analysis of D. Hamberg (1952), the work on long range projections at the Central Planning Bureau in the Netherlands, e.g., P.J. Verdoorn (1956), and furthermore the more disaggregated analysis by Wassily Leontief (1953), and other authors in the field of input-output analysis. (c) Models with explicitly expressed possibilities of substitution between labour input and capital stock in a traditional production function. This type of model is exemplified by the publications of Jan Tinbergen (1942), Trygve Haavelmo (1954), Robert Solow (1956) and Stefan Valvanis-Vail

(1953)" (Johansen, 1959, 157).

There is no mention of Joan Robinson's work, which was certainly familiar to Johansen.[2] He did not, we must conclude, see any relevance of her particular viewpoint (to be dealt with below) for his problem (in contrast to Salter and Solow, as we shall see).

Johansen reports having the feeling that many economists in the three groups worked with a "guilty conscience" with respect to the realism of their assumptions about substitution (he found the expression "guilty conscience" in Domar (1957, 7). Substitution is not *always possible*, but neither is it *never possible*. So, nobody is right, and Johansen's solution, called "synthesis" in the title of his paper and "compromise" in the text, consists of assuming perfect substitutability if dealing with new investments, and complete rigidity if dealing with capital goods installed as a result of investment in the past.

The production at time t is obtained by adding the production at t of the remnants of capital vintages installed in earlier periods, plus the production of the new capital vintage installed at t. To determine the growth path of production over time, Johansen needs a production function, a function describing the shrinkage of capital over time (in order to determine the remnants at each time t), the magnitude of the labour force over time, and the rate of saving, that is, roughly, the percentage of production at t that is not used for consumption at t, and which, therefore, determines the size of the new layer of capital to be installed.

Johansen's model was meant to be a contribution to growth theory in which the relationships studied are between saving, labour force, and productivity on the one hand and the growth of production on the other hand. His crucial conclusions are about the effects of the introduction of his specific layer structure of capital on these relationships: "it seems that the conclusions [of growth models generally] are in some respects more sensitive to shifts in the *form* of the production than they are to the shift from the assumption of substitutability in the usual sense to our assumption of substitutability only 'at the margin'." His message, therefore, was that *economists could do away with some of their unrealistic assumptions without doing away with the conclusions previously drawn from the models that contained these assumptions*. And Johansen ends his paper as follows: "If the study had been directed more specially towards such subjects as, say, the importance of the rate of investment for the possibilities of adopting new techniques, the importance of obsolescence in the process of growth, the relation between population growth and "structural" unemployment, etc., then the conclusions would depend more specifically on the choice of what kind of substitutability one assumes".

For methodology the following observations seem relevant: in a sense Johansen presumes earlier growth theories to be "empirically false," but neither Johansen, nor the editors of *Econometrica*, who decided to publish the paper, saw the relevance of demonstrating this supposed falsity with any results of empirical research. Apparently, the underlying lack of correspondence between older growth theories and what the economic process is like in reality, was considered to be *obvious*. Johansen also presumes that many economists in his groups (a), (b) and (c) realized this state of affairs and he illustrates this by invoking Domar's "guilty conscience".

Prior to Johansen's attempt to improve upon existing theory, there is no such thing as a falsification of growth theory by the results of empirical research.[3] Instead, there is, for a whole lot of different reasons, a fluctuating degree of dissatisfaction with the correspondence of existing models to what the economist *a priori* considers to be the obvious essentials of the real world processes, for which the model's interesting theorems are supposed to be relevant.

We can safely suppose that the editors and readers of *Econometrica* knew very well that Johansen's suppositions are false too: even if investment in capital is realized, some substitution possibilities remain, and even a readily disposable investment fund of the utmost liquidity does not yield perfect substitution possibilities. Nevertheless, it is quite reasonable to consider Johansen's model as an improvement upon existing theory at the time and it is quite understandable that it was recognized as such.

There was, then, no "empirical research," but there were many things everyone "knew," pressing more or less on the economist's conscience. This pressure was felt with respect to the dilemma between rigidity and substitution, and Johansen saw the way out.

ROBINSON AND THE PROBLEM OF TIME, CAPITAL, AND GROWTH

Why was the pressure felt exactly there and not on some other place in the jungle of growth theory assumptions, many of which are at best only approximately true—and any case of approximate truth is a case of falsehood? And why was it felt so clearly that three economists set out independently to solve the problem?

Joan Robinson certainly is part of the answer. The two other inventors refer to her as early as on their first page. She tells the story of the "student of economic theory" in her paper of (1953), and it does not really end well: "He is instructed to assume all workers alike, and to measure L in man-hours of labour; he is told something about the index-number problem involved in choosing a unit of output; and then he is hurried on to the next question, in the hope that he will forget to ask *in what units C is measured*. Before ever he does ask, he has become a professor, and so sloppy habits of thought are handed on from one generation to the next" (Robinson, 1953, 18).

Her mode of formulation already makes clear that the reader is requested to take a fundamentally different point of view. Let a country, to simplify, have no distinction between profit and interest. There is only "return to capital," which we call, for convenience, the interest rate. Robinson's problem with the way neoclassical economists use aggregate production functions for the determination of wage rates and interest rates is that not only total labour input has to be given, but also the total "amount of capital," in order to process the calculation: ceteris paribus, the quantity of capital determines the marginal productivity of capital, which in its turn determines the interest rate, in the neoclassical mode of thought. But if we have two industrial areas, I and II (at different times and/or places), how should we determine which one represents the larger amount of capital? It would be convenient if of all means of production in I, there would be exact copies in II (just as old, and used with the same intensity in the past), and if in II would be some additional ones with no counterpart in I. But everyone knows, quite independently of any empirical research, that such cases are so rare as to be virtually nonexistent. How, then, should the "quantity of capital" be measured, if it cannot be added up in terms of physical units? If some *value* could be attributed to every stock of capital, these values could be used in the neoclassical production function, thus determining the marginal product of a "unit of capital" in terms of the chosen unit of value. But this requires some choice of bookkeeping philosophy. Robinson considers two such philosophies. The first one she took from Keynes' investment function (see postscript). In this approach, the value of a piece of capital equipment is the sum of future earnings, discounted at some interest rate. The bookkeeper, therefore, will need a given interest rate in order to calculate the value of capital, which the neoclassical economists, however, need to calculate the ruling interest rate.

Robinson showed that the same cirularity arises if we apply a second type of bookkeeping philosophy that she borrowed from Sraffa's interpretation of Ricardo's *Principles* (see postscript). According to this philosophy, the value of a piece of capital equipment is the sum of outlays in the past that were needed to produce it. But, of course, these outlays are also spread over time and have to be discounted at some interest rate. Yet, it is the interest rate that the neoclassical economist wants to calculate on the basis of the result of the bookkeeper's work.

The neoclassical rules for the determination of wage rates and interest rates do not really work in practice, she claims, because the result of their calculation has to be given if the calculation is to be carried out at all, and Robinson does not only want to change the rules, but even to change the target of the game. We had better not try to calculate wage rates and interest rates, she ventures to claim. They are economically undetermined and given by the cultural characteristics of society, such as class division and power. What we can calculate is the effect of some *given* wage interest ratio on the accumulation of capital and the growth of production. If a theory determining the wage-interest ratio itself is possible at all, then it is the sociologist's job to find it.

This new game, the calculation of rates of accumulation and growth of production, requires a new type of abstraction as a starting point. We should start by analysing economic states of "tranquillity." Such a state is characterised by a constant interest rate in the entire foregoing period in which the physical capital now in use was built up (and managers and bookkeepers know this) and by an exactly equal and constant interest rate for the future periods in which the physical capital resulting from present investment decisions will be in use (and managers and bookkeepers expect this). "Tranquillity," therefore, does not merely pertain to a certain moment of an economy, but to a period of the history of an economy. If such a period of history satisfies the requirement of tranquillity, then Robinson calls it a Golden Age. In Golden Ages, Keynes and Sraffa's Ricardo agree on the value of capital.

In other ages—and Robinson of course realises that Golden Ages are not likely ever to be observed—we can calculate the "quantity of capital" only under very restrictive assumptions. She occupies herself with the key questions of the 1950s: what determines economic growth? And she answers the question in terms of *comparative dynamics*. Take two countries, both in the midst of a Golden Age, equal in all aspects except the wage-interest ratio, or except the state of technique, or except labour supply (which is a determinant that receives more attention from her than usual in the period). Then calculate the accumulation of capital and the growth of production of the respective countries and compare the resulting growth paths. This kind of analysis may appear quite abstract, but according to Robinson, there is no other way than to rebuild economics from these foundations.

Robinson's critique on the neoclassical concept of capital was well received in the circles of theoretical economists, but her point—changing the target of the game—was missed, or abhorred. Economists were not ready to hand over the job of explaining the wage-interest ratio to another academic discipline.

It cannot always be inferred whether or not economists were explicitly reluctant to change the target of their game because of the widespread misunderstanding of the intentions Robinson had in her paper of (1953) and in her book (1956). She managed to create some confusion, but the new order she advocated only created a small undercurrent in economics.

SALTER

The second inventor of the vintage model, Wilfred Salter, puts a lot of Robinson in the introduction of his (1959) paper. The "sloppy-habit-of-thought"-Robinson, to be sure, and not the Robinson who wants to change the aims of economic theory. He presents his vintage model as a solution of Robinson's problem of how to measure the quantity of capital in a neoclassical production function, a solution less radical than her own. For the meaningful use of this production function, he claims, we need not calculate the value of the *whole* capital stock, because the production function is only relevant for today's investments. If we analyze investment *decisions*, we only care for the marginal additions and replacements of the capital stock. Only there is the production function—which is really a planning function in a world of blueprints—*relevant*. Capital goods already existing are simply there, and what they produce is simply being produced because we happened to possess these capital goods, and it would be irrational not to use them. We do not need a production function for this, because nothing is decided upon. We did need such a function at that moment in the past when these capital goods were decided to be installed by means of a choice of technique and given an investment fund. Since then, the production function relevant at that moment has become history.

This introduction is Salter's motivation for writing a paper about these periodic decisions about what to do with a *given* investment fund, taken independent of any knowledge about what is left of the capital goods installed in previous periods. The only "capital" in his production function is today's gross investment fund, and it is thus "cast in terms of investment rather than the ambiguous concept of capital" (Salter, 1959, 47). This way, he saves himself from Ricardo, but Keynes remains there (see section 2): interest rate expectations influence the capital intensity of the new vintage (Salter calls it "items of capital equipment") preferred by the investor for reasons of profitability. As a result, he considers the duration of technically realizable capital goods to be relevant for the decision, and adds this as a variable to his "marginal-additions-and-replacements"-production function. He proves that the duration chosen will be shorter under higher interest rates, under higher risks, and under faster economic obsolescence.

In 1960 Salter's book *Productivity and Technical Change* appeared. "The ideas on which this book is based were developed at Cambridge between 1953 and 1955" (Salter 1960, xiii). The central idea is the vintage model, and Robinson's student would be quite astonished. His famous "Salter diagram" is reproduced here as fig. 1.

Total output is disaggregated into output due to each vintage of capital goods, and every vintage has its own labour intensity. This allows the representation of the quantity of labour used by a vintage as a rectangular surface. He also uses integral calculus to describe this function.

One year before, in his paper of (1959), Salter did not introduce any figures, and like Robinson (1953) and Robinson (1956), he did not refer to any statistics. He only explained how to interpret a production function without having to assume a known quantity representing "the" capital stock as a whole.

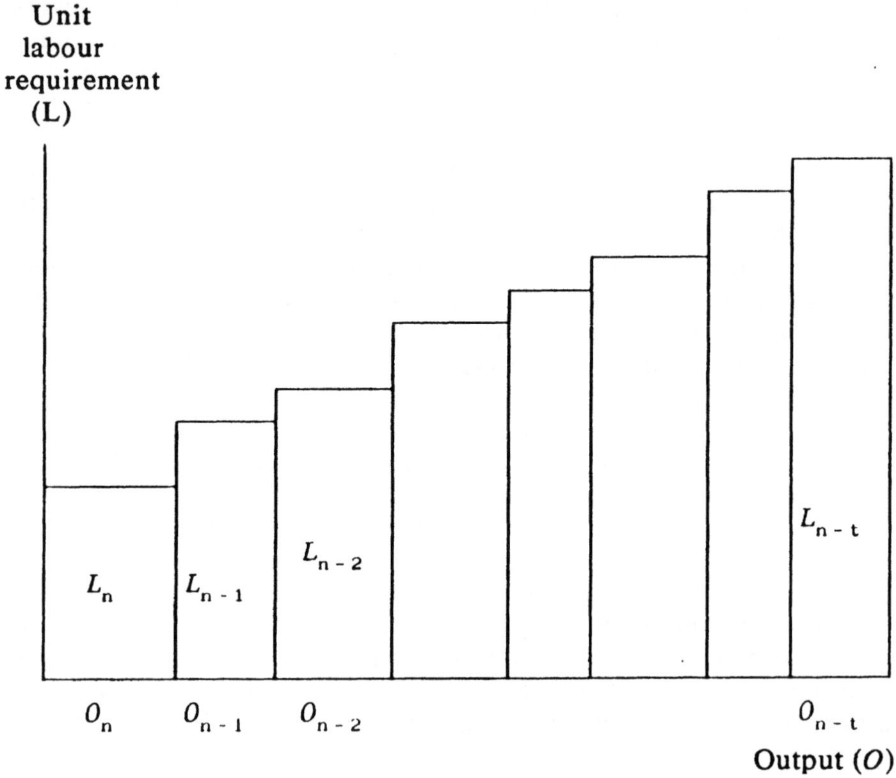

Figure 1: The "Salter diagram"

In the book, references to Robinson are rare. (Salter was a student of W.B. Reddaway in his Cambridge years.) The book almost starts with a summary of his (1959) paper, but the story about the "marginal additions and replacements"-production function is omitted there and left for his crucial chapter IV entitled: "A Model of the Delay in the Utilization of New Techniques of Production".

His book is largely based upon the principles explained in this chapter and it thus seems very probable that the vintage idea belongs to "the ideas . . . developed at Cambridge between 1953 and 1955." At the time he published his book (1960), he did not seem any more to attach much interest to the problem of "capital" for the theory of his book; he repeats in the introduction that for all practical purposes the problem has been solved, his production function having been "cast in investment instead of the ambiguous concept of capital" (Salter, 1960, 9).

His book contains not only theoretical results, but also very many statistical and econometric results: he provides a cross section analysis of a selected sample of British industries, calculating correlations and linear regression equations between indices of volume of output, employment, prices, unit labour costs and related variables of the industries, repeats the analysis for the United States and interprets and compares the results. His introduction is about the relationship of theory and observation and he writes: "the empirical analysis is in no sense meant as a test of the theory. In fact, I am *deeply conscious* of the gap between the empirical and theoretical approaches" (Salter, 1960, 9, italics mine). He distinguishes *definition* and *measurement*, that is the collection of figures, sharply from *interpretation*, which begins "once we ask what such figures mean" (3).

As in the case of Johansen, econometrics plays no role in Salter's invention of a vintage model. Neither is the model tested by means of econometrics. The idea is the result of pure thinking about the aggregate neoclassical production function in a world with growing output per head, full employment and a rising labour productivity. What is technique, and what does technique do? The answers to these questions are given in an act of interpretation of such a world. His econometrics (the estimation of the parameters of assumed functional relationships between variables relevant to production) comes only afterwards and is in no sense meant as a test of the theory.

SOLOW

Solow's exercises with capital theory in the 1950s have always been inspired by the neoclassical theory of which he wanted it to form a part. In that he differs from Salter and Johansen. Solow clearly recognizes Robinson's charge and first sets out to find in his paper of (1955), the conditions under which a disaggregate production function (containing the amount of each kind of capital good as a separate variable) can be simplified to an aggregate production function (containing a single variable for the "quantity of physical capital" as a whole). These conditions, the solution of a mathematical problem,[4] turn out to be very restrictive. In a comment by Robinson (1955) he is, apart from this, criticized for having dealt only with the index problem and not with the problem of the time it takes to build capital goods, which involves the interest rate. In this way Robinson tries to force Solow to set forth the question in such a way that the neoclassical target of the game has to be given up (see section 2). But Solow does not like that. Measuring the quantity of capital in a time-dependent way as units of labour input plus cumulated interest has, Solow holds, "a faintly archaic flavour" (Solow, 1955, 101).

Nonetheless, the restrictiveness of the conditions he found made Solow feel uncomfortable, as we shall see. As long as he knew of no better way, he went on doing empirical research based on the assumption that the conditions were satisfied, implying that the aggregate production function as a tool for econometricians has economic meaning. This sets the stage for an empirical research program in mathematical trouble that, nevertheless, attracted much attention, a stage, therefore, that is quite worthy of being observed by methodologists.

Some remarks on the supply of data in the early fifties should be made in order to delineate the logic of the problem situation. Schmookler (1952) constructs indexes for land, labour and capital input and output of the American economy (1869 to 1938). His aim is to combine these indexes to finally measure the growth of "output per unit of input." Such a unit of input is a weighted index obtained from the input indexes of land, labour and capital. His resulting index is meant to mirror "the changing efficiency of the American economy," and to describe "the pattern and magnitude of technical change for the United States as a whole from 1869 to 1938" (214). His conclusion is that "The efficiency increases were unevenly distributed, the maximum technical change transpiring in 1874-88 and 1919-33 . . ." and that "the increase in gross national product over the period reflected in roughly equal parts an increase in resources and an increase in efficiency" (230).

Schmookler neither thought nor wrote in terms of "O=f(L, C)" (see section 1. But to everyone who did, his study must have been much more puzzling than the kind of study, more usual at the time, in which efficiency was measured as output per unit of labour only: in the latter type of study, efficiency growth could, in principle, be attributed to "C". If we were to believe Schmookler, however, half of the efficiency growth had to be attributed to "f," which, in neoclassical theory, usually was treated as a fixed function, as if reflecting the laws of nature that govern production. A little earlier, and in quite a different setting, that of the Heckscher-Ohlin trade model, Samuelson

(1948) wrestles with the problem as follows: "laws of nature may be the same 'everywhere,' but the laws of nature and the economically relevant production function relating maximum output obtainable from specified concrete inputs are two quite different things." 'Knowledge' is not something you can store in 'C', Samuelson argues. "It would be artificial in the extreme to explain any . . . empirical case by saying that 'knowledge' is 'scarce' in one place relative to the other . . . Knowledge is not an input such that the more you use of it, the less there is left" (Samuelson, 1948, 180-183).

Abramovitz (1956) improved upon Schmookler's (1952) study by using the new figures of Kuznets and Kendrick, and improving the method of indexing. He writes, "the source of the great increase in the net product [since the Civil War] was not mainly an increase in labour input per head, not even an increase in capital per head... Its source must be sought principally in the complex of little understood forces which caused productivity, that is, output per unit of utilized resources, to rise" (6). That is, by 1956, "f" is even suggested to carry the main burden of the growth of output. "This result is surprising in the lopsided importance which it appears to give to productivity increase, and it should be, in a sense, sobering, if not discouraging, to students of economic growth" (Abramovitz, 1956, 11).

Solow's seminal work on this particular problem is his "Technical Change and the Aggregate Production Function" (1957). Here, Solow uses an aggregate production function for long term estimation. The function is allowed to shift over time, and it is precisely the shift that he wants to estimate. He estimates on the basis of time series on U.S. employment, "stock of capital" (!),[5] share of property in income, and private nonfarm GNP per manhour—1909-1949. Estimating the shift of the production function is made possible by *assuming* neoclassical theory to be correct in that factors of production are paid their marginal products. This assumption is not testable, but *under* this assumption, the following function can be estimated.

$$O = A(t) \cdot f(L, C)$$

in wich f is linear homogeneous, O output, L labour, C capital and A a parameter changing over time. The result of the estimation is a value of A(t) for each year.

What is Solow's reason for doing this? What makes shifts of aggregate production functions interesting? They are, he answers, relevant for the discussion about the determinants of economic growth. The question is: to what extent is growth effected by a simple increase over time of the quantity of capital per head, and to what extent is it effected by technical change?

What is "technical change"? Standing by itself it seems a rather vague concept, but it gets a very precise meaning as soon as we decide to interpret it as the *shift of a production function.* The concept then is loaded with neoclassical theory. Which technician of which factory would see much difference between carrying out orders that result in a substitution along the factory's production function and orders that involve a shift of the factory's production function? The jobs will probably not be of too different a nature, and since they are both done by a technician, there seems to be no reason to reserve the term "technical change" for only one of them. As soon as you use a neoclassical production function, however, the distinction between "increasing the quantity of capital" and "technical change" becomes inevitable. Solow was not the first to think about technical change as drift of the production function. By 1957, it had become usual in growth theory to *assume* A(t) as a parameter representing technical change and influencing the growth rate. A(t) represented, as it was called, "Hicks-neutral" technical change. (Swan (1956) is an example of this.) Solow now adds to this an econometric technique, or as he called it, a "wrinkle," with first order differences to sort out the growth effects resulting from increases in the quantity of capital per head and those resulting from technical change. The test is clear: if A(t) turns out to be relatively constant over time, the aggregate production function would not have shifted much, and those would have been right who sought to explain growth mainly from an increase of C/L, the quantity of capital per head. If, on the other hand, A(t) had increased over time, we would have *observed* technical change determining growth. This is how Solow's A(t) turned out to evolve over time (figure 2).

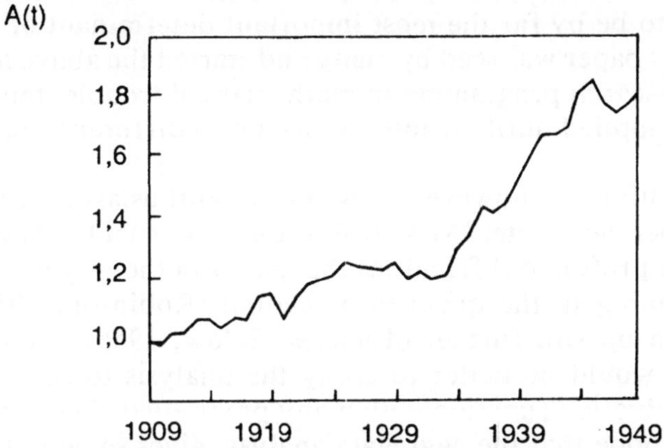

Figure 2. The development of "technique"?

Does figure 2 depict the development of the state of technique? There is no way to test that. There is no report on the "real" development of technique that we could use to compare with figure 2 and see whether the two differ or not. How, then, do we judge whether A(t) represents the state of technique?

Solow: "I was tempted to end this section with the remark that the A(t) series, which is meant to be a rough profile of technical change, at least looks reasonable. But on second thought *I decided that I had very little prior notion of what would be "reasonable" in this context. One notes with satisfaction that the trend is strongly upward; had it turned out otherwise I would not now be writing this paper*. There are sharp dips after each of the World Wars; these, like the sharp rises that preceded them, can easily be rationalized. It is more suggestive that the curve shows a distinct levelling-off in the last half of the 1920's. A sustained rise begins again in 1930. There is an unpleasant sawtooth character to the first few years of the A/A curve, which I imagine to be a statistical artifact" (Solow, 1957, 316 (italics mine)).

If A(t) represents the state of technique, Solow concludes, then it follows from the time series that "gross output per man hour doubled over the interval (1919-1949), with 87½ per cent of the increase attributable to technical change and the remaining 12½ per cent to increased use of capital" (Solow, 1957, 320).

One and the same "wrinkle" thus gave a very specific neoclassical meaning to the concept of technical change in 1957 and turned out right away to be by far the most important determinant of economic growth! This paper was read by many and started the above mentioned empirical research programme in mathematical trouble: the "wrinkle" was widely applied until far into the sixties to different countries and time series.[6]

Solow himself, however, was not so enthusiastic at all. In his famous paper he wrote: "Mrs. Robinson in particular has explored many of the profound difficulties that stand in the way of giving any precise meaning to the quantity of capital (Robinson, 1953), and I have thrown up still further obstacles (Solow, 1955). Were the data available it would be better to apply the analysis to some precisely defined production function with many precisely defined inputs. One can at least hope that the aggregate analysis gives some notion of the way a detailed analysis would lead" (Solow, 1957, 312).

Two years later, Solow presents his vintage model (Solow, 1959). This is what he came to think about: technical change, explaining 87½ percent of growth, should relate in some way to the stock of capital goods. If, however, we use an aggregate production function, we cannot imagine any process by which technical change comes about but that "it floats down from the outside" (Solow, 1959, 90). "The striking assumption is that old and new capital equipment participate equally in technical change. This conflicts with the *casual observation* that many if not most innovations need to be embodied in new kinds of durable equipment before they can be made effective. Improvements in technology affect output only to the extent that they are carried out into practice either by net capital formation or by the replacement of old-fashioned equipment by the latest models with a consequent shift of equipment by date of birth" (italics mine).

Endowed with his magnificent solution of the problem, he criticizes his own paper of 1957. About shifting aggregate production functions he now writes: "it is true that the notion of time-shifts in the function is a confession of ignorance rather than a claim to knowledge . . ." (Solow, 1959, 90).

New techniques are "embodied" in new capital goods resulting from the spending of gross investment funds. This is a "casual observation," by which Solow means that he does not regard it to be his task to test the statement. No: "My object is to reconstruct the model to *make allowance for this aspect of reality*" (Solow, 1959, 91, italics mine). He simply *knows* it is an aspect of reality.

"To this end," he writes, "it becomes necessary to distinguish capital of different dates of construction or vintages" (Solow, 1959, 91). With his new model he does some exercises in estimation, which is a bit more complicated econometrically.[7] But the "numerical values suggested," together with the model used to estimate them, allow Solow to show how capital investment (Solow, like Salter, now starts to prefer the term investment), in his paper of (1957) only responsible for 12½ percent of growth, is now rehabilitated, and Solow pregnantly writes why: "capital formation is the vehicle for carrying technical change into effect" (Solow, 1959, 97).

A routine theoretical task within the framework of neoclassical research programmes is performed in Solow (1962): "to demonstrate that, even in the absence ex post substitutability between labour and 'capital', the neoclassical categories of thought make sense and even the neoclassical theorems continue to hold" (217).[8]

SUMMARY AND CONCLUSION

The ways in which Johansen, Salter, and Solow found the vintage solution, and the respective intentions they had with this solution, are understandable once we realize the *logic of the problem situation*: explaining growth of output in combination with a rising labour productivity, starting from a traditional aggregate production function as the main tool at the time for the analysis of this kind of problem.

Johansen (1959) manages to avoid Scylla and Charibdis in the discussion, in growth theory, about substitution in aggregate production functions by construing a model that fortunately allows the derivation of growth paths similar to the ones derivable from existing models.

Salter (1959) finds a method to employ production functions in the usual way without having to assume the "stock of capital" as a measurable quantity. It is highly probable, however, that he found the method several years earlier in the context of his empirical research on productivity and technical change that he finally presented in his book (1960). He needed the vintage idea in order to explain the *delay* in the utilisation of new techniques with the help of production functions.

Solow (1957) finds an appealing method to measure the shift of aggregate production functions over time. His first inclination is to interpret the "place" of the production function in a certain year as the "state of technique." This causes him problems because in this framework there is no natural way to imagine *how* exactly technical change comes about. Since it comes about through the installation of new capital goods, Solow is forced to disaggregate and consider the technical composition of the capital stock. Solow's question in his paper of (1957)—"to what extent is 'capital' responsible for growth and to what extent should growth be explained by technique?"—turned out not to be answerable with the help of an aggregate production function.

The invention of vintage models was clearly an important event (the two decades following the year 1959 witnessed over 100 publications concerning vintage models in the international literature).[9] Very precisely can we see, in these three examples of finding an idea that attracts attention and stimulates research, what rôle observation and empirical research plays in trailblazing economic science.

Underlying Johansen's paper is the question to what extent substitution is possible in the real world. Johansen simply knows, just like everyone else, that freedom of substitution before installation of capital goods is much greater than afterwards. This may certainly be called an observation. But for this observation it is not necessary to estimate structural parameters of some econometric model, neither does Johansen do so. There is no number at all in his paper, and he rightly supposes that everyone understands the problem he is solving.

Neither does Salter need any parameter values to convince us of the force of the vintage idea, he writes about a "simple, but often neglected point." Such simple points should, according to Salter, be dealt with independently of the "collection of figures." Salter could not be charged with neglecting the activity of collecting figures, for it is the main purpose of his paper of (1960) to report on that. Theory, however, is according to Salter, quite a different activity, that starts once we ask what such figures mean; therefore not only the "figures" matter, there are also "very simple points".

Such "simple points" are also found at the crucial moments in Solow's papers. Though he bothered about an *estimation result*, the great significance of time shifts of the aggregate production function as a "variable" explaining growth (87½ percent) in the period 1909 to 1949, his real problem was that he had no natural way to interpret this significant technical change in terms of the aggregate production function. Where does technical change come from? "It flows down from the outside," he concluded in his paper of (1959). It is true that exactly this problem would not have bothered Solow if he had found 0 percent instead of 87 percent%. Then, however, he should have been forced to conclude in his paper of (1957) that from 1909 to 1949 we have lived in a world with a growing capital intensity of production and *without significant technical change*. And if the trend of A(t) had turned out to be downward, he would not, as he already makes clear in his paper of (1957), have written his paper at all. It was *a priori* impossible that some plausible parameter value would result. There were only three logically possible results: a technical progress as *deus ex machina* (A(t) increasing), or technical stagnation from 1909 to 1949 (A(t) remaining stable), or technical regress (A(t) decreasing), whatever that may be. And Solow knew, just like everyone else, that there had been technical progress (though he was, of course, not sure to get this as result of applying his "wrinkle"), that labour productivity had increased and that this must have something to do with capital goods installed in the course of the years. These observations, "very simple points" as Salter calls them (Solow calls them "casual observations" (Solow, 1959, 91)), do the work, and the work had to be done *before* meaningful parameters could be estimated. Without solving this first, Solow encountered problems in answering the question as to what his numbers meant (which he would also have had with *any* other number resulting). This general type of problem must have suggested the vintage solution to him.

For economic methodology it seems necessary to distinguish between two kinds of factual economic knowledge. First, we have the general kind of knowledge that we acquire by just living our life, reading newspapers, and perhaps looking over some very simple statistics. Second, we have econometric results, that is, the results of the estimation of parameters. In the cases dealt with in this chapter, satisfactory econometric results were achieved *after* a theory was contructed that had a clear relationship with the "very simple points" (Salter) and "casual observations" (Solow), with our general kind of factual knowledge, therefore. Before this was achieved "consciences" felt "guilty" (Johansen, Domar). Econometrics was, in our cases, not a means to find the solution, nor was it a means to test the validity of the idea. This might be expressed by saying that the vintage theories of capital, basic to a specific research line in econometrics, are themselves accepted on the ground of their *plausibility*.

POSTSCRIPT 1: PRECURSORS

First dealing with the history of the problem of measuring the quantity of capital: Ricardo (1821, ch. XXXI, "On machinery") understood Robinson's problem of the role of the interest rate in measuring the quantity of capital on the basis of its cost of production in the past very well. Sraffa (1951) brought this again to attention.

Keynes' marginal efficiency of capital schedule (Keynes, 1936, 135-37) contains the essence of measuring the quantity of capital as the present value of the future earnings of the capital goods: today's interest expectations determine which new investments are judged to be profitable. This can be found in Wicksell (1901-06, 206-238; 1893, 71-127). The first English edition of Wicksell (1901-06) appeared in the thirties. Wicksell (1898) appeared in English in 1936. Robinson was not the only one after Keynes to pursue this subject. It can also be found in Knight (1944) and Lerner (1953). Lerner distinguishes "investment" and "capital" in Salter's (1959) way, but he does not introduce the vintage idea.

Robinson writes about her theory of accumulation that it "presented itself to me as a generalisation of the General Theory, that is, an extension of Keynes' short-run analysis to long run development. But I was very much illuminated by Piero Sraffa's Introduction to Ricardo's *Principles*" (Robinson, 1956, vi).

In the years before the "capital debate," also, Wicksell (1893) is translated into English. Robinson refers to it in her *Accumulation of Capital*.

But much earlier, Marx wrestles with the problem, from a Ricardian perspective:

> [Die] "fortschreitende relative Abnahme des variablen Kapitals im Verhältnis zum konstanten und daher zum Gesamtkapital ist identisch mit der fortschreitend höhern organischen Zusammensetzung des gesellschaftlichen Kapitals in seinem Durchschnitt. Es ist ebenso nur ein andrer Ausdruck für die fortschreitende Entwicklung der Gesellschaftlichen Produktivkraft der Arbeit, die sich gerade darin zeigt, daß vermittelst der wachsenden Anwendung von Maschinerie und fixem Kapital überhaupt mehr Roh- und Hilfstoffe von derselben Anzahl Arbeiter in derselben Zeit, d.h. mit weniger Arbeit in Produkte ver-

wandelt werden. Es entspricht diesem wachsenden Wertumfang des konstanten Kapitals—*obgleich er nur entfernt das Wachstum in der wirklichen Masse der Gebrauchswerte darstellt, aus denen das konstanten Kapital stofflich besteht*—eine wachsende Verwohlfeilerung des Produkts" (Marx, 1867, III, 222, italics mine).

Now proceeding to precursors of the vintage idea itself, we can identify Marx as a fourth independent inventor. For Marx (1867) it is a "circulation" problem, and he treats the "Umschlagszeit" of fixed capital and its relationship to the speed of technical change in the following way: "Ein Teil des vorgeschoßnen Kapitalwerts ist in diese, durch die Funktion der Arbeitsmittel im Prozeß bestimmte Form *fixiert.* Mit der Funktion und daher der Abnutzung des Arbeitsmittels geht ein Teil seines Werts auf das Produkt über, ein andrer bleibt fixiert im Arbeitsmittel und daher im Produktionsprozeß. . . . Dieser im Arbeitsmittel fixierte Teil des Kapitalwerts zirkuliert so gut wie jeder andre. . . . Aber die Zirkulation des hier betrachteten Kapitalteils ist eigentümlich. Erstens zirkuliert er nicht in seiner Gebrauchsform, sondern nur sein Wert zirkuliert, und zwar allmählich, bruchweis . . . Durch diese eigentümlichkeit erhält dieser Teil des konstanten Kapitals die Form: *Fixes Kapital*" (Marx, 1867, II, 159). Hjalmarsson (1975) quotes the central passage in Marx: "Die Arbeitsmittel werden großenteils beständig umgewälzt durch den Fortschritt der Industrie. Sie werden daher nicht in ihrer ursprünglichen Form ersetzt, sondern in der umgewältzten Form. Einerseits bildet die Masse des fixen Kapitals, die in einer bestimmten Naturalform angelegt ist und innerhalb derselben eine bestimmte Durchschnittslebenszeit auszudauern hat, einen Grund der nur allmählichen Einführung neuer Maschinen etc., und daher ein Hindernis gegen die rasche allgemeine Einführung der verbesserten Arbeitsmittel" (Marx, 1867, II, 171). (N.B. The title of Salter's Chapter IV is: "A Model of the Delay in the Utilisation of New Techniques of Production"!).

Johansen (private correspondence) found a passage in Heckscher (1918, 134-35). It shows a Salter diagram like figure I. Every rectangular surface represents a "fabrik," in an import-competing industry. Those "fabriker" in the industry that have a high labour productivity will find it advantageous to form a trust in order to lengthen the economic life of some weak-home competitors with low labour productivity. If they do so, any decrease of home-market price by lowering import tariffs, immediately leads to unemployment as a result of this weak edge going out of business. As long as the government eschews this effect of the facilitation of international trade by means of lowering tariffs, it keeps the tariff high enough to avoid it. The rest of the industry then profits from the resulting high margin. This makes Heckscher the fifth independent inventor of the vintage idea.

There is something of the vintage idea in Lerner (1953, 10-11) where he fears that new capital equipment, requiring lower running expenses, is also a cheaper investment, thus reducing the volume of investment, if no offsetting rise of demand is expected.

Robinson (1956) sometimes returns from her voluntary exile to comparing Golden Ages in order to make very complicated attempts to analyse changes in one economy over time, resulting from, for example, changes in wage-interest ratio or technique. In doing so, she needs a lot of additional assumptions to derive any results. One of them is: "The length of life of individual capital goods is short so that an individual entrepreneur can readily change his stock of capital goods from one form to another, without loss of value, by refraining from renewing items that have ceased to be profitable and investing accrued amortization funds in items wich he expects to be profitable" (Robinson, 1956, 139). She clearly recognized the situation.

Salter (1960, 4) mentions Hicks (1932, 183): "an entrepreneur by investing in fixed capital equipment gives hostages to fortune. So long as the plant is in existence, the possibility of economising by changing the method or scale of production is small; but as the plant comes to be renewed it will be in his interest to make a radical change."

Johansen mentions as his sources of inspiration: Svennilson (1954, 208) and (1956, 325), Maywald, Baran (1957, 21) and 78/79 and Strumilin (1951, 175). At least some of these authors are known to have read Marx very well.

NOTES

*Tilburg University. The author benefitted from helpful comments by M. Abramovitz, N.B. de Marchi, R. Janssen, the late L. Johansen and R.M. Solow.

1. Johansen (1959), Salter (1959), Solow (1959). Prof. Johansen and Prof. Solow confirmed this in private correspondence.

2. At the time Johansen submitted his paper to *Econometrica* (Spring term 1959), he was in Cambridge. (In a letter dated February 22, 1982, he mentions that Salter was in Australia by that time.)

3. We shall deal with empirical research by Smookler and Abramovitz in section 4. Their findings do not falsify models with aggregate non-vintage production functions but imply shifts of those functions.

4. This is a "conditions for conditions result" (Hamminga, 1983, 68).

5. Solow writes: "The capital time series is the one that will drive a purist mad," Solow (1957, 314).

6. Blaug (1980, 195); McClelland (1975, 194).

7. Some more details are in my reply to Weintraub, below.

8. This is "field extension" (Hamminga, 1983, 67).

9. Some of these publications were very critical concerning usefulness of the vintage approach. Denison (1964, 1967) claims that vintage models under usual assumptions severely overestimate the effects of the pace of investment on the overall growth of production. He argues that the reduction of the average age of capital by (say) one year, does not, under normal circumstances, mean adding one year's average quality improvement to the stock of capital goods. And he also argues that a very large increase in the pace of investment is needed for a relatively small reduction in the average age of capital equipment, so that "under reasonably normal circumstances" changes in the average age have no more than "a negligible effect on output" (Denison, 1967, 145-46); see also Abramowitz (1962, 773-74, 779-80). Apart from the critical contributions, the activities that the publications report on can be classified into: theory development (generalization of the model and weakening of the conditions for its basic theorems to hold); disaggregation into branches of industry; development of appropriate estimation techniques; application to estimation techniques to data sets of specific countries and branches of industry; the use of the foregoing results for applied economic analysis, prediction, and recommendation of specific economic policies for countries and branches of industry (which list will be the subject of further methodological research).

REFERENCES

Abramovitz, M. (1956), "Resource and Output Trends in the United States Since 1870," *American Economic Review*, 46, 5-23.

________________. (1962), "Economic Growth in the United States," *American Economic Review*, 52, 762-782.

Baran, P.A. (1957), *The Political Economy of Growth*. New York: .

Blaug, M. (1980), *The Methodology of Economics*. Cambridge: Cambridge University Press.

Brems, H. (1957), "Constancy of the Proportionate Equilibrium Rate of Growth: Result or Assumption?" *Review of Economic Studies*, XXIV, 131-138.

Denison, E.F. (1962a), "How to Raise the High-Employment Growth Rate By One Percentage Point," *American Economic Review*, 52, 67-75.

________________. (1962b), *The Sources of Economic Growth in the United States*. New York: Commission for Economic Development.

________________. (1964), "The Unimportance of the Embodiment Question," *American Economic Review*, 54, 90-94.

________________. (1967), *Why Growth Rates Differ*. Washington: Brookings Institute.

Domar, E.D. (1957), *Essays in the Theory of Economic Growth*. New York: Oxford University Press.

Eisner, R. (1952), "Underemployment Equilibrium Rates of Growth," *American Economic Review*, 52, 820-831.

Haavelmo, T. (1954), *A Study in the Theory of Economic Evolution*. Amsterdam: North-Holland.

Hamberg, D. (1952), "Full Capacity vs. Full Employment Growth," *Quarterly Journal of Economics*, 66, 444-49.

Hamminga, B. (1983), *Neoclassical Theory Structure and Theory Development*. Berlin: Springer Veslag.

Harrod, R.F. (1939), "An Essay in Dynamic Theory," *Economic Journal*, 49, 14-33.

Heckscher, E.F. (1918), *Svenka Produktionsproblem*. Stockholm: A. Bonnier.

Hicks, J.R., (1932), *The Theory of Wages*. London: Macmillan.

Hjalmarsson, L. (1975), "A Note on Marx and Putty-Clay," Memorandum nr. 47, University of Gothenburg, Department of Economics.

Johansen, L. (1959), "Substitution versus Fixed Production Coefficients in the Theory of Economic Growth: A Synthesis," *Econometrica*, 27, 157-176.

Keynes, J.M. (1973 [1936]), *The General Theory of Employment, Interest and Money*. Cambridge: Macmillan, for the Royal Economic Society; vol. of *The Collected Writings of J. M. Keynes*, ed., D. Moggridge.

Knight, F.H. (1944), "Diminishing Returns from Investment," *Journal of Political Economy*, 52, 26-47.

Lakatos, I., (1970), "Falsification and the Methodology of Scientific Research Programmes," In Lakatos, I., and Musgrave, A. (ed.). *Criticism and the Growth of Knowledge*. Cambridge: Cambridge University Press.

____________________. (1971), "History of Science and its Rational Reconstructions," *Boston Studies in the Philosophy of Science*, VIII, Buck and Cohen (ed.). Dordrecht: Reidel.

Lerner, A.P. (1953), "On the Marginal Product of Capital and the

Marginal Efficiency of Investment," *Journal of Political Economy*, 61, 1-14.

Leontief, W., et al. (1953), *Studies in the Structure of the American Economy*. New York: Oxford University Press.

Marshall, A. (1982 [1890]), *Principles of Economics*. London: Macmillan.

Marx, K. (1975 [1867]), *Das Kapital*. East-Berlin: Dietz.

Maywald, K. (1957), "The Best and the Average in Productivity Studies and in Long-Term Forecasting," *The Productivity Measurement Review*, No. 9 (Reprint Series No. 132, University of Cambridge). Cambridge: Department of Applied Economics.

MacClelland, P.D. (1975), *Causal Explanation and Model Building in History, Economics, and the New Economic History*. Ithaca: Cornell University Press.

McMullin, E. (1970), "The History of Science: A Taxonomy," *Minnesota Studies in the Philosophy of Science*, V. Minneapolis: University of Minnesota Press.

Nowak, L. (1980), *The Structure of Idealization*. Dordrecht: Reidel.

Popper, K.R. (1959), *The Logic of Scientific Discovery*. London: Hutchinson.

Ricardo, D. (1951 [1821]), *Principles of Political Economy and Taxation*, in Sraffa, P. (ed.). *The Works and Correspondence of David Ricardo*, Vol I. Cambridge: Cambridge University Press.

Robinson, J. (1953), "The Production Function and the Theory of Capital," *Review of Economic Studies*, 21, 81-106.

__________________. (1955), "The Production Function and the Theory of Capital—A Reply" (to Solow (1955)). *Review of Economic Studies*, XXIII, 247.

_________________. (1956), *The Accumulation of Capital*. London: Macmillan.

Salter, W.E.G. (1959), "The Production Function and the Durability of Capital," *Economic Record*, 35, 47-66.

Salter, W.E.G. (1960), *Productivity and Technical Change*. Cambridge: Cambridge University Press.

Samuelson, P.A. (1948), "International Trade and the Equalization of Factor Prices," *The Economic Journal*, 59, 181-197.

Schmookler, J. (1952), "The Changing Efficiency of the American Economy, 1869-1938," *The Review of Economics and Statistics*, 34, 214-231.

Sneed, J.D, (1971), *The Logical Structure of Mathematical Physics*. Dordrecht: Reidel.

Solow, R.M. (1955), "The Production Function and the Theory of Capital," *Review of Economic Studies*, XXIII, 101-108.

_________________. (1956), "A Contribution to the Theory of Economic Growth," *Quarterly Journal of Economics*, XL, 65-94.

_________________. (1957), "Technical Change and the Aggregate Production Function," *Review of Economics and Statistics*, 39, 312-320.

_________________. (1959), "Investment and Technical Progress," in Arrow, K., Karlin, S., Suppes, P. *Mathematical Methods in the Social Sciences*, Stanford: Stanford University Press, 1960.

_________________. (1962), "Technical Progress, Capital Formation and Economic Growth," *American Economic Review*, 52, 76-86.

_________________. (1962), "Substitution and Fixed Proportions in the Theory of Capital," *Review of Economic Studies*, XXIX, 207-218.

Sraffa, P. (1951), Editorial introduction to Ricardo (1821).

Strumilin, S.G., (1951), "The Time Factor in Capital Investment Projects" (Transl. from the Russian). *International Economic Papers*, No. 1, London, New York: Macmillan.

Svennilson, I. (1954), *Growth and Stagnation in the European Economy*. Geneva: United Nations.

__________________. (1956), "Capital Accumulation and National Wealth in an Expanding Economy," in *Twenty-Five Economic Essays in Honour of Erik Lindahl*. Stockholm: Ekonomisk Tidskrift.

Swan, T.W. (1956), "Economic Growth and Capital Accumulation," *Economic Record*, 32, 334-361.

Tinbergen, J. (1942), "Zur Theorie der langfristigen Wirtschaftsentwicklung," *Weltwirtschaftliches Archiv*, 55, 511-49.

Valvanis-Vail, S. (1953), "An Econometric Model of Growth: U.S.A. 1869-1953," *American Economic Review*, 45, 208-221.

Verdoorn, P.J. (1956), "Complementarity and Long Range Projections," *Econometrica*, 24, 429-450.

Wicksell, K. (1954 [1893]), *Ueber Wert, Kapital und Rente*, Neudruck der Ausg. Jena 1893. Aalen: Scientia Verlag, 1969. English Translation, *Value, Capital and Rent*. London: Allen and Unwin.

__________________. (1898), *Interest and Prices*. London: Macmillan.

__________________. (1901-06), *Vorlesungen über Nationalökonomie*, 2 Vols. Neudruck der Ausg. Jena 1913 (Vol. 1) und 1922 (Vol. 2). Aalen: 1969. English Translation, *Lectures on Political Economy*. London: Routledge & Kegan Paul, 1934-35.

COMMENTARY BY E. ROY WEINTRAUB[1]

INTRODUCTION

Hamminga begins by specifying that his is a narrow conception of methodology: its task is "to contribute to the growth of empirical knowledge about what the professionally successful economists of the real world actually do and how they do it." The first point to recognize is that this position is wildly at variance with the "established" view that methodology is to economics as the philosophy of science is to physics. Traditionally, methodology is that subdiscipline in economics that is concerned with the philosophy of the social sciences as it is or may be applied to economics. Consequently the methodologist is a philosopher-manque whose primary concern is to translate into economics the variety of understandings generated in the more philosophical literatures.[2] In contrast, Hamminga's essay here represents somewhat of a redirection of philosophers' concerns, and like any such intellectual realignment, deserves to be taken most seriously; few of us will change our minds on major issues capriciously. Hamminga's chapter will help methodologists begin to think through the implications of refocusing their attention. What I intend to suggest in the pages to follow is that neither Hamminga, nor those who choose to move away, with him, from traditional methodological concerns, need to think of themselves as a solitary travellers, for the road is well lighted, and safe, and the scenery is spectacular—indeed, the road is even more beautiful than Hamminga appears to now imagine.

HISTORIOGRAPHY

"Economic methodology can, I hold, not be more than a branch of the history of economic thought. It is the branch that seeks answers to methodological questions in case histories, that tries to generalize these answers into empirical theories, that tries to test the resulting generalisations by digging out new case histories, and so on, and so forth." Hamminga takes on the issue of vintage capital goods theory, developed in the 1950s by Leif Johanson, Wilfred Salter, and Robert Solow, and frames the questions: "what exactly suggested the vintage idea to the three economists? Which theoretical intentions did they have with the idea? Which problems did they want to solve? What role did 'empirical observation' play in the process? We are especially interested in the role of econometrics . . ." (328).

Suppose I were to answer the first of those questions with the phrase "The Tooth Fairy." Would that answer suffice for Hamminga? Under what circumstances would it suffice, and for whom would it suffice?

The point is that only certain arguments will carry weight in certain communities, and an argument that "The Tooth Fairy" came to Robert Solow in a dream and whispered "vintage capital" in his ear might be interesting to a psychologist, but not to a philosopher interested in the "logic of discovery." As economic methodologists have been the ones to mine the case studies written by historians of economics, the sense that philosophical concerns must structure the narratives has grown apace. Hamminga is thus in a bind, and it is a real one of constructing a history, the audience for which consists of professional economists and methodologists. If his audience were to be instead construed to be historians, or psychologists, or radical feminists, he would have told a different story.[3]

History is not a neutral recitation of facts linked temporally. Histories are constructed, and the materials out of which that construction grows are themselves constructed. What constitutes a fact is not independent of the story; for Hamminga, what Salter ate is probably a fact, but is not an historical fact. And how the historian constitutes an historical fact is not independent of the story being told. The harsh treatment economists have given the remarkably able biography of Keynes, written by the historian Robert Skidelsky, with its attention to Keynes's family and his personal interrelationships, makes economists uncomfortable.

At issue is the difficulty of the enterprise that engages Hamminga's attention. Writing history is not easy and is certainly not straightforward. Besides the choices about audience, and the construction of facts, or in sociological terms "the nature of facticity," there are a host of issues about what is and what is not a source. Are the sources in the history of economics the published articles alone, or are the reminiscences of the economists a source too? Are the finished products of the scientific activity the only, or best, or rather completely unreliable "texts"; indeed, how are the texts to be read? Do we believe that the meaning resides in the writing, or that we construct the meanings of the text in the same way that the author constructs the meanings of the phenomena? What constitutes evidence for the historian is not given but is the result of decisions taken.

These matters should be understood by economists writing in the history of economics, but too frequently are not even considered. It is a scandal that economists have to take seriously the uninformed musings of the eminent on historical issues, such as the recent piece by Paul Samuelson on "Out of the Closet: A Program for the Whig History Of Economic Science." The issues in historiography are understood by historians, and that branch of History called the History of Science, of which the History of Economics is a sub-sub-specialization (of the History of Social Science) has its own set of historiographic writings.[4]

SOCIOLOGY OF SCIENTIFIC KNOWLEDGE

The other major set of issues that should be addressed prior to considering Hamminga's case study, and the questions he puts to it, are those associated with the consitution of scientific disciplines, even social sciences, as social organizations. That is, science is a social activity with certain social objects served by the activity and the products of the activity. Just as a case study may be structured by a philosopher's concerns, so too may that case study be structured by the concerns of sociologists of science. Put another way, historians of economics seem to have as an audience not only the methodology community, but also a community of sociologists who study science as a social enterprise. There is not, however, a subdiscipline within economics based on the sociology of science that corresponds to that subdiscipline called Methodology, which is based on the philosophy of science. Whether this is because economists at root disbelieve in sociology as in Leijonhufvud's phrase, "a lesser tribe without a 'modl' as totem," or whether this is because it is too difficult for neoclassical economists to think about groups as social actors, is in the end of no matter. There are just a few historians of economics who have an interest in the sociology of the economics profession.[5]

Which is not to say that there is not a sociology of science lurking in the background of the histories of economics. Citation studies, patterns of influence, who taught whom, what got published where, are all issues of importance to the Mertonian generation of sociologists of science. That group took the products of science as given and asked questions about the production process as it were, particularly the social or professional elements of that process. This is the sociology of science that is implicit in most case studies. But there is an alternative to this view and that is the set of ideas associated with those modern sociologists who have redefined their field as the "sociology of scientific knowledge." That is to say, these individuals do not assume that the knowledge is "out there" and that the social process called science gathers that knowledge so that the task of sociology is to study how that knowledge is disseminated and rewards allocated on the basis of new knowledge.

This new way of looking at the scientific enterprise is based more fully on the idea that scientific knowledge itself is constructed socially in communities of scientists, and that that knowledge is indeed constructed and not found. From this perspective, the relevent question to ask is not "What is the most efficient organization of science for discovery?"; nor are they concerned with "Who discovered the phenomenon or fact or theory first?" Rather, the analysts' attention is directed to science as an activity that produces "scientific knowledge," and asks: how is that knowledge produced, what is the role of the observor, what role do instruments play in constructing knowledge, how is knowledge agreed upon in the sense that consensus is reached on the facticity of an event or observation, how are others persuaded, how does the community train its apprentices, etc. Writers in this tradition have been interested, for example, in how theory and data interact, exactly how experimental anomalies are treated, the rhetoric of the scientific paper, etc.[6]

Now just as Hamminga chose to write his history to elicit "answers to methodological questions . . . [so that one may try] to generalize these answers into empirical theories . . .," so too Hamminga accepts a particular view of the enterprise of science, a particular view of the sociology of science. He accepts the position that the vintage capital idea was "discovered" simultaneously by three economists, from three separate perspectives, and asks most of his questions about the intellectual context in which those individuals discovered what they did. He thus tracks in the public record, in books and articles, backwards in time from the "discovery," in an attempt to uncover in

Popper's phrase, the logic of discovery. I, instead, in the pages to follow, will ask different questions of the vintage capital episode. I will suggest that the kind of micro-history that Hamminga attempts to construct must be viewed not as a datum on which one may "test the resulting generalisations," but rather as an interesting, though necessarily fragmentary, piece of a code that changes with every attempt at decryption.

HAMMINGA'S HISTORY

Hamminga's history itself is straightforward in a temporal sense. He first discusses Leif Johansen's 1959 growth theory survey, a survey that looked backwards to the reasons for the concern with the idea of vintage capital. He notes in passing the role of Joan Robinson's puzzle about the measurement of capital and the implications that had for thinking about growth. This section itself focuses on Johansen's idea of the layered form of capital: Hamminga quotes from Johansen who wrote "it seems that the conclusions [of growth models generally] are in some respects more sensitive to shifts in the form of the production function than they are to the shift from the assumption of substitutability in the usual sense to our assumption of substitutability only 'at the margin'" (330). He goes on to point out that Johansen's "solution" of the vintage problem, a problem of attributing output growth to some "cause" in order to explain differential rates of output growth both intertemporally for a particular society, and at a time across societies, was a theoretical solution. That is, there were no empirical tests that supported the vintage idea and no decisive refutations of previous nonvintage models. Rather, there was a sense of "a fluctuating degree of dissatisfaction with the correspondence of existing models to what the economist a priori considers to be the obvious essentials of the real world processes for which the model's interesting theorems are supposed to be relevant" (331).

The next section of Hamminga's chapter goes on to consider Joan Robinson's formulation of the capital measurement problem and her method of calculating rates of accumulation and growth from the perspective of the history of an economy and comparative dynamics. But the fact that an explanation of the wage-interest ratio required a sociological theory, or some other exogeneous factor, to explain wages—for marginal productivity would not do for her analysis—caused problems: "Robinson's critique on the neoclassical theory of capital was well received in the circles of theoretical economics, but her point: changing the target of the [modelling] game, was missed, or abhorred...She managed to create some confusion, but the new order she advocated only created a small undercurrent in economics" (334).

Hamminga then examines the contribution of Salter, and notes that Salter's vintage capital model, where each vintage has its own labor intensity, can indeed lead to a theoretical model that is estimable by econometric techniques; the point is, however, that the model was developed not to confirm or disconfirm any theory, or theoretical proposition, but rather to solve a theoretical problem of relating outputs to inputs in such a way that growth could be conceptually isolated, and the notion of "technique of production" could be given an unambiguous interpretation.

Hamminga's final historical section is concerned with Robert Solow and his important 1957 and 1959 papers. This section places Solow in a tradition of work by Schmookler, Kuznets, Kendrick, and Abramovitz. Solow was concerned to "explain" different growth patterns and make sense of the idea that productivity might be considered to have increased over time and to differ among societies at any one time. His aggregate production function analysis was an attempt to give one consistent set of interpretations to the various ideas and to provide a framework in which some empirical work could be carried out to allow "testing." His later incorporation of vintage ideas about capital allowed him "to demonstrate that, even in the absence ex post [of] substitutability between labor and 'capital', the neoclassical categories of thought make sense and the neoclassical theorems continue to hold" (343: from Solow, 1962, 217).

Hamminga draws but one real conclusion from his history, and it is best to repeat it explicitly here:

> For economic methodology it seems necessary to distinguish between two types of factual economic knowledge. Firstly, we have the general kind of knowledge that we acquire just living our life, reading newspapers, and by looking over some very simple statistics. Secondly, we have econometric results, that is, the results of the estimation of parameters. In the cases dealt with in this paper, satisfactory econometric results were achieved after a theory was constructed that had a clear relationship with the 'very simple points' (Salter) and 'casual observations' (Solow), with

> our general kind of factual knowledge therefore. Before this was achieved 'consciences' felt 'guilty' (Johansen, Domar). Econometrics was, in our case, not a means to find a solution, nor was it a means to test the validity of the idea. This might be expressed by saying that the vintage theories of capital, basic to a specific research line in econometrics, are themselves accepted on the ground of their *plausibility*" (345).

AN ALTERNATIVE METHODOLOGICAL PERSPECTIVE

Hamminga's conclusion is rather a cautious one but is consistent with a cautious positivist's notion that theory should be tested, and that progress should arise through the testing of and refutation of conjectures. That is of course the folklore of economic methodology, at least in its most naive forms presented in introductions to elementary economics textbooks. Hamminga simply says, "let's look"[7] and finds, in fact, that the theory developed autonomously, constrained only, it appears, by a much "lower" level of empirical evidence. He draws this conclusion and makes little of it, as if saying that methodology must recognize that "a good line of work" did not proceed in the fashion which methodological folklore suggests.

But there is one way to rationally reconstruct this sequence of papers, to produce a philosophically coherent history as it were, without having to cast doubt on the validity of methodologists' accounts of acceptable economic science.

In particular, if we take the philosopher Imre Lakatos's view of the Methodology of Scientific Research Programs seriously, we can have, I suggest, a perfectly coherent account of the progessive nature of the sequence of papers studied by Hamminga. Elsewhere (initially in (Weintraub, 1979), but extensively in (Weintraub, 1985 and 1988)), I argued that there is a neoWalrasian research program, and it is characterized by its hard core, its heuristics, and its protective belts of theory sequences.

In these terms, the growth literature was diffuse prior to Robinson. She challenged the economics profession to create a coherent neoWalrasian account of growth; her own account was articulated within the neoMarxian program. Salter, Johansen, and finally Solow provided that account, and vintage capital was the unifying idea. The models, instantiations of the hard core of the neoWalrasian program in the context of growth theory, were modified by successive theoretical investigations, each providing some excess empirical content. The role of econometrics is very easy to understand here. Is is not, of course, the role that Hamminga thinks econometrics must have, a function based on "the estimation of parameters." [8] In an earlier paper I noted that:

> Whatever its defects, the research program idea allows two related points to be aired: a sequence of models is the unit in which applied economics is in fact appraised within the economist-community, and empirical work is associated with partial corroborations of theories, and not falsifications...Analysis ...suggests that theoretical progress can be appraised by attention to those heuristics...[And] empirical work, applied economics, is not an activity in which 'facts falsify theory' but is rather associated with 'bringing evidence to bear on the excess content of theory sequences' (Weintraub, 1988, 225).

Thus I have no problem with Hamminga's questions about the role of econometrics, for to me it is not a puzzle at all. The failure to see econometric tests as crucial for refinements of theory is problematic only if one misperceives, in a general way, the nature of econometrics. Such confusion also seems to go along with a misperception of the nature and function of experiments in science.

The MSRP view has some additional explanatory power in the reconstruction of this history, for it accounts for the fact, which Hamminga emphasizes, that there was "widespread misunderstanding of the intentions Robinson had in her paper of (1953) and in her book (1956). She managed to create some confusion, but the new order she advocated only created a small undercurrent in economics" (334). Alternatively, we can argue that Robinson, working as she was from within the neoMarxian program, could not effect changes in the conceptual underpinnings of particular theories associated with the neoWalrasian or neoclassical research program. The only criticisms that can be incorporated in the theories are criticisms that point to ways in which Ti may be modified to yield a theoretically progressive Ti+1. Since Robinson's views on production functions allowed a refinement of the notion of "capital" in the neoclassical account to the notion of "vintage capital," her work was important and "her critique on the neoclassical account of capital was well received." But since her larger point, that class and the sociology of workers and capitalists determined the wages/profit ratio, was a point associated with another program distinct from that of neoclassical economics, that point could not have much impact at all.

ECONOMETRICS AS ECONOMICS'S EXPERIMENTS

Hamminga's concern that econometrics was not really used to refine the theories of capital and growth is misguided. This notion seems to come, as I have suggested, from the idea that theories are presented in science, and it is the job of the experiment to sort out better from worse theoretical accounts. At a more naive level, at the level of high school science textbooks say, or science texts based on the discovery principle (by rolling marbles down inclined planes our children "discover" acceleration and velocity), experiments prove or disprove, or at least discriminate between, theories. Thus dropping a pebble and a rock off the Leaning Tower of Pisa is still on a par with Newton getting hit on the head with the apple and Archimedes displacing water in his bath. The analog in economics is, of course, the belief that econometrics should allow, or facilitate, our ability to discriminate between theories. Textbooks suggest that the choice between Monetarism and Keynesianism or New Classical Economics and NeoKeynesianism could, but more importantly should, be based on the "evidence," where that evidence is in the form of econometric tests that reject one hypothesis without rejecting another.[9] Even the best of economists accept this kind of logic:

> Unfortunately, we lack both reliable data and powerful techniques for distinguishing sharply between valid and invalid propositions in positive economics, and the professional pressures to 'publish or perish' continually encourage a 'game playing' approach to econmetric work that does nothing to improve the data base or the standard techniques that are regularly employed for testing economic hypotheses...In many areas of economics, different econometric studies reach conflicting conclusions and, given the available data, there are no effective methods for deciding which conclusion is

correct (Blaug, 1980, 261).

The difficulty one has maintaining this sense of failure about econometrics is the sheer exhuberance of its practitioners, and the outsider's sense of its richness and complexity and, dare we say it, its success. That success is not based on settling theoretical controversies. Neither is an overwhelming love of particle accelerators, or radio astronomy, or X-ray crystallography, based on their potential use as theory dispute adjudicators. Scientific experiments function in much more complex ways, and our understanding of experiments has been greatly modified in recent years. This reconceptualization has some real implications for economists understanding of empirical work.

ECONOMETRICS AS SKILLFUL PRACTICE[10]

In his book *Changing Order* (1985), the sociologist Harry M. Collins develops a view of the nature of scientific experimentation that accords well with the observed features of actual laboratory practice. In contrast, the positivist view, that experiments that can be replicated are the means by which theories are confirmed or disconfirmed, is at best incomplete and at worst misleading. In Collins's presentation, based on some detailed case studies of laboratory work, the nature of experiments is wrapped together with the idea of science as a craft. If we identify, for a particular line of work in a scientific discipline ("people working in the area of neoclassical growth theory in the 1950s"[11]), that group as the "core set," we note that

> Core sets certify new knowledge...The knowledge which emerges from a core set is the outcome of an argument that may have taken many forms not normally viewed as belonging to science. All these 'negotiating tactics'...are attempts to break the experimenters' regress. Some 'non-scientific' tactics must be employed because the resources of the experiment alone are insufficient. In the absences of an algorithmic recipe for proper replication of an experiment, these tactics are ways of trying to establish what is going to count as 'going on in the same way' in the future. Nevertheless, the outcome of these negotia-

> tions, that is, certifiable knowledge, is in every way 'proper scientific knowledge'. It is replicable knowledge. Once the controversy is concluded, this knowledge is seen to have been generated by a procedure which embodies all the methodological proprieties of science. To look for something better than this is to try to grasp a shadow. (Collins, 1985, 143)

The experimenters' regress, for Collins, is the problem that an experiment, to be successful, must be "replicable," which means that it must be seen to be identical to an original experiment in all essential features. But what is an "essential feature," and what is not, are precisely the theoretical issues that the experiment is designed to illuminate; this leads to a regress in which the experiment itself is "negotiated" and argued within the core group. The result of an experiment is thus a social construction in which individuals achieve consensus about an initially unsettled feature of a phenomenon or event. In negotiating their way to an outcome, the members of a core set construct both theory and evidence.

> Scientists do not act dishonorably when they engage in the debates typical of core sets; there is nothing else for them to do if a debate is ever to be settled and if new knowledge is ever to emerge from the dispute. There is no realm of ideal scientific behavior. Such a realm—the canonical model of science—exists only in our imaginations (ibid.).

From this view of the role of experimentation as intertwined with theory and argumentation and the certification of new knowledge, socially constructed, we can recognize the role of econometrics in economic argumentation. In particular, we can address the Hamminga case study of the growth/vintage capital controversy and identify the nature of the evidence used in negotiating a successful resolution of the controversy. Thus, Hamminga mistakenly dismisses econometrics in Salter's attempt to ground new knowledge claims about vintage capital. Hamminga quotes Salter as saying that "the empirical analysis is in no sense meant as a test of the theory. In fact I am deeply conscious of the gap between empirical and theoretical approaches" (Salter, 1960, 9; cited by Hamminga, 337). Hamminga goes on to comment that this means that "As in the case of Johansen, econometrics plays no role in Salter's invention of a vintage-model. Neither is the model tested by means of econometrics" (ibid.).

But why is this even worth commenting upon? That is, why would Hamminga even suggest that the absent testing is worth noting except from a perspective that links econometrics with testing in the first place? Despite his having suggested that testing was not really present in the discovery process, Hamminga appears to have a residual belief that econometrics, like experimentation in physics, is concerned with testing empirically autonomous theories. But since econometric work itself is part of a complex social negotiation by which arguments are developed to achieve concensus within the core set, and those arguments are variously theoretical, econometric, ideological, metaphorical, and even personal,[12] we can reject the simple view that econometrics plays no role in such theoretical debates. There is often no closure to a controversy without a full reconstruction of the set of interrelated ideas and their empirical grounding.[13]

This view makes sense as well of Solow's econometric work, work that puzzles Hamminga. For when Solow identified technical change with shifts in a neoclassical production function and embarked on econometric procedures to estimate rates of technical change, he was not attempting to test neoclassical theory at all; rather, he was engaged in a process in which what could constitute evidence about technical change itself was open to reinterpretation, and theory, evidence, and even the central metaphor of an aggregate production function had to be argued about in the core set. This is at the heart of the capital theory controversy, or the Two Cambridges Controversy, for since Solow was interested in applied work, he used neoclassical theory and evidence that had no meaning apart from that theory. Robinson was continually irritated that Solow used measured capital to discuss growth issues, and her constant refrain was that that concept was meaningless; Solow's response, that within neoclassical theory capital means thus and such was never understood as a perfectly reasonable argument by Robinson and her supporters. Hamminga's noticing that econometric tests could not provide independent support for the neoclassical theory, nor could it be used to disconfirm that theory, is of interest only if econometrics plays the same role that experiments do in those old fairy tales about science.

It is not the case then that econometrics played no role in leading Solow from his 1957 paper to his ideas about vintage capital in 1959. To be sure, it was not the case that he was led by an econometric test to reject his simpler "theory." But neither was it the case that econometrics played no role. Hamminga quotes Solow to the effect that

> The striking assumption is that old and new capital equipment participate equally in technical change. This conflicts with the casual observation that many if not most innovations need to be embodied in new kinds of durable equipment before they can be made effective" (Solow, 1959, 90; cited in Hamminga, 342).

But the point here is surely that in his econometric work that involved constructing series for capital aggregates, Solow was led naturally to vintage ideas. The casual observation itself could not have changed anything. It required a reinterpretation of data as having been generated by different capital vintages, and it required a theoretical framework rich enough to allow a reinterpretation of that evidence so that it could be used persuasively to negotiate with others in the core set to achieve a consensus about the determinates of economic growth.

> . . . one can see how the outcome of core set debates is affected by . . . 'socially contingent' factors [like non-scientific negotiating tactics[14]] but one can also see how the output is nevertheless what will henceforth be proper knowledge. The core set gives methodological propriety to social contingency" (Collins, 1985, 144, italics in original).

CONCLUSION

Bert Hamminga has provided a case study to draw some methodological conclusions, among them the "fact" that in the development of the vintage capital idea, econometrics played no real role. His major point, too little understood, that methodological argumentation must be well based on what can be inferred from "successful" economics, should not be lost in my critical remarks. But all case studies are selections, and the evidence they develop is related to some view of the enterprise called science, or economic science. Accepting Hamminga's rationalist position, I suggested that a Lakatosian framework could make sense of the role of econometric work in the sequence of papers that culminated in the acceptance of vintage capital models.

But Hamminga's rationalism provides a too restricted view of science, one in which knowledge is "found" or "gained." If, instead, we accept that knowledge is constructed, then we focus instead on the means by which individuals, in what Collins calls the core set, are lobbied to change their positions, and we ask questions about the ways in which individuals are persuaded to accept a consensus position. I have tried to suggest that such a view makes Hamminga's own narrative coherent with respect to the role of econometrics in ways that a positivist vision does not. In his "science as discovery" picture, econometrics is problematic in that it did not "confirm or disconfirm" the "discovery" of vintage capital, which role econometrics is "supposed" to have. On the "construction of knowledge" view, econometric arguments were used to convince members of the growth theory community that the interrelated set of ideas in neoclassical growth theory indeed had evidentiary support, in that econometric studies could be carried out using the neoclassical theory.

NOTES

1. This chapter was written during a Fellowship year at the National Humanities Center, Research Triangle Park, North Carolina. Support from the NHC is gratefully acknowledged.

2. I have taken up this set of issues, in a rather negative way, in a (1989) paper titled "Methodology Doesn't Matter, But The History Of Thought Might," *Scandinavian Journal of Economics*, 91, 477-93.

3. For example, it is surprising to me that no one has yet written about Joan Robinson's career, and her economics, from a gender-theoretic perspective.

4. At least there was one piece critical of Samuelson, and that was Kurdos (1988); but see Samuelson's reply, which withdrew somewhat from his overstatements but failed entirely to understand the difference between intellectual history and economic theory (Samuelson, 1988). One of the early explicit treatments of such topics is to be found in George Sarton's Harvard Inauguaral Lecture of 1935,

published as *The Study of the History of Science* (Cambridge: Harvard University Press, 1936). For the present state of the literature see, for example, the sixteen page (agate-typeface) bibliography in Helge Kragh's *An Introduction to the Historiography of Science* (New York: Cambridge University Press, 1987).

5. My colleague A. W. Coats has been almost alone in his research activity on the history of the discipline of economics, where that history has been focused not so much on the great ideas, or the great men (not women), but on the organizations like the American Economic Association which shaped and formed many features of the profession "Economics."

6. Two excellent collections of papers in this tradition are K. Knorr, R. Krohn, and R. Whitley (eds.) *The Social Process of Scientific Investigation* (Boston: Reidel, 1981), and K. Knorr-Cetina and M. Mulkay, (eds.) *Science Observed* (London: Sage, 1983). For an extended, and fascinating, exemplar of such analysis, see H. Collins *Changing Order: Replication and Induction in Scientific Practice* (London, Sage, 1985). A short exposition of the major themes, engagingly written, is S. Woolgar's *Science: The Very Idea* (London: Tavistock, 1988).

7. This recalls Wittgenstein's "look and see . . . don't think, but look." (Wittgenstein, 1958, sec. 66, 31) For a discussion of this point, see M. H. Abrams who annotated Wittgenstein's words with the remark "It soon appears, however, that what we find when we look depends upon what theorist we look at, where in his writings we look, and with what expectations, categories, and aims." (Abrams, in Bloomfield, 1972, 13)

8. It is astounding how this notion that econometrics is fundamentally concerned with the testing of theories has taken hold in the minds of those economists who are not econometricians or applied economists. I blame the positivists for this bit of nonsense; it comes, of course, from the related confusion that holds that experiments in science are concerned with testing, and refuting, well-defined theoretical conjectures. On this, see directly, Collins (1985) and Galison (1987). I shall take this up in greater detail below.

9. "Friedman always said that, in principle, the demand [for money]

should be elastic but that empirically the elasticity is not large enough to matter. He used his pseudo reduced form expression to show that money and nominal income are highly correlated, and he dismissed all the evidence acquired with structural equations. Eventually he abandoned that tactic . . ." (James Tobin, interviewed in Klamer, 1983, 106)

10. The central argument of this section is based on the view of experiments in the sciences developed by Harry M. Collins in a number of writings, but particularly in his book *Changing Order* (1985). I do not, however, wish to suggest that Collins would necessarily endorse my interpretation, and extension to economics, of his views on science.

11. This group is akin to "adherents to a particular scientific research program."

12. The first economist to point this out was Arjo Klamer in his dissertation "New Classical Economics: A Methodological Examination of Rational Expectations Economics" (Duke University Mimeo, 1981). In that discussion, Klamer identified what he termed "discourses," among them theoretical, empirical, metaphorical, etc. Klamer suggested that all of the discourses are employed to persuade, perhaps, different members of the community of economists to accept new knowledge claims. This line of argumentation, of course, led Klamer to join with McCloskey in detailing a concern with how economists persuade one another, an enterprise that has adopted McCloskey's language of *The Rhetoric Of Economics* (1985).

13. Could Keynesian Economics have succeeded in supplanting the alternative 1930s views on unemployment with an entire rearrangment of what constituted data and what that data "meant," etc.? For example, the meaning of "unemployment" changed over time and thus what constituted the "problem" was itself negotiated. The historian Alex Keyssar has examined this in (Keyssar, 1986).

14. Recall Solow's bon mot to the effect that "Everyone except Joan Robinson knows what we mean by capital."

REFERENCES

Abrams, M. H. (1972), "What's the Use of Theorizing About the Arts?," in Bloomfield, Morton (ed.) *In Search of Literary Theory*. Ithaca: Cornell University Press.

Blaug, M. (1980), *The Methodology of Economics*. New York: Cambridge University Press.

Collins, H. A. (1985), *Changing Order*. Beverly Hills: Sage.

Galison, P. (1987), *How Experiments End*. Chicago: University of Chicago Press.

Johansen, L. (1959), "Substitution versus Fixed Coefficient Production Coefficients in the Theory of Economic Growth: a Synthesis," *Econometrica*, 27, (April), 157-176.

Keyssar, A. (1986), *Out of Work: The First Century of Unemployment in Massachusetts*. New York: Cambridge University Press.

Klamer, A. (1981), "New Classical Economics: A Methodological Examination of Rational Expectations Economics." Unpublished Ph.D dissertation, Duke University.

__________. (1983), *Conversations With Economists*. Totowa: Roman & Allanheld.

Knorr, K., Krohn, R., and Whitley, R. (eds.) (1981), *The Social Process of Scientific Investigation*. Boston: Reidel.

__________, and Mulkey, M. (eds.) (1983), *Science Observed: Perspectives on the Social Study of Science*. Beverly Hills: SAGE Publications.

Kragh, H. (1987), *An Introduction to the Historiography of Science*. New York: Cambridge University Press.

Kurdos, C. (1988), "The 'Whig Historian' Adam Smith: Paul Samuelson's Canonical Classical Model," *History of Economics Society Bulletin*, X, 1, (Spring).

Lakatos, I. (1970), "Falsification and the Methodology of Scientific Research Programs," in Lakatos, Imre, and Musgrave, Alan (eds.) *Criticism and the Growth of Knowledge.* New York: Cambridge University Press.

McCloskey, D. (1985), *The Rhetoric of Economics.* Madison: The University of Wisconsin Press.

Robinson, J. (1953), "The Production Function and the Theory of Capital," *Review of Economic Studies*, XXI, 2.

__________________. (1956), *The Accumulation of Capital.* London: Macmillan.

Salter, W. (1960), *Productivity and Technical Change.* Cambridge: Cambridge University Press.

Samuelson, P. A. (1987), "Out of the Closet: A Program for the Whig History of Economic Science," *History of Economics Society Bulletin*, IX, 1, (Fall), 51-60.

__________________. (1988), "Keeping Whig History Honest," *History of Economics Society Bulletin*, X, 2, (Fall), 161-167.

Sarton, G. (1936), *The Study of the History of Science.* Cambridge: Harvard University Press.

Solow, R. (1960), "Investment and Technical Progress," in Arrow, K., Karlin, S., and Suppes, P., *Mathematical Methods in the Social Sciences 1959.* Stanford: Stanford University Press.

__________________. (1962), "Substitutions and Fixed Proportions in the Theory of Capital," *Review of Economic Studies*, XXIX, 207-218.

Weintraub, E. R. (1979), *Microfoundations.* New York: Cambridge

University Press.

__________________. (1985), *General Equilibrium Analysis: Studies in Appraisal.* New York: Cambridge University Press.

__________________. (1988), "The NeoWalrasian Program Is Empirically Progressive," in de Marchi, Neil (ed.) *The Popperian Legacy in Economics.* New York: Cambridge University Press, 213-227.

Wittgenstein, L. (1958), *Philosophical Investigations.* Oxford: Basil Blackwell.

Woolgar, S. (1988), *Science: The Very Idea.* London: Tavistock Publications.

REPLY BY BERT HAMMINGA

Weintraub quickly climbs the stairs of abstraction to deal with background assumptions that determine the flavour of my history, but he ends back on earth, asking whether my claim concerning the role of econometrics is tenable: "The point here is surely that *in his* [my] *econometric work which involved constructing series of capital aggregates*, Solow was led naturally to vintage ideas" (Weintraub's italics).

I do not know what evidence makes Weintraub so sure, but his claim is relevant. If true, it would falsify my conclusion that the problems to which the idea was a solution were quite clearly observable without the aid of econometrics, and that the econometrics in itself provided no material "leading" to the idea, in short, that econometrics was an "after the event" affair in the history of the introduction of vintage models. Evidence against Weintraub's point is that estimating aggregate production functions is far easier technically (far more "natural" if Weintraub likes) than estimating a vintage production function. About the simple aggregate production function that he used in his paper of (1957), Solow wrote later (1959), "The empirical use . . . is easy; all the parameters can be estimated by linear regression from time series of the logarithms of [O, C and L]" (Solow, 1959, 94, notation adapted). After introducing vintage parameters, "No such simple routine will work" (94) because the time dependent variables of the production function are themselves defined in terms of the parameters of which Solow wants an estimate. The parameters stand for 1) average life time of capital goods; 2) the (Cobb-Douglas) form of the production functions; and 3) the "technical progress" determining the productivity of all vintages, expected to increase if we go from the oldest capital vintages still in use to the most recently installed types of equipment. Solow uses time series of roughly the same type as he used in his study of (1957), and first order changes in time of the variables of these series allow him to estimate only one of the three parameters on the basis of assumed values (or, as Solow calls them: "outside estimates") for the other two. He chooses to estimate "technical progress," and assumes for that purpose an average life time of twenty-five years and a Cobb-Douglas parameter of value 2/3 and 3/4, "which bracket most of the previously published estimates" (95). Solow is not satisfied with his procedure. Neither is the fit impressive, "but it is at least fair and could probably be improved by careful rectification of the underlying data, and perhaps by an alternative choice of [the average life time of capital]" (95). *With respect to the problem of estimating the parameters using existing time series, therefore, things got worse than they were in Solow's (1957).* This evidence suggests that Solow was not, as Weintraub claims, led naturally to vintage ideas by econometric work, but that, on the contrary, he forced himself into a lot of trouble to give *a priori* desired "vintage" meaning to his econometric results.

Now for Weintraub's more general points: haven't I been forced to bow for what my audience of economists and methodologists considers to be relevant facts for histories like mine? Wouldn't I have presented different facts to an audience of sociologists and psychologists?

Indeed, a different audience would probably have made me ask different questions. Sociologists and psychologists have different questions about the history of, say, chess than those likely to be asked by chess players. The latter probably do not care much whether or not Arthur was a king and who came to him in his dreams. They will be interested in the rules and strategies of the time ("What were the rules for moving pawns?"; "Did Arthur usually open with e2-e4?"). I try to write for players and close observers of the game "economics." Weintraub may criticize their concerns. I find it rewarding to take them as given and to supply material that I hope is interesting to this specific group.

That does not mean I deny relevance to Collins' "sociological" views of scientists sticking together in "core sets" that aim at consensus (on what is replicable knowledge), using a great variety of arguments, partly seeming methodologically "improper," in debates that really are contingent processes of "negotiation," followed by cover ups meant to give "methodological propriety" to the consensus reached. But I tend to judge the applicability of Collins' views as limited. Let me illustrate some of the problems with my case study on vintage models. Did the independent publication of the three first vintage models in 1959 mark a point where "consensus" was reached? Consensus about what? Certainly not about the vintage structure of a country's stock of capital, because this would probably have been conceded by every economist before and after that year. If any consensus was reached, it was about the *fruitfulness* of vintage productions functions in getting rid of obviously false, but hitherto, indispensable assumptions in growth theory: a consensus about what were nice things for economists to do in the near future. Can this be seen as a consensus on what is "replicable knowledge," as Collins' views suggest? I find this very hard to push further. What is the "replicable knowledge" involved? Parameters were not calculated at all by Johansen and Salter. Their papers contained pure theory. Solow calculated some parameter values by making a host of qualitative and quantitative assumptions that he himself found partly unattractive. He meant to show *a way to do it*, rather than a set of values candidate for the title "replicable knowledge".

But adepts of the Collins hypothesis would certainly find the cover-ups it predicts, called "methodological folklore" by Weintraub. In general, one should never believe what some economist says another economist has said, nor even what he says he said himself. This holds for primary literature of the kind that features in my case history, but especially for the secondary literature (review articles, text books), that tends to lead us further away from the intriguing factual problem situations of economists working at the frontiers of research lines. Finally, the philosophers come often to deprive the whole discussion on economics of any factual content it still might have had.

I do not, as Weintraub claims I do, "ask that econometrics play the same role that the fairy tales about science have consigned to experiments," in fact, I do not waste any time making methodological demands of my object of enquiry. My history is indeed intended to show, as Weintraub nicely puts it "that a good line of work did not proceed in the fashion which methodological folklore suggests," but I also tried to describe exactly how it did proceed, and I tried, as well as I could, to bring out the logic of the process (the sociologist Collins may be satisfied by discovering "social contingency"; I find this paradoxical because I think the whole idea of doing sociology is to find laws in what appears socially contingent, so "discovering social contingency" seems to me like confessing failure). I did not mean to create a "puzzle." If Weintraub wants to see it as a "puzzle" that fades once you look with Lakatosian eyes, I do not object to his attempt as such (I have, however, elsewhere produced precise historical evidence on economics against the hypothesis that its method looks like the one described by the methodology of Lakatos (Hamminga, 1983, especially 119-123).

NAME INDEX

SUBJECT INDEX

MIX
Papier aus verantwortungsvollen Quellen
Paper from responsible sources
FSC® C105338

If you have any concerns about our products,
you can contact us on
ProductSafety@springernature.com

In case Publisher is established outside the EU,
the EU authorized representative is:
Springer Nature Customer Service Center GmbH
Europaplatz 3, 69115 Heidelberg, Germany

Printed by Libri Plureos GmbH
in Hamburg, Germany